A decade after the *Titanic* was loc— — — — — half miles under the North Atl— — — — — — — — Dan van der Vat presen— — — — — — — — — ent of one of the greatest— — — — — — s of the twentieth century. They show— — — technological triumph of the discovery and exploration of the wreck has raised more problems than it solved, as well as a lot of debris.

While trenchantly re-examining all the great issues raised by the most poignant disaster of modern times, the authors bring out other intriguing questions:

Why was the man at the helm when she hit the iceberg packed off to South Africa?

Why did her reluctant Chief Officer "still" feel uneasy about a ship on which he had never sailed before?

Why did one of her stewards "wish the bally ship at the bottom of the sea"?

It was not only the sea that covered up the *Titanic* ...

THE RIDDLE OF THE
TITANIC

Robin Gardiner & Dan van der Vat

ORION

An Orion Paperback
First published in Great Britain by Weidenfeld & Nicolson in 1995
This paperback edition published in 1996 by Orion Books Ltd,
Orion House, 5 Upper St Martin's Lane, London WC2H 9EA

Copyright © 1995 Robin Gardiner and Dan van der Vat

Second impression 1998
Third impression 1998
Fourth impression 1998
Fifth impression 1998
Sixth impression 1998

The right of Robin Gardiner and Dan van der Vat
to be identified as the authors of this work has been
asserted by them in accordance with the
Copyright, Designs and Patents Act 1988

A CIP catalogue record for this book is available
from the British Library.

ISBN: 0 75280 167 8

Typeset at Selwood Systems, Midsomer Norton

Printed and bound in Great Britain by Clays Ltd, St Ives plc

CONTENTS

ILLUSTRATIONS

Reading the news: crew's families scan the lists of survivors at White Star, Southampton[2], as a newsvendor sells the story in London[2].

Section three

The first Senate hearing at the Waldorf-Astoria hotel in New York[6].

Philip A. S. Franklin, New York vice-president of International Mercantile Marine, with his chief, Ismay, on the way to the hearings[6].

Robert Hitchens, helmsman of the *Titanic*[2].

Attorney-General Sir Rufus Isaacs questions Ismay at the British Inquiry, chaired by Lord Mersey[2].

Sir Cosmo Duff Gordon[8], one of his £5 cheques for a rescuer[8], and his wife, "Lucile"[2].

Guglielmo Marconi and the chief executive of his British company, Godfrey Isaacs, brother of the insider-dealing Attorney-General[9].

The bow of the *Titanic* two miles beneath the Atlantic[10].

Robert D. Ballard[11].

Artefacts recovered from the wreck and displayed at the National Maritime Museum, Greenwich[12].

The starboard propeller of the *Titanic* as it is today. The arrow shows the number '401'[10].

Photographic credits:

1   Ulster Folk and Transport Museum, Harland and Wolff Collection
2   Illustrated London News (Sphere)
3   Mary Evans
4   Ulster Folk and Transport Museum
5   National Maritime Museum
6   Illustrated London News (ILN)
7   Cork Examiner/Southampton City Heritage Collection
8   Illustrated London News (Sketch)
9   Marconi
10 Imax Corporation/Undersea Imaging International Ltd & TMP (1991) I Limited Partnership
11 Wood's Hole Oceanographic Institute
12 Press Association
13 Hulton Deutsch Picture Library

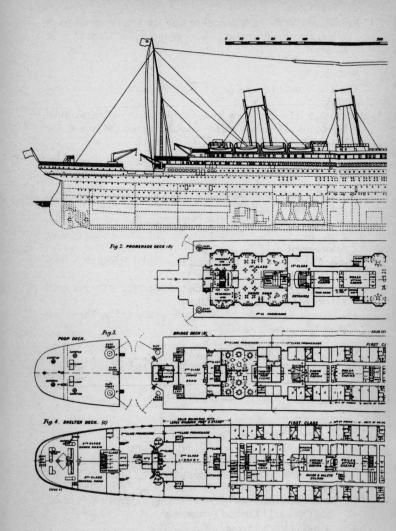

Fig 2. PROMENADE DECK (A)

POOP DECK. Fig. 3. BRIDGE DECK (B)

Fig. 4. SHELTER DECK. (C)

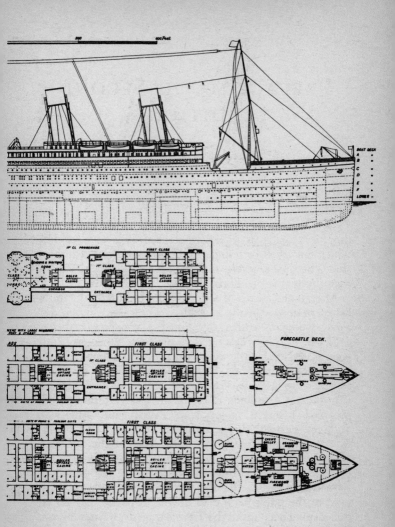

Plan of the *Titanic*, 1911 (Note that B deck was altered in 1911).

PREFACE TO THE SECOND EDITION

THE LIVELY DEBATE provoked by the first edition of this book leads us to describe the origins of a volume which may well be unique in the history of joint authorship – because the two authors differ radically about the hypothesis that prompted it.

After many years of studying the mountains of published material on the eternally memorable *Titanic* disaster, Robin Gardiner developed a conspiracy theory about it, which is described in the text. When his draft was passed to Dan van der Vat as a professional writer and maritime historian, he realised that life was too short to catch up with Gardiner's breadth of knowledge. So van der Vat examined in depth the less voluminous but plentiful primary material in British and American archives, particularly the thousands of pages of evidence to the official inquiries on either side of the Atlantic. He found (with regret!) no conclusive, courtroom-quality evidence for the Gardiner hypothesis, but recognised its seductive appeal. After the tumult between the authors (and at the publishers) died down, all parties agreed on the ensuing account of the *Titanic* tragedy, written by van der Vat with the line-by-line consent of Gardiner.

The result is first and foremost a root-and-branch re-examination of the catastrophe, which we have tried to clarify both by incorporating the latest discoveries and by including the mysteries that are unresolved and likely now to remain so. Our agreement to differ enables us to present the Gardiner hypothesis, to explain its attraction – and to give the arguments against it. Gardiner expressed himself satisfied because all he had wanted was to see the theory published and await developments; van der Vat, the professional sceptic on the team, was satisfied with his freedom to deploy both sides of the argument. The most amusing result was how those reviewers who opposed the conspiracy theory of the *Titanic* found all the ammunition they wanted to use against it within the book they were reviewing. One critic reproduced part of the Epilogue almost verbatim (without acknowledgment) in his ringing rejection. Others, we were pleased to see, gave us a very fair hearing and recognised why Robin Gardiner's theory (on which he is still hard at work) progressed as far as it has.

If there is one thing on which the authors wholeheartedly agree, it is that readers should decide for themselves as they study a book which aims above all to be the most thorough general reappraisal of the *Titanic* legend ever published.

This new edition contains a few corrections as well as some fresh material that has come our way in the intervening year. We should like to thank warmly those readers who have contacted us with information and suggestions.

R.G. D.v.d.V.   April 1996

PREFACE

COVER-UPS UNCOVERED

Since the wreck of the *Titanic* was located by a Franco-American expedition in 1985, public interest in the tragedy not only survives intact but also shows every sign of remaining insatiable – as we were reminded by the extensive coverage of London's first memorial to the disaster, unveiled at Greenwich on 15 April 1995.

We need only consider the striking evidence of this from the last quarter of 1994: an exhibition of *Titanic* artefacts at the National Maritime Museum in Greenwich was mobbed on its opening in October; the following month a Japanese company announced the building of a replica of the *Titanic* as a "floating hotel and conference centre" for £100 million; in December the London revival of Gavin Bryars's curious 1969 musical documentary (docutorio?), *The Sinking of the Titanic*, was sold out.

In the same period we were brutally reminded of the eternal dangers of seafaring. Some 900 people were lost on the ferry *Estonia* in the Baltic Sea; the cruise-liner *Achille Lauro* caught fire and sank in the Indian Ocean (mercifully only three people died). And yet another ferry catastrophe struck the Philippines (where the *Titanic*'s seventy-five-year record as the worst peacetime sea-disaster was surpassed when 4,375 people went down with a ferry in 1987).

In the decade following the discovery of the wreck of the *Titanic*, two and a half miles under the North Atlantic, half a dozen descents took place upon its hulk and some 3,600 objects were brought up. Yet it soon became clear that lingering doubts attaching to the myth of the *Titanic* ("myth" is used here in the narrow sense, of a story whose truth may be secondary to its symbolism) would not be resolved by dives alone. Indeed one can argue that by yielding spectacular photographs and films and by allowing us to stare at objects from the ship and her passengers' effects, no matter how little they have added to the sum of human knowledge, the dives actually distracted our attention from the abiding mysteries. Even the crow's nest bell which sounded the ship's death-knell turned out to be just a bell: it does not bear the name of the world's largest and most luxurious liner of her time.

Short of an all-out dig over the wreckage, which would be prohibitively costly and a controversial assault on what is, after all, a mass grave, the hulk of the great liner that was once the pride of the White Star Line has probably told us all her secrets.

We need, therefore, to look elsewhere for answers to the mysteries that have fascinated writers and readers alike ever since the *Titanic* went down on the night of 14–15 April 1912. The long crack we assume the iceberg made in the ship's side is deeply buried in sand and invisible. But what of the new conundrum of a hole near the bow, which looks consistent with an explosion? There is no record of one; but nor is there hard evidence of any other cause.

In our root-and-branch reappraisal of the legend we have tried to take as little as possible for granted – not even the identity of the hulk. Careful searches on several dives have failed to find the stern name-plate with its embossed letters eighteen inches high. What is more, when he returned to conduct the first exploration in 1986, Dr Robert Ballard, leader of the American research team, saw nothing with the name *Titanic* on it, as he told one of the authors. But while on his search he met a bulkhead that should not have been there ...

That particular puzzle is insoluble because the official plans of the *Titanic* were destroyed by an air-raid during the Second World War, but we shall return to the implications in a moment. The very position of the wreck itself also raises new questions. Fixed by the latest satellite-aided navigation, it does not accord with the one given in the *Titanic*'s calls for help, even after allowing for current and drift. The importance of this will become clear.

Our purpose in *The Riddle of the Titanic* is to examine these and other mysteries, old and new, in the light of the latest discoveries, while keeping the survivors' evidence, much of it disputed then and now, very much in mind.

The resulting theories range from the mundanely explanatory to the apparently fantastical. As an example of the former, we argue that White Star evaded a charge of gross negligence by paying off key witnesses. In the latter category we examine the idea that the *Titanic* was a ringer.

Rather than balking at the very idea, even the most sceptical reader may be as surprised as we were to learn how much evidence seems to point to a switch between the *Titanic* and her older sister-ship, the *Olympic*.

We go into this in the body of the book. But to whet the reader's appetite we cite a few of the salient facts here. Both liners were owned by the White Star Line, whose records have vanished as completely as the *Titanic*'s plans (but with no Luftwaffe to blame this time). In her first few months afloat, the *Olympic* had been seriously damaged through her own fault in a catastrophic collision with a naval cruiser, and again when she shed a propeller-blade. Her owners, their insurance invalidated and their costs mounting as the *Olympic* spent months in dock under repair instead of taking the lead on the fiercely competitive North Atlantic route, fought the Royal Navy for damages all the way to the House of Lords – and lost.

As we shall show, to this motive could be added (a) opportunity, when the two sister-ships were side by side for the last time in Belfast in March 1912; and (b) means, given that little more would have been needed than changing a few name-plates to swap identities. Even the crockery, cutlery and linen were interchangeable White Star standard issue.

Close study of the mass of evidence from the two official inquiries into the disaster, American and British, and of the extra material discovered elsewhere and since, leaves a powerful sense of unfinished business, queries unanswered, missing facts and contradictions unresolved. For example:

Why was the true role of J. Pierpont Morgan, the banker and tycoon who was the real owner of the *Titanic*, covered up at the American inquiry?

How did the Attorney-General, who dominated the British inquiry, get away with insider-trading in shares of the Marconi Company at the very moment its value was boosted by the key role of wireless in the rescue?

We take a new look at the scapegoats thrown up by the inquiries: Captain Stanley Lord of the *Californian*, which spent the night of the disaster hove-to just a few miles from the *Titanic* without going to her aid; and J. Bruce Ismay, chief executive of the White Star Line who coolly stepped into a lifeboat, leaving hundreds of women and children to drown.

We also show that Captain E. J. Smith of the *Titanic* was an even greater danger to navigation than has been established hitherto. His record of mishaps matches that of White Star as a whole: the line, of which he was commodore, had the worst safety record of the leading transatlantic shipping companies. Here are two further mysteries about its conduct:

Were two of the surviving crewmen who were on watch at or near the bridge of the *Titanic* when she struck her iceberg bribed by White Star to keep their mouths shut, both at the inquiries and long afterwards? What guilty secret did they share?

Did the officer of the watch ignore three earlier warnings of ice from the crow's nest?

Amid these and other puzzles large and small, we cannot forget that the central mystery of the *Titanic* remains what it has always been:

> Why did Captain Smith *accelerate* into an exceptionally large and southerly icefield of which he had been warned repeatedly, both before and during his last voyage?

We also reassess and throw new light upon many further points, among them:

> the disappearance of the lookouts' binoculars;

> the fire, covered up by Captain Smith, that raged below in a coal bunker from before the maiden voyage began to within hours of the disaster;

> the attested reluctance of Chief Officer Henry Wilde to take up his duties;

> the fifty-five passenger cancellations (including J. P. Morgan's) shortly before departure;

> the massive alteration to the *Titanic*'s superstructure days before she set sail; and

> the conundrum of the 'mystery ship(s)' which may – or may not – have passed near the scene of the tragedy as it was still being played out, raising the possibility that far more than one in three of those aboard could have been rescued.

Wherever these persistent and eternally fascinating questions and theories may lead in the pages that follow, and whatever the problems still unresolved among the many riddles left by the *Titanic*, her story remains the most unforgettable tragedy in the history of human transport.

Robin Gardiner
Dan van der Vat

Oxford and London, April 1995

PART ONE

BEFORE THE FACT

They that go down to the sea in ships: and occupy their
   business in great waters;
These men see the works of the Lord: and his wonders in
   the deep.

Psalm 107, Book of Common Prayer

Was not the weltering waste of water wide
   Enough for both to sail?
What drew the two together o'er the tide,
   Fair ship and iceberg pale?

A Tryst by Celia Thaxter, 1874

I

THE "OLYMPIC" CLASS

The *Titanic* legend was born in 1907 in Mayfair, London, in an after-dinner conversation between Lord Pirrie, chairman of Harland and Wolff, the Belfast shipbuilders, and his host, J. Bruce Ismay, chief executive of the White Star Line. Pirrie proposed the construction of three liners, much larger and more luxurious than anything then afloat. Ismay agreed that this was the only way White Star could hope to oust the Cunard Line from domination of the Anglo-American North Atlantic route, then as now the most important and competitive in international passenger transport. As a subsidiary of International Mercantile Marine (IMM), over which Ismay also presided, White Star had access to funds controlled by J. Pierpont Morgan, proprietor of IMM through one of his notorious trusts and thus the real owner of the *Titanic*. Pirrie was the prime mover behind an alliance which united Morgan's money, White Star's prestige and the technological supremacy of Harland and Wolff behind the "Olympic" class of liners, the world's largest for a quarter of a century. The *Olympic* was the pioneer; and her early misfortunes are essential not only to the story of the *Titanic* disaster itself but also for a proper understanding of it. We therefore begin with the class leader, the Royal Mail Steamship *Olympic*.

On 16 December 1908 work began on keel number 400 at the new number-two slipway in the Harland and Wolff shipyard at Queen's Island, Belfast. Keel number 401, the future *Titanic*, was laid at slipway three, also specially built, as early as 31 March 1909. The world's largest gantry loomed over the two ways. The *Olympic's* keel was complete by 1 January 1909. The "skeleton" of the ship – the vertical frames from stem to stern plus transverse bulkheads and criss-cross of beams, girders and pillars ready to receive the ship's mild-steel plates – was completed on 20 November. The frames were a yard apart along a hull measuring 882 feet nine inches from stem to stern by, at broadest, ninety-two and a half feet. Intervals between frames were reduced to two feet at the bow and two feet three inches at the stern.[1]

The ship's five-foot, three-inch double bottom was almost flat between the keel and the sides, giving the main body of the hull a strong and very capacious pencil-box shape. The cellular double bottom contained water-tanks for storing boiler and non-potable tap water. The inner skin was called the tank top; the outer skin of the bottom consisted of overlapping strakes (fore-and-aft rows) of plates. Half a million rivets weighing 270 tons were used for the bottom alone, one sixth of the total needed to hold the ship together. She was hydraulically riveted, a new technology conferring more strength than the old hand-riveting method (welded construction was still some twenty years away). Amidships on either edge of the bottom was a pair of 300-foot bilge-keels to reduce rolling in heavy seas. Special steel castings, which would not have looked out of place (except for their grotesque size) in a display of abstract sculpture, had to be made to brace the stern and support the three propellers and the cast-steel rudder (seventy-eight feet eight inches high; its six sections weighed a total of 101 tons).

A key feature of the structure commanded inordinate attention during the two official investigations of the *Titanic* disaster: fifteen watertight bulkheads across the hull, equipped with automatic watertight doors which could also be closed from the bridge by a single electric switch. These, according to a special issue of the *Shipbuilder* magazine devoted to the sisters *Olympic* and *Titanic* in summer 1911, "make the vessel practically unsinkable".[2] Less sober journals dispensed with the adverb and thus gave rise to the hubristic legend of the "unsinkable *Titanic*". Even her builders and owners never went quite that far in their claims before the fateful voyage. But that some of them believed it at least some of the time was shown by a remark from J. Bruce Ismay, chief executive of the White Star Line, during the British inquiry: "We thought she was unsinkable."[3]

The class had eight principal decks: the boat deck, with the navigating bridge at its forward end, and decks A (uppermost) to G (lowest), not counting the orlop deck over the bottom. B deck consisted of three "islands" separated by well decks: forecastle, bridge deck and poop. The shelter deck (C) was the highest within the hull; but of the fifteen watertight bulkheads one extended from the bottom only as far up as F deck, eight rose to E and just six to D deck. The fact that all these bulkheads stood at least two and a half feet above the waterline was held to be enough for safety purposes.

But, unlike the latest Cunarders, the "Olympics" had no watertight *compartments* in the true sense, immune from flooding if undamaged, or watertight longitudinal bulkheads. As this combination of safety features could make a ship list severely and even capsize when seriously damaged (the *Lusitania* turned over and sank in eighteen minutes when torpedoed in May 1915) the absence of longitudinal bulkheads was less crucial.[4] But the lack of a watertight main deck connecting all fifteen watertight bulkheads from above turned out to be fatal; the Cunarders had one, as well as a double bottom rising eight feet up the sides.[5] The "Olympics" were meant to stay afloat even if any two of the sixteen transverse compartments formed by the bulkheads filled with water; they would probably float even with four sections open to the sea in fair weather. Indeed they ought to have been able to survive a direct torpedo hit, provided it did not cause a "sympathetic explosion" inside the hull (as on *Lusitania*). The designers had in mind collisions between the bow and the side of another vessel or object, or vice versa (startlingly commonplace in the days of steam, as we shall show). The rigid keel and the double bottom would withstand a grounding. What other kind of collision could there be?

Early in April 1910 the shell of the *Olympic* was fully clad in plates one inch thick, mostly thirty feet long and six feet high, weighing up to three tons each, while the "ribcage" of her sister to her right had already taken shape. A single plate towards the bow on each side, just below the forecastle, and a third at the stern, already bore the proud name *Olympic*.[6]

Like almost all White Star ships since 1871, her name ended with the suffix *-ic*, just as nearly all Cunarders ended with *-ia*: by such detail did the front-runners on the North Atlantic route seek to keep their corporate identities distinct in the minds of the public. The ship's name[7] is an adjective derived from Mount Olympus in Thessaly, where the ancient Greeks believed their gods lived (with hindsight the name *Titanic* was even more portentous: it was the adjective for the previous gods who were unseated and, when they sought revenge, overwhelmed by the Olympians under Zeus).

By this time the citizens of Belfast were becoming accustomed to an ever-changing skyline as the twin shapes rose over 100 feet above the slipways. Out of view (but not of earshot) was the simultaneous work of fitting the steel decks and the main internal subdivisions, soon to be dressed with the finest materials available, including 40,000 square yards of synthetic interior deck-lining.

The *Olympic* was launched into the River Lagan stern first on 20 October 1910 before an array of dignitaries. There was no champagne christening; but the intricate mechanical arrangements, supervised by Lord Pirrie himself, went without a hitch. By this time she weighed 24,600 tons. Her passage into the water was eased by twenty-three tons of grease; in her first minute of motion, in which she travelled barely her own length, she reached a speed of 12.5 knots before being brought up short by six anchors and eighty tons of cable. But once she was freed of these restraints a gust of wind blew her against the dry dock nearby, denting some of her plates. This might usefully have been seen as a clear warning of how dangerous the movement of an object of such unprecedented mass in a confined space could be; but it was not.

The *Olympic*'s hull at this stage bore a light-grey undercoat along the sides and red-ochre, anti-fouling paint along and below the waterline. Everything from the massive propulsion machinery to the main superstructure was in place save the four tall funnels and the two masts. A 200-foot floating crane was brought up to lower the boilers into her hull; the ship was then towed into the great Thompson graving (dry) dock, specially built by the Belfast Harbour Commissioners for the new giants, the only one in the world capable of taking them. Harland and Wolff needed just seven months and ten days between launch and completion, a startling achievement considering that the new White Star flagship was half as large again as any vessel previously built.

The *Olympic* was a ship of 45,324 gross register tons (GRT). These units of measurement are universally used for merchant ships. GR tonnage however is a measure not of weight but of volume, reflecting the amount of space contained within the outline of the ship, including the superstructure. If the proportion of GRT taken up by machinery, bunkers, tanks, crew quarters and the like is deducted, the result is the net register tonnage (NRT; in effect the total of commercially usable space), 20,847 tons in the case of the *Olympic*. Largely because the *Titanic* alone had the forward half of her A-deck promenades enclosed, she measured 46,328 GRT and 21,831 NRT; but she was not an inch longer, broader, taller or in any sense "bigger" than the *Olympic* and had exactly the same claim to the title of "the world's largest ship" as her elder sister. The *weight* of each ship was expressed by the water she displaced when fully loaded ("displacement tons", the measure always quoted for warships). This amounted to about 52,000 tons unladen for the *Olympic* and 250 more for her sister. In terms of quantity the *Titanic* was thus the world's *heaviest* ship and in quality the greatest in terms of her facilities. Fully laden the ships displaced (weighed) about 66,000 tons each.

In a bustling yard, work proceeded intermittently on the *Titanic* (but at an even faster pace, stage for stage, thanks to lessons learned on the *Olympic*), as well as on three liners for other shipowners and two tenders for White Star. In dry dock the *Olympic*'s hull was painted black and the superstructure white, the three great bronze-bladed propellers were fitted, the two masts stepped and four buff funnels put up, topped with black-painted "collars" to mask the effect of smoke. Masts and funnels were dashingly raked aft at an angle of one in six. During and after the period in dock a host of fitters, joiners, carpenters, electricians and others turned the interior of the ship into a floating town. The first-class section with its squash-court, gymnasium, pool and Turkish bath, its broad promenades and raised glass roofs over some public areas, was a complete post-Victorian spa.

The *Titanic* may have been much vaunted for her superior luxury; yet the overwhelming majority of illustrations of her interior that have come down to us show the *Olympic*, including those in the *Shipbuilder*. Even such oft-cited items as the *Titanic*'s provisioning lists were "borrowed" from the *Olympic*.[8] From the first, therefore, the sisters were freely interchangeable for publicity purposes and were in fact often mistaken for one another. This is hardly surprising as they were identical but for the forward half of the sides of their A decks and the pattern of windows on their B decks, plus some adjustable internal partitions and other details. This confusion factor will perforce recur.

The *Olympic* was a colossus; but her design was deceptively simple and elegant, something which becomes apparent if her picture is placed alongside those of the contemporary big Cunarders, which look top-heavy by comparison. The White Star liners were conceived by Pirrie but planned in detail by a Harland and Wolff team led by Alexander Carlisle, Pirrie's brother-in-law, the company's general manager and principal naval architect, who retired in 1910. He was assisted and then succeeded by another Pirrie relative, his nephew Thomas Andrews, a director and the chief draughtsman (there were clearly no blushes about nepotism at Harland and Wolff; but both men were well chosen and accomplished). Edward Wilding, a naval architect, was assistant chief of design and would succeed Andrews, lost in the disaster; Carlisle and Wilding were important witnesses at the British inquiry. For the "Olympics" Carlisle expanded upon his hull design for the second *Oceanic*, built by Harland and Wolff in 1899 (the first ship longer than the freak *Great Eastern* of 1858). He also designed the interior.[9]

The *Olympic*'s main power came from two four-cylinder, triple-expansion, reciprocating steam-engines built by Harland and Wolff. Aft of them was a 420-ton Parsons low-pressure turbine which drove the third, central propeller by recycling steam from the main engines. The two outer propellers had three blades each and a diameter of twenty-three and a half feet; the centre propeller measured sixteen and a half feet and had four blades. The main engines delivered 15,000 horsepower each at seventy-five revolutions, enough without the turbine engine's further 16,000 horsepower (for forward propulsion only) to produce 21 knots. The turbine was an afterthought prompted by a successful experiment in 1909 with this form of mixed propulsion, which brought useful economies in fuel. The extra horsepower implied a potential top speed well in excess of 21 knots. Steam came from a total of twenty-nine boilers, arranged in six boiler-rooms numbered from aft to forward and including a total of 159 furnaces. They were fuelled from coal bunkers arranged across the ship forward and aft of each boiler-room (except the aftermost, which contained five single-ended boilers fed from forward only). The bunkers rose from the tank top to the underside of F deck and had a combined capacity of over 8,000 tons.

Two refrigeration engines stood in the port engine-room; four 400-kilowatt, steam-powered generators with dynamos to produce electric current for, among other things, 150 separate electric motors aboard, were arranged in pairs aft of the turbine engine-room. By the standards of the time, unprecedented and lavish use was made of electricity in the running of the ship. Cranes, winches, passenger and service lifts, heaters, cookers, clocks, telegraphs, watertight doors, a fifty-line, internal telephone exchange and hosts of other gadgets depended on it. So also did the Marconi wireless set with its guaranteed range of 350 miles (many more at night). The apparatus, installed in a "wireless house" on the boat deck, was connected to a double aerial slung between the two masts, 205 feet above the sea, and had two separate circuits plus reserve storage-batteries (accumulators) in the event of a power failure. Hundreds of miles of cables and wires ran through the ship to supply all the electrical devices, including 1,500 bell-pushes for summoning stewards. When disaster struck, this "nerve system", as the *Shipbuilder* magazine's special issue on the "Olympics" called it, was not found wanting.

The "Olympics" carried a crew of almost 900.[10] Of these, in round figures, 500 looked after the passengers, 325 cared for the engines and just sixty-six including the master and his seven deck officers, sailed the ship. The Captain's suite was on the starboard side of the boat deck, aft of the wheelhouse which stood immediately behind the bridge. The deck officers had their cabins in the same section of superstructure, built round the foremost funnel and known as the "officers' house". At its after end on the port side was the Marconi room or wireless house. The Chief Engineer and his principal minions were accommodated on the starboard side of F deck above the main engines, but they had their own small section of promenade on the port side of the boat deck between the third and fourth funnels. Their messing facilities were on E deck above their cabins, handy for the long, broad passage which ran the length of the port side of E deck and linked all the main working departments directly or by means of side-passages and companionways or spiral stairs. This busy main gangway was known to the crew as "Scotland Road" after a lively working-class thoroughfare in Liverpool, the port of registration of the "Olympics". It also linked forward and aft steerage sections; a narrower passage to the starboard of E deck was for first-class use, named "Park Lane" after a street in London's wealthy Mayfair area.

The firemen or stokers lived in the forecastle on five decks (C to G); the seamen's mess was on the port side of C deck and their "glory hole" (dormitory) on E deck; the stewards and caterers lived on the port side of the same deck. All the main divisions of crew thus had their own separate facilities: the size of the *Olympic* enabled the builders to conceal a maze of passageways and stairs inside her honeycombed structure, to such effect that personnel could move about the ship without being seen by passengers. Just as the public sections of the "Olympics", strictly segregated by class, reflected the rigid social structure of the period before the First World War, so the behind-the-scenes service network imitated the hidden passages and stairways of a stately home. The ship's post office was down on G deck near the bow, over the mail room on the orlop deck deep down in the hull.[11]

Although there were first- and second-class promenades (forward and aft respectively) and a gymnasium on the boat deck, there were no cabins at that level and only a few on A deck, which carried the spacious first-class lounge, reading/writing and smoking rooms, complete with palm court and verandah. The large, central section of B deck was also devoted to first class except for the second-class smoking room aft. More first-class cabins and a library for second-class were sited on C deck; right aft were the third-class promenade and some public rooms. Saloon deck D had more first-class cabins and the first-class dining saloon forward, plus second-class cabins and saloon aft.

The third-class accommodation began on D deck, right forward, with more right forward and right aft on E and F decks. The great distance between fore and aft enabled the shipping line to segregate unmarried emigrants by sex; there were 164 "open berths" (dormitory bunks for men) forward. The *Olympic* could carry 735 first-, 674 second- and 1,026 third-class passengers, a total of 2,435. By moving, removing or adding partitions these allocations could be adjusted according to need. With her crew, the ship was certified safe for transporting some 3,300 people.

The official capacity of the fourteen purpose-built life-boats, two emergency cutters and four Engelhardt collapsible boats was 1,178, enough places for one-third of those aboard.[12] This was somewhat *more* than the Board of Trade required at the time; but the ship with her water-tight bulkheads was meant to be her own lifeboat. Only after the night of 14–15 April 1912 was the principle of lifeboat accommodation for all aboard universally adopted; before the disaster on that darkest night, nobody had thought of it, although the Germans and the Americans already required more lifeboat provision than the British. Even in the 1990s, lifeboats for all are no guarantee of survival for all, but there can be no doubt which option passengers and crews prefer.

Carlisle's earliest plan envisaged sixty-four boats, enough for all; later he proposed forty, then thirty-two, but that was scaled down to twenty after discussions between builders and owners, who apparently preferred to use the space for more expansive promenades.[13] This consideration may have lain behind Ismay's decision to use much of the *Titanic*'s B-deck promenade space for extra cabins after the *Olympic*'s maiden voyage. Each pair of manually activated, Welin patent davits was capable of lowering three boats in succession (and could have been adapted to lower four). The foremost of the eight pairs of davits on either side were permanently swung out, each carrying an emergency cutter which doubled as a lifeboat. A and B collapsibles were stowed on either side of the roof of the officers' house, while C and D rested on the forward ends of the officers' promenade on either side, immediately abaft of the bridge. For ease of stowage, the collapsibles had shallow wooden bottoms topped by canvas sides, to be raised and propped into place in an emergency. None of the twenty boats was motorized.

The mighty engines turned for the first time on 2 May 1911 with the *Olympic* tied up in the fitting-out basin. Towards the end of the month Harland and Wolff were able to raise a substantial donation to Belfast's hospitals by throwing the giant ship open to the public. People fell over themselves to pay five shillings – a day's wages for some – in the morning and mobbed the ship in the afternoon, when admission was reduced to two shillings. The public's awe was palpable.

On 29 May 1911 the *Olympic*, aided by five tugs, set off for two days of sea trials on Belfast Lough. The tenders *Nomadic* and *Traffic*, built at Harland and Wolff in the same period for serving the "Olympics" at Cherbourg (the former for first and second class, the latter for third), went with her. The test-speed was not announced, but the *Shipbuilder* "understood" that the official design-speed of 21 knots was exceeded by three-quarters of a knot. Francis Carruthers, the Board of Trade surveyor at Belfast who had carried out about 2,000 inspections during construction, had no hesitation in issuing a certificate of seaworthiness valid for one year. RMS *Olympic* was ready for sea.

In the early morning of 31 May she lay gleaming in

the Lough when a chartered steamer from Fleetwood, Lancashire, brought several hundred distinguished guests to Harland and Wolff to watch the launch of the *Titanic* and the ensuing departure of the *Olympic* for Liverpool. More than 100,000 people, a third of the city's population, also turned out to watch. A ferry charged two shillings for a cruise past the *Olympic* and back in time for the launch; the Belfast Harbour Commissioners enclosed the best view from the County Antrim side and exacted a few more pence per head for city hospitals. Spectators swarmed into the area round the shipyard and climbed anything climbable to get a better view. Admission to the three stands erected in the yard itself for the occasion was by invitation only, for the launching party, dignitaries and the press. Ireland had never seen a crowd like it: a mighty roar of approval erupted as the second giant began her slide by the stern down the slipway, greeted by the whistles of ships in the harbour.

The VIPs included J. P. Morgan, ultimate owner of the ships, his executive, J. Bruce Ismay of White Star, and Lord Pirrie of Harland and Wolff. This day was special for the yard but even more so for its chairman: it was not only his birthday but also his wife's. After a boardroom lunch at the yard (lesser guests had to make do with a banquet at the Grand Central Hotel in the city) this trio of financier, operator and constructor of the largest ships so far built headed a special group invited aboard the *Nomadic* for transfer to the *Olympic*. As the crowd began to disperse, she set off majestically for Liverpool at teatime, twenty-nine months since her keel was laid. Moored in the River Mersey, the world's finest liner was open to more crowds of admirers on 1 June.

That evening she sailed to Southampton for provisioning and final preparation for her maiden voyage to New York, via Cherbourg in France and Queenstown (now Cobh) on the south coast of Ireland. When the *Olympic* left Southampton on 14 June she was fully booked,[14] which is rather more than could be said for her sister ten months later.

The maiden voyage ended on a jarring note. Manoeuvring alongside White Star's Manhattan pier fifty-nine on 21 June, the *Olympic* trapped and almost sank the tug *O. L. Halenbeck* under her stern. Her own damage was superficial and her programme was unaffected.

Bestriding the bridge in command of the leviathan was Captain Edward John Smith, commodore of the White Star fleet, to whom we shall return. After her maidenly embarrassment the *Olympic* settled into a three-weekly rhythm with the previous-generation liners *Majestic* and *Oceanic*. Each ship left Southampton every third Wednesday, called at Cherbourg and sailed to Queenstown overnight, normally reaching New York in the early hours of the following Wednesday. She would set off again in daylight on Saturday for the return leg, calling at Plymouth in south-west England (Queenstown was mainly an emigration port) and Cherbourg again before reaching Southampton on Friday night.[15] Much of the three-and-a-half day turnaround at each end was spent coaling, the most hated job at sea in the age of steam, on revictualling the ship and loading a fresh set of laundry. This routine was shattered less than four months later, at lunchtime on 20 September 1911.

Southampton lies at the head of Southampton Water, which runs from north-west to south-east towards the Isle of Wight off England's central southern coast. A ship coming down the waterway can turn either south-west, down a broader seaway, the Solent, or else south-east, along an even wider channel called Spithead, to the north of which lies Portsmouth, principal harbour since time immemorial of the Royal Navy. The three waterways meet in an area notorious for treacherous shoals and sandbanks, most notably the Bramble, marked by buoys. These broad expanses of sheltered water are thus much more dangerous than they look, and the larger the ship, the trickier the manoeuvres. For merchant ships a pilot is compulsory.

Captain Smith was on the bridge as the shining *Olympic* was passing smoothly down Southampton Water after casting off by noon for her fifth run to New York. But the man giving the navigation orders was George William Bowyer, a pilot of thirty years' experience appointed by Trinity House, the ancient corporation which also looks after lighthouses, lightships and navigational buoys. Bowyer's services were "appropriated" (reserved) for the White Star and American lines.[16] As the *Olympic* approached the Bramble, around which she would have to execute a long, inverted S-turn to pass into Spithead, the armoured cruiser HMS *Hawke* (Commander William Frederick Blunt, RN) was concluding routine engine tests as she sailed up the Solent towards Portsmouth at about 15 knots.

The *Hawke* was twenty years old, prehistoric by contemporary naval standards in a period of extraordinary technological upheaval. Described as an "excellent steamer",[17] she could probably still muster her design speed of 19.5 knots, though she might have needed the help of a following wind. She was one of six in the "Edgar" class, and was armed with two 9.2-inch, ten six-inch and seventeen smaller guns, all obsolete, plus two underwater torpedo tubes. Her side armour was five inches thick. On this day her most relevant armament was of ancient origin: an underwater ram, a steel casting packed with concrete, attached to her forward-raked bow. To contemporary admirers of the latest warships she may have looked like a wreck before she hit anything.

The *Olympic* slowed down from 18 knots to about 11, swung to starboard and then, signalling her intention with two blasts from her deep-throated whistle, turned to port south of the Bramble and accelerated. Before this second turn the liner was presenting her port side to the cruiser's at a distance; after the turn she presented her starboard side to the *Hawke*'s port at a rapidly narrowing range. As they converged the cruiser was initially travelling faster, on a north-easterly course; the naval veteran for a few moments was set to pass the spanking new liner, over eight times her weight.

But, watching the cruiser begin to fall back, Captain Smith said to the pilot:[18] "I do not believe he will go under our stern, Bowyer." The pilot replied: "If she is going to strike let me know in time to put the helm hard a-port ... Is she going to strike us, sir?"

"Yes, Bowyer, she is going to strike us in our stern ... He is starboarding and he is going to hit us."

Bowyer sang out to the quartermaster at the wheel: "Hard a-port!" But it was too late. *Hawke* had drawn up about as far as the *Olympic*'s bridge before the liner's gathering speed made her fall back. The ships may have been 100 feet apart when the cruiser's sharp bow shifted abruptly to port as if to swing across the liner's wake. It should be noted here that in those days helm orders were confusingly reversed, as if ships were still steered by an oar or tiller rather than a wheel linked to a steering engine which operated the rudder: to "starboard the helm" caused a turn to port (left), and to "port the helm" meant a turn to starboard (right). This confusing practice, abandoned in 1928, will arise again, not only in the present context.

On the bridge of the *Hawke* watching the liner swinging round towards him, Commander Blunt said to his navigation officer, Lieutenant Reginald Aylen: "If she is going east she will not have much room to turn; we will give her as much room as possible." He ordered port helm, which meant a turn to starboard.[19] Noticing the ensuing sudden lurch to port of four to five points (up to fifty-seven degrees), Blunt shouted: "What are you doing? Port, port, hard a-port! ... Stop port [engine], full astern starboard!"

But Petty Officer First Class Ernest Hunt, the quartermaster at the wheel, now sang out: "Helm jammed!"

Lieutenant Geoffrey Bashford, the officer of the watch, and Leading Seaman Henry Yeates, a helmsman, sprang to his aid and tried to force the wheel round. Having delivered a turn of only fifteen degrees, it would not budge. The very violence of the turning motion had caused its gearing to seize up; when the pressure on the wheel was relaxed after the collision, it responded normally once again. The Captain meanwhile leapt down the ladder from bridge to wheelhouse and himself swung the handle of the engine-room telegraph to "Full Astern".

It was all to no avail. Sucked into the looming flank of the huge, accelerating liner by imperfectly understood physical forces (something else we shall meet again), the submerged steel proboscis of the cruiser buried itself in the starboard quarter of the *Olympic*. The point of contact was below the waterline some eighty-five feet from her stern. The full force of the impact of 7,350 tons of steel travelling at seventeen statute miles per hour was transmitted through the hard tip of the ram and the thin edge of the bow. The warship's stem sliced another big hole above the waterline. The ram fell off; the *Hawke* canted over alarmingly before righting herself and falling back. The *Olympic* reeled with the impact and her stern swung away three compass points (about thirty-four degrees) to port. Two of her aftermost compartments were flooded, but the watertight bulkheads functioned exactly as intended, containing the water and enabling the ship to stay afloat on an even keel, only slightly down at the stern. The cruiser's bow was mangled and bent to starboard. *Hawke* was able to limp to Portsmouth under her own power, behind her watertight collision bulkhead. *Olympic* crept back to Southampton on one main engine. Both ships were wirelessing reports of the collision to their respective headquarters as they withdrew from the scene of an accident deeply embarrassing to both parties.

Blunt's first signal reached his Commander-in-Chief in Portsmouth by wireless at 1.40 p.m., just over fifty minutes after the collision: "*Hawke* has been in collision with SS *Olympic*. Both severely damaged. Now at anchor. Further report will follow." Three hours and ten minutes later a telegram from White Star, signed by its chief executive, arrived from Liverpool on the desk of the Secretary to the Admiralty in London: "Referring serious collision between *Olympic* and *Blake* [*sic*: a mistaken identification aboard the *Olympic*] will greatly appreciate your instructing Portsmouth afford *Olympic* any assistance required. Ismay." In fact the liner managed on her own, anchoring off Cowes until the tide rose enough to allow her to return to Southampton. Blunt put in his written report late the same afternoon.

Two days later the Navy convened a court of inquiry (obligatory after any collision) at Portsmouth, conducted by Captains Henry W. Grant (presiding) and Edward L. Booty, RN.[20] The whole swift proceeding smacks of an efficient "stitch-up" and pre-emptive strike by the Navy. Statements were taken from seven witnesses on the bridge at the time of the crash, in ascending order of rank: a signalman, an able-bodied seaman, a leading seaman, a petty officer, the navigation lieutenant, the first lieutenant and finally Blunt himself. There was no witness from the liner or her owners.

The commander described how his ship was engaged on a three-fifths power trial with the engines on eighty-two revolutions. "By her turn to the eastward the *Olympic* had brought her starboard side to my port, rendering herself, under Article 19 of the Regulations for the Prevention of Collisions at Sea, the ship to give way. When *Hawke* had passed the Eastern Conical Buoy, by which time the *Olympic* was round and running abreast of *Hawke* at a distance of under half a cable [i.e., less than 100 yards] and gaining steadily, I again ordered the course to be altered so as to give the *Olympic* as much room as possible." Blunt concluded: "In my opinion the collision was caused by the *Olympic* misjudging her turn round the Bramble Bank and thereby coming so close to the

Hawke that as she forged ahead past her the suction due to her great mass drew the *Hawke* in on her. The *Hawke* could give no more room owing to the proximity of the Prince Consort Shoal." Blunt claimed that his ship cleared the latter hazard by a mere thirty yards and the ships were less than sixty yards apart when his veered off course and they crashed. His essential argument was that in the circumstances he had the right of way under the navigational "rule of the road" giving priority to the starboard ship.

The naval inquiry's unsurprising finding was that the *Olympic* was entirely to blame and the *Hawke* entirely blameless. The Hydrographer of the Navy to whom the papers were referred concurred in this conclusion. Oceanic Steam Navigation, owners of the White Star Line, however, issued a writ on 21 September against Commander Blunt (the Admiralty being immune) for damages in the High Court, whereupon the Admiralty decided one week later to make a cross-claim against the owners of the *Olympic* for damage to its cruiser.

The two suits were heard as a single case by the president of the Probate, Divorce and Admiralty Division – that curious ragbag of a High Court section – Sir Samuel Evans, sitting not with a jury but with two technical assessors, both master mariners from the Elder Brethren of Trinity House. White Star was represented by Mr F. Laing, KC (King's Counsel, a senior barrister); the Admiralty by no less a figure than the Solicitor-General, Sir Rufus Isaacs, KC, MP, the Government's most senior law officer but one, assisted by Butler Aspinall, KC, and instructed by the Treasury Solicitor. The leading lawyers in this case were all, did they but know it, to participate in the British inquiry into the loss of the *Titanic* a few months later. "Olympic versus Hawke" meanwhile commanded special legal attention at every stage of its passage through the English judicial system. Something more important seemed to be at stake than a collision (albeit serious) between the world's most famous liner and a warship, in which neither vessel was lost and nobody was hurt. The case was to become an epic.

The Admiralty went so far as to seek out, at great cost in fees, fares and other expenses, an expert American witness on the mysterious effects of suction: Mr D. W. Taylor, a ship constructor for the United States Navy from Washington, DC. The British naval witnesses, presumably thoroughly rehearsed, gave a disciplined impression of collective competence and confidence which the civilians from the *Olympic* could not match. The liner's helmsman, Haines, for example, had been confused in the witness-box and gave self-contradictory evidence on the course of his ship, telling "a very extraordinary story", the president thought. "The pilot with this huge vessel made too large and sweeping a turn round the Bramble," he found. The court recognized suction as the immediate cause of the collision.

Other witnesses for the Oceanic Steam Navigation Company, the legal personification of the White Star Line, included Captain Smith, who said his ship had been sailing at her "reduced maximum speed" (for coastal waters) of 20 knots before she slowed for the Bramble turn. She was under compulsory pilotage at the time. Pilot George Bowyer told the court he thought the cruiser had been "making rather a tricky move to pass under our stern" which Blunt had misjudged. It was the fifth time Bowyer had piloted the *Olympic* out of Southampton. He had sounded the proper warning of his port turn by whistle. He had never experienced the suction phenomenon.

The opposing sides fully agreed on the independent assessment of the damage to both ships by Harry Roscoe, a consultant naval architect of the Liverpool firm of Roscoe and Little. He examined each in dry dock, the cruiser in Portsmouth and the liner in Belfast. On the latter he found, above the waterline and eighty-six feet forward of the stern post, an inverted triangular hole some fourteen feet wide at the top, extending from immediately above D deck to fifteen feet below. The deck had been penetrated to a depth of eight feet by the cruiser's bow. The ram had made a separate hole, shaped like an inverted pear, below the waterline between G and orlop decks. Eighteen feet of the upper surface of the starboard bossing (the projection from the hull containing the starboard main propeller shaft) had been badly indented and torn. All three manganese-bronze blades of the propeller had been damaged. Traces of them were found embedded in the cruiser's forward end and a length of eight feet had been knocked off her ram (found in time for the Appeal Court hearing). Part of the starboard crankshaft on the liner was strained and out of true (two sections out of four).

An earlier internal inspection of the liner's after end by surveyors from the Navy and Harland and Wolff had revealed a crack between a crank arm and the shaft, which was bent, an event which must have jolted the starboard engine. The aftermost section of the shaft could be withdrawn quite simply, but to get at the others plating would have to be removed. "The *Titanic*'s shafting is available if necessary but if used would entail considerable delay in that ship's completion, as the engines are now being put into her" (12 and 13 October 1911, date of this inspection).[21] Nonetheless, as will be seen, this was how the job was done.

The foregoing report accompanied the statements of claim for the High Court hearing. So did that of a Mr Steele, an independent surveyor, who diagnosed damage to the plating on the liner's D, E, F and G decks and the tunnel giving access to the shaft. Ten strakes (rows) of plates showed tears, indentations or scrapes near the stern. A refrigerated store between G deck and the tunnel had been damaged by sea-water soaking its insulation. Many of the frames holding the plates in place had been buckled and thousands of rivets started (dislodged).

The nub of the judgment, as delivered on 19 December 1911 and summarized for the benefit of the appeals, was: "The President [Sir Samuel Evans] accepted in all material respects the evidence from the *Hawke* and found that the collision was solely due to the faulty navigation of the *Olympic*. He consequently dismissed the action brought by her owners against Commander Blunt, but as he held that the defence of compulsory pilotage set up by them had been made out, he also dismissed the action brought by the Admiralty against the *Olympic*." Evans embellished his judgment with more colourful words of his own choosing:

> One of the colliding vessels was the largest and finest product of the shipbuilding enterprise and skill of the first maritime nation of the world; the other was one of the protected cruisers of her Navy. The contemplation of the calamity, and of the damage which resulted from it, cannot but produce a feeling of regret, and even a sense of pain.

White Star had to foot the bill for the pilot's navigational error. Neither side was compensated for the damage to its ship. The *Olympic* was blamed for the crash even though her owners, captain and crew were blameless as the pilot was in charge at the time. The law then in force, since changed, was quite clear: "An owner or master of a ship shall not be answerable to any person whatever for any loss or damage occasioned by the fault or incapacity of any qualified pilot acting in charge of a ship within any district where the employment of a qualified pilot is compulsory by law."[22] Evans said he thought the defence of compulsory pilotage should be repealed. But George Bowyer stayed in post long enough to pilot the *Titanic* out of Southampton on her one and only voyage. The Navy promoted Blunt to captain and gave him HMS *Cressy*, another obsolete cruiser but half as big again. Captain Smith was promised command of the *Titanic* as soon as she was ready for sea.

White Star meanwhile won a petty victory over the burgeoning trade-union movement of the day. Members of the *Olympic*'s crew were paid off when the lamed ship docked, receiving only three days' wages instead of the twenty-one payable for a complete return voyage. Some of the ship's firemen, always a turbulent element in the White Star fleet as will become clear, took the company to Southampton County Court, which referred the case to the High Court. On this occasion the Admiralty division was more sympathetic to the embattled line and found in its favour.

On the main issue of damage to its flagship, White Star refused to accept Evans's judgment in favour of the Navy and went to the Court of Appeal. Lords Justices Williams, Kennedy and Parker delivered their judgment on 5 April 1913. They allowed new evidence resulting from the recovery after the first hearing of the *Hawke*'s lost ram. They deduced from this that the cruiser had been up to seventy yards further off the Prince Consort Shoal at the time of the accident than the mere thirty claimed by Blunt, perhaps 100 yards in all, which meant that the cruiser could have made more room for the liner than she did. But they thought the *Olympic* witnesses generally unreliable, and unanimously dismissed the appeal, with costs. Their lordships decided that there was no question of overtaking; the vessels were crossing, which meant *Hawke* had right of way as the starboard vessel.

Although legal expenses were now making another significant contribution to the big deficit run up by the *Olympic*, White Star decided to take the case all the way to the House of Lords, urged on by Captain Smith above all (although he was pushing at an open door). Lord Haldane, the Lord Chancellor (a member of the Cabinet who presides over both the judicial system and the upper house of Parliament), took the case himself, supported by Lords Atkinson, Shaw and Sumner. Sir Robert Finlay, KC, now led for White Star (as he had by this time done at the *Titanic* inquiry), supported by Mr Laing; the Attorney-General, Sir John Simon (new in the post held by Isaacs at the time of the inquiry), led for the Admiralty, supported by Mr Aspinall. The heaviest artillery of the English Bar available to White Star could, however, make no impression on the findings of the lower courts: the Lords were as one in upholding the earlier judgments, unanimously dismissing this final appeal with costs on 9 November 1914.

The ships had been crossing each other's courses, they ruled; the cruiser, a slower ship in any case, had not been overtaking or trying to overtake the liner, the Lord Chancellor said. "It seems to me that the real explanation of what happened is that her pilot thought that the *Olympic* would come round into the channel well ahead of the *Hawke*. He appears to have misapprehended the speeds of the two vessels and their relative positions ... He took the *Hawke* to be on a parallel instead of what was a converging course." The fact that the cruiser's helm had jammed was irrelevant; no action by the cruiser could have averted the collision.[23]

By this time the three-year-old damage to the bow of HMS *Hawke* was sadly academic: she had gone down in six minutes with most of her crew of 550 in the northern North Sea on 15 October 1914. Torpedoed at noon by the German submarine *U9* (Lieutenant-Commander Otto Weddigen), the old cruiser, her stem straightened and her ram unreplaced after the collision with the *Olympic*, blew up.

The impartial observer, while accepting that Bowyer's swing round the Bramble was too fast and too wide and was the main cause of the crash, will surely discern two contributory acts by the *Hawke*: her steering jammed because the wheel was wrenched round too violently; and she could have given the *Olympic* fifty yards more sea room than she did without much risk. Had *neither* of these factors arisen, the collision might have been avoided.

But it is beyond speculation that the accident on 20 September 1911 was a fateful and crucial moment in the story of the *Titanic* disaster. White Star had been about to announce 20 March 1912 as the date for her maiden voyage to New York.[24] Her sister's accident threw an already tight schedule at Belfast into disarray: White Star must have been crossing their fingers on 11 October 1911, when they gave out the new date of 10 April, a delay of exactly (but only) three weeks.

The *Olympic* after all had to be repaired, and only the yard which built her, with access to Belfast's single, outsize dry dock (occupied by the *Titanic*), could do that. The Harland and Wolff repair and maintenance facility at Southampton took two weeks to fit temporary covers over her two mighty wounds: steel plating for the underwater hole caused by the ram and wood for the one above the waterline. Thus patched up, the liner left for Belfast on 4 October, proceeding at 12.5 knots on her port engine and arriving safely the next day. The repairs proper took another six and a half weeks; the *Olympic* left Belfast for Southampton only on 20 November, having missed three transatlantic return voyages, and went back to work at the end of the month. Repairs and lost fares cost White Star an extra £250,000, one-sixth of the original building outlay.[25]

The *Olympic* was insured for only two-thirds of its construction cost, or $5 million (£1 million),* with the Atlantic Mutual Insurance Company of New York, the usual practice of International Mercantile Marine (IMM), which had owned White Star since 1902. Atlantic Mutual spread the risk among many other American and foreign insurers, including Lloyd's of London, a normal procedure. The oddity in IMM's insurance arrangements was the proportion of risk borne by the group itself, which sometimes ran even higher than one-third. "I do not believe there is any company crossing the Atlantic that carries such a large proportion of its own insurance as the subsidiary companies of [IMM]," Philip Franklin, US vice-president of the group, told the American inquiry on its third day. Ismay even boasted on day sixteen of the

---

* For rough 1995 equivalents, multiply dollars by twelve and pounds by forty.

British inquiry that "no other line paid lower premiums" than White Star – or carried such a large excess. But as the collision with the *Hawke* was blamed on the *Olympic*, her owners could not recover anything and had to bear all the expenses incurred, direct and indirect, themselves.

To save time, the *Titanic*'s starboard propeller shaft, fortunately ready for fitting but not yet installed, was cannibalized while substitute sections were manufactured with all speed for the newer ship. She of course had to be towed out of dry dock to make way for the *Olympic*.

By this time it would have been very hard to tell from outside the yard which ship was in dock and which afloat nearby. Contrary to the impression given by some photographs of the ships, touched up at the time or later, the names on the bows were not picked out in white but in burnished-gold paint. They would not be discernible from a distance except through binoculars or telescope, or on a photograph unless taken from close to.

The bent crankshaft, the distorted frames, the twisted bossing, the gashed deck-plates, the chipped propeller-blades and the broken hull-plates were removed and replaced, the consequential damage to the propulsion system and other features put right. Ships are built from the bottom up but these repairs, awkwardly, had to be done from the stern or the side or underneath. On the other hand, the sheer size of the *Olympic* and the dock gave the repairers elbow-room; and ships were damaged so often in the age of steam that difficult tasks of this kind were a routine challenge to the skilled Harland and Wolff workforce of 15,000 men.

On Thursday 29 November, 1911, the *Olympic* returned to the transatlantic run, one day late because of heavy fog; George Bowyer piloted her out of Southampton without incident as Captain Smith stood by on the bridge. Any unease the master might have felt about the presence of the old pilot would surely have been offset by his painfully acquired personal knowledge that worse things happened at sea. The three-weekly cycle continued smoothly, apart from an almighty shake-up on 14 January in a mid-Atlantic storm the like of which even Captain Smith had never experienced. But on 24 February 1912 the hapless *Olympic* suffered her third accident in less than nine months. Eastbound for home after leaving New York on the 21st, the liner was steaming across the Grand Banks 750 miles off Newfoundland when she passed over a submerged obstruction and shed one of the three blades of her port propeller, which weighed twenty-six tons. "The shock was felt throughout the ship."[26] The *Olympic* arrived at Southampton on the due date (28 February), but not without further incident: a man deported from the United States in third class as a dangerous lunatic gave his attendant the slip on the 26th and was never seen again. James Kneetone was logged as having gone overboard.[27]

Ships were constantly shedding propeller-blades in the heyday of steam. But this was one of the world's biggest blades, and its abrupt removal from the world's longest propeller shaft while the world's largest ship was making more than 20 knots (her customary speed on the open sea) would have had a commensurate effect on shaft, engine and the surrounding area of the hull. No matter how quickly the cause of the sudden shudder was diagnosed and the affected engine stopped, the consequent stress would have been serious on a ship whose stern had been extensively repaired just three months earlier.

It was only in 1993 that another reason was revealed for taking the damage to the *Olympic* more seriously than hitherto. Since this newly discovered factor clearly played a key part in the *Titanic*'s loss, we shall explore it here, on its first appearance in our narrative.

The 1910 steel used to build the class was a lot closer in its properties, molecular structure and strength to cast iron than modern steels. A paper delivered to the United

States Society of Naval Architects and Marine Engineers said in connection with the *Titanic* disaster: "... the low water temperature (*circa* thirty-one degrees Fahrenheit) would have put contemporary steel of that vintage into the brittle-fracture zone ..."[28] The authors, reinterpreting how the ship broke up after hitting the iceberg on the basis of photographic evidence from the wreck, went on to conclude:

> Tests done on steel recovered from the wreck site ... have indicated that the type of steel used in the *Titanic* became brittle when exposed to the water temperature of thirty-one degrees. The brittle nature of the steel in the icy cold waters of the Atlantic ... could have contributed to the hypothesized rivet and plate failures ...
>
> The plausibility of this brittle-fracture theory is underscored by experiences of the *Olympic* and *Britannic*, sister-ships of the *Titanic*. [In her collision with *Hawke* the *Olympic*] was struck abreast of the mainmast and the opening was mainly below the waterline. The plate tears in the area of impact exhibited a brittle-fracture type of failure ... many of the plate tears were unusually sharp in their extent and had the appearance of brittle fracture ... The extent of such damage would have been magnified many times by ... the collision damages sustained by the *Olympic*, a consequence of the sensitivity of [her] plating and stiffener-systems to impact.

The paper asserts that the brittleness of the steel used to build the "Olympic" class peaks at thirty-one degrees Fahrenheit (minus one degree Celsius). It is worth noting that the *Hawke* collision, which apparently caused brittle fractures, took place in southern English waters in September, when mean temperatures are up to thirty Fahrenheit degrees warmer. It is even more noteworthy that the *Olympic*'s blade-shedding shudder occurred in

February, the very depth of winter, in an area of the North Atlantic whose temperature is affected by the chill Labrador Current – to say nothing of icebergs and ice-fields. It would be more than merely surprising if those Grand Banks waters were much above thirty-one degrees at the time of the *Olympic*'s third accident.

Small wonder then that the consequent second return to Belfast for repair took nearer a week rather than the single day[29] envisaged when she arrived at Southampton on one main engine on 28 February, after the customary halts at Plymouth and Cherbourg. She left for Belfast on the 29th (Leap Year Day) but was too slow to catch the tide there on Friday 1 March. Her next scheduled departure for New York on 6 March was simply cancelled. There seems to have been no White Star sailing at all that day, which suggests that the extent of the damage and the consequent, unduly long stay at Belfast came as a nasty surprise to the owners. The shed propeller-blade thus added another substantial operating loss as well as a new repair bill to the already lengthy debit side of the *Olympic*'s account. A few minor additional alterations and adjustments were made to her before she rejoined White Star's normal service from Southampton on Wednesday 13 March. Work on the *Titanic* was disrupted once again as she was on the verge of completion: she had to be hauled out of the graving dock to make way for her distressed sister. The pair were photographed together for the last time on 6 March, on the eve of the *Olympic*'s return to Southampton.

Yet it was at this period of maximum inconvenience for Harland and Wolff and White Star alike that Ismay, as the owner's representative, decided that a steel-framed screen with sliding windows, to protect first-class passengers from spray, must be fitted to the forward half of the promenades on *Titanic*'s A deck before her sea trials, scheduled for 1 April.[30] "It is seldom in the history of great liners that such a major modification was made at so late a stage in construction."[31] Ismay said it was a response to passenger comments made to him on the *Olympic*'s maiden voyage. It was so urgent that even though the latter's essential repairs had kept her already delayed sister out of dry dock, it could not wait for a quieter time. But such screens were not "essential" enough to be fitted to the *Olympic* herself: she had to rub along without them for a quarter of a century.

The A-deck screens are the most obvious external feature enabling the observer to tell the *Titanic* from the *Olympic*. The other large-scale difference is less well known: the enclosed sides of B deck were longer on the *Titanic* and had a distinctly less uniform pattern of windows. A close examination of the profusion, probably the vast majority, of *Titanic* souvenir postcards (over 170 separate issues, one or two actually showing the *Lusitania*!) on sale before and *after* the disaster reveals the *Olympic*, with no side-screens on A deck, standing in for the *Titanic*. The last recorded photograph of the two sisters together shows them in echelon, in the process of changing places yet again in the graving dock.[32] Neither sports a screen on A deck. Ironically, the windows in the Ismay screens needed a spanner to open them, a fact which was to make it more difficult for some first-class passengers to board the lifeboats when the time came.

The record of SS *Olympic*'s first nine months after completion shows that she came close to sinking a tug, ran onto a cruiser, had a propeller-blade knocked off at high speed and spent nine weeks under repair. For the vast majority of the damage to herself, to say nothing of the consequential and indirect costs, she was uninsured. We now know that she was not as strong as she looked because her steel was brittle. We also know she was routinely confused with the *Titanic*, often deliberately. This makes the publicity[33] for her re-launch in spring 1913 after a massive safety refit seem ironic, if not downright disingenuous: "The new *Olympic* – virtually 'two ships in one'."

Since she plays only a supporting role in the rest of our story, we may anticipate the remainder of her career here. Seven weeks after her sister hit an iceberg and sank, the *Olympic* narrowly avoided hitting something rather larger: England. Abysmal navigation having put her many miles north of where her officers thought she was, she only just missed running onto the rocks north of Land's End on the south-western tip of England, a promontory she should have been passing on the south side, early in June 1912. Only a violent reversal of engines to 'Full Speed Astern' saved her at the last moment, a mishap which was kept secret for seventy-five years.[34]

The *Olympic* had an adventurous First World War as a troop-ship in the Mediterranean and Atlantic, evading air and submarine attacks (but ramming and sinking a U-boat in April 1918). After a massive, £500,000 refit in 1919–20, when she was converted to oil (but still got no spray-screens for A deck), she sailed on until retired in 1935 and broken up in 1937. During this period she backed into the SS *Fort George* in New York harbour in 1924 and crushed the Nantucket Lightship, killing seven aboard, in a fog in 1934. Nonetheless for most of her life this remarkable ship bore the nickname "Old Reliable".

The *Olympic* left Belfast on 7 March 1912 after the second unscheduled return to her birthplace, arriving at Southampton the next day. Five days later she was once again coaled up and revictualled, ready to reclaim her slot in White Star's three-week, three-ship transatlantic cycle. On 23 March she left New York for the eastbound leg, carrying as much extra coal as she could to help her sister as well as herself to overcome the effects of a long coal strike in Britain (settled on 6 April, although supplies did not return to normal for many days). On 3 April she started her seventh round trip, twelve hours before the

Titanic took over her berth at Southampton. The *Olympic* left New York for home again on 13 April and was about 750 miles out into the Atlantic when she picked up her sister's cry for help. Her new master was Captain Herbert James Haddock.

2

ROOTS OF DISASTER

One of the many distortions of history in the *Titanic* myth is that she was perceived as a fateful phenomenon of her time *before the disaster associated with her name*. Had it not been for the disaster we would clearly never have heard of the premonitions (which hindsight nonetheless renders staggering) or of the Jonahs who intoned, "No good can come of this" whenever human inventiveness produced a new sensation.

Another historical distortion is that the Edwardian era which inspired the "Olympics" came to be (and often still is) presented as a Golden Age of peace, prosperity and progress doomed to founder in the Flanders mud.[1] The age was bound to seem golden from a post-1914 perspective. Yet for the United Kingdom of Great Britain and Ireland the period was one of decay, made up of widespread poverty, unemployment, internal and international tension – a relative decline which had begun with the unification of Germany in 1870 and was to continue throughout the twentieth century, an age of rust rather than gold. Abroad, Britain's Empire had lost face and self-confidence in lumbering to a hollow victory by half a million imperial troops over a few thousand Boers after three years of war in South Africa. America and Germany were forging ahead economically, industrially and commercially, and the latter was also openly challenging the supremacy of the Royal Navy. As a result the British gave up their "splendid isolation" and concluded alliances: in 1902 with Japan, to protect their Far East interests while concentrating their fleet in European waters; and in 1904 with the "old enemy", France, in the Entente Cordiale, which became the Triple Entente when a tottering Russia joined them in 1907.[2]

Domestically there were issues such as Home Rule for Ireland, votes for women and a coagulation of discontents known at the time as "the Social Problem" with capital "S" and capital "P". Together they made the age seem anything but golden to all but the privileged minority presiding over a class-ridden society in what was still very much the richest country in the world. Social provision remained abysmal five years after the Labour Party first won seats in the House of Commons. At the very time the two great sister-ships were under construction side by side in 1911, the rising tide of discontent threw up first a violent coal strike in South Wales, source of the best steam-coal, and then a ten-week nationwide rail strike marked by riots and arson. Industrial unrest was a constant theme in the last three years of peace and beyond; a national coal strike seriously affected shipping and threatened to disrupt the *Titanic*'s maiden voyage.[3]

If the myth of the Golden Age was invented after the First World War, before it the myth was still very much alive of "British is best", the overweening attitude which led entrepreneurs to pursue amazing but erratic advances in technology at breakneck speed. The shipping and ship-building industries went to the limit in encouraging and exploiting progress in such fields as steam power, turbines, steel construction, electrical engineering and wireless. The result was a procession of ever larger vessels for rapidly expanding trade and passenger markets, especially in North Atlantic liners. Fierce competition, particularly between Britain and Germany, in speed, luxury and sheer size developed on this principal prestige-route over the turn of the century. The speed was to appeal to the go-ahead, the luxury to attract the rich, the size to cope with the masses of European emigrants fleeing the "Golden Age" in steerage class for a new life in North America.

As in ballistic technology much later in the century, when missile research blazed the trail for space exploration, so at its beginning bounding progress in marine technology followed in the wake of even greater leaps in warship construction. At an accelerating pace the leading fleets had switched from wooden vessels to ironclads, then steel and armour-plated ships, from sail to steam and turbines, from muzzle-loading cannon to turreted, long-range breech-loaders while adopting torpedoes, submarines and wireless. Then Britain launched HMS *Dreadnought* in 1906, heralding a new generation of big battleships, the strategic armaments of the period. Their overwhelming combination of massive "all big-gun" broadsides, heavy armour and high speed rendered every earlier capital ship obsolete at a stroke. In 1907 the Anglo-German naval arms race escalated sharply on the delivery of three more such ships to form the first "dreadnought" squadron in the Royal Navy.[4]

In the same year the "Olympic" class was conceived by the chairman of Harland and Wolff, Lord Pirrie, who conveniently happened to be a director of the White Star Line that ordered them, and of its American parent, IMM, which funded them on behalf of J. P. Morgan.

During that *annus mirabilis* in the history of naval architecture the great liner race culminated for the time being in the triumph of the British-owned Cunard Line's two super-fast, 30,000-ton, transatlantic ships, the *Lusitania* and the *Mauretania* (which, after her sister's brief reign, held the Blue Riband for fastest crossing from 1907 to 1929). The *Mauretania* remained the fastest even when surpassed from 1911 in both size and luxury by the White Star's 45,000-ton "Olympics".[5] Yet the Board of Trade, the British government department which supervised shipping, had not adjusted its regulations on ship construction and life-saving provision since the first 10,000-ton liner appeared two decades earlier.[6]

Another inherited distortion of history is the impression left by a mountain of *Titanic* literature that the ship

commanded special attention long before her maiden
voyage. Prior to the disaster it was naturally the *Olympic*
that came first in every sense: not only in chronological
order as pioneer of her class but also in public interest.[7]
The largely overlapping construction of a pair of colossal
and identical ships then took over as the focus of a degree
of public attention unmatched until the age of the astro-
naut. This phase culminated in the launch of the *Titanic*
on the same day (31 May 1911) as the *Olympic* first set
sail – a flamboyant early example of manipulative public
relations. The latter's maiden voyage was, however, over-
shadowed by the imminent coronation of King George V.
Finally the emphasis switched to the *Titanic* as her builders
and her owners proclaimed that she would be the world's
largest and most luxurious ship, even more lavish than
the German liners, even more opulent than her sister.[8]

The *Titanic* disaster was not the first time but the second
that a flagship of the White Star Line hit an iceberg – and
not the first but the second time that the line produced
the world's worst peacetime shipwreck.

These are just two of many startling facts about an
extraordinary company whose erratic and dramatic
history was exceptional, even by the buccaneering standards of the heyday of industrial capitalism and the steam
which drove its machines. The line's record before and
after the most notorious disaster of them all is a unique
catalogue of dubious or illegal business practice, recklessness, bad luck, accident and catastrophe. All this is
made clear in a by-product of the thorough work on the
Titanic by the American writers John P. Eaton and Charles
A. Haas: their well-named *Falling Star*, a history of the
line calamity by calamity. Not the least arresting feature
of this book is the small print between the chapters, listing
"accidents and incidents" too minor (in this breathtaking
context) to rate more than a passing mention. It is overwhelmingly clear that living on the edge, whether of ruin

or the latest shipping development, was essential to the ethos of the White Star Line throughout its unhappy history.

The line was founded in Liverpool, then Britain's principal port, in 1845 by Henry Threlfall Wilson and his first partner, John Pilkington. By 1852 it was established in the Australian trade, taking migrants and manufactures out and bringing wool, gold, whale-oil and other raw materials back. Wilson acquired another partner, James Chambers, in 1857, and six years later they went into steam propulsion for the first time with the *Royal Standard*.[9]

Two weeks out from Melbourne after an uneventful maiden voyage, under sail and roughly halfway to Cape Horn, the 2,033-ton part-steamer, part-sailer was suddenly enveloped by thick fog on the morning of 4 April 1864. As Captain G. H. Dowell wrote to the owners:

> ... at the same moment the lookout sang out, "Broken water ahead". The next moment saw a large iceberg close under [sic] the starboard bow ... The helm was immediately put hard a-starboard ... bringing the ship parallel with the berg ...
>
> The sea gradually settled her down upon it ... thus bringing the yards in contact with the berg. Before they broke they struck the berg several times, bringing down large masses of ice on the deck.[10]

Amazingly there was no sign of a leak after the ship was bounced by the wind all the way along the side of an immense mass of ice showing over 600 feet above sea-level. Dowell was able to get steam up and reach Rio de Janeiro on 9 May, the ship's spars, rigging and upperworks badly damaged but her hull entirely sound and her steam-engine in fine fettle. Pausing only three days to complete with coal, the *Royal Standard* resumed her homeward voyage, arriving in Liverpool on 19 June.

She was rather sounder than her owners' finances in 1864. White Star had decided to throw in its lot with two other lines to form a new company with three steamers on its books. Whispers of insider-trading in its shares and illegal holdings by directors through nominees led the London Stock Exchange to investigate and the merger was aborted. But the same directors decided to use the same £2 million of capital to set up a similar company under another name. Not surprisingly a sceptical public wanted nothing to do with it and this scheme too collapsed. White Star meanwhile had seriously overextended itself by borrowing to finance a second steamer, which had to be sold on delivery. Chambers left and Wilson took on his third partner, John Cunningham. Two of the company's banks collapsed in 1866–7, when a trial run on the New York route also failed. White Star's assets were sold off: they included such goodwill as remained and the company's pennant, a five-pointed white star on a red background. These were snapped up for £1,000 by Thomas Henry Ismay, aged thirty-one, senior partner in Ismay, Imrie and Company, who went on to found the Oceanic Steam Navigation Company Limited on 6 September 1869 – henceforth the official name of the owners of the White Star Line. Six weeks earlier Ismay's partner, G. H. Fletcher, had reached agreement with Harland and Wolff for the construction of four advanced steamers, the first to be named *Oceanic* like the new company. The second was all but identical if even more luxurious: the *Atlantic*.[11]

With these, two more of the same class and then two slightly bigger liners (to join the rapidly increasing company fleet inside a year), White Star planned to concentrate on the already highly competitive and expanding New York run, but without abandoning Australasia. The money to fund Oceanic's swift and ambitious expansion was raised by a Liverpool financier of German extraction called Gustavus Schwabe. His nephew, Gustav Wolff, was an engineer and later junior partner at Harland and Wolff (another case of nepotism justified by events). Such was the origin of the enduring alliance of White Star and its builder. The basis of the deal promoted by Schwabe was that the line would order ships exclusively from the one yard, although the builder naturally remained free to construct for other lines. White Star was the monogamous partner in this marriage of convenience; both Wolff and Edward Harland bought shares in Oceanic alongside Ismay.

The *Atlantic*'s vital statistics describe a hull with a deep keel (to steady her spread of sail) but otherwise quite modern in shape, despite the mixed propulsion (sail and steam). She was 420 feet long and forty-one across the beam – the ratio, good for speed and fuel economy, of roughly ten to one overwhelmingly favoured for merchant steamers thereafter, including the "Olympics". Her gross register tonnage exceeded 3,700 and she was capable of 13.5 knots, very competitive for the time.[12] She cost about £120,000 and could carry 166 in saloon class plus 1,000 in steerage. Her maiden voyage to New York began on 6 June 1871. The press enthused about the unprecedented luxury of her appointments ...

Her nineteenth westbound crossing began at Liverpool on the afternoon of Thursday (then the customary sailing day for the passenger service to New York) 20 March 1873. The master was Captain James Agnew Williams, aged only thirty-three; this was his second voyage in command. After stopping at Queenstown the ship mustered just a few dozen cabin passengers but some 800 in steerage, including 200 children, looked after by a crew of 140. There were also fourteen stowaways, found after departure and made to work their passage, giving a total aboard of about 1,000, say three-quarters full.

On Tuesday 25 March the *Atlantic* ran into a great storm which constantly buffeted the ship and seriously slowed her down for six days. Worried about his coal supply after fighting massive waves and adverse winds for so long, Williams decided on 31 March, while 460 miles east of New York, to turn north for Halifax, Nova Scotia, only 170 miles away. At about 3.15 a.m. on 1 April the *Atlantic* ran hard aground, some fifteen miles south-west of the entrance to Halifax: slipshod navigation and bad weather had combined to place the ship at least a dozen miles due west of where her officers thought she was. Williams was asleep in the chart room at the time.

The lifeboats were smashed to pieces by the ship's grinding movements, the rocks, the wind and the surf as steerage passengers fought their way out of the bowels of the deep-hulled ship. The *Atlantic* heeled over at an angle of fifty degrees as desperate people scrambled up the rigging and the hull filled with water. When it reached the hot boilers, they exploded. The ship capsized onto her starboard side. About 250 men got ashore by means of ropes bravely dragged through the surf by seamen and slung between the rigging and some rocks. Two men swam 200 yards through rough water to raise the alarm on the offshore island the ship had struck. Local fishermen courageously launched their frail boats to go to the rescue. On the rocks, the ship broke in two and the stern section sank out of sight. Captain Williams ordered Third Officer Cornelius Brady to go by boat to the mainland and then walk to Halifax to get more help. He arrived in a state of exhaustion and shock at the Halifax office of Cunard, then White Star's local agent, late in the afternoon of 1 April; a Cunard liner, a government steamer and a tug were sent to the rescue. A total of about 400 survivors were brought back to Halifax, including the master: at least 546 people, including all but one of the 200 children, died in the worst mercantile casualty then on record. More than 400 bodies were found up to fifty miles from the scene. They were buried in mass graves nearby.

A formal inquiry for the British Board of Trade started at Halifax on 5 April and reported on the 18th. The tribunal attributed the disaster to sloppy navigation, recklessness by the Captain in choice of course and speed, as well as failure to take soundings in coastal waters. There had been too little coal aboard. The Captain's conduct after the grounding, however, had been such that his master's ticket was suspended for two years rather than revoked. He said he had gone to sleep fully dressed, leaving orders to be called at 3 a.m.

White Star appealed against the coal-skimping verdict and another hearing started on 28 May. This merely confirmed the original finding on 11 June. The line had enough influence in London to be able to persuade the Chief Surveyor of Shipping at the Board of Trade to look at the matter a third time. He found that "the question of fuel supply cannot ... have had anything to do with the loss of the *Atlantic*".[13] Indeed the coal stock had actually been rather underestimated and misreported to the Captain by Chief Engineer John Foxley. There was enough on board to get to New York, even in bad weather, with seventy tons to spare (her coal capacity was about 960 tons). But even the Chief Surveyor left the original verdict of bad seamanship untouched. This tragedy seems all the more poignant for having happened so close to land, just a few miserable miles from the port in a storm unnecessarily chosen by Captain Williams. Not surprisingly, White Star expunged the very name *Atlantic* from all its publicity material – to such effect that it is not mentioned in the table in the *Shipbuilder* listing the line's ships up to and including the "Olympics".[14] This form of suppression of all reference to a disaster was common practice at White Star and elsewhere, as will become clear.

Among other major setbacks for White Star (what follows being far from exhaustive) is the unexplained disappearance in the North Atlantic of the cattle-steamer *Naronic* (6,594 tons), then the largest cargo-ship in the world, on her thirteenth voyage in 1893. Six years later the 1874 liner *Germanic* (5,008 tons) sank under the weight of the ice on her upperworks in New York harbour – only to be resurrected and to sail on, and on and on, ultimately in Turkish livery, until 1950 (only

Cunard's *Parthia*, scrapped at the age of eighty-six, out-lasted her). In 1907, on her way home from Australia, *Suevic* (12,500 tons) ran aground near Land's End in Cornwall. The forward third, stuck fast, was amputated and the rest towed to Southampton. A new, 212-foot bow was built at Belfast and brought down to join the rest of the ship: it was a perfect fit. Two years later the *Republic* (15,378 tons) collided in fog with the liner *Florida* off Massachusetts and eventually sank; thanks to an early triumph of wireless, which brought White Star's *Baltic* to the rescue, only a few of about 1,650 passengers and crew aboard the two stricken ships were lost.[15] This catalogue of disasters stood out even among the vicissitudes of the many companies that suffered marine casualties over the turn of the century.

There is no reference to the *Titanic* in the article by Archibald Hurd on Joseph Bruce Ismay in the British *Dictionary of National Biography* (*DNB*),[16] even though the great disaster was the central event in the subject's life. His father, Thomas Henry, died in 1899. Born the eldest son at Crosby near Liverpool in December 1862, J. Bruce, as he was usually styled, took over as head of both White Star and Ismay, Imrie and Company. The latter acted as a ship-management company for Oceanic, the line's owners.

Ismay Senior was a wealthy man and showed his affection for his son in the manner long since established among the British *grande bourgeoisie* spawned by the Industrial Revolution: he sent the boy away to boarding school at the age of eight, to Elstree in Hertfordshire. From there at thirteen he went to Harrow. He did not go to university, but spent a year living with a tutor in France before entering on a four-year apprenticeship in his father's office. Then came a year travelling round the world (presumably not in steerage). Now aged twenty-four, Ismay was sent to work in the New York office of White Star for five years, rising seamlessly in a year to the status of agent for the line at its principal destination.

Now thoroughly cognizant of the family business, he returned to England in 1891 as a partner in Ismay, Imrie and Company, where he worked until his father's death. On that occasion he became chief executive of the firm and of White Star. Only three years later he sold the line. The *Dictionary of National Biography* uses strangely tortuous language in describing how it happened: "Ismay became head of the business and his management was most brilliant and successful." But in 1901 he was "approached by American interests towards forming an International Shipping Company, and after lengthy negotiations between him and J. P. Morgan ... the International Mercantile Marine Company [IMM] was formed" (the word "towards" jars here).

What really happened was that Morgan, the most powerful financier in American history, made Ismay an offer he was unable (or too weak) to refuse, from a company (IMM) which, before and after the transfer, did not pay its shareholders a dividend, unlike White Star. Morgan valued the line at ten times its 1900 earnings (swollen by Boer War contracts). Even so, one cannot imagine Ismay's much respected father, who was made of sterner stuff, just selling off White Star, then doing well, to such a foreign predator. Morgan, principal target of United States anti-trust legislation (against monopolies and cartels), wanted to dominate the transatlantic route. Ismay remained chief executive of White Star and in 1904 was made president of the IMM group as well, until his resignation in 1912. He was also a non-executive director of four British insurance and three transport companies.

His biographer in the *DNB* describes how Ismay founded and funded the Merchant Navy training-ship *Mersey* and later gave £11,000 for the widows of drowned seamen and £25,000 for mercantile veterans of the First World War. According to the *DNB* Ismay had a "striking ... overpowering personality" and "arrested attention ...

and dominated the scene" in social company. A hard exterior was the "outward veneer of a shy and highly sensitive nature, beneath which was hidden a depth of affection and understanding which is given to but few". He always showed sympathy for anyone in trouble, apparently, and had an "intense dislike of publicity". Ismay, a crack shot, enjoyed tennis, golf, motoring and (especially) fishing at his country home in Ireland. His London house was at 15 Hill Street, between Berkeley Square and Park Lane, in the most expensive district of Mayfair. He died in obscurity in London, in October 1937 – only one month after the *Olympic*'s hulk was towed to Inverkeithing in Scotland for breaking up.

The American whose British poodle and shipping agent he became, John Pierpont Morgan, ultimate owner of White Star and the "Olympic" ships, was so rich and powerful that he was able single-handedly to save the United States from defaulting on the gold convertibility of the dollar in 1895.[17] He was born to Junius Spencer Morgan, general merchant and director of an insurance company, and his wife Juliet, née Pierpont, at Hartford, Connecticut, on 17 April 1837. He inherited the prominent Pierpont nose, not the only anatomical protuberance that was to play a disproportionate part in his life. At fifteen rheumatic fever left him with a slight but permanent limp. Other teenage afflictions included eczema, migraines and fits of fainting and lethargy; but he took part in sports, notably yachting. His father went to London as agent for the American magnate George Peabody. Morgan completed his education at a Swiss school and then went to Göttingen University in Germany in 1856–7, emerging as a polished, polyglot young man of the world with a very good head for figures. Like Ismay, he was put to work at his father's office, where he started as a clerk in New York. In 1859 he moved to New Orleans to learn the cotton trade. Two years later he wed his first wife, the consumptive Amelia Sturges, the great love of his life, and was shattered when she died after only four months of marriage. Even seven years later he was toying with the idea of retiring, at the age of thirty-three, because of his persistent melancholy.[18]

Nonetheless he put his undoubted gifts and excellent start in life to optimal use, building up his father's business interests into the largest and most powerful private banking house in America. With the Morgan Guaranty Trust Company behind him he moved into, and eventually controlled, the booming American railways, forming United States Steel along the way as an instrument for dominating that industry also. He was not infallible: he once rejected a chance to buy General Motors for half a million dollars. But first, last and all the time he was a banker, undoubtedly the most powerful member of that profession there has ever been. He also became a major philanthropist and collected works of art on the vacuum-cleaner principle. On his death in 1913 they formed a vast bequest to the Metropolitan Museum of Art in New York. He served as president of the museum and also as commodore of the New York Yacht Club.

Ismay's father, fully aware of Morgan's ambitions in the Anglo-German-dominated transatlantic shipping trade and of his own company's vulnerability, tried to rally other British shipowners into a defensive, patriotic alliance.[19] Although he had retired in 1892, Ismay Senior did all he could to stem the tide, but his erstwhile colleagues and competitors did not respond and he died a disappointed man seven years later. The Americans duly got their transatlantic foothold when the International Navigation Company of New Jersey (itself owned by the Fidelity Trust of Philadelphia, Pennsylvania, a Morgan holding company) bought up the ailing Inman Line of Liverpool in 1893, alongside the American Line and the Belgian Red Star Line. Inman gave the Americans an entrée to British shipbuilding, the best in the world. Morgan changed the name of his conglomerate to IMM in 1902, also acquiring the Atlantic Transport, Leyland and Dominion lines.[20] His ambition was to construct an alliance with the Germans to break the British lead and achieve American supremacy on the transatlantic routes; doubtless he would have seen off the Germans similarly had he succeeded.

But the key purchase that made IMM a major force in transatlantic and world shipping was Morgan's acquisition for £10 million of Oceanic and its White Star Line, whose shares were transferred to a newly created subsidiary of IMM, confusingly named International Navigation Company (of Liverpool, not New Jersey). To compound the confusion, IMM then transferred the shares to two Morgan trusts as security for new bond issues. The Byzantine takeover was completed in 1902–3 against the initial opposition of the Ismays (J. Bruce and his brother James): but the shareholders took Morgan's dollars and ran, very wisely as it turned out.

The British Government woke up late to the threat to one of the country's most important invisible-export earners and decided to do all it could to keep White Star's great rival, the Cunard Line, British – encouraged by Cunard's opportunist chief, Lord Inverclyde. It sanctioned cheap loans for building the *Lusitania* and *Mauretania*, on condition that they would be available, with decks strengthened for guns, to the Government in case of war. There were fears that "British" ships owned by American interests could be whisked out of reach of requisition in a crisis (but Morgan's son fortunately proved to be an Anglophile). Cunard found no difficulty in accepting this windfall: the company was to become the undisputed market leader and enjoy a total triumph over its Americanized rival.

James Ismay and William Imrie (Thomas Ismay's erstwhile partners) and one other left the Oceanic board, but J. Bruce Ismay (chairman and managing director) and Harold Arthur Sanderson stayed on. So did William James Pirrie of Harland and Wolff. Ismay (as £20,000-a-year president) and Pirrie later joined Morgan himself on the board of IMM among its five "voting trustees",[21] once Ismay had won undertakings on White Star's survival.

Billionaire tycoons tend to require that everything, including the tiniest subsidiary of their conglomerates, must show a profit to justify its existence. In his youth J. P. Morgan[22] kept a detailed note of every cent he spent (in later years, when his wealth swelled out of sight as if in sympathy with his all too visible bottle-nose, he retained rafts of accountants and lawyers for such purposes, but it is a racing certainty that he always knew exactly how much he was worth).

Morgan took an active personal interest in the affairs of White Star,[23] the prestige jewel in IMM's crown and by far its biggest earner. We can be certain that, as Morgan's only noteworthy business failure, IMM's poor performance must have rankled: imagine a Morgan company which paid no dividend ... Thus the great man, chubby, balding and, as ever, preceded by the nasal beacon which was the real reason why he shied away from publicity, came to Belfast in February 1910 to look at the plans for the *Titanic*.[24] He examined every detail, down to the choice of furniture, in the uniquely opulent suite on B deck earmarked for him in her plans. She and her sister were, after all, being constructed with his money, in the struggle to build up White Star as the locomotive to pull the loss-making IMM into profit. Morgan supported Ismay's policy of going for size and luxury rather than the speed pursued by Cunard and the Germans. He was in the city again on 31 May 1911 for the razzmatazz of the *Titanic*'s launch and the *Olympic*'s departure: Morgan, returning to Britain at the very end of 1911, promised to join the *Titanic* for her maiden voyage.

Given his formidable personality and the ruthlessness with which he used his limitless financial resources in the pursuit of power and profit, it is at least surprising that he permitted the complaisant, money-no-object arrangement between Harland and Wolff and White Star not only to continue but to flourish. There was no contract but only a letter of agreement for the construction of the "Olympics". Morgan kept Ismay on as chief executive of White Star and persuaded him to run IMM itself from 1904 for as long as he was willing to, even though neither company produced the kind of profit Morgan had been looking for when he took over. Ismay left both after the disaster, having decided at about the time of the *Olympic*'s collision with the *Hawke* to retire at fifty.

The reason behind Morgan's indulgence was William James Pirrie, chairman of Harland and Wolff, director of White Star and IMM. It was Pirrie who helped and encouraged a willing Morgan to break into British shipping, undertaking soundings and negotiations on his behalf – and it was Pirrie who put up the idea of building the three "Olympics", after dinner at Ismay's London house. Pirrie, in short, brought off a marriage between British technical prowess and American money (this union ended in disillusion and divorce, whereas that between Harland and Wolff and White Star lasted until the latter's death). His motive was to secure the future of his beloved yard, in deepening financial trouble and desperately short of capital, by means of orders from all IMM lines.

Yet of the leading figures behind the genesis of the giant ships and the 1912 disaster, Pirrie came closest to escaping the attention of history[25] – even though he was the only one to have a personal and financial stake in both IMM/White Star and Harland and Wolff. Lord Mersey, the judge at the British inquiry, though very keen to trace connections between builder and owner, could find no other.[26] The "Olympics" were Pirrie's idea, his broad design, his products; but illness spared him both the fateful voyage and interrogation at the British inquiry. Unlike the other two in the *Titanic* triumvirate, Pirrie was not at all shy of publicity, as shown by his readiness to accept one high-profile public appointment after another. How ironic it is that Ismay was reviled for surviving the disaster and

Morgan for the luxury of his suite on a ship with "no lifeboats for steerage passengers", while Pirrie, their go-between and the prime mover in the whole story, hardly got a mention.[27]

Pirrie was born in Quebec in 1847, the only son of James Alexander Pirrie and Margaret, née Montgomery, both of the Scots-Irish stock which was the backbone of the Protestant minority in Ireland (and since 1921, the majority in Northern Ireland). The parents returned to the Belfast area soon enough to put the young William James into the Royal Academical Institution, a grand Belfast school. No academic, he became an apprentice at Harland and Wolff in 1862. It took him only twelve years to become a partner in the expanding yard; and after its founder, Edward Harland, died in 1895, Pirrie was made chief executive, turning it into a public company. When Harland's partner, Wolff, retired in 1906, Pirrie became chairman as well, initiating a great modernization and expansion with two huge new slipways under a colossal gantry: clearly the "Olympics" were already more than a gleam in his eye, although he did not put up the idea to a compliant Ismay until 1907. By then he was comfortably established both as a pioneer in design and a shrewd businessman in a tough industry: "For half a century he was identified with all the important developments which took place in naval architecture and marine engineering ... In a sense he may be said to have been the creator of the big ship."[28] Among his many honours and awards, he was a Knight of the Order of St Patrick and a Privy Councillor (1897), an honorary Doctor of both Laws and Science; he became Baron Pirrie in 1906 on taking sole (and dictatorial) control of the yard.

We can complete Pirrie's history briefly here by noting that the flow of Establishment baubles continued unabated after the great maritime disaster with which he was so intimately concerned yet scarcely associated by the public. He was promoted to Viscount in 1921, when King George V came to Belfast to open its new provincial parliament after the partition of Ireland. In the meantime, among his string of public appointments, Pirrie served as a Justice of the Peace; as Lord Mayor of Belfast in 1896–7; as His Majesty's Lieutenant for the city in 1911; and for many years as Pro-Chancellor of Queen's University, Belfast. In March 1918 he was appointed Controller-General of shipping in succession to Sir Joseph Maclay, with dictatorial powers to speed up construction after the great shipping crisis brought on by the U-boats in the previous year. He also took a hand in modernizing and expanding dock and harbour facilities nationally. Before that he had supervised a rapid expansion in the production of merchantmen, warships and even aircraft at Harland and Wolff for the war effort. Employment at the yard peaked at 50,000.

Pirrie died at sea without issue in 1924, still in harness as chairman and on his way home from an inspection of South American ports, where he had made recommendations for modernization. Once again the *Dictionary of National Biography* makes no mention of the *Titanic* in his entry. Given that Lord Pirrie is the "Teflon" man of the story to whom nothing stuck, this seems a less surprising omission in his case than in Ismay's. Yet it is a big gap, and a distortion of the historical record. Harland and Wolff papers in the Northern Ireland Public Record Office show that Pirrie accumulated debts of about £1 million in his declining years and was effectively bankrupt when he died.

His company was founded by Edward Harland, who in 1858 bought Hickson's yard on Queen's Island, Belfast. Like Ismay a few years later, he needed finance and got it from his friend Gustavus Schwabe; the latter's nephew Gustav Wolff duly became a partner in the yard in 1861. Harland's many technological breakthroughs included the box-shaped hull with steadying bilge-keels, providing much more room for cargo and comfortable accommodation. The yard and its future principal client were thus linked by the Schwabe connection before Ismay and Harland met.

When they did, they developed, with Schwabe's blessing, a remarkable way of doing business which survived them both. There was no detailed contract for a given ship but only the letter of agreement. Harland and Wolff would build the vessel on a "cost-plus" basis, regardless of the price of labour and materials, but closely consulting and obtaining the agreement of White Star at every stage; the yard then added a commission of five per cent to the final bill. The result was a long list of supremely large and luxurious ships which had to work long and hard to pay for themselves: an undamaged *Olympic* would have needed six years of intensive use to recover her construction costs. Harland and Wolff, however, could not lose on their White Star deal as they took on work for other clients, including the Bibby, Royal Mail and Peninsular and Oriental lines and even some of their German competitors. Having indirectly sold his main client to Morgan, Pirrie helped the American organize a price-cutting cartel with the Germans to undermine Cunard (no customer of Pirrie's, so doubtless seen as fair game) which had to be rescued by the British taxpayer. In the peculiarly British tradition of the "Great and Good" still with us today, Pirrie let this shark loose on his country while accepting every honour it could bestow.

Harland and Wolff soldiers on to this day, 136 years old and now the only major, home-owned general shipyard in the United Kingdom. The Morgan Guaranty Trust Company of New York seems to flourish. White Star however is long gone, but its later history was scarcely less dramatic than its earlier record and is therefore summarized here.

The decision to build the third "Olympic" was taken in summer 1911 and announced on 1 September. There is no formal confirmation, but many contemporary press reports said she was to be named the *Gigantic*.[29] In May

1912 Ismay flatly denied this and on the 30th the name *Britannic* was announced. It was obviously changed after, and because of, the disaster.[30] The word "gigantic" is familiar enough, deriving from the ancient Greek for giant; in classical mythology, the Giants were another preternatural race who, like the Titans, took on the Olympian gods and lost.[31] White Star had doubtless had enough of portents; instead of turning to ancient divinities they fell back on the spirit of the nation. And it was exclusively the nation that the new monster served: she never carried a fare-paying passenger. Launched in February 1914 as the latest "world's largest ship" (48,158 tons; 889 feet by ninety-four), she was not completed, thanks mainly to wartime factors, until November 1915. That autumn, once again and for the last time, two "Olympics" were together in the Harland and Wolff yard (the other being converted into the war's most successful troop-transport).

The *Britannic* was requisitioned as a hospital ship as soon as she was ready and was commissioned in December. In five return voyages to the Mediterranean she brought back 15,000 sick and wounded – more than enough men for an infantry division. On her sixth voyage to the Mediterranean HMHS *Britannic* struck a German mine in the Aegean off Kea Island on 21 November 1916, her fate probably sealed by a "sympathetic explosion" in a coal-bunker. She took fifty minutes to go down by the head; only twenty-one people died, mostly caught in the swirling propellers as engines were re-started in an attempt to beach the ship. The only survivor of one lifeboat thus sucked under was Violet Jessop – who had been a stewardess on the *Titanic*. Fireman John Priest also served on all three "Olympics" and lived. Of the thirty-five ships in the White Star fleet in 1914, ten were lost in the war. After it, the accidents and near misses continued, though with hardly any loss of life.

IMM lost interest in the transatlantic rat-race in 1926, selling White Star to the venerable Royal Mail Line for about £8 million, a loss of £2 million. Its chief, Lord

Kylsant, had succeeded Pirrie in the chair at Harland and
Wolff and also had interests in the Union Castle Line, the
Southern Railway and the Midland Bank; but he was no
J. P. Morgan. With Harold Sanderson, the only survivor
of the pre-Morgan years on the board, as his deputy, he
set up a new company called White Star Line Limited
and used its high turnover and occasional profits to help
finance the purchase of two other lines, recklessly over-
extending himself. Then came the Slump. Parliamentary
questions in 1931 led to a government inquiry into the
Royal Mail group. Kylsant was subsequently convicted of
issuing a false prospectus for a 1928 share issue. He was
sentenced to a year in prison.

In 1933 the British Government once again offered
Cunard a subsidy, to help what was long since the leading
transatlantic line to complete the first of its two colossal,
80,000-ton "Queens" (the *Queen Mary*) – not to fend off
White Star this time but to take it over. An enabling act
was rushed through Parliament in 1934 and White Star
was wound up a year later; its debt of over £11 million
was written off. The defunct Oceanic was dissolved in
1939 and Kylsant's no less redundant White Star Line
Limited in 1945: Cunard–White Star then happily sawed
the second barrel off its name. Cunard plain and simple
thus had the last laugh, after a long and bitter commercial
struggle. According to the National Maritime Museum
at Greenwich, even White Star's company records have
vanished.[32] Cunard sailed on, still operating the world's
best-known liner, *Queen Elizabeth II*, or "*QE2*" for short,
in 1996 (despite a disastrous Christmas cruise when she
set sail in the midst of major repairs because a German
yard fell behind with a refit in 1994). The line, reflecting
the shrivelled circumstances of British shipping, was by
then however owned by the Trafalgar House property
group. One White Star vessel survives (if without its
funnel): the *Nomadic*, the tender for first and second
classes built for the "Olympics" in 1911, now a floating
restaurant in Paris.

Sanderson has already featured twice in our story. Since he appears again, notably in a cameo role at the British inquiry, and since he was with White Star longer than anyone except Ismay, he deserves a little space. The usual sources are unhelpful. This professional company director and dedicated clubman appeared in *Who's Who* annually, but as subjects control their entries we perforce rely unduly on the man himself.[33] He suppressed his age, parents, education and address. He was born in Bebington, Cheshire, not far from Liverpool, to "Richard Sanderson of London". His mother is not mentioned. In 1885 he married Maud Blood "of New York" (who died in 1927); they had two sons and a daughter. He was thus probably in his seventies when he died in February 1932.

After rising to a partnership in Sanderson and Son of New York, presumably his father's firm, he became a partner in Ismay, Imrie and Company in 1899. He had a seat on the board of half a dozen other shipping and associated companies and on the Mersey Docks and Harbour Board. He was a down-table director of all these corporations but became president of the Liverpool Shipbrokers' Benevolent Society and captain of Formby (Lancashire) golf club. Like his mentors, Morgan and Ismay, he was fond of such commercially useful avocations as motoring, hunting and yachting. His clubs included the Royal Yacht Squadron (Cowes, Isle of Wight), the Royal Thames (London) and Larchmont (New York) yacht clubs, as well as the Constitutional, City of London and White's gentlemen's clubs. His *Who's Who* reference included this cryptic note: "M: YP4724". The italic "M" means member: the number suggests a masonic lodge, which suits an obviously secretive operator who wanted the cachet of a *Who's Who* entry without giving anything away to strangers.

Having also introduced the *Titanic* triumvirate of Ismay, Morgan and Pirrie – agent, owner and builder – together with the line, the trust and the yard behind the catastrophe, we can return to 1911 and the completion of the *Titanic*, keel number 401, hot on the heels of the *Olympic*, keel number 400, and related matters.

Ever after the disaster there has been a hunt for portents, omens, auguries and Awful Warnings in the period between the laying of the keel and the fateful voyage. However sceptical one may be about the paranormal, it has to be admitted that the superstitious and the paranoid are presented with plenty of ammunition by attested events. Take, for example, the *Titanic*'s hull number, 390904. It is possible to imagine, especially if one is waylaid by a conspiracy theorist, that when handwritten with an open figure four and straight-legged nines and then held up to a mirror, this number spells out the phrase NOPOPE. It probably helps to be on a galloping horse at the time. How often the number was thus viewed is not recorded; but Roman Catholic workers at the yard are said to have complained to the management and were solemnly assured that it was a coincidence. Some saw it as a portent of disaster.[34]

This is not the place to go into Northern Ireland's longstanding ethnic division, but it expresses itself in religious terms. To oversimplify, the descendants of the Anglo-Scots settlers of the seventeenth century are Protestant and Unionist (in favour of the British connection) in their politics, while the indigenes are Roman Catholic with Irish Nationalist views. The trouble with the foregoing anecdote is that the vast majority of Harland and Wolff workers have traditionally been Protestant, and if they noticed the mirror effect they would have regarded it as a great joke and no reason for unease. Given the discrimination in most fields, including labour, against Catholics prevalent in those hard times (and not yet extinct), it is hard to imagine industrial unrest arising over something so arcane, even in the unhappy province's most paranoid moments. Eaton and Haas, who record the "No Pope" story, retail another rumour: that the speed of work on the *Titanic* caused workers to be sealed up inside the hull (probably inspired by the "unexplained" tapping of an inspector).

When researching his book on the disaster, Michael Davie met a Harland and Wolff veteran whose grandfather and uncle had worked on the "Olympics".[35] The old man produced another conspiracy theory based on the fact that at the time of construction Home Rule (internal autonomy) for the whole of Ireland was one of the main issues in British politics. Pirrie was a committed Home Ruler, unusually for a Protestant; furthermore the "Olympics" were being built for an "English" company. The bulk of the mainly Protestant workforce would have had some sympathy for the treasonable threat by the Irish Unionist leader, Sir Edward Carson, to resist Home Rule by force (he was disastrously appeased with a Cabinet seat and a peerage). The old welder did not say it in so many words, but left Davie with a hint of politically motivated sabotage, deliberate carelessness or at least shoddy work. Anyone who has spent any time looking at the politics of Northern Ireland, as one of the present authors has, will recognize this for what it is: a classic manifestation of that special local paranoia, commonplace but not universal, which sees absolutely everything in ethno-religious, party-political terms. The flaw in this theory is that the class leader, the *Olympic*, despite her poor steel, survived many further adventures in peace and war, remaining afloat for a quarter of a century. This was no record; had she avoided her early mishaps she might, with better steel (and modernized), have lasted much longer. Both monster "Queens" and the *QE2* worked for well over thirty years each (the *Queen Mary* was still tied up at Long Beach, California, in 1995 after more than sixty years afloat). Twenty-five years at sea thus argue the opposite of bad workmanship.

We can safely ignore the American poetastrix Celia Thaxter, who wrote a McGonagallesque dirge in 1874 about a ship hitting an iceberg: her "premonition" that all aboard died was fortunately exaggerated. We can pass over the British spiritualist and great newspaper editor, W. T. Stead, who died in the disaster: he had written a short story in 1886 about a sea collision made worse by a lifeboat shortage, and another in 1892 about the rescue of survivors of a ship that hit an iceberg.

But we cannot ignore the most astounding coincidence in the *Titanic* canon (and probably in all literature): the novella *Futility*, by the American amateur mystic Morgan Robertson (1861–1915), published in 1898. Robertson, a former Merchant Navy officer, was worried by the widespread and cavalier disregard of the iceberg threat to the ever larger and faster ships of his day. No other "premonitions" are recorded under his name. The similarities between his fictional SS *Titan*, which also hit an iceberg and sank, and the real ship show up best in tabular form:

	Titanic	*Titan*
Flag	British	British
Time of voyage	April	April
Displacement	60,250 tons	70,000 tons
Length	882 feet	800 feet
Top speed	24 knots	24 knots
Capacity	3,000+ people	c. 3,000 people
No. aboard	c. 2,200	2,000
Propellers	Three	Three
Lifeboats	20 (1,178 places)	24 (500 places)
W/t bulkheads	15	19
Side hit	Starboard	Starboard

It would be very satisfying to be able to say whether any of the key figures in the *Titanic* saga knew of this Awful Warning before the event it "foresaw", but we found no such indication. It seems unlikely because the story became famous only on serialization after the real-life disaster.

As we saw, work began on the *Titanic* on 31 March 1909,

three and a half months after the *Olympic*; the time-lag grew to seven and a half months by launching and over ten months by sailing. There is nothing untoward in this expanding gap, which indicates only that effort was focused on the class leader to have her in service as soon as possible. It took just over seven months to complete the *Olympic* from launch while the *Titanic* took ten months to fit out; but there was plenty of other important work going on at the yard throughout the period. There was obviously room for flexibility: witness the bravura orchestration of the *Titanic*'s launch and *Olympic*'s departure on 31 May 1911. More than seven weeks of unexpected and extensive repairs to the *Olympic* set back the date announced for the *Titanic*'s maiden voyage by a mere three weeks, when there was only one dry dock available for both – even though Ismay insisted his promenade screens be fitted to the latter at the eleventh hour, as well as ordering minor alterations to the *Olympic* while she was laid up.[36] The efficiency with which Harland and Wolff, confidently rolling back the frontiers of technology, built these pioneering superliners is still amazing to contemplate. No ship of theirs is known to have been lost to intrinsic mechanical or structural failure; the undoubted design and safety shortcomings were due at least as much to government as to them.

The list of specifications for the fitting out of the *Titanic* was even longer than her sister's, a huge, thick book of nearly 300 pages dealing with everything from the panelling of the public rooms to paintbrushes, candelabras to cots, masts to mops.[37] Three bells were fitted, one twenty-three inches in diameter at the foot of the foremast to sound the watches for the benefit of the crew in the forecastle, one of seventeen inches in the crow's nest on the same mast to enable the lookouts to sound warnings and one of nine inches on the bridge. Some 3,560 cork lifebelts were supplied, more than enough for a full complement of passengers and crew. As vessels of over 10,000 tons (the largest category recognized by the Government

in the 1894 Merchant Shipping Act) with watertight transverse bulkheads, the "Olympics" were legally required to
provide lifeboats for 960 people. As we have seen, there
were places for 1,178, a voluntary "bonus" of nearly
twenty-three per cent over the minimum – but 2,369 too
few to accommodate everybody legally permitted to be
carried on the *Titanic*. Even without the benefit of hindsight, the lifeboat provision seems illogical. Either the
legal minimum was adequate or it was not. If it was
adequate, why exceed it by a quarter – unless there was
an unspoken awareness that it was inadequate? And if it
was inadequate, why limit the margin to a quarter,
especially when Carlisle, the original designer, had initially
wanted places for all?

Even as this multifarious work proceeded at a frenetic
pace – an X-ray of the ship would have revealed an
extraordinary hive of activity involving swarms of men –
the *Titanic* had to be hauled out of the graving dock and
the *Olympic* edged in for examination and refitting of her
port propeller. Then the double manoeuvre was repeated,
to provide turning room for the departing ship. There was
to be no time for a quick visit to Liverpool, the ships'
nominal port of registration (chosen because White Star's
head office was there): the last chance for that vanished
when high winds kept the *Titanic* waiting an extra day in
Belfast for her sea trials.

Captain Haddock had taken over the *Olympic* with effect
from her 3 April sailing so as to free White Star's commodore, Captain Smith, to command once again, as was the
custom, the company's latest liner and *ex-officio* flagship.
Some authorities on the disaster say that Smith was only
to captain the maiden voyage before retiring at sixty-two;
others say he would have retained command and retired
only after taking the *Britannic* on her first sailing, when
he would have attained the usual pension age of sixty-
five; the missing White Star archives would presumably

have settled this matter along with other puzzles. There is no record of a successor to Smith being chosen for the *Titanic* before she sailed. The voyage was undoubtedly Smith's last, but there is no indication whether it was intended to be.

Haddock was new to the superliners whereas Smith was not, which makes the decision abruptly to deprive the former of the services of Chief Officer Henry Wilde as well as the *Olympic*'s First Officer, William McMaster Murdoch, seem strange. It appears as unhelpful as Ismay's eleventh-hour insistence on promenade screens – especially as Wilde himself was reluctant to change berths.[38] As a result Murdoch, promoted as the *Titanic*'s designate Chief Officer, was bumped down to First Officer and Charles Herbert Lightoller, designated First, to Second Officer. David Blair, who came aboard in Belfast as Second Officer, was doubtless not sorry later that he was dismissed at Southampton and reassigned to a berth elsewhere. The command reshuffle was not completed until the very morning of the departure from there on 10 April. But if Smith (as distinct from White Star) requisitioned Wilde as a trusty deputy for the special voyage he was about to command, the caution which this may be seen to indicate is far from typical of the master.

Edward John Smith, known to the Merchant Navy as "E.J.", was born in 1850 at Hanley, in the Potteries conurbation of Staffordshire, not quite as far from the sea as it is possible to get in England. Nonetheless on leaving school at thirteen he went to Liverpool to serve an apprenticeship under sail with Gibson and Company, before joining White Star as a junior officer in 1880. He rose rapidly to his first command in 1887.

Less than two years later he had the first of a series of maritime mishaps, when the *Republic* ran aground off Sandy Hook at the entrance to New York harbour on 27 January 1889. She was stuck for five hours before being floated off and entering port to unload her passengers. No sooner was this complete than a furnace flue over a forward boiler fractured, killing three crewmen and injuring seven. At the end of a very trying day, a bluff Captain Smith commented only that the damage was minor. (This was not the *Republic* lost in 1909 but her 1872 predecessor, which was sold off later in 1889.)

Smith's next accident occurred after less than two years, when he ran the homeward-bound *Coptic* aground off Rio de Janeiro in December 1890. Damage again was minor.

All apparently went well for "E.J." over the next eleven years, during which he served with distinction in the Boer War, captaining troop-ships and earning the Transport Medal, the Reserve Decoration and the rank of Commander in the Royal Naval Reserve (which is why his ships latterly flew the "Blue Duster" of the RNR rather than the "Red Duster" of the British Merchant Navy).

In 1901 he found himself in command of the *Majestic*, built in 1890. A fire, attributed to a wiring fault, broke out in a linen closet at five in the morning of 7 August 1901, as she was approaching New York. Water was poured through a hole cut in the deck above; but five hours later the blaze restarted, exuding choking smoke and fumes into adjacent cabins. The fire was finally extinguished by injecting steam. The protracted incident was not unique, but it was odd for at least one reason: Smith said afterwards that nobody had alerted him at the time so he knew nothing until it was all over. There being no hazard at sea worse than fire, the omission seems as bizarre as Smith's apparent insouciance.

Commodore from 1904, Smith captained White Star's current flagship exclusively for the rest of his career, starting with the second *Baltic*. While he was still her master on 3 November 1906, a fire broke out in number five hold, in Liverpool dock. The hold was flooded and the blaze put out, but 640 bales of wool were destroyed or damaged by fire and/or water.

Having transferred from the *Baltic* in 1907, Smith was in command of the *Adriatic* (24,541 tons) on 10 October

1908 when four members of the crew were caught systematically looting passengers' baggage of goods worth $15,000, stashed away in various parts of the ship.

Thirteen months later when approaching New York once more, the *Adriatic* ran hard aground and stuck for five hours at the entrance to the Ambrose Channel, on 4 November 1909.

On 8 August 1910 firemen, volatile as usual, went on strike aboard the *Adriatic*, still White Star's flagship, while she was in Southampton.

We have already seen how the *Olympic* under Smith's command ended her maiden voyage to New York on 21 June 1911 by trapping and almost crushing a tug; how she collided with HMS *Hawke* on 20 September (under pilot's orders, but with Smith on the bridge and in a position to act, which he did not); and how she ran over a wreck on 24 February 1912, losing a propeller-blade.

That and no fewer than three groundings of liners are more than enough to make Smith's record stand out, even by the happy-go-lucky standards of the high summer of steam. It was customary to pay masters and officers a substantial annual bonus if the ships on which they were serving managed to escape damage during the year, a fact which shows how common mishaps were in those days. By the time Smith achieved command of the world's largest ship, the first of the "Olympics", he was the world's best-paid seaman on a salary of £1,250 per annum. His no-collision bonus would have meant an extra £200, or a handsome sixteen per cent. He could hardly have claimed to qualify in 1911.

During the customary lay-over after he had brought the *Adriatic* into New York in mid-May 1907 on her uneventful maiden voyage, Captain Smith granted the city's and America's leading newspaper, *The New York Times*, the favour of an interview. The reporter naturally asked him if he had ever been involved in any dramatic incidents in his long career. Apart from bad weather, the grizzled captain cheerfully replied, he had never had any trouble at sea, nor did he anticipate any.[39] "I will say that I cannot imagine any condition that would cause a ship to founder ... Modern shipbuilding has gone beyond that," he said. Beyond what was not made clear, but the underlying implication is that the latest ships were indestructible. In the light of the foregoing catalogue, leaving aside the serious incidents that occurred after the interview and allowing for the gung-ho approach of contemporary masters working to narrow margins and tight schedules, the denial is an egregious example of British understatement – or, in plainer English, a lie. Somewhere around this time, Senator William Alden Smith was shown round the *Adriatic* during a New York stopover by Captain Edward John Smith. The two men were not yet related.

It was of this frock-coated buccaneer that the Attorney-General, Sir Rufus Isaacs, said at the British inquiry in his opening address: "He took charge of the *Titanic* because, as one would gather, the White Star Line had complete confidence in his skill and judgment. He had been many years in their employment and in command of vessels belonging to the White Star Line; and I believe I am right in saying that, except for the occurrence between the *Hawke* and the *Olympic*, there had never been any collision in any vessel which he had commanded ... " Strictly speaking this was true apart from one tug; but a lawyer is only as good as his brief. The Attorney-General's colleague, Butler Aspinall, said Smith was "a man with a good record"; and one of the heroes of the disaster, Captain Arthur Rostron of the rescuing liner *Carpathia*, told the inquiry on its twenty-eighth day that he had known Smith, a man of "very high standing".

Smith's wife was called Eleanor and their only daughter, born at the turn of the century, was named Helen. The family lived in an imposing, detached and double-fronted house, "Woodhead", in Winn Road, in the outlying Southampton suburb of Westwood, as befitted a man at the pinnacle of his respected profession.[40] He also looked the part, in his braided peaked cap and long, navy-blue coat with the two medals over the heart and four gold rings on each sleeve – a solid, even majestic figure with a neatly trimmed, King George V full beard, radiating good humour and confidence, hardly ever raising his voice. Despite attaching great weight to deference and discipline, he managed to be both popular and highly respected among his superiors at White Star, his peers and subordinates at sea and with the passengers, a rare feat in any context.

He also had *élan*, as Second Officer Lightoller, senior survivor from the crew in the disaster, vividly recalled: "It was an education to see him conn his ship up through the intricate channels entering New York at full speed. One particular bad corner ... used to make us flush with pride as he swung her round, judging his distances to a nicety, she heeling over to the helm with only a matter of feet to spare between each end of the ship and the banks."[41] The landlubber's mind boggles nevertheless: no wonder he ran ships aground so often.

Such was the master of his craft who walked aboard the *Titanic* at Belfast on 1 April 1912 to take command for her sea trials in Belfast Lough, a long bay opening eastward into the North Channel of the Irish Sea. Stormy weather forced a twenty-four-hour postponement. Lord Pirrie had wanted to come but was ill with prostate-gland trouble and was represented by Thomas Andrews, now managing director of the yard, as well as Edward Wilding, senior naval architect; Ismay had a previous engagement and was represented by his partner, fellow IMM and White Star director Harold Sanderson. This was, after all, the second time an "Olympic" had been tested and deputies were surely quite appropriate for the occasion.

There is also an air of the blasé about the trial itself. Whereas the first "Olympic" had been put through her paces over two days, the second apparently needed only one: more precisely, just twelve hours at sea. Five tugs took the liner from the yard via the River Lagan and the Victoria Channel into open water, as steam built up in her boilers. The Board of Trade surveyor at Belfast, Francis Carruthers, who had made 2,000 visits during her construction, was once again calling the shots, although Captain Smith was in command. Rather less than half a full crew was aboard; a complete one, including the large stewards' department, would be signed on at Southampton. But, despite the general hardship among seafarers caused by the long coal strike, only one fireman of those who had joined in Belfast before the trials signed on again at Southampton for the voyage proper – Thomas McQuillan.

As with the *Olympic*, the *Titanic* was put through her paces, stopping and starting with various engine combinations, but was not required to run a measured mile or make maximum revolutions and does not appear to have surpassed 20.5 knots for more than a few minutes. At that speed her turning circle was found to have a diameter of just 3,850 feet (while the ship moved forward 2,100 feet, or getting on for two and a half times her own length), a performance which impressed Carruthers. In the "emergency stop" test begun at 20 knots, the ship needed 850 yards or almost half a mile, after her engines were thrown from "Full Ahead" through "Stop" to "Full Astern", to come to a halt. The ship maintained a modest average speed of 18 knots for her two-hour, straight-course running test, although she touched 21 knots for a few minutes. On the return run, she was swung rapidly from side to side to test her handling, slalom fashion.

While these trials were taking place the two wireless operators, John "Jack" Phillips and Harold Bride, his junior, were tuning in and testing the ship's Marconi apparatus. Although subject to the ship's articles and classified as junior officers, the two men were employed and paid by the Marconi Company, as was the custom in those early days of marine wireless. The set functioned flawlessly. The ship's compasses were also fine-tuned and calibrated on the open sea, free from the many magnetic distractions of the shipyard. The last requests from Carruthers, sixteen years in his job and a former ship's chief engineer, to Captain Smith were that both main anchors be dropped and the lifeboats swung out and back, though not lowered.[42] Fourth Officer Boxhall personally ensured the boats were properly equipped when the ship left Belfast; but he, like all the other officers, had apparently not been told that the davits and boats were strong enough to take a full load of passengers before launch.

After that the inspector happily signed the certificate declaring the ship suitable for passengers and emigration for one year. Andrews and Sanderson signed the papers formally transferring the ship from builder to owner. Although Andrews and eight assistants would stay aboard as the builders' "guarantee group" to make final adjustments and deal with teething troubles on the first voyage, the vessel was now the property of the White Star Line. The weather having already delayed the trials for a day and put paid to a viewing stop at Liverpool, the ship weighed anchor just an hour after Carruthers, Sanderson and other supernumeraries had gone ashore. She averaged slightly more than 20 knots (and briefly touched 23.5) for the untroubled 570-mile run to Southampton, where she docked in the first few minutes of 4 April.

Because of the coal strike the port was inordinately crowded with idle ships whose passages had been cancelled or postponed. Demand had slackened as passengers postponed their travel and emigration plans amid the uncertainties caused by the fuel shortage. This was solved for Smith's next voyage by contributions from the *Olympic* (she had brought extra coal from New York in sacks piled up in some of her public rooms) and by plundering the bunkers of other IMM ships marooned in Southampton. To assemble a moderately respectable complement of passengers, even for the 10 April first sailing to New York of the world's most luxurious ship, White Star found it necessary to divert, not to say pirate, many travellers from other ships. They included people booked first class on older liners, who had to rest content with second-class cabins on the new one: the standard of comfort may have been greater but the cachet of "first class" was still missing.[43] Even so, the ship was barely half filled.

No doubt the coal famine was the obvious explanation for many a last-minute change of plan, vacillation and cancellation by many intending travellers, who were in any case in short supply in spring 1912 because of a whole series of strikes affecting shipping. But at least fifty-five people changed their minds about sailing on the *Titanic* in particular at short notice.[44]

By far the most interesting was John Pierpont Morgan, who had promised that he would be aboard. He pleaded ill health. A former business partner of his, Robert Bacon, the departing American Ambassador to Paris, and his wife and daughter, also cancelled, some time after Morgan had called on him en route to Aix-les-Bains in the South of France. Bacon said he had to stay on to help his delayed successor to settle in.

Henry C. Frick, a steel magnate and anti-union ally of Morgan's, had earlier cancelled his reservation of "millionaire suite" number B52 with private promenade merely because his wife had sprained her ankle on a cruise to Madeira. The suite was reallocated to Morgan, until he made his excuses. It was then assigned to Mr and Mrs J. Horace Harding, who decided to go home on the faster *Mauretania*. In the end J. Bruce Ismay inherited it by default.

On 9 April, the very eve of departure, George W. Vanderbilt of the railway and shipping family and his wife cancelled on the urging of her mother, who reminded them of all the fuss and bother associated with maiden voyages. Their servant, Frederick Wheeler, and their luggage however sailed as planned and were lost with the ship. A telegram to relatives after the sinking reporting the Vanderbilts safe on another ship may have played a part in a garbled interception and an erroneous deduction and announcement that the *Titanic* herself was safe.

The "Olympics" were conceived, proposed, planned and built by a man who lived beyond his means and would stop at nothing to promote himself and his beloved ship-yard when it fell victim to a cash-flow crisis. He unleashed a rapacious J. P. Morgan, of a higher order of ruthlessness altogether, on an unprepared Britain and helped to sell his own principal customer down the river. The latter, the White Star Line that commissioned the ships on Lord Pirrie's proposal, Morgan's money and Ismay's approval, had a record before and during the relevant period of dubious business ethics and slap-happy seamanship. Its hereditary chief was a weak character, as dazzled as Pirrie by Morgan's wealth and power. And White Star's commo-dore was not just a showman who made the passengers feel good but also a show-off who drove the world's biggest liners as if they were gigantic speedboats. So much for Smith, Ismay, Morgan and Pirrie, the quartet behind the loss of the steamship *Titanic*.

3

ALL ABOARD

On her departure from Belfast there were binoculars in
the crow's nest of the *Titanic*.[1] There was also a fire in
number ten coal-bunker in number six boiler-room. On
departure from Southampton eight days later, the binoculars had gone – but the fire had not.[2] From 1 April
in Belfast the Chief Officer was William McMaster
Murdoch, master's certificate number 025780; but on the
eve of departure from Southampton he was ordered to
step down as the Captain's deputy in favour of Henry
Wilde, master's certificate 027371.[3]

However bizarre it may seem, there were no binoculars
in the crow's nest of the world's most luxurious liner as
she set out across the Atlantic on a heavily advertised
maiden voyage in an extended ice-season known to be
exceptionally bad, when there were no fewer than five
pairs lying around on the bridge, according to Charles
Lightoller. There was even a binocular storage-box built
into the nest. George Hogg, a lookout, recalled that the
pair available to him and his five colleagues between
Belfast and Southampton, when the Second Officer was
David Blair, were marked "Second Officer, *Titanic*". Hogg
had been ordered to lock them away in the Second Officer's cabin after the run to Southampton, where Lightoller
took over as Second Officer: Hogg said he had asked him
in vain for their return.[4] Ismay told the British inquiry
that White Star had invariably provided binoculars for

the lookouts until 1895; after that it was left to each master's discretion.

Anyone who has ever looked for, or at, anything at sea or in open country will be aware of the value, and the limitations, of binoculars. In keeping an eye out for anything untoward the best instrument is the naked eye: any distant object or phenomenon which strikes it, whether a ship, an iceberg or unidentified speck, can be examined and identified with binoculars. If looking for a specific object – an island or a landscape feature, for example – it is best to establish the general direction in which to look with the unaided eye before using the glasses. Scanning a land- or seascape, or the horizon, with glasses, which achieve their magnifying effect by severely *restricting* the field of view, can easily mean missing something in the middle distance, or vice versa. It is most efficient to let the eye roam systematically over the entire scene, using glasses to examine any individual features. Besides, holding binoculars clamped to the head for anything longer than a few seconds is hard on the eyes and arm-muscles. And even with the finest night-glasses, these effects are redoubled after dark.

But in all the *Titanic* literature a simple but important point, a secondary advantage of having binoculars in this context, appears to have been overlooked. It needed Frederick Banfield, a retired Royal Navy lieutenant whose father died on the *Titanic* before he was born, to point this out.[5] The crow's nest was completely open, and even though there was no wind on the night of the disaster, the ship was travelling at 22 knots, which meant the lookouts faced a constant flow of frosty air coming towards them at 25 statute miles per hour. Their eyes would have been streaming; at least binoculars brought out from under a coat from time to time would have provided some relief. Indeed it is legitimate to infer that the lookouts must have been forced to turn their heads away or duck below the rim of the nest at frequent intervals if they were to see anything at all ahead of them. This is something they could conceivably have taken turns to do, but that is speculation unsupported by evidence. It is beyond dispute that those keeping watch on the glassed-in bridge, including the First and Sixth Officers, the helmsman and his relief, were at least as likely to see an object ahead as the lookouts. So much, until chapter 8, for the Mystery of the Missing Binoculars, one of the most intriguing sub-plots in the *Titanic* story.

Fire at sea has traditionally been the sailor's worst nightmare; even before fossil fuels were used on ships their hulls were made of wood. The world was reminded of this ever-present danger late in 1994, when the Italian cruise-liner *Achille Lauro* caught fire off the Horn of Africa and sank; fortunately only three lives were lost, thanks to a massive rescue operation. Steam-power changed the nature of shipping for ever, not just technologically but also by making it possible to sail to a timetable. Coal, however, is a surprisingly volatile substance, notoriously capable of apparently spontaneous combustion in enclosed spaces, especially in ships' bunkers. A routine precaution was to spray the coal with water as it was loaded, which also kept the dust level down. But if a fire started and took hold in a bunker nonetheless, the safest method of dealing with it was to send a reinforced group of stokers to empty the fuel store completely from the stokehold with their shovels. Their normal job was to shovel coal in this way straight from the stokehold at the bottom of the bunker into the voracious furnaces heating the boilers, at the best of times a hellish job commonly carried out in a temperature of 100 degrees Fahrenheit (thirty-eight degrees Celsius) or much more.

So the fact that a bunker fire was detected on the *Titanic* soon after the sea trials is not remarkable in itself, if still particularly unfortunate on the eve of a highly publicized, prestige voyage. The ship left Belfast with 1,880 tons of coal, barely enough for three days' steaming, because of the strike, the intention being to collect nearly 5,000 tons more at Southampton from the *Olympic*'s extra delivery and from the bunkers of lesser IMM ships crowding the port. The coal loaded in Belfast would, however, have had to be distributed fairly evenly among all eleven bunkers (about 170 tons in each) if all twenty-nine boilers were to be available for use. Coal would have had to be available in bunker number ten, which supplied boiler-room number six. The bunkers, like the boiler-rooms, were numbered from amidships forward and, except for the foremost bunker, number eleven, were arranged in pairs "back to back" with a watertight bulkhead between each pair. The fire was seated in the starboard side of bunker ten, at the after end of the sixth and foremost boiler-room and forward of watertight bulkhead number five (bulkheads, confusingly, being counted from the bow).

It is at least curious that the fire was allowed to burn on, not only at Belfast (where time was admittedly short) but also for a whole week in Southampton, when it would have been most obvious, natural and convenient (not to say prudent) to extinguish it while in port. But it is even more remarkable that the blaze escaped the attention of Maurice Harvey Clarke, a nautical surveyor, the Board of Trade's assistant emigration officer and inspector at Southampton. His job was to supplement and complete the inspections carried out by his Belfast colleague, Francis Carruthers. In three visits to the vessel, the last consuming the whole of the morning before departure, Clarke checked the accommodation, the boats and the entire crew, assisted by medical officers. As an official examining ships for their suitability as emigrant vessels he would surely have taken a special interest in third-class accommodation, a sizeable proportion of which was immediately above the burning bunker on decks E and F.

But, having noticed nothing untoward on the lower decks, Clarke proceeded to the boat deck and had two lifeboats crewed, swung out, lowered away, rowed round the dock and hauled back aboard before signing the clearance certificate and countersigning the survey report. Clarke told the inquiry that he did not notice the fire, nor had it been drawn to his attention. "If it was a serious fire, it should have been reported to me," he declared. Views may differ about the seriousness of a bunker fire, however commonplace such outbreaks may have been; but to conceal it from Clarke when it had been burning for over a week comes across as cavalier, if not worse. If the blaze was unimportant no harm would have been done by mentioning it; if it was important, it should have been mentioned.

In the light of that intriguing omission, it seems positively reckless on the part of the ship's firemen, who must have known of the blaze, to refuse to take part in boat drills at Southampton before sailing. Clarke was at least aware of their refusal and told the inquiry that such reluctance was unique to the White Star Line. Not even the offer of an extra half-day's pay, 2s. 4d. per head for ordinary firemen, could persuade them to turn up.

The Government was no less complacent in the matter of boats, as we have seen. Board of Trade officials told the British inquiry that watertight bulkheads, wireless and the "safe" transatlantic sailing tracks agreed among all the shipping lines in 1898 were the main factors behind the low lifeboat provision accepted before the disaster.[6] In the decade ending with 1881, 822 passengers and crew had been lost in shipping casualties on the Anglo-American route (including White Star's *Atlantic*); in the ten years to 1891, 247 people were lost (seventy-three passengers out of three and a quarter million carried); to 1901, during the safe transport of six million people nine passengers were lost; and in the ten years to 1911 there had been fifty-seven fatal casualties among passengers and crew.

Henry Tingle Wilde, the Chief Officer who went down with his captain and their ship, presents us with a mystery just as intriguing as the curious incident of the binoculars in the night-time. His entry in the crew list drawn up by White Star at Southampton[7] shows him to have been thirty-eight years old, born in Liverpool and still resident in the city, at 24 Grey Road, Walton, an inner suburb best known for its prison. He is shown to have signed up on 9 April 1912 but to have been due to report aboard at 6 a.m. on the 10th, sailing day, the last possible moment for assuming his duties. His monthly pay was £25, a quarter of the Captain's but £7 10s. more than the man he displaced, now First Officer Murdoch; Second (hitherto First) Officer Lightoller was docked £3 10s. per month and had to rest content with £14. Only these three were senior enough to take charge of the watch, which they normally did on the basis of four hours on and eight off. To complete the reshuffle Second Officer Blair left the ship on 9 April; the four junior deck-officers (Third to Sixth) stayed put. Second, Third, Fourth and Fifth Officers survived.

Wilde's belated appearance is curious because it cannot have been the consequence of mere overnight whim, whether on Captain Smith's part or that of his employers. It is simply inconceivable that a master, even the commodore of the line, could or would deprive a senior colleague of his chief mate, especially against the will of them both. Smith's record also strongly suggests that he was not the sort of man who would adopt the "belt and braces" approach of demanding that both his most senior officers (Wilde and Murdoch) should, like himself, have experience of the *Olympic*. Nor could Wilde's transfer have been ordered on the spur of the moment, because the *Olympic* had left for New York on 3 April. Captain Haddock therefore, new to the superliners and already deprived of his Chief Engineer, Joseph Bell, and his First Officer, Murdoch (who fondly imagined he had been promoted to Chief Officer on the *Titanic*), was also obliged to leave without Wilde. If Smith did not "kidnap" Wilde, as we conclude he did not, then only White Star's management can have decided that Captain Smith must be given his support willy-nilly and have organized the consequent changes on both ships. That Haddock might have benefited from experienced support was shown some seven weeks after the loss of the *Titanic*, when he narrowly missed running aground on Land's End. As we saw, this was covered up at the time, but Haddock was subjected to the humiliation of being watched by a White Star monitor for his next few sailings.[8]

Yet the apparently indispensable Wilde, removed from the *Olympic* by 3 April (when she sailed for New York), was not on hand in Belfast for the trials or in Southampton for loading and other final preparations. Instead he joined the *Titanic* as late as he possibly could, not long before the master himself arrived to issue his sailing orders. Even Smith had been visiting the ship daily from 6 April at the latest, as the crew list attests. Perhaps Wilde had extracted some Easter leave in exchange for the imposed move.

That Wilde's appointment was anomalous is confirmed by the testimony of Second Officer Lightoller and Fourth Officer Boxhall to the American inquiry on days one and three respectively. There had been no sign of Wilde in Belfast; Murdoch was still Chief and Lightoller First Officer on 9 April, when Captain Clarke was busy not noticing the fire down below on his penultimate visit.

That the position was unwelcome to the appointee was proved by Wilde's last letter, to his sister. It was posted at Queenstown, a day and a half into his unwanted assignment: "I still don't like this ship ... I have a queer feeling about it."[9] He must therefore have discussed his transfer with his sister while on leave, or else the word "still" does not make sense. The other inference is that he had been aboard the *Titanic* previously, something which could only have occurred before she was completed, presumably when the *Olympic* was making one of her unscheduled returns to Belfast for repair. While it is entirely possible to imagine him taking the opportunity of inspecting the new ship out of professional interest, it is impossible to imagine why he would feel hostile or be overcome by misgivings about his own ship's stablemate before she was even ready for sea. In any event his is surely the most poignant presentiment of them all.

Those who believe in portents will also seize upon one of several letters from Steward George Beedem, held by the British Titanic Society. He was one of many seafarers who transferred from the *Olympic* to the *Titanic* between one voyage and the next. Writing to his mother on the evening of Good Friday, two days after his transfer, Beedem says: "I have done two days . . . You can hardly tell the difference between the two boats. I have been standing by the ship today to see she doesn't run away." One letter in particular, sent to his wife, Lill, on the eve of departure from Southampton, is full of life's cares and concerns. "This is the last night and thank goodness we are off tomorrow." He hated his time ashore but away from his family, spent looking for a place in Southampton for them to live between shifts on the *Titanic*. He was short of money, worried about his wife, who had a painful swelling on her neck, and about his discharge certificate which he had forgotten to bring, and was also feeling unwell himself:

> I have no news to tell you only the last 3 days I've felt rotten & what with no dusters or anything to work with I wish the bally ship at the bottom of the sea.[10]

The uxorious Beedem wrote another letter to his wife and their child Charlie for posting from Queenstown, by which time he was feeling a little better. He did not live to rue the day he wrote those innocent words.

White Star faced an uphill struggle to lure passengers onto the "maiden voyage of the world's largest and most luxurious ship", as we have seen. The company managed to fill only just over half the available passenger accommodation as J. P. Morgan, his friends and half a hundred other cancellations reduced the total expected aboard by more than four per cent. As part of its efforts to muster a respectable total for 10 April, the line plastered the press with notices – in which the oddly persistent tendency to confuse the two "Olympics" manifested itself embarrassingly once again. Proclaiming that the "*Titanic* sails from Southampton and Cherbourg on first voyage to New York April 10, 1912", the newspaper advertisement said that the "palatial Royal Mail steamers *Olympic*, 45,324 tons, and *Titanic*, 45,000 tons [*sic*], are the largest in the world". The gross register tonnages, it will be noted, have been reversed, making the *Olympic* surpass her sister's GRT. This was doubtless no more than a copywriter's or compositor's error; but it adds to the long list of such slips.

Southampton began to displace Liverpool as the premier British port for transatlantic liners at the turn of the century. It was much handier for London and the Home Counties, principal catchment area for first-class passengers (whether rich natives or returning foreign visitors) and for Cherbourg, where ships could collect continental voyagers before making a last call at Queenstown on the south coast of Ireland for the sadly endless stream of Irish emigrants. White Star transferred its main Anglo-American service to the southern English port in 1907. It was as ever Captain E. J. Smith who led the way, taking his latest command, *Adriatic*, from Liverpool to New York in May but bringing her back to Southampton on 5 June. The Liverpool–New York route remained in being, however, and the *Adriatic* was sent back to it in June 1911, when the *Olympic* entered service on the Southampton–New York run with *Oceanic* and *Majestic*.

To cater for the superliners, White Star acquired a new dock (later known as Ocean Dock) next to the local Harland and Wolff repair yard: berths forty-three and forty-four, with a combined length of nearly 1,500 feet. The *Titanic* arrived there at midnight on 3 April with 1,880 tons in her bunkers (part of it on fire). Her sister had left what coal she could behind on her departure some twelve hours earlier, having not only stocked up in New York but also made the eastbound crossing at reduced speed to conserve fuel; a total of 4,427 tons were gleaned from this source and from the stokeholds of the *Oceanic*, *Majestic*, *New York*, *Philadelphia* and *St Louis*, all owned by IMM companies. In the aftermath of the strike, the port was still crowded with ships moored in pairs or even threes.[11] On 5 April, Good Friday, the ship was dressed overall in bunting; the Easter weekend was presumably the main reason why the *Titanic* needed a whole week in Southampton rather than three to four days.

White Star had no difficulty in completing the crew on 6 April, after so much shipping had been idle for so long. Many jostling for berths had already seen service on the *Olympic* and seem to have been favoured. The majority came from Southampton, the city which would be devastated as no other by the tragedy; but Liverpool, London, Belfast and Dublin were strongly represented. There were also five postal clerks (three American, two British) to sort the mail during the voyage; eight musicians supplied by a Liverpool agency to entertain the passengers in the ship's palm court; and dozens of staff from Gatti's of London to work in the à la carte restaurant, an expensive innovation in transatlantic luxury. None of these groups was employed by White Star, but all, like the two Marconi operators, were bound by the ship's articles. So were Thomas Andrews, a director of Harland and Wolff, and his eight assistants in the guarantee party.

The crew finally mustered 892: seventy-three in the "deck department" but including two doctors, two window-cleaners, two stewards to look after the officers and seven "pursers and clerks"; 325 in the "engine department", including twenty-eight engineers, eight "refrigerator and electrical" engineers and 289 engine-room crew;

and 494 in the "stewards' department", including two telegraphists, 471 "Chief Steward and staff", twenty stewardesses and one matron. One man introduced himself as Thomas Hart, fireman, of 51 College Street, Southampton, and produced the indispensable paybook ("certificate of continuous discharge") to prove it. He was taken on. Spare crew were waiting aboard to be signed up as replacements for the inevitable handful (twenty-two, mostly from the engine department) who missed the boat, some of them having probably ordered one pint too many in dockside public houses. Some were listed as "deserters" and a few as "departed by consent"; thirteen substitutes were thus signed on at the twelfth hour while the disappointed remainder were sent ashore via the tugs.

Fewer than 1,000 passengers boarded at Southampton (427 in the "cabin" or first and second classes, 495 in third or "steerage" for an official total of 922). The cargo was not up to much either, some 11,500 items totalling 559 tons (consigning cargo on liners was expensive, but also fast, and was regarded as the safest and swiftest means of international transport). Wilde came aboard at 6 a.m. on the 10th to prepare for Smith's arrival by taxi at 7.30; the Blue Ensign of the Royal Naval Reserve was run up at the stern at 8 a.m.; the third-class boat-train drew up alongside at 9.30 and the train for first and second classes at 11.00, both from London's Waterloo terminus. Since no *Titanic* provisioning list survives, we can pass over the attempts to synthesize one from the *Olympic*'s earlier lists; we can be certain that there were lakes of wine and milk and mountains of butter and cereals. The commodious refrigerated stores aboard ensured that more than enough fresh food was available for six days of gluttony on the part of those so inclined. Rich people of the time ate exceedingly well.

The à la carte and first-class restaurants (and the entire "Olympic" class of luxury liners) had been built for conspicuous consumers and inordinately wealthy people above all. The richest person aboard by a large margin was

Colonel John Jacob Astor, reputedly worth £30 million (a great deal less than the absentee owner, J. P. Morgan; but Astor was only one member of a fabulously wealthy family). Aged forty-seven, he owned a large portion of Manhattan and had recently married an eighteen-year-old second wife, after a grand scandal over the divorce from his first, which had led him to take refuge abroad until the American press found somebody else to "doorstep". Another of the plutocrats aboard (with his blonde mistress) was Benjamin Guggenheim who, though not as rich as he was cracked up to be, was a member of another outstandingly wealthy immigrant dynasty which made its fortune in mining, metals and machinery. Like Morgan, the Guggenheims sought immortality by collecting and endowing entire museums full of art. An undoubted multi-millionaire among the passengers was Isidor Straus, owner with his brother of Macy's department store in New York, the world's largest, travelling with his wife. Their enormous personal wealth did not save this couple's lives – or prevent them from acquiring heroic stature in the coming catastrophe. Serious railway money was represented by such as Charles M. Hays, the great Canadian transcontinental pioneer, and John B. Thayer of the Pennsylvania Railroad Company. Also aboard were George D. Widener of Philadelphia, Pennsylvania, member of a banking family grown rich on building urban tramways, and his wife. Not rich, but seriously powerful, was Major Archie Butt, chief aide, adviser and friend of President William Howard Taft of the United States.[12]

After Captain Clarke signed the papers for the Board of Trade, Smith handed over a brief, formal Captain's Report to the owners, represented by their marine superintendent at Southampton, Captain Benjamin Steele. "I herewith report this ship loaded and ready for sea. The engines and boilers are in good order for the voyage, and all charts and sailing directions up to date. Your obedient servant,

Edward J. Smith."[13] No need, apparently, to mention the fire in bunker ten.

Thomas Andrews had come aboard at the same time as Wilde and put his baggage in first-class cabin number A36, created by repartitioning just before departure from Belfast and one of many features of the ship not included in her original plans. J. Bruce Ismay had shown his wife and children something of the ship that morning before bidding them farewell as they left via the first-class gangway. He then took possession of suite B52, which incorporated cabins B54 and B56, all included in the port-side millionaire's apartment, the most luxurious accommodation on the entire ship. B52 itself was the sitting room designed to J. P. Morgan's wishes. Ismay's valet, Richard Fry, was allocated inboard cabin B102, almost opposite the suite. His secretary, Mr W. H. Harrison, was also aboard. All three travelled free. The equivalent accommodation on the starboard side, B51, was the other millionaire's suite, but was actually a little smaller than the accommodation intended for Morgan. It was occupied from Cherbourg by Mr and Mrs Thomas Cardeza.

Among the early boarders on the 10th was the pilot, the selfsame George Bowyer who had been in charge of the *Olympic* in her brief encounter with the *Hawke*. The *Titanic* had been berthed stern first to make her departure from the congested port easier. Six tugs pulled her out of the White Star dock in a forward and sideways movement, to clear the dockside, take her through a wide turn to port and place her in the middle of the dredged channel in the River Test. The great ship, released by the tugs, came under her own power and was slowly gathering speed against the incoming tide as she passed berths thirty-eight and thirty-nine, about to make another turn to port into the River Itchen.

Alongside this pair of berths were the liners *Oceanic* and *New York*, tied up in tandem, the latter outboard of the former; normally only one ship would have been tied up there, leaving more room in the channel. As the *Titanic* approached the *New York* from astern and to starboard, the latter's six mooring lines first slackened, then tautened – and then twanged apart like overstretched guitar-strings. A 517-foot ship was now loose and swinging by the stern to starboard, across *Titanic*'s path, disturbed by the sheer bulk (not the propellers) of the bigger ship in the narrow channel, only forty feet deep. With splendid presence of mind, Captain C. Gale of the tug *Vulcan* saved the situation. Realizing that an attempt to push the *New York* back would simply turn his powerful but tiny vessel into the mincemeat in a looming steel sandwich, he swung the tug behind the *New York*'s stern and got a line over her at his second attempt. This enabled him to pull, rather than push, the ship back towards the dockside; but the errant stern, having been hauled out of her path, came within four feet of hitting the *Titanic* as other tugs joined the battle to bring the *New York* under control. The drifting ship's bowsprit brushed along the side of the *Oceanic*, causing superficial damage: the gangway was pulverized. People on the decks of all three ships watched the drama in helpless horror as the tugs pulled their lines taut and the *New York*'s motion was arrested. George Beedem was watching:

> As we left today the American boat *New York* broke her moorings & drifted right across our bows[,] missed the *Oceanic* by about a foot[,] we had to reverse engines sharp & one of our tugs got her under control before any damage was done, anyhow it was a narrow squeak for all of us.

On the bridge of the *Titanic* the two white-bearded seadogs, having apparently learned nothing and forgotten nothing about suction, reacted more swiftly and skilfully than when helplessly watching the approach of HMS *Hawke*. Bowyer ordered "Stop Engines" and then "Full Astern"; Smith had the starboard anchor lowered to just above water-level, ready for dropping in aid of an engine-assisted turn to port, to help swing the stern to starboard round the ship's centre of gravity and avoid or minimize a collision. All this delayed the *Titanic*'s exit from the port by an hour after casting off at noon. The fact that the ship had caused the *New York* to break loose (the *Oceanic* came close to doing the same) speaks for itself: Smith and Bowyer were sailing too fast for the overcrowded conditions in port, however much skill they showed in helping to avert a crash. What would have happened, or more precisely what would not have happened, had they failed and collided with the *New York*, is a matter for speculation: but it is highly likely that the name *Titanic* would have been forgotten by history.

Unfazed, as the ship's bugler blew for lunch, the elderly mariners took the ship ahead again, if somewhat more circumspectly this time, and brought her south-eastward into Southampton Water, bound for Spithead and Cherbourg. Judging by his past record, the iron-nerved Captain Smith was not a man to cry over spilt milk, and was even less likely to cry over milk that had, by the narrowest of margins, not been spilt at all. It took an hour to secure the runaway *New York* and to get the *Titanic* clear of the harbour. No attempt was made to recover lost time on the short leg to Normandy, less than eighty miles or four hours steaming away to the south.

Andrews and the guarantee party from Belfast had started work even before the ship left Southampton; but although the nine men were on call round the clock they had little enough to do once the ship was under way.[14] Some fitting-out workers had been disembarked with the unwanted crewmen on the tugs.

Cherbourg, a much smaller port than Southampton, was unable to take large liners, which therefore had to drop anchor outside the harbour and await service by the two purpose-built White Star tenders, segregated by class and introduced with the *Olympic* in 1911. The *Train transatlantique* brought only 142 first-, thirty second- and 102 third-class passengers from St Lazare station in Paris. The tenders were thus very lightly loaded.

Among the first-class contingent, apart from the Cardezas, were several extremely rich Americans, including the business magnates Emil Brandeis and Benjamin Guggenheim. The most sociologically interesting, however, were British, a couple who chose to travel incognito as, of all things, "Mr and Mrs Morgan". Perhaps this was their little joke; people of their standing must have known who really owned the ship they were about to embark upon. Their passports revealed them to be Sir Cosmo and Lady Duff Gordon.

Sir Cosmo Edmund Duff Gordon, Baronet, owed his social distinction and wealth to the unearned privilege of descent from a man who ran some useful errands during the Napoleonic Wars. The fifth holder of the title, he inherited it from a cousin who had died childless. Sir Cosmo (1862–1931) did not rate an entry in the *Dictionary of National Biography*, and his entry in *Who's Who* mentions no activity of any kind, whether intellectual, business or even pleasure. He was educated at Eton and maintained households in fashionable Kensington, London, and Kincardineshire, Scotland.

The most interesting fact about this drone was his choice of wife. In 1900 he married Lucy, widow of James Stewart Wallace and daughter of Douglas Sutherland of Toronto, Ontario. She was also the elder sister of the *risquée* novelist Elinor Glyn, mistress of Lord Curzon, diplomat, politician and Viceroy of India. Lucy had made a name for herself as an exclusive fashion designer, trading under the name "Lucile" from discreetly stylish premises in London's Hanover Square. They had no children. His photograph shows a stolid face with a dimpled chin, "handlebar" moustache and sandy hair *en brosse*; hers reveals a lively and attractive face topped with a fringe of dark hair and reminiscent of her notorious sister. If the choice of soubriquet was a joke it was probably her idea. Morgan is hardly an unusual name but, since the press was probably expecting John Pierpont of that ilk, the Morganissimo of Morgans, to be on board for this special voyage, it was not a choice offering much chance of real disguise; it could easily have had the opposite effect by drawing attention to the wealthy, middle-aged couple. But this did not transpire; their anonymity, if that is what they wanted, was preserved – for the time being.

Their ship dropped anchor off Cherbourg an hour late at 6.30 p.m. local time and left some ninety minutes thereafter, having loaded passengers, luggage and mail from the two tenders. Thirteen fortunate first-class and seven second-class cross-Channel passengers (and possibly two from third) were safely conveyed ashore. A remarkable picture survives of the ship lying off Cherbourg in the gathering dark, all lights blazing from seven decks, looking as she must have looked from the lifeboats after the collision (the picture was not entirely accurate: it shows heavy smoke coming from the aftermost of the four funnels, which was a ventilator rather than a chimney).

It was up the ladder inside this dummy funnel that a stoker, in need of some air or merely to indulge his sense of fun, climbed during the *Titanic*'s short and final stop-over at Queenstown, Co. Cork.[15] The brief appearance of his coal-blackened face over the rim of the tall funnel made some of those who saw it laugh; others, inevitably it now seems, regarded it as a bad omen, even a Mephistophelean manifestation. Queenstown also was much too small for such a big ship; the *Titanic* therefore anchored two miles out to sea and awaited the arrival of two paddle-steamer tenders, segregated by class as usual and appropriately named *America* and *Ireland*. There were 120 passengers, third-class except seven for second, joining here at the last port of call before New York.

There were also 1,385 sacks of mail, eloquent testimony to the numbers of Irish emigrés living in the United States.

Only seven passengers were disembarking, all from second class, six of them in one party. One of the latter was Francis Browne, teacher, student-priest of the Society of Jesus and a keen and prolific photographer. He snapped the last surviving pictures taken aboard the ship, including the final extant shot, fittingly dramatic, of Captain Edward John Smith looking down from his lofty bridge.

The tenders also collected some mail sacks from England to take ashore. Amid the confused toings and froings of passengers, reporters, crew and officials recorded by Browne and the *Cork Examiner*'s photographer on the tenders, a certain John Coffey slipped aboard, unseen by their cameras, with intent to desert his ship. Coffey, a fireman aged twenty-four, hid in the pile of mailbags and smuggled himself ashore undetected.

According to the crew list, he had served on the *Olympic* and lived at 12 Sherbourne Terrace. The space for his address gives only the house number and the street; it has merely been assumed that the latter must have been in Queenstown.[16] But it is much more likely to have been Southampton because the register quite clearly gives the town as well as the street in all cases except for the largest segment of the crew – those who lived in Southampton. On Coffey's page all the addresses lack the name of a town except the last, where Liverpool has been added in the clerk's handwriting (unlike the rest of the address, inscribed by the crewman himself).

The crew list also reveals that Coffey had been born in Queenstown, which most obviously suggests that he signed aboard the *Titanic*, perhaps after a long lay-off because of the coal strike, to go home free of charge for a break or to settle some personal or family business. Unfortunately Coffey soon vanished without historical trace. He was obviously not afraid of the sea or hard work in the stokehold because he signed aboard the *Mauretania* as a fireman when the Cunarder called at Queenstown only a few days later, the last that is known about him. How he did it without getting his paybook signed before leaving the *Titanic* is unexplained. Perhaps such a resourceful man would have had no trouble in forging the necessary entry in his "certificate of continuous discharge". Perhaps too he had seen something which convinced him, as a fireman, that it would be in his best interests to be off the *Titanic* rather than on it ... Regrettably the best (and enthusiastic) efforts of John Clifford in the library of the *Cork Examiner* on our behalf failed to unearth any more information on John Coffey, the *Titanic*'s last deserter, the Queenstown boy who at least lived to stoke another day on another great ship.

At Queenstown E. J. Sharpe, the local immigration officer, countersigned the "Report of Survey of an Emigrant Ship" issued by Carruthers in Belfast. He also issued the last "Clearance Certificate" giving the official final total aboard. Unaware naturally of Coffey's desertion, he once again wrote down a total of 892 for the crew. His figure for the passengers was 1,316, giving a total aboard of 2,208. He counted 606 in the cabin classes and 710 in steerage. One of the many curiosities of the tragedy, irritating because beyond satisfaction by proven fact, is that the numbers aboard have never been settled beyond dispute. The British inquiry Report[17] gives a crew of 885 (sixty-six deck, 325 engine, 494 "victualling") and counts the eight bandsmen as passengers, on whose total number it agrees with Sharpe: 1,316. White Star and Sharpe made the crew 892, the discrepancy being entirely in the deck department, which totals seventy-three on Sharpe's and White Star's lists but seven fewer in the Report. Perhaps the latter discounted the seven "pursers and clerks" – or the deck officers (but not Captain Smith, it seems).

As the liner lay off Queenstown, J. Bruce Ismay by his own admission sought out Chief Engineer Joseph Bell, late of the *Olympic*, for a private discussion. Nobody else was present; no other witness attested to the meeting. "It was our [sic] intention, if we had fine weather on Monday afternoon or Tuesday, to drive the ship at full speed," he told the American inquiry when it opened in New York.[18] He admitted he never consulted Captain Smith about this, or anything else to do with the movements of the ship; nor had the master consulted him on such matters. But he went on to say: "The *Titanic* being a new ship, we were gradually working her up." Note the "we". Recalled to testify on the tenth day in Washington, Ismay denied any attempt to influence the Captain on the running of the ship.[19]

Ismay told the British inquiry[20] that full speed meant seventy-eight revolutions; but "our intention" in New York had become "the intention" in London six weeks later, where he denied responsibility for the idea of a speed trial. But later he said that "we [sic] were to run her at full speed on the following Monday"; that the *Olympic* had logged 22.75 knots in perfect conditions and: "We [sic] were hoping that [the *Titanic*] would do a little better than that."[21] Ismay, chief executive of the line and of the conglomerate which owned it, sailing free of charge (a privilege he said even the deadly rival Cunard would grant him as a courtesy) with his staff in the most lavish accommodation available aboard, also insisted at the British inquiry that he was just an ordinary passenger, to the incredulity of the Attorney-General.

But we can discount out of hand at this juncture suggestions from a number of survivors that the ship was trying to break the average-speed record of 27.4 knots won in 1907 by the *Mauretania*. The holder of the Blue Riband for fastest crossing had two-thirds the gross register tonnage and three-quarters the displacement of an *Olympic* but boasted turbines of 70,000 horsepower, compared with the 46,000 delivered by two less efficient reciprocating engines and one turbine aboard the larger ship. Ismay himself pointed out that there was no possibility of bringing forward the scheduled ceremonial arrival of the

Titanic off New York in the early hours of Wednesday 17 April. In fact ships often arrived there up to twelve hours early, although this would undoubtedly have been embarrassing on a maiden voyage for which White Star hoped to gain much favourable publicity after recent setbacks – the coal strike and the losses on the *Olympic*. But the latter, under Smith's command, arrived off New York several hours early on her own maiden voyage, a fact which was masked by a long delay at quarantine before docking.[22] Such considerations need not have prevented a brief run by the *Titanic* at full power, which could have been balanced by reducing speed later in the voyage.

Outrunning the *Olympic* was incontrovertibly Ismay's intention, for which he sought the concurrence of Captain Smith and Chief Engineer Bell. The ship increased her speed day by day, and on Sunday 14 April the last three main boilers out of twenty-four were fired, giving a speed, final as it turned out, of 22.5 knots; the remaining five auxiliary boilers would have had to be brought into the propulsion system the next day for the top-speed run (she had already touched 23.5 between Belfast and Southampton but was then lightly loaded). The run would have had to be brief because there was not much coal to spare. Be that as it may, those responsible for the safe running of the ship had their minds focused on speed instead of the icefield they knew lay across their path.

After two hours at Queenstown the ship weighed anchor at 1.30 p.m. on Thursday 11 April. Steerage passenger Eugene Daly had brought his Irish bagpipes aboard and stood on the third-class promenade aft, playing "Erin's Lament" as Ireland's gateway to America receded astern of the westbound ship. No doubt this musical phenomenon was received with the usual mixed feelings by those not accustomed to it. One cannot help wondering what the many Dutch, Scandinavian, Mediterranean and Balkan emigrants made of the kilted Celt and his plangent pibroch.

Another dubious reflection on Ismay's "ordinary-passenger" status and purported non-intervention in the running of the ship is provided by his curious role in connection with a crucial wireless message from the White Star liner *Baltic*, received at 1.42 p.m. on 14 April. Smith not only showed him this warning of ice across their track but let him put it in his pocket for five hours instead of pinning it up in the chart room at once.

The central mystery of the *Titanic* saga, amid the mountains of often contradictory evidence and subsequent library of books, is the undoubted fact that Captain Smith, commanding the world's largest and most celebrated liner, *accelerated* out of Irish waters into an area of the North Atlantic known to be infested with ice – much more of it and rather further south than usual. Beating the *Olympic*'s performance was undoubtedly the most natural ambition for a man like Smith to conceive, and obviously Ismay felt the same; but pressing ahead without taking account of the freak ice conditions seems so disproportionately reckless that it remains a conundrum. It had been the mildest winter in Greenland and the far north for thirty years. This had resulted in more icebergs (giant fragments of glacier), ice floes and field ice breaking away and drifting southward, encouraged by the cold, sub-surface Labrador Current, and/or north-eastward on the urging of the warm Gulf Stream, into the internationally agreed transatlantic sea-lanes. This unusually high risk of ice was common knowledge at the time of the voyage; such information was spread with increasing facility by wireless. The ether was thick with ice reports; it was proved beyond doubt at the British inquiry that the doomed ship (as distinct from her officers) received no fewer than six ice-warnings on 14 April, her last day afloat.[23] The texts are in the next chapter.

A framed notice behind glass in the chart room of every White Star liner drew the attention of officers to a series of principles, the first of which was "the vital importance of exercising the utmost caution in navigation, *safety outweighing every other consideration*" (the document's own emphasis). The "Ship's Rules" contained the following order: "The Chief Officer is held jointly responsible with the Commander for the safe and proper navigation of the steamer, and it shall be his duty to make a respectful representation to the Commander if he apprehends danger, when his responsibility shall cease. Any neglect in this respect will not be excused."[24]

There is no means of knowing whether Wilde made any representation to Smith; but if he was uneasy before the voyage began, indeed before he joined the ship, one cannot help wondering how he felt when he heard, as he must have done, of the specific ice-warnings received as the liner pounded westward. The Chief Officer, who of course followed his captain in going down with the ship, is a curiously shadowy figure, seldom coming out of the background in the evidence to the two inquiries; but when he is mentioned by witnesses he emerges as a powerful, calming presence, supervising the loading of the boats while quelling indiscipline and panic by sheer force of personality. Not the kind of man, one would think, to be overcome by "queer feelings" *before* taking up his berth on a ship where he could never previously have worked – the brand-new *Titanic*.

From Wilde's letter to his sister it is absolutely clear that he felt unhappy about the ship before he took up his post, and that his misgivings were not dispelled when he boarded her "for the first time", at any rate since she had been officially commissioned on 2 April 1912. The unease of Henry Wilde is another of the tantalizing mysteries in the *Titanic* myth. Could he have seen or heard something that escaped the attention of others (with the possible exception of John Coffey)? Or was this experienced, imposing man in his prime just a superstitious wimp?

The *Titanic* started work with a fire burning in her bowels, no binoculars in her crow's nest, no lifeboats for half of those aboard and an uneasy Chief Officer, dragooned on board against his will, on her bridge. He, the First Officer, the Chief Engineer and a large slice of the rest of the crew were veterans of the *Olympic*, as of course was the Captain himself. The latter once again allowed his ship to go too fast in narrow waters, only just evading, thanks mostly to the skill of a tug skipper, yet another mishap. Although the ship's coal problem was solved at the expense of other vessels, passengers were few and a significant number cancelled at the eleventh hour. The official inspections were perfunctory; and the owners' chief representative held a secret conclave with the Chief Engineer to plan a speed-test and then kept a vital ice-warning in his pocket for five and a half hours. Neither he, nor the master, nor the officers (nor indeed the generality of the Merchant Marine) apparently felt any special caution was necessary, although all of them knew in a general sense before they set sail that the great ship was heading for an extremely unusual, not to say unique, concentration of ice, in an area where ice should not have been such a hazard on the main Atlantic liner route at that time of year.

PART TWO

DURING THE FACT

The safety of all those on board weighs with us beyond all other considerations, and we would once more impress upon you and the entire navigation staff most earnestly that no risk is to be run which can be avoided by the exercise of caution ... and by choosing, whenever a doubt exists, the course that tends to safety.

IMM Company Instructions to Captains

"Over-confidence", a most fruitful source of accident, should be specially guarded against.

From framed notice in chart room

4

NEMESIS ON ICE

Pausing only to whistle in apologetic salute to a French trawler which came perilously close to being swamped by her bow-wave, the *Titanic* turned away from land in the early afternoon of 11 April, passing over the horizon in about an hour.[1]

Ice-warnings for the north-western Atlantic notwithstanding, the weather in the eastern and central regions of the ocean was delightful – mid-ocean spring at its best. The wind was light and the swell smooth and moderate, the sun was out all day except for a patch of fog which took ten minutes to clear, and the absence of both cloud and moonlight by night allowed the stars to put on a rare and splendid display, the like of which the many urban people aboard would seldom have seen.

From noon on Thursday the 11th to noon on Friday, a period which included the two-hour stop at Queenstown, the ship covered 464 sea-miles with her engines running at seventy revolutions. The distance was posted up in the smoking room as transatlantic steam-liner tradition demanded. In such weather the officers had no difficulty in fixing the ship's position, the *sine qua non* of accurate navigation, by sighting their sextants at the sun daily at noon. With no stops, the vessel managed 519 miles on Friday to Saturday at seventy-two revolutions and 546 from Saturday to Sunday noon at seventy-five, only two miles short of the *Olympic*'s best day's run.[2] The ship's clocks were put back daily on the westward leg, in keeping with the changing longitude (New York time being five

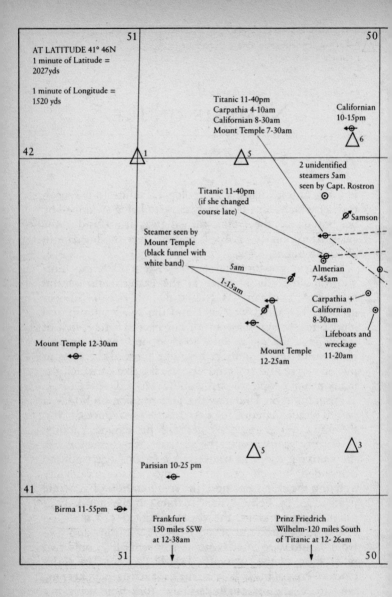

AT LATITUDE 41° 46N
1 minute of Latitude =
2027yds

1 minute of Longitude =
1520 yds

51

50

Titanic 11-40pm
Carpathia 4-10am
Californian 8-30am
Mount Temple 7-30am

Californian
10-15pm

6

42

1

5

2 unidentified
steamers 5am
seen by Capt. Rostron

Titanic 11-40pm
(if she changed
course late)

Samson

Steamer seen by
Mount Temple
(black funnel with
white band)

5am

Almerian
7-45am

1-15am

Carpathia +
Californian
8-30am

Mount Temple
12-25am

Lifeboats and
wreckage
11-20am

Mount Temple 12-30am

5

3

Parisian 10-25 pm

41

Birma 11-55pm

Frankfurt
150 miles SSW
at 12-38am

Prinz Friedrich
Wilhelm-120 miles South
of Titanic at 12- 26am

51

50

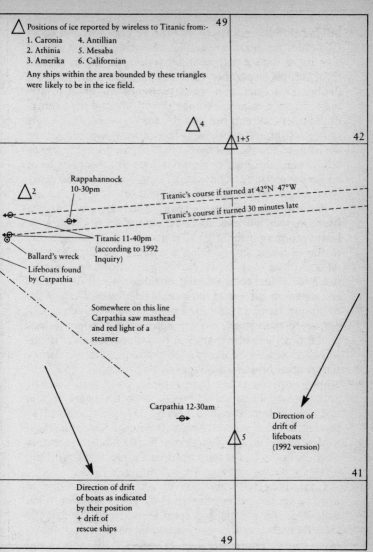

Map showing position of ships between 10.15pm and 11.20am on the night 14/15th April 1912

hours behind London), so that the average speed in knots (sea-miles per hour, a sea-mile measuring 2,000 yards or 240 more than a statute mile) was not quite as fast as these figures imply. But each day brought a distinct and deliberate acceleration which was not modified in any way. On the Sunday afternoon twenty-four of the twenty-nine boilers were in use and the ship reached 22.5 knots in her last hours; as we have seen, Ismay was behind the decision to fire the last five boilers on the Monday, to see what speed the engines would deliver at seventy-eight to eighty revolutions.[3] Quite clearly the *Titanic* would easily have surpassed her sister's performance.

Phillips, aged twenty-four, and Bride, twenty-two, the Marconi men working six hours on and six off, were kept busy recording incoming and transmitting outgoing signal traffic. Sending or receiving a wireless message in mid-Atlantic had even more cachet (and much less public-nuisance value) than making or taking a call in a smart restaurant in the age of the mobile telephone. Even at the minimum fee of 12s. 6d. or $3 (for ten words; 9d. or 35¢ per word thereafter), extortionate for the money-values of the time, wealthy first-class passengers fell over themselves to send a Marconigram from the *Titanic*. Ismay sent routine business messages to his Liverpool and Southampton offices. Other than several "good luck" signals and the notorious ice-warnings from his peers at sea, Captain Smith received no messages. Outgoing traffic had to wait from 11 p.m. on Friday, when the Marconi transmitter broke down. The best efforts of both operators over six hours fortunately restored the set to full working order by 5 a.m. on Saturday, according to Bride.

Composing self-important messages was just one of many distractions on offer aboard. There was not much to look at outside the ship apart from the sea by day, the stars by night and the very occasional passing ship. While organized entertainment such as parties, balls, dances and games were, with forbearance, not imposed by the ship's company, there was an eight-man ship's "orchestra", the band of the *Titanic* with its enormous repertoire, and an electric organ on A deck, where the first-class lounge and smoking room were also to be found. These, with their florid, over-ornate décor, were worthy of the grandest hotel and even had raised roofs arching over the boat deck; there was also a glass dome over the main first-class entrance, leading down to the smoking room, immediately aft of which was a bar and the verandah with palm court. There was provision for deck games, left to the passengers to organize for themselves.

Down on F deck there were Turkish and "electric" baths, open to ladies and gentlemen at different times of the day for four shillings, which included use of the adjacent swimming pool measuring thirty-two feet by thirteen. A swim alone cost one shilling. One deck below, next to the post office, was a squash court, complete with resident professional (Frederick Wright), where half an hour's strenuous exercise could be had for two shillings. The first-class gymnasium with the latest exercise apparatus was located on the boat deck, on the starboard flank of the second funnel. Less strenuous activity was to be had in the reading and writing room next to the lounge. Lifts were provided for second- as well as first-class passengers.

The second-class facilities on the "Olympics" were as lavish as anything in first on most of the previous generation of transatlantic liners. The smoking room on B deck was directly above the large library on C deck. The third-class public areas also set new standards, with chairs rather than benches in the dining saloons, which had bright, white walls. There were two bars forward on D deck and one aft on C by the third-class smoking room, which was not unlike a public house with its oak panels, hardwood tables, chairs and benches. The "general room" had white-painted walls embellished with pine and boasted a piano for sing-songs as well as tables for card and bar games. All classes had their promenades, strictly segregated like everything else.[4]

Meals were noisily announced by Bugler P. W. Fletcher

and were served at the same times (but naturally in different dining saloons) for all classes. Breakfast could be had between 8.30 and 10.30 a.m., lunch between one and 2.30 p.m. and dinner from six to 7.30 p.m. The first-class saloon was enormous, capable of seating 532 amidships on D deck. The Captain's Table, with seating for six, was amidships at the forward end of this huge room, the largest covered open space on the ship. Smith took breakfast in his quarters, might or might not take lunch in the saloon, alone or with a guest or two, and was most likely to be seen at dinner, either at his own table or as the guest of a distinguished passenger. On the evening of Sunday the 14th he dined in the à la carte restaurant as guest of honour of Mr and Mrs George Widener of Philadelphia.[5]

The second-class saloon was rather better than modest, with a capacity of 394, and the two third-class saloons on F deck could cope with a total of 473 at a time. The à la carte restaurant was available to first class only and was open continuously from 8 a.m. to 11 p.m. First-class passengers, mostly Americans, who elected to use it throughout the voyage instead of the dining saloon were given a rebate of $15–$25 on their tickets. The Café Parisien, also exclusively first class, was adjacent to the restaurant on the starboard side of B deck, offering a meeting place for a floating café society. All these elaborate eating and drinking places were supplied from the vast refrigerated stores.

The printed third-class bill of fare offered generous portions if a limited choice, which varied according to the day of the week. In keeping with the social and class norms of the time, the main meals were labelled "dinner" and "tea" (rather than lunch and dinner respectively). Breakfast consisted of cereal, kippers or boiled eggs, bread, marmalade and tea or coffee; dinner, the main meal taken at midday among the lower orders, consisted of soup, a substantial meat dish such as roast pork and vegetables, a cooked dessert and fruit; tea was a cooked course, bread or buns, cooked fruit or other light dessert and tea. A late supper of cheese and biscuits or gruel and coffee was on offer daily.

Breakfast in the two cabin classes was on the colossal, contemporary scale, hugely elaborate in first class; second class missed nothing of substance on an only slightly simpler menu. Sunday dinner in second class (menus of all types of meal survive: no need to borrow from the *Olympic* for these), taken in the evening unlike in third class, consisted of clear soup, a fish course, curried chicken and rice, spring lamb or roast turkey with vegetables and potatoes or rice, various desserts, nuts and fruit, cheese and coffee. The seven-course dinner on the same day in the first-class dining saloon included hors-d'œuvres variés or oysters; a choice of two soups; salmon; filet mignon, a chicken dish or stuffed marrow; lamb, duckling or roast beef plus vegetables; a choice of four light savoury dishes; and four desserts. The à la carte restaurant offered the kind of fare available in such traditional London favourites as the Café Royal or the Savoy Grill – international cuisine with a British accent. "Draught Munich lager beer" could be had for sixpence a pint in the first-class dining saloon. Bottled beers and of course wines were also on offer all over the ship.

As the passengers, cosseted according to class by the stewards' department, ate and drank, dozed, promenaded, read, exercised, conversed, listened to music or just stared out to sea, the deck and engine departments soon settled into their familiar professional routines. Around morning-coffee time Captain Smith received the daily reports from the heads of departments – Chief Officer, Chief Purser, Chief Steward, Chief Surgeon, Chief Engineer – and then, in full dress uniform and escorted by his acolytes, proceeded in state round the ship on the detailed tour of inspection required of White Star masters every day except Sunday, from bridge to boilers and forepeak to poop, via the public rooms and service facilities of all three classes.

On the bridge the three senior officers took it in turns to command the watch (under the master, officially never off duty and actually always on call). The officers of the watch were assisted by the junior officers on the bridge in a rota of four hours on and four off.[6] The seniors had their four hours on watch and eight off, but had other responsibilities which ate into their off-watch time: the Chief Officer, for example, was responsible for the ship's log, which was lost in the disaster. The log could so easily have been entrusted to one of the officers assigned to the lifeboats: in our view, conspiracy theorists are right to be suspicious about the fact that it was not, given the duration of the ship's death-agony and the obvious importance of the record.

The Second Officer would seem to have been responsible for the lookouts. The original holder of this post, David Blair, had supplied the crow's nest with "his" binoculars; and when he left at Southampton, they were reportedly stowed in his cabin. His successor, Lightoller, was the man sought out in the officers' mess by lookout George Symons,[7] who asked for their return, only to be told that there were none available. Symons said Lightoller had apparently gone to First Officer Murdoch's cabin and found none; he would have been better employed searching his own room for the pair originally handed to the lookouts by Blair. Lightoller also said he had mentioned the lookouts' request to Chief Officer Wilde, who had said the matter was "in hand". The continuing absence of glasses from the crow's nest undoubtedly aroused genuine, understandable and abiding resentment among the lookouts (but may also have been a comfort to Fleet, who sighted the iceberg seconds too late to save the ship), yet that was where the matter was left.

Fleet's sense of grievance may well have had a deeper and more disturbing cause than this. George M. Behe, a vice-president of the American Titanic Historical Society (THS), made out a strong, circumstantial case in 1993 that Fleet reported ice ahead to the bridge *three separate times* in the half-hour before the warning immediately preceding the collision – only to be ignored by the officers on duty, Murdoch and Moody.[8] Behe cited hearsay evidence from several witnesses who heard Fleet telling this tale after the rescue – decidedly different from what he said at the two official inquiries. He and his mate, Lee, were also heard to say that First Officer Murdoch had shot himself, precisely because he had ignored their earlier warnings. These assertions were tantamount to common gossip aboard the rescue ship *Carpathia*, Behe writes.

He goes on to postulate, though on less substantial evidence, that Fleet was offered financial security by White Star to suppress the earlier warnings at the inquiries. Fleet was certainly an awkward and highly defensive, not to say paranoid, witness, obviously under enormous stress (and the eye of Ismay). An unhappy life after the disaster ended in suicide in 1965 when he was seventy-seven, thirty years after he retired from the sea with the *Olympic*, his last ship. It is possible that he blamed himself for the disaster, or at least for surviving it, as participants in great catastrophes often do, especially when they played a central role.

Less speculative is Behe's account of an alleged confession by Robert Hitchens, the helmsman at the time of the collision, that he had been offered a well-paid job in return for suppressing certain unspecified events on the bridge of the *Titanic*. He became a harbourmaster at Cape Town, South Africa, where he made the purported statement to a British seaman on a ship which called in there in 1914. Anyone on the bridge could not fail to have heard ice-warnings from the crow's nest. This story was first revealed by Don Lynch, historian and a vice-president of the Titanic Historical Society, in *Titanic: An Illustrated History*.

The first ice-warning known to have reached the bridge of the *Titanic* and the cognizance of the Captain on Sunday

14 April was from Cunard's *Caronia* (Captain Barr): "[To] Captain, *Titanic*. Westbound steamers report bergs, growlers [small icebergs] and field ice in 42 degrees north from 49° to 51° west, 12th April. Compliments – Barr." The addressee had reached latitude 43° 35' north, longitude 43° 50' west by the time he received this two-day-old warning at 9 a.m. on Sunday. But the area indicated was only a few miles north of his intended course, and there was a constant southward drift of up to 1.5 knots to consider. Smith himself dictated the acknowledgement of this message, as he did the following one.

The second warning of the day was placed in the hand of the master at 1.42 p.m. when his ship was at 42° 35' north, 45° 50' west. It came from the *Baltic*, one of his former commands: "[To] Captain Smith, *Titanic*. Have had moderate, variable winds and clear, fine weather since leaving. Greek steamer *Athinai* reports passing icebergs and large quantities of field ice today in lat. 41° 51' N, long. 49° 52' W … Wish you and *Titanic* all success – Commander." This warning delineated an area even closer to the ship's course (and to the position eventually given by her as the site of the collision).

"It appears that the master handed the *Baltic*'s message to Mr Ismay almost immediately after it was received," says the British Report. "This no doubt was in order that Mr Ismay might know that ice was to be expected. Mr Ismay states that he understood from the message that they would get up to the ice 'that night'. Mr Ismay showed this message to two ladies, and it is therefore probable that many persons on board became aware of its contents. This message ought in my [the Wreck Commissioner's] opinion to have been put on the board in the chart room as soon as it was received. *It remained, however, in Mr Ismay's possession until 7.15 p.m., when the master asked Mr Ismay to return it. It was then that it was first posted in the chart room* [authors' emphasis].

"This was considerably before the time at which the vessel reached the position recorded in the [SOS] message," the Commissioner and chairman of the inquiry, Lord Mersey, went on. "Nevertheless I think it was irregular for the master to part with the document, and improper for Mr Ismay to retain it." In his next breath, however, Mersey uncritically accepted the proposition that this "incident" had no effect on Smith's navigation of the *Titanic* even though it surely destroyed any residual belief that Ismay was an "ordinary passenger" ...

It is not Ismay's retention (careless – or calculated?) of the vital ice-warning that stands out but rather Smith's decision to give it to him and let him walk away with it. To have read it out, to have shown the telegram form on which it was written, even to let the chief of the line hold it and read it for himself – any of that would have been entirely understandable. But to let him slip it in his pocket and go off for a late lunch, rather than recovering it and putting it on the chart-room board where it belonged, beggars belief.

Meanwhile the ice was closing in. The German liner *Amerika* reported at 1.45 p.m. to the United States Navy's Hydrographic Office in Washington, DC, that she had "passed two large icebergs in 41° 27' N, 50° 8' W on the 14th April". The Office acted as a clearing house for ice-warnings, logging and relaying them to North Atlantic shipping. The message was picked up as a courtesy by the *Titanic* for forwarding to Washington via Cape Race, Newfoundland, when the ship came in range of the latter that evening. Though not addressed to the ship, the message contained vital navigational information and should have gone to the bridge. Jack Phillips did not mention it to his junior, Harold Bride, or give it to an officer as he should have done, according to Bride.

At 7.30 p.m. another message was intercepted, from the Leyland (IMM) ship *Californian* (of which much more later) to the same line's *Antillian*: " ... lat. 42° 3' N, long. 49° 9' W. Three large bergs five miles to southward of us. Regards – Lord." Bride said he gave this to an officer, but could not recall which.

At 9.40 p.m., by which time Smith had retired, the ship received a message from the SS *Mesaba*, with a warning intended specifically for her: "From *Mesaba* to *Titanic* and all eastbound ships. Ice report in lat. 42° N to 41° 25' N, long. 49° to 50° 30' W. Saw much heavy pack ice and great number large icebergs. Also field ice. Weather good, clear." The area indicated completely surrounded the spot where the ship was to meet her doom. There is no evidence that the message reached the Captain or the bridge; there is every reason to believe that even if it had, it would have made no difference. Smith would not have slowed down.

The sixth warning came by signal-lamp at 10.30 p.m. from SS *Rappahannock* (Albert Smith, acting master, no relation), a British cargo-ship passing a few miles to the north, eastbound from Halifax, her steering gear actually damaged by ice: "Have just passed through heavy field ice and several icebergs." This was acknowledged by lamp from the *Titanic*'s bridge, proof that an officer received it, as he would have had to order the reply: "Message received. Thank you. Good night."

Twenty-five minutes later, the aforementioned *Californian* addressed the *Titanic* directly with the message: "We are stopped and surrounded by ice ..." but was brusquely interrupted before she could give her position: "Keep out, shut up. You're jamming my signal. I'm working [communicating with] Cape Race." This exchange was not reported to the bridge; but we can be certain that Captain Smith had received at least two warnings of ice across his true course on Sunday 14 April, 1912. He would have known that the ocean area marked on the route chart with the warning "field ice between March and July" lay some twenty-five miles north of the westbound transatlantic shipping track he was on; but the chart also showed an irregular line, 100 to 300 miles *south* of the track, labelled: "Icebergs have been seen within this line in April, May and June."[9]

*

As officer of the watch until ten o'clock on Sunday night, Lightoller ordered Symons and his partner, Archie Jewell, on duty in the crow's nest, at 9.30 p.m. to keep a sharp lookout for ice (but still without benefit of binoculars). The order was transmitted by Sixth Officer James Moody, accompanied by the instruction to pass it on to the next pair of lookouts. The Second Officer had done a thumbnail calculation on the basis of the *Caronia*'s ice-warning and concluded they would sight ice at about this time. The Sixth Officer performed a similar exercise in mental arithmetic, probably drawing on a different warning or warnings such as the *Baltic*'s, and worked out, rather more accurately, that they would reach the ice-infested area at about 11 p.m.[10]

One nagging nuisance at least was finally disposed of by Saturday evening: the ten-day-old fire in number six boiler-room mentioned in the previous chapter.[11] Leading Stoker Frederick Barrett at last succeeded with his colleagues, and an extra gang of a dozen firemen *specially enlisted at Southampton for the task*, in clearing the burning bunker of all its coal. Chief Engineer Bell had told him that the Harland and Wolff guarantee party, led by Thomas Andrews, urgently wanted to inspect the damage. Barrett said the fire had darkened ("dinged" was the slang he used) watertight bulkhead number five: "the hose was going all the time," he said. Leading Fireman Charles Hendrickson said the fire had started in Belfast, but there had been no attempt to tackle it until after leaving Southampton. The bulkhead had become red-hot and looked scorched and warped, but the damage was simply covered up. "I just brushed it off and got some black oil and rubbed over it," he said, "to give it its ordinary appearance."[12] One is left wondering whom this simplistic exercise was intended to impress. Shipwright Edward Wilding said in evidence that the fire would have made the bulkhead more brittle (just as we now know a very low temperature would have done).

Clement Edwards, for the Dock, Wharf, Riverside and

General Workers' Union, suggested on day twenty-five of the inquiry that number five bulkhead gave way to incoming water because it was weakened by the fire. Thomas Lewis, for the British Seafarers' Union, had unearthed the fire and the damage to the bulkhead in examining Barrett on day three of the British inquiry.

In his closing address on day twenty-nine Edwards also made the interesting suggestion that Smith gave Ismay the *Baltic* ice-message as a tacit warning against the speed-trial proposed by the latter for Monday 15 April (the Captain's way of telling the "owner" to slow down?) and that Ismay kept it in the hope it would be forgotten, so that the test would go ahead. This is not consistent with the picture of the gung-ho "E.J." we have come to know from his record; but at least, as Edwards argued, the incident proved Ismay to be no "ordinary passenger" – as did the fact, also highlighted by Edwards, that he went straight to the bridge after the collision with the iceberg.

Meanwhile the *Titanic* was still being steered across the broad Atlantic along the "Outward Southern Track", the agreed westbound course followed by liners between 15 January and 14 August each year. White Star's "rule" that a lifeboat drill should be held every Sunday morning was honoured more in the breach than the observance. It was cancelled on this occasion because a strong breeze was blowing at the time, although it died away quite soon; for the rest of the day, exceptionally, the only wind was made by the passage of the ship.[13] Captain Smith, excused his weekday tour of the vessel, preferred to conduct a religious service lasting forty-five minutes in the first-class dining saloon, starting at 10.30 a.m. – the one occasion when the lower orders were allowed to cast their eyes over the opulent accommodation laid on for their betters. The band accompanied the hymns. Since there were by a large margin not enough lifeboats for all aboard, not even for all the passengers, a drill might well have done more harm than good and been the opposite of reassuring. English law did not require Smith to hold one and firemen in particular (clearly the most unruly element of ships' crews, at any rate in White Star's experience) regarded such extra chores as no part of their duties.[14] Trimmer George Cavell bluntly told the British inquiry on day five that he had never experienced a lifeboat drill on White Star liners except on a Sunday morning if the ship happened to be in New York harbour (a time and a place at which there would be no passengers to alarm).

The agreed transatlantic track the ship was following was a "great circle" route from the Fastnet Rock at the south-western tip of Ireland to a position at latitude 42° north and longitude 47° west known as the "turning point". A great circle route is the shortest distance between two points on the globe, i.e., the arc of a circle joining them whose centre coincides with that of the earth. Ships would descend upon the turning point on a broadly south-west-erly course (S62W true or 242° in the case of the *Titanic*) and then turn almost due west for the run to New York (S86W true or 266° in this instance).

Captain Smith, however, left instructions in the night-order book, kept for the benefit of the officer of the watch (Wilde was on duty at the time), that this turn should be made at 5.50 p.m. on Sunday 14 April – thirty minutes later than due. Assuming, as we can from the evidence, that the ship was maintaining a speed of not less than 22 knots, she would have continued for another eleven sea-miles on her old course, which would have put her two to four miles further south at the moment of the turn than would otherwise have been the case. This would have placed her somewhat southward and to the west of the ice mentioned by the *Baltic*, and even further to the south of the *Caronia* ice.[15] But in the context of warnings indi-cating a field of ice not less (and quite possibly rather more) than seventy-eight miles wide across her path,[16] the change of course is too slight to justify our deducing a consciously evasive manoeuvre by Captain Smith: at the time of the collision his vessel was only two miles south of the customary route. One would have expected a decisive turn to the south-west, away from the continental shelf off Newfoundland and Nova Scotia, then to westward a good while later, if such had been his intention. There is no proof that it was.

Lightoller relieved Wilde at 6 p.m. on Sunday; Sixth Officer James Moody came on duty at 8. The air temperature was registered in the early evening as an uninviting forty-three degrees Fahrenheit and falling quite noticeably. First Officer Murdoch was on his rounds; at 7.15 p.m. he noticed that the forward forecastle hatch was partly open and emitting light. He ordered a lamp-trimmer, Samuel Hemming, to close it to preserve the night-vision of the lookouts at the bridge and crow's nest. By nine o'clock the air temperature had fallen to a decidedly cold thirty-three, a drop of ten degrees in two hours.

By this time Smith was at dinner with the Wideners. Lightoller had been shown the *Caronia* ice-warning by his captain earlier in the day and had it in his head, as we have seen, that they would be up to the ice at about 9.30 p.m. whereas Sixth Officer Moody thought they would meet it at 11 p.m. Either Lightoller, who denied it, or one of the junior officers on duty on the bridge must have received from Harold Bride at about 7.30 p.m. the *Californian*'s ice-message to the *Antillian*, intercepted and brought to the bridge by the Marconi man. At this stage of the voyage there was ice only fifty miles ahead of the ship. At 8.40 p.m. Lightoller warned Ship's Carpenter J. Maxwell, responsible for the fresh-water tanks, that the water in them might freeze because the sea temperature was down to thirty-one degrees (one degree below the freezing point of fresh water but not of sea-water). A similar message went to Chief Engineer Bell, who would need to look to his boiler-water.

Smith made his excuses to the Wideners and their distinguished guests, including the Thayers and Major Butt, left table early and went up to the bridge, arriving at about 9 p.m. and engaging Lightoller in a discussion which lasted at least twenty minutes. "There is not much wind," said the Captain. "No, it is a flat calm, as a matter of fact," the Second Officer replied. "A flat calm," Smith repeated. All the nautical witnesses questioned on this at the British inquiry agreed that such conditions were so rare in the North Atlantic that they were unlikely to recur in a lifetime's experience at sea. Lightoller regretted aloud that there was not even a breeze as they entered the icy region because this meant there would be no tell-tale, phosphorescent ripple against an iceberg, helping to reveal its presence.

The two officers debated the other indications of bergs, including reflected light (this would have to originate from the ship herself or the stars as there was no moon). Even if the iceberg was only showing its "blue" or dark side (if it had just rolled over, perhaps), it ought at least to reveal itself by a white outline. Lightoller was confident on such a clear, calm night of seeing an iceberg, even a small one or growler, at one and a half to two miles, giving plenty of time to avoid it. There was, however, no discussion of the ice-warnings or of the two deck officers' differing calculations of likely times for encountering ice. At about twenty past the hour, Smith announced his intention of retiring for the night, but fully dressed and only as far as the bunk in the chart room. His parting words to the officer of the watch were: "If it becomes at all doubtful, let me know; I shall be just inside." Lightoller had no doubt that this was an order to call the Captain if ice was sighted.[17] The context of their discussion indeed allows no other conclusion.

At half past nine Lightoller told Moody to order the two men then in the crow's nest, Jewell and Symons, "to keep a sharp lookout for ice, particularly small ice and growlers" and to pass the word to their reliefs, Fleet and

Lee, due on at 10 p.m. when the watch changed. At that moment First Officer Murdoch relieved Lightoller in charge on the bridge; the air temperature was at freezing-point; the "Cherub" patent log showed that the ship had covered forty-five sea-miles in the past two hours, an average speed of 22.5 knots. The weather remained clear and absolutely still, the sea dead calm. Moody stayed on duty. From their actions and conversation, all these three officers and their master were actively aware that they were approaching ice and had in their different ways prepared for it. The Captain had delayed his turn, conceivably as a concession to caution, and definitely left orders to be called if anything untoward arose; Murdoch closed the hatch fifty feet below the crow's nest; Lightoller ordered a special alert at the moment from which he anticipated seeing ice; Moody had worked out that ice might appear any time from 11 p.m. At half past ten, the sea temperature was still down to an unusually low thirty-one degrees (the temperature at which, it will be remembered, the metal of the hull was at its most brittle).

At 11.30 p.m., according to Fleet and Lee, the two lookouts then on duty, but supported by only one other witness at either official inquiry, a slight but definite haze appeared dead ahead of the ship. They did not report it. Ten minutes later, without consulting his colleague, Frederick Fleet suddenly reached across and sounded the death-knell of the *Titanic*: three strokes on the crow's-nest bell, meaning an object was dead ahead of the ship. He told the American inquiry he had seen "a black mass ... a little bit higher than the forecastle head" – more than fifty-five feet. There had been a faint haze for ten minutes until the collision, he insisted at the British inquiry. His mate, Reginald Lee, also said there had been a haze, as did off-duty Fireman Alfred Shiers, who came on deck to investigate: "The berg was in a haze." Mersey chose not to believe them.

As he tolled his bell Fleet also telephoned the bridge seventy feet aft; Sixth Officer Moody answered.

Fleet: Are you there?
Moody: Yes; what do you see?
Fleet: Iceberg right ahead!
Moody: Thank you.
[To First Officer Murdoch:] Iceberg right ahead!
Murdoch [to Helmsman Hitchens]: Hard a-starboard!

In evidence on the twelfth day in London, Lightoller made
the startling suggestion that the *Titanic* had begun to turn
to port *before* Fleet rang down from aloft; but Lightoller
was in bed at the time and out of touch with the bridge.
Be that as it may, Quartermaster Robert Hitchens, aged
thirty, at the helm since 10 p.m., wrenched the wheel hard
over as far as it would go, trying for a southward swing
from 289° or "north seventy-one west" of 40° (just over
three and a half compass-points). Murdoch meanwhile
was ordering first "Stop" and then "Full Astern" on the
engine-room telegraph; in the same flurry of action he
pushed a bell-button for ten seconds to warn those below
of his intention to close all watertight doors and then
pulled the switch which automatically did so.[18]

It was all too late. Some forty seconds had elapsed from
Fleet's warning and the ship had veered some two points
(22.5°) to port – more than enough, unfortunately, to
ensure she did not hit head-on – when she struck the
iceberg a glancing blow. A ridge or other underwater
protrusion scraped along the side of the hull at about ten
feet above the keel, causing straggling damage some 300
feet long but only a few inches wide at most. Ship and ice
were in contact for a maximum of ten seconds; the ship
had travelled about 500 yards between the alarm and the
impact. It will be recalled that the ship had taken 850
yards to stop from 20 knots on her trials. The evidence
suggests that Fred Fleet saw the iceberg at barely 500
yards.[19]

What passengers and crew sensed of the collision, if
anything – many slept through the moment which killed

the *Titanic* – depended on where they were, their experience of life and/or their imagination.

To Third Officer Herbert Pitman, giving evidence to the American inquiry, it sounded like "a chain running over a windlass". In London he said it was as if the anchor was being lowered.

Major Arthur Peuchen of the Canadian Militia (equivalent to the British Territorial Army or the American National Guard), "felt as though a heavy wave had struck our ship. She quivered …".

Lightoller had many occasions to describe how the impact seemed to him, not least in his book. But his first opportunity was at the American inquiry (as in the case of the two quoted above): "A slight shock, a slight trembling and a grinding sound." In London this had become "a jar and grind … a slight bumping", not at all violent.

Mrs J. Stuart White, a passenger, said imaginatively but convincingly: "It was just as though we went over a thousand marbles." George Harder, also a passenger, only observed "a dull thump".[20]

Impressions were just as varied, and more numerous, at the British inquiry. Able Seaman Joseph Scarrott said accurately that it felt like a sudden full-speed astern: "just a trembling".

Down below it was a different story. Fireman George Beauchamp, in number ten stokehold at the time, said the crash was "like a roar of thunder".

James Johnson, a steward in the first-class saloon, said: "I did not feel much because we thought she had lost her wheel or something, and somebody passed the remark, 'another Belfast trip' [for an unscheduled repair]." Obviously old *Olympic* hands …

Trimmer Thomas Dillon (trimmers kept coal level in the bunkers), on duty in the engine-room, felt only "a slight shock". So did Thomas Ranger, a greaser: "A slight jar [which] lifted us off our feet." (No such name appears on the crew list.) Trimmer Cavell had a nasty experience in a bunker when the coal shifted and trapped him for a while. Fireman Shiers merely "felt a bump", got out of bed and went to the forecastle head.

Bathroom Steward Charles MacKay was off duty and playing cards when he felt a shock, not at all severe. Lookout George Symons, AB, said: "What awakened me was a grinding sound on her bottom. I thought at first she had lost her anchor and chain and it was running along her bottom."

J. Bruce Ismay, chief executive of the White Star Line, was awakened by the collision and thought that "we had lost a blade off the propeller". This was an astute reaction from someone who had not been on the *Olympic* or, as far as can be discovered, any other ship when such an event had taken place.[21]

Martha Eustis Stevenson said she was fast asleep in first class when "I was awakened by a terrible jar with ripping and cutting noises which lasted for a few moments."

In second class, the young teacher Lawrence Beesley, who later wrote a painstaking account of the disaster, was awakened but felt "nothing more than an extra heave of the engines and a more than usually obvious dancing motion of the mattress".[22]

Bump, grind, rumble or roar, it brought Captain Smith to the bridge within a minute. "What have we struck?" he asked Murdoch. "An iceberg, Sir. I hard-a-starboarded and reversed the engines and I was going to hard-a-port around it, but she was too close. I could not do any more. I have closed the watertight doors."[23] Fourth Officer Boxhall had also rushed to the bridge and Smith ordered him to go below forward on the starboard side, establish the whereabouts and extent of the damage and report back. Ismay also appeared on the bridge, to be told that the ship had struck.

Leading Stoker Fred Barrett was on duty forward of number five watertight bulkhead on the starboard side of the foremost boiler-room, number six, and was one of the very first to receive a most dramatic demonstration of the extent of the damage. Even as he was deafened by a thunderous roar, a huge horizontal jet of water instantaneously burst in through an opening in the ship's side, two feet forward of his position and two feet clear of the orlop deck. He had to make his escape by the emergency ladder because the watertight door had closed.

Boxhall needed a quarter of an hour to go below, look around, call out Lightoller and Pitman on his way back and return to the bridge. He had been able to determine in that time that there was no water on F deck but the orlop deck was flooded forward of number four watertight bulkhead. The five postal clerks were already moving their precious sacks from the mail room to the post office on G deck above. Ten minutes after the collision, water had risen as much as fourteen feet above the keel in the first five "watertight" compartments (a misnomer, as we have seen). Over a period of some minutes after the impact the ship first moved astern then stopped, then went half-speed ahead – or vice versa, depending on whether you believe the evidence to the British inquiry of Trimmer Thomas Dillon (day five) or Greaser Frederick Scott (day six), both on duty in the vicinity of the business end of the engine-room telegraph connected with the bridge.

By midnight, as Captain Smith and Thomas Andrews of Harland and Wolff went below for a hurried inspection, the mailbags were floating twenty-four feet above the keel. Andrews knew the *Titanic* was mortally wounded and gave her an hour to an hour and a half to live, possibly two hours. Once four compartments were flooded, the sea would spill over each bulkhead in turn, in the way that water flows down a tilted ice-cube tray, and send the liner down by the head. In fact five compartments had been opened to the sea by the brush with the iceberg and were filling simultaneously.

Andrews was pessimistic in his first thumbnail calculation of the hours and minutes left to the stricken liner – but not unduly so. Twenty minutes after the collision with the iceberg, Captain Smith was sure that his ship was lost. By five minutes past midnight on the morning of Monday

15 April (ship's time, which was one hour fifty minutes ahead of New York time) the floor of the squash court forward on F deck was awash, thirty-two feet above the keel. Water was coming into boiler-room number five, the sixth "watertight" compartment from the stem. The ship was already noticeably down by the head.

Boxhall was kept busy. No sooner had he delivered his damage report than the Captain ordered him to check the dying ship's position. Lightoller had taken the last "fix" on the stars at 7.30 p.m. on Sunday, a calculation which Smith had later entered on the chart. To obtain the position four and a half hours later Boxhall used "dead reckoning" (an expression whose origin is lost but which has nothing to do with death). Starting from his 7.30 "fix" he took account of all subsequent notations of course and speed recorded in the ship's log to calculate her position when she struck. He may or may not have got these absolutely right; he may or may not have allowed for the southerly Labrador Current the ship had met some time after 7.30.

How he arrived at the famous position of latitude 41° 46' north, longitude 50° 14' west, which was undoubtedly a few miles out, we shall never know in the absence of the log. Each erroneous minute of latitude put the calculation one sea-mile out; each miscalculated minute of longitude represented roughly 1,100 yards at this latitude (lines of latitude are parallel to the Equator; lines of longitude converge towards the poles). He could have taken another fix on the stars to make sure, but perhaps time and instruments were lacking. At any rate the position was accurate enough to bring rescuers and would-be rescuers up to the lifeboats; and when Commander Joseph Groves Boxhall, RNR (retired), died fifty-five years later at the age of eighty-three, his will requested that his ashes be scattered at the spot: "41° 46' N, 50° 14' W."

Captain Smith himself took the slip of paper on which Boxhall had written the co-ordinates to the wireless room and ordered repeated broadcasts of the international distress signal, adding this revised final position. The earliest recorded signals, some thirty-five minutes after the collision (transmission of these must also have been ordered by the master), had given the co-ordinates 41° 44' or 41° 46' north, 50° 24' west. These were now corrected under the *Titanic*'s call sign MGY. Cape Race in Newfoundland logged a distress call containing the amended position at 12.25 a.m., ten minutes after the Marconi shore-station and two ships, *La Provence* (French) and *Mount Temple* (Canadian) had picked up the first known requests for assistance from MGY. The international call for help was in the process of changing from "CQD" (colloquially rendered as "come quick, danger") to "SOS" (informally "save our souls"); the sinking ship used both. "CQ" was the Marconi code for "all stations"; the addition of "D" signified an emergency call to all stations. SOS was introduced in 1908 as being more memorable, and also easier to transmit and recognize, in Morse code: three short, three long, three short.

By this time the ship was under a cloud of excruciating noise and steam as pressure was released from most of the boilers, in order to forestall explosions when the ship sank low enough in the water for the sea to reach them. A few were kept going to the end to power the generators providing light and current for the radio. Phillips and Bride could barely hear the acknowledgements of their calls for help amid all the uproar. "MGY says CQD. Here [is the] corrected position ... Require immediate assistance. We have collision with iceberg. Sinking. Can hear nothing for noise of steam," SS *Ypiranga* heard at 12.26 a.m.[24]

The chill air was full of messages that night. The British Report records sixteen ships and Cape Race as having received the distress messages from MGY, several of which replied with offers of help. But the court's compilation of messages is not complete and the list of ships mentioned in it not exhaustive. The American inquiry placed twelve named ships (all included in the British seventeen) and one unidentified sailing ship in the vicinity of the disaster. The *Rappahannock* cannot have got far to the east with her damaged rudder after her exchange of lamp-signals, perhaps fifteen miles; but she had no wireless and was not counted. We shall return to this vexed question of who was where in due course.

One ship that did not hear the electronic call for aid was the liner *Californian*; she was a modest, 6,223-ton, eleven-year-old cargo-ship and had only one wireless operator, Cyril Evans, twenty years old and with just six months' experience. The concept of manning the wireless round the clock did not become the norm until after the catastrophe. Having been rebuffed when warning the *Titanic* of ice, he turned in at 11.30 p.m. (ship's time, twelve minutes ahead of the *Titanic*'s time). The two facts are not connected: Evans, quite reasonably, was tired after a long day at Morse key and earphones. He went out of his way at the British inquiry (day eight) to insist that he had not felt insulted by the impatient dismissal of his half-delivered ice-warning. The convention was that the faster and/or larger ship took precedence, he pointed out. Captain Lord brought the ship to a halt for the night at 10.21 p.m. (10.09 on the *Titanic*) because she was completely surrounded by ice. He gave his position as 42° 5' north, 50° 7' west, some nineteen and a half miles north-north-east of the scene of the collision (and one and a half hours before it happened). Evans heard nothing more until about a quarter to six on Monday morning. We shall come back to his ship.

There was no public address system on the *Titanic* so news of her plight spread slowly round the ship, transmitted by word of mouth as stewards sought out passengers in their cabins. The ship's eight-strong band, led by Wallace Hartley from Colne, Lancashire, started playing cheery ragtime numbers in the first-class lounge at a quarter past midnight. Shortly afterwards they took up station on the boat deck by the port-side entrance to the first-class grand staircase. By this time the water was forty feet above the keel in the seamen's accommodation forward on E deck.

It was 12.25 a.m. ship's time. At this moment, Captain Smith issued the order to prepare the lifeboats for loading women and children; and the eastbound Cunard liner *Carpathia* (Captain Arthur Rostron) acknowledged receipt of the amended distress signal, saying he was on his way at full speed. He started from a position about fifty-eight miles to the south-east, reversing his course and piling on steam.

The attitude of Ismay, Captain Smith and his officers to the ice they knew was approaching presents an extraordinary mixture of the cavalier and the fatalistic. The ship had accelerated day by day. A crucial ice-warning was forgotten or ignored for more than five hours. The master and his watch-officer had a long and detailed discussion about how hard it might be to spot icebergs with no wind, no swell and an all but unique, flat calm. Yet the crow's nest was deprived of binoculars and it was also planned to sail even faster the next day. Early sightings of icebergs from the crow's nest were apparently ignored by the officers of the watch, determined to beat the *Olympic*'s best time for the crossing. And when disaster struck, reaction on the bridge was curiously slow: thirty-five minutes before the first SOS; forty-five minutes before starting to *prepare* the lifeboats.

All this shows that if White Star felt it had something to hide for fear of being found negligent, with all that this would legally imply, its fears were entirely rational. Up to and at the moment of the collision there were six men on watch. Fleet and Lee were in the crow's nest; on the bridge were the officers Murdoch and Moody, both dead; and the two quartermasters, Hitchens at the wheel and Alfred Olliver on stand-by (every watch had two quartermasters on duty, taking the wheel for two hours each). Olliver, not called at the British inquiry, told the American one (day six) that he had been trimming the lamps of the ship's standing compass aft of the bridge until just before the impact and had first seen the iceberg as it passed aft of the bridge. Fleet (called by both inquiries) and Lee (British inquiry only) told the same story and had plainly agreed to testify to a haze round the iceberg which just one other witness, Fireman Shiers (British only), supported while many others, including Lightoller, said there had been no such thing. Hitchens was the only witness to what happened on the bridge itself just before and during the impact; and Fleet and Lee the only witnesses on how, when and to what effect the alarm was sounded. Of these three, two may have been rewarded for their silence while the third sturdily went back to sea. According to the Rev. Mrs Pat Thomas, his granddaughter, Reginald Lee probably served out the First World War before taking a series of jobs ashore, always in the Southampton area. He regaled his children and grandchildren with tales of the disaster, attended the annual commemorative survivors' dinner given by Cunard-White Star and died peacefully in the mid-1960s.

Having thus raised a more than merely reasonable doubt that White Star's version of events was the whole truth, one is entitled to speculate about what else might have been concealed by a company with a uniquely dubious business and damage record in an industry historically notorious for fraud. We have described White Star's murky past and its own and its commodore's astounding mishaps; we also mentioned the fact that emigrant ships such as the "Olympics" were subject to government inspection. This was because shipowners in the early days of steam blatantly overloaded and overinsured vessels in poor condition ("coffin ships") – until Samuel Plimsoll, MP, roused public opinion against them and inspired the first Merchant Shipping Act of 1876, lending his name to the line on ships' hulls showing maximum permitted load.[25]

As our researches went deeper and the unresolved mysteries in the *Titanic* legend accumulated, a truly startling theory emerged to "explain" many anomalies, entailing a fundamental revision of the story. Given that White Star was no stranger to the underhand and that its new owner, J. P. Morgan, was utterly ruthless in business, what lengths would they go to if they found that their principal shipping asset, the *Olympic*, was not just damaged but crippled when it hit a cruiser? What if the low-grade steel of her stern, which needed a month and a half to repair as Cunard cleaned up on the North Atlantic, laid her open to redoubled damage when she ran over a wreck a few months later, in water of a temperature at which the steel was at its most brittle?

The ship returns to Belfast for an overnight replacement of a lost propeller-blade but is still there five days later, missing another round trip to New York at great expense and embarrassment to her owners. In the same yard, taking turn and turn about with her in the one dry dock available, is the all but complete, all but identical *Titanic*. So similar are the two ships that they are often confused, as we have seen – sometimes accidentally, sometimes deliberately (nearly all the internal illustrations – photographs and drawings alike – of the *Titanic* which have survived are in fact of the *Olympic*). Even Harland and Wolff manage to mix up the two ships in the minutes of their board meetings.[26]

The simultaneous presence of the pair in the yard represents the opportunity. The means are surprisingly modest, perhaps as little as exchanging the ship's nameplates and the odd loose item such as lifebuoys (very few items bore the ships' names) – a task for a small team of men acting under the cover of all the work going on aboard both liners. The motive? A mixture of wounded pride and money: White Star fought vainly and beyond all reason to extract damages from the Admiralty (adding heavily to the *Olympic*'s uninsured losses).

So why not switch the two ships, patching up the

Olympic enough to stand gentle sea trials and a "maiden voyage" which would end in a known icefield, with other IMM ships on hand to rescue all aboard – except that the ever-impetuous Smith gets it wrong and crashes early. The *Olympic* is written off on the *Titanic*'s insurance while the latter sails on as her sister for twenty-three years. The most surprising aspect of this seductive speculation proved to be not so much the fact that it had arisen but how far it could be taken.

5

THE QUICK AND THE DEAD

The absence of a definitive list of all passengers and crew when over 2,200 people were aboard the *Titanic* is irritating but hardly surprising: passenger lists remain just as unreliable in the computer age, as many an air disaster has shown. The confusion over the fate of some of the lifeboats, however, when there were only twenty to consider, is highly frustrating. There is no need to labour the discrepancies between the various sources on the exact numbers of passengers and crew aboard until disaster struck: there is both too much and too little information for us to be able to resolve them. There is, for example, a much bigger difference between the number said by witnesses to have been aboard all the lifeboats taken together, calculated by the British inquiry[1] as 914, and the number rescued (most likely 705, but even this figure is not beyond doubt).

The saddest shortfall, apart from the one between the total aboard and the number of lifeboat places, is the difference between the 705 saved and the official capacity of the boats, 1,178. Considering the calm weather, the boats could probably have coped with a good 500 more than managed to get into them, which would have reduced the fatalities in the world's worst peacetime sea disaster by a third and made the total saved larger than that of the lost. But, as will emerge in this chapter, it is not altogether clear what happened to some of the boats or what happened inside them. Eyewitnesses are renowned for their unreliability; when there are so many, their numbers increase rather than reduce the inconsistencies so that it only remains possible to approximate. The prospect of death may well concentrate the mind; but not, it seems, on fact.

The temperature of the sea round the ship, slowly sinking in the icefield, was twenty-eight degrees (minus two degrees Celsius), boding ill for anyone forced to spend more than a few minutes in the water. The iceberg that mortally wounded the *Titanic* seems to have borne a superficial resemblance above the waterline to the Rock of Gibraltar, although everyone who saw it and left a description, drawing or even photograph (taken from other ships after daybreak) retained a somewhat different memory of its shape, size and other features. Somehow considerable quantities of ice fell on to the well deck, C, between forecastle and bridge. There were too many witnesses to this phenomenon for it to be dismissed as imaginary, but there is no explanation for it. Since the bridge extruded about a foot and a half over the side of the ship, it is just possible to imagine this projection scraping the berg and knocking some ice forward onto the deck below; or the outward-curved edge of the starboard bulwark on the forecastle might have dislodged some ice in passing. But emergency boat number one was kept permanently swung out further than either of these features and there is no evidence of damage to it from the iceberg – on the contrary. All this leaves the possibility that the ice was dislodged by the impact from the rigging (mast and funnel stays) or the great, four-stranded wireless antenna slung between the masts. Several black jokes were made about putting some of this ice in drinks or taking it home as a souvenir.

Because water expands when it freezes, ice is lighter than water. The part of an iceberg visible above the sea is only one-ninth of its total mass: the *Titanic* might as well have sideswiped Gibraltar itself at full tilt because the iceberg she struck was, as far as she was concerned, an immovable object, a floating island weighing many hundreds of thousands of tons. Short of a nuclear explosion, nobody has found a means of breaking up an iceberg to this day: all one can do is leave it to melt when it is ready and steer clear in the meantime. The world's heaviest ship would not have affected the berg's slow but remorseless drift by as much as a millimetre. Most icebergs in the northern hemisphere are "calved" (broken off from a glacier) in the huge Disko Bay in Greenland. They may take as much as two years to reach the Grand Banks off Newfoundland; in mild weather they may fragment, shedding "growlers" or small icebergs and thus increasing the hazards to navigation.[2]

The "guilty" berg therefore went on drifting after the disaster, probably at about one mile per hour, and would have been a few miles south, and some lesser distance east, of the scene of the disaster by the time it was sighted some six to eight hours later. This means that we cannot be certain beyond doubt that it was identified or even seen the next morning; the most likely suspect among the bergs described by witnesses was a twin-peaked one which seemed to have a red-ochre line at water level, suggesting contact with a ship's anti-fouling paint. Descriptions of the lethal iceberg by passengers and crew vary wildly: it was enveloped in haze; it was no such thing; the face it showed to the ship was black or dark blue; it was high above the ship; it was barely as high as her side; it was white when seen from the ship afterwards; it was tall; it was squat.

It undoubtedly stank, many said: icebergs often contain indescribably ancient mineral, vegetable, fish and even animal matter which reeks primevally when exposed to air for the first time in millennia. This unpleasant fact rather militates against the idea that it was berg ice on the forward well deck that people put in their drinks. But, no matter what the iceberg looked or smelt like, and no matter how indifferent his judgment of distance may have

Changing places: *Olympic* and *Titanic* (right) take turns at the Thompson graving dock in Belfast on their last meeting early in March 1912.

The men behind the superliners. Above: the partners in Harland and Wolff in its heyday (1876-1885): from left to right, Gustav Wolff, W.H.Wilson, William James (later Lord) Pirrie, Edward Harland; inset, Thomas Andrews, the shipwright who went down with the *Titanic*. Below right: Lord Pirrie (left), and J. Bruce Ismay, managing director of White Star, inspecting the *Titanic*. Below left: J. Pierpont Morgan, financier of the *Titanic*.

The sisters under construction at Harland and Wolff.

The sisters completed: the *Olympic* (top) with her open A deck promenade, and the *Titanic*, with enclosed A deck and irregularly spaced windows on B deck.

The great propellers:
before and after
Olympic's collision
with HMS *Hawke*.

The hole in the stern and the damaged propeller of the *Olympic*.

Titanic leaving Belfast for the last time.

been, the authorized version of the legend says that lookout Frederick Fleet saw it first, before his mate Reg Lee and before anyone on the bridge, all of whom were meant to be on special alert for ice.

One first-class passenger, Marian Thayer, whose husband was lost but whose son was saved, saw something most peculiar on going up on A deck immediately after the collision and looking over the starboard side:

> I saw what looked like a number of long, black ribs, apparently floating nearly level with the surface of the water, parallel with each other [and the side of the ship] but separated from each other by ... two or three feet of water ... the nearest one being probably twenty feet from the ship, and they extended from near the bow to about amidship. I saw no high iceberg at the time.[3]

It took about twenty minutes to get the first lifeboat into the chill, still water from when Captain Smith ordered preparations for loading women and children. This was a less than dazzling performance with the latest equipment by a crew of purported professionals, manifestly undertrained in emergency procedures. Nor was the ship systematically scoured for them so as to be able to get them off efficiently, boat by boat. The senior officers had a half-formed plan of having the boats lowered with a few people aboard and telling them to row to the big gangway doors in the side of the ship to fill up, but these doors were not opened in the ship's last hours. Boatswain Nichols and a party eventually went to open them on the orders of the supervising officers but were never seen again.

At approximately a quarter to one, ship's time, on Monday 15 April, lifeboat number seven was lowered on the orders of First Officer Murdoch, assisted by Fifth Officer Harold Lowe. This was one of the fourteen purpose-built lifeboats, some thirty feet long with an official capacity of sixty-five. There were up to twenty-eight aboard, not even half full, and the true figure may have been nearer twenty, less than a third of capacity. Boats with odd numbers were on the starboard side and those with even to port. It will be remembered that there were two Engelhardt collapsible boats on each side, A and C to starboard, B and D to port, each intended for forty-seven passengers; and there were the two "emergency boats", the cutters nearest the bow on each side, kept swung out at all times and also intended to serve as lifeboats for forty people apiece, number one to starboard, number two to port. The boats were not lowered in numerical order but rather when they were deemed ready by the officers in charge of loading. We adhere to chronological order; only when two boats were launched simultaneously do we fall back on numerical order.

According to the evidence – at the British inquiry, care was taken to question witnesses from every single boat, which somehow only made confusion more confounded – number seven had just three crew members, including two lookouts (Hogg and Jewell). Eight female and ten male passengers were definitely located aboard by witnesses. One of them, Mrs Helen Bishop, of Dowagiac, Michigan, who had travelled first class with her husband, Dickinson, aged twenty-five (they gave evidence at the American inquiry on day ten), went out of her way to praise the conduct of Hogg, who was in charge, and a crewman whose name she gave as Jack Edmonds. No such name appears on the crew list, a classic example of the difficulties thrown up by the evidence, especially that concerning the lifeboats.

Archie Jewell, having gone off duty at 10 p.m., had heard and felt the collision and rushed out onto the well deck forward, where he was one of the many who, with varying degrees of amazement, saw ice on the starboard side of the deck. He returned to his bunk for his clothes and Boatswain Nichols appeared, ordering all seamen on deck.[4] Jewell, just eighteen, was one of the few crewmen aboard who knew his boat-station, number seven; lists were posted up in the various crew quarters assigning men (firemen and stewards as well as the relatively few seamen aboard) to boats, but many clearly never read them, whether out of illiteracy, indifference or faith shared with their master in the "unsinkability" of their ship. Crewmen were needed to row and steer, but not a few of those assigned to various boats, such as firemen and stewards, had no experience of either: the evidence of neglect of lifeboat drill by White Star is overwhelming. Many of the boats lacked a light, water or biscuits, or all such items, when launched, although they were supposed to have them and did have them when inspected in Belfast. Only a few boats had compasses, but that was an intentional economy as groups of boats were expected to stay together. Some lights were distributed as boats were being lowered, and the bakery staff handed out loaves. Number seven pulled clear of the ship and stood by.

Number seven was soon joined by boat five, commanded by Third Officer Herbert Pitman, not one of the heroes of the drama. Pitman had been working under Murdoch and alongside Fifth Officer Harold Lowe, helping to load up to forty-one passengers, including several men, into number five when it became clear there were no more women in the vicinity at the time lowering began (12.55 a.m.). J. Bruce Ismay decided to take a hand in matters, urging passengers aboard the boat and then telling Lowe to "lower away, lower away!" rotating his arm like a windmill. Lowe, an excitable character who, like the other officers, had armed himself with a loaded pistol, told his company chairman to "get the hell out of the way". The twenty-nine-year-old junior officer shouted: "You want me to lower away quickly? You'll have me drown the whole lot of them!" Ismay sloped off.[5]

Pitman apparently was one of the many aboard who would have preferred to stay on the ship and await rescue, but was ordered by Murdoch to take charge of the lifeboat: "You go away in this boat, old man, and hang around the after gangway. Goodbye, good luck," said Murdoch, shaking hands. Many passengers adopted the same attitude, believing perhaps until it was too late that their ship really was unsinkable, which was probably one of the main reasons why most of the boats were so tragically underfilled. That was an especially bitter irony given that lifeboat provision was so inadequate in the first place.

Another reason was the erroneous but apparently universal belief among the officers that the boats were not strong enough to be lowered full and would buckle; only the last few boats were comparatively crowded, when it was clear that the ship was about to sink. Wilding, the naval architect, said in evidence[6] that the lifeboats had been tested with weights for lowering full; had he been aware of the officers' ignorance of this, he would have rectified it in Belfast. This constituted a strange as well as tragic oversight, all part of the common underestimation of the purpose and potential importance of lifeboats. It still seems astonishing that Thomas Andrews of Harland and Wolff did not notice the underloading and tell the officers it was unnecessary. Andrews was very active in clearing cabins of passengers and helping in other ways, even if he seemingly lapsed into shock near the end.

Dr H. W. Frauenthal, meanwhile, having seen his wife take a seat in number five, decided with his brother to jump from the deck to join her as the boat began to be lowered away barely two-thirds full. Even so the doctor managed to land on Mrs Annie Stengel, a first-class passenger who until then doubtless thought she was safe from immediate harm. His boots broke two of her ribs and knocked her unconscious; but despite the cold and the extra pain, she lived to dine out on the story. Pitman ordered the crew to row away from the ship and stand by, joining and then making fast his boat to number seven. There he resolutely ignored the cries of the dying, claiming that passengers had protested, for fear of being swamped, when he had turned lifeboat number five round earlier with a view to filling it from the people in the water. At least it caused him some distress when he was pressed over his conduct on the witness-stand ("I would rather you did not speak about that"); and two passengers, a woman and a man, had transferred from his boat to number seven when they got the chance, apparently in disgust at his refusal to order a return to the scene of the wreck. The American inquiry gave Pitman a hard time over this; the British inquiry did not press him.[7]

The first to be launched on the port side was boat six, which was lowered under Lightoller's supervision at about the same time as number five, 12.55 a.m. There may have been twenty-eight aboard, all women except for two crew members (Quartermaster Hitchens who had been at the helm on impact was in charge, supported by Fred Fleet, the lookout who sounded the alarm) plus two male passengers, the Canadian Major Arthur Peuchen and an Italian "stowaway" with a broken forearm. Lightoller had allowed Peuchen to board because he had the wit to present himself as a keen amateur yachtsman with useful experience. Lightoller thought there were forty-two aboard but can surely be forgiven any confusion as he was involved in loading some seven boats that night. Captain Smith came by and ordered Hitchens to row in the direction of a ship whose lights could be seen roughly five miles away and two points off *Titanic*'s starboard bow. Lightoller repeated the order. The American inquiry alone came up with sixteen witnesses who saw this "mystery ship", a subject to which we shall return; it apparently vanished from the scene of the disaster. Hitchens, who counted thirty-eight women aboard, stuck to the tiller, leaving Fleet and Peuchen to row; he refused to go back for those in the water and took swigs from a flask. Some time during the night the boat came up to number sixteen: they tied themselves together and a stoker from sixteen crossed over to help with the rowing on six. There was no compass in the latter. Some of the women took a turn at the oars in an attempt to keep warm.[8]

Murdoch and Lowe were doing distinctly better filling and lowering boats on the starboard side than Lightoller and Moody to port. This was at least partly due to the fact that the ship at first listed somewhat to starboard, having been damaged on that side; the water took its time to break down non-watertight partitions and cross the ship, whereupon a great accumulation in the broad "Scotland Road" alleyway probably caused the subsequent list to port. A list to one side naturally made it harder to lower the boats on the other; a pronounced list would cause them to grind against the ship's side. At the same time the boats on the listing side might swing out too far from the ship to be boardable from decks other than the boat deck, unless they could be hauled in somehow or reached by an improvised "bridge". These problems arose several times and slowed down the hesitant evacuation.

Murdoch and Lowe were working their way forward from amidships; having launched boats seven and five, they loaded boat three. There may have been twenty-five women and children and ten male passengers aboard; there was undoubtedly an unusually high proportion of crew, perhaps fifteen, far more than were needed to steer and row. One of the latter, George Moore, AB, said the officers allowed the men and crew to board because there were no more women or children in sight. Number three was lowered from the boat deck to A deck but first-class passengers could not get aboard because the windows in Ismay's screen had not yet been opened with their special spanner; the lifeboat was then lowered all the way to the water, losing two oars in the process. One of the first-class passengers aboard was Mrs Charles M. Hays, who remained distraught and called out for her husband whenever another lifeboat came into view. But he was one of the gallant men who refused to leave the ship so long as women and children remained aboard.[9]

While his colleagues were busy supervising the loading or part-loading and lowering of the boats, Fourth Officer Boxhall, on the orders of the Captain and with the assistance of Quartermaster George Rowe, started firing socket-signals (not rockets) from the starboard end of the bridge. As the two men worked they could see a pair of red and green navigation lamps approaching to about five miles off, indicating a ship coming head-on; later Boxhall saw her red light and two white masthead lights, indicating that she had turned away to starboard. Between firings he vainly tried to raise her by signal-lamp.

The powerful socket signals were launched from mortars, firing a missile 800 feet into the air where it exploded into twelve slowly falling white stars. Boxhall may have launched eight at roughly five-minute intervals, starting at 12.45 as the first boat was launched and finishing at 1.20 a.m. as numbers nine and ten took to the water. There was no uniform international procedure for distress signals of this kind; there was, however, an established custom and practice of firing rockets at regular intervals, as in this case, to indicate an emergency. White rockets were recommended and favoured for this purpose, but a few lines had their own rocket signals for non-emergency communication, mostly coloured but not excluding white ones.

It seems clear now, after many years of fierce dispute still not resolved, that most of these signals, if not the *Titanic* herself, were seen from the *Californian*, said by her master and his chief mate alone to have halted in the icefield for the night at 42° 5' north and 50° 7' west, or a good nineteen miles north-north-east of the wreck. The signals as seen from her bridge were so far away that they appeared not even to reach as high as the masthead of an intervening ship seen by some *Californian* witnesses before the white lights fell back. A steamer was definitely sighted (in the general direction of the *Titanic*, it was established later) from the hove-to *Californian*, but did not respond to lamp-signals. Both official investigations spent a lot of time putting two and two together from these disparate facts, initiating an almighty controversy and arriving at an answer rather different from four, as will be revealed in due course. None of the many unsolved mysteries associated with the *Titanic* legend has aroused so much conflicting passion.

As the signals burst over their heads, Murdoch and Lowe, initially supported by the Boatswain, moved on in the direction of the palpably sinking bow to tackle boat one, the emergency cutter-cum-lifeboat, whose normal position was to hang swung out from the forward, starboard end of the boat deck. After some difficulty in bringing it within reach of passengers (eloquent testimony to the general lack of practice with lifeboats among the crew), this boat was launched at ten minutes past one, or a quarter of an hour after number six, whose crew had been ordered to steer towards a ship two points off the starboard bow. The man in charge of boat one, the self-important lookout George Symons, AB, saw a white (stern?) light a point or two off the *port* bow, suggesting that the mystery ship had passed westward – or that the *Titanic* had swung round. The crew pulled towards it for a time.

Boat number one (capacity forty) was by a large margin the least laden of them all, mustering no more than a dozen: two women, three male passengers and seven members of the crew (two seamen and five firemen). Fifth Officer Lowe confirmed that the boat had been lowered with so few aboard because there was nobody else to be found within reach on boat or A decks at the time. Hovering in the hope of being included among the lucky dozen were our noble friends Sir Cosmo and Lady Duff Gordon. The baronet, who could see with only one eye, clearly had it fixed firmly on the main chance. He and his wife, and her secretary, Miss Laura Francatelli, had hung around in the vicinity of first lifeboat number seven and then number three in the hope of being allowed to board conveniently as a party. Sir Cosmo, who was a considerable bridge player and had fenced for England at the 1908 Olympic Games, finally asked Murdoch as he looked for passengers for number one: "Can we get in that boat?" The First Officer allegedly replied: "With the greatest pleasure," or words to that effect. Two American males also stepped aboard, still leaving crew outnumbering passengers by seven to five.

The evidence from people in this boat is perhaps the most contrary of all, despite the lack of numbers. Either it turned round and went back to the scene of the disaster or it did not. It pulled away from the ship for anything between 100 and 1,000 yards and stood by awaiting a recall or further orders which never came, as instructed by the lost Murdoch. The passengers or the two ladies either did or did not object to the idea of going back when one or two of the crew raised the idea.

One of the few facts that is undisputed was that Sir Cosmo, while in the lifeboat, offered each of the seven crewmen aboard a cheque for £5, or a month's pay (excluding board) for a seaman. This was the sensational revelation of day five of the British inquiry, made by Leading Fireman Charles Hendrickson, who was in number one. As we shall show when describing that inquiry, this led to not altogether illogical allegations, notably in the American press, that Duff Gordon bribed the crewmen not to go back to those in the water for fear that the boat might be swamped. The baronet insisted his offer was a gesture of sympathy for the fact that the crewmen had lost their berths, their pay and all their gear and he "wanted to do something for them". In the few days between Hendrickson's evidence and Duff Gordon's, an unnamed person from London "representing Sir Cosmo Duff Gordon" sought out Symons for interview at his home in Weymouth, Dorset, and also Fireman James Taylor in Southampton, who corroborated Hendrickson's evidence. Taylor was paid seven shillings in expenses, more than a day's pay, for attending an interview at White Star's Southampton offices. The two crewmen mentioned the visits in evidence under oath on day ten of the British inquiry.

The £5 per man (not in cash to spend in New York but in cheques convertible only in England) were for them to buy new kit, Duff Gordon said. He handed out the drafts on his London bank aboard the rescuing ship *Carpathia*, written out by Miss Francatelli on blank notepaper and signed by the baronet himself. Understandably, this dubious episode became a separate cause célèbre within the grand sensation of the British inquiry, as will be made clear.[10]

Launched at the same time as number one but on the port side was boat eight, under the supervision of the physically imposing, calm and collected Chief Officer Wilde, aided by Lightoller. Captain Smith was also on hand for a minute or two. Some witnesses thought this boat was launched before number six as the first port-side lifeboat into the water, but the British Report, which is quite shameless about rounding the time up or down to the nearest five minutes, is definite: number eight was launched, like number one, at 1.10 a.m.

But not before a poignant drama was played out on the boat deck nearby. Aware of the Captain's original "women and children only" order, Mr and Mrs Isidor and Ida Straus (he of Macy's store in New York) stood by and watched as women were ushered into lifeboat number eight. Colonel Archibald Gracie, their friend, was also watching. Invited to step in, Mrs Straus said: "No, I will not be separated from my husband. As we have lived, so will we die, together." Someone then suggested that they both get in as nobody would object to a man of Mr

Straus's advanced age being saved. The old man however stood firm, saying: "No, I do not wish any distinction in my favour which is not granted to others." So they died together. Ellen Bird, Ida's tearful maid, got into number eight with her mistress's fur stole as a parting gift.[11]

Boat eight's load was put at thirty-nine by the British inquiry. There were four crewmen (Thomas Jones, AB, in charge; two stewards and a cook), no male and apparently thirty-five female passengers. On the opening day of the American inquiry, Steward Alfred Crawford said of Captain Smith: "He gave us instructions to pull to a light that he saw and then land the ladies and return, back to the ship again. It was the light of a vessel in the distance. We pulled and pulled, but we could not reach it." Thomas Jones described on day six how a "talkative lady … a countess or something" had a lot to say for herself, so he put her in charge of the tiller while the crewmen and some of the women rowed. This was the elegant Lucy-Noel Martha, Countess of Rothes, travelling with her maid (Miss Mahoney) but without her noble Scottish husband, and clearly not the parasitic type of aristocrat. When she was not steering, she insisted on plying an oar; she also comforted a broken-hearted, keening Italian woman who had lost her husband. Several other women took up oars. Jones had managed to "acquire" one of the number-boards from their boat aboard the *Carpathia*; later he had it framed and sent it to Lady Rothes as a token of his undying admiration.[12]

The next to go down from starboard was boat nine, at 1.20 a.m., attended by Murdoch and Moody. Albert Haines, the Boatswain's Mate, was in charge, supported by two quartermasters, a seaman and four stewards. This lifeboat at least appears to have had a more acceptable total aboard; the British inquiry arrived at fifty-six, including the eight crewmen, six men and forty-two women. The six men were allowed aboard because no more women could be found; one elderly woman broke down, refused to step aboard and retired below. The French novelist Jacques Futrelle, aided by an officer, forced Madame May Futrelle into the boat against her will: "It's your last chance: go!" her anguished husband cried. Otherwise, number nine cleared the boat deck of women and apparently stopped at A deck for more on the way down; this far astern there was no Ismay screen to get in the way. Nor was there compass or light in the boat. Quartermaster Walter Wynn saw a steamer's red (port navigation) and white (masthead) light; he thought the ship that was showing them must have been seven or eight miles away. When these lights disappeared, he made out another white light in the same direction.[13] After some difficulty in removing the lashings round the oars, boat nine slowly pulled away from the ship.

Having helped Murdoch with number nine, Moody crossed the boat deck, rounding the dome over the first-class main entrance, to give Lightoller a hand with boat ten, its equivalent on the port side. The British Report has this boat going into the water at the same time as number nine, 1.20 a.m. In charge was Edward Buley, AB, a Royal Navy veteran, assisted by another seaman and three non-seaman crew members. No male passengers joined this boat under the eagle eyes of the officers; but an Armenian and a Japanese had managed to conceal themselves aboard as stowaways and were discovered after launching. Those permitted to board consisted of forty-one women of all classes and seven children.

The ship's Chief Baker, Charles Joughin, assigned to number ten, had thirteen men under him and sent them up to the boat deck with forty pounds of bread each for the boats at about half past midnight. Joughin helped to throw children across the gap of a yard and a half between the boat and the listing ship's side, which several women were reluctant to leap. In the end Joughin missed this boat and all the others, floated off the sinking ship and was able to scramble aboard one of the collapsibles.

Able Seaman Buley had the impression that boat ten was the last to be launched, which was far from accurate; but told the American inquiry at great length (day six) of the steamer that passed across the bow of the *Titanic* only three miles off, pausing for three whole hours before slowly sailing away. Buley believed it was the knowledge that a ship was in the area and would surely come to their aid which kept the passengers quiet: crew members told many that "there is a steamer coming to our assistance". This may also have persuaded many passengers to stay aboard and wait for rescue rather than making for, and possibly overrunning, the lifeboats.

Number ten joined collapsible D and boats four, twelve and fourteen, which later formed a flotilla, linked by ropes and commanded by Fifth Officer Lowe.

Next to go down the starboard side at 1.25 a.m. was boat eleven, once again supervised by Murdoch and Moody. According to the evidence at the British inquiry this lifeboat was actually overloaded on launching, with seventy people, five more than capacity, on board. This claim is to be treated with scepticism; we already know that the total saved was significantly less than the sum of its parts, as represented in the boat-by-boat estimates of the witnesses. And although the officers must have had an increasing sense of urgency as the ship inexorably went down at the head, they may have started with the belief that the boats were not strong enough to be lowered full and had the idea of filling them up from the gangways rather than while they hung from the davits.

Able Seaman Humphries was given charge of this crowded boat, in which some people were forced to stand; he was joined by seven other crewmen and Mrs Annie Robinson, a first-class stewardess who had been on the Canadian *Lake Champlain* when it was lost to an iceberg collision in 1907. There may have been one male passenger aboard, Philip E. Moch from first class (or there may have been three); and there were up to sixty women and children. Since there was nobody left on the boat deck as it was being filled, more people were taken from A deck.

As the boat reached the water in its heavily laden condition it was almost swamped by the outflow from the ship's overworked pumps. There was a struggle to free it from its falls, the long ropes by which it was lowered from the davits, when the after tackle-block jammed. Elsewhere, a number of boats were cut free of their ropes in the water because the sea was so calm there was no swell to lift the boat and allow ropes to be unhooked when momentarily slack. Evidently the "quick-release" gear connecting the ropes to the boats either failed or was unfamiliar to the crew. On the other hand, had there been anything like a normal Atlantic swell running, boats could have got into difficulties of a different sort.

Mrs Robinson noted that the gallant ship's band were still playing their hearts out as the lifeboat began its descent. In the boat, women complained about having to stand, and one distraught woman repeatedly wound up and set off an alarm clock during the night.[14]

On the other side of the ship at around the same time as number eleven, port-side boat twelve began its descent to the water with Lightoller and Lowe in attendance at 1.25 a.m., according to the British Report, which placed a modest forty-two in the boat. There were only two seamen aboard, John Poingdestre (in charge) and Frederick Clench, both ABs. Once again the boat appears to have been launched underfilled for lack of women and children in its vicinity at the time. A large number of men from second and third classes tried to get aboard, but they were fended off by Lightoller and Poingdestre.

A Frenchman was said by Seaman Clench to have leapt into the boat as it was being lowered past B deck. When it reached the water, the two seamen were unable to unhook it from its falls until third-class passenger Margaret Devaney produced a pocket-knife, enabling Poingdestre to cut the ropes. This boat, the tenth to be launched if we follow the British inquiry order, eventually joined the Lowe flotilla mentioned above (and again below).

Events away from the boat deck aboard the enormous ship, lit up from stem to stern, against a background of loudly hissing steam, rockets bursting overhead, bandsmen playing familiar tunes and mysterious lights passing in the distance, have come down to us as a confusing kaleidoscope, a slow-motion bedlam. Since no witness was in a position to take an overview – Lightoller and Boxhall as the most active surviving officers came closest – this is hardly surprising.

The resulting impression is an eerily fragmented one, of boats being lowered half empty for lack of passengers while elsewhere crowds had to be held back; of people, both passengers and crew, returning to their accommodation for a while after coming on deck to find out what had happened; of groups of Catholic emigrants reciting the rosary together in one of the third-class dining saloons, passively awaiting whatever their God might have in store; of Chief Officer Wilde stalling a rush on the boats by 100 crewmen through sheer force of personality; of that same officer (a less likely tale on a 45,000-ton ship) ordering a rush from one side to the other by hundreds of people in order to correct a list; and of the terrible penultimate scene, well attested (for example, by Colonel Gracie), when a tide of humanity, including hundreds of women, surged up from steerage astern and made for the poop deck in the last minutes.

The cameos of the dying hours culled from witnesses at the inquiries and the more or less reliable newspaper articles, memoirs and books written immediately after the disaster or many years later became the legendary bricks from which the *Titanic* myth was built over time. Quite a few were false: a man who allegedly dressed himself as a woman in order to get into a boat was just wearing a shawl over his head in the cold. Captain Smith, who was issued with a pistol, like other officers, by Lightoller, did not shoot himself and almost certainly did not tell all and sundry to "be British". All this was merely to gild the lily of a legend already sufficiently awesome.

Yet there were attested scenes of both gallantry and eccentricity as well as cowardice and sheer terror. Many people not unreasonably fortified themselves with spirituous liquors; one male passenger was seen to swill a bottle of gin while a crewman disposed of a bottle of brandy. Chief Baker Joughin said he went below to drink half a tumbler of whisky from his private bottle and met one of the surgeons on a similar errand. An orderly queue formed at the purser's office on C deck to withdraw valuables, whereas Major Peuchen, perhaps more aware that you cannot take it with you, calmly left a box of securities with a face value of £60,000 in his cabin, preferring to put on his warmest clothing. The ship's safes were not crammed with treasure, as dubious recent trawls of the wreck seem to have proved. Colonel Gracie, meeting the squash-professional Frederick Wright amid all the pandemonium, wryly cancelled his Monday morning half-hour on the court, by then full of water.

Down in the torn guts of the ship, Leading Stoker Barrett, who had been so shocked to see a jet of water burst in upon him in foremost boiler-room number six, got into boiler-room number five to help some junior engineers with pumping, as he later told the journal *Marine Engineer*.[15] One of them was lying helpless with a broken leg when the fire-damaged bulkhead number five suddenly gave way under pressure and a great mass of water burst in, forcing him to climb to safety. All others in the boiler-room were drowned.

By 1.30 a.m., approximately one hour fifty minutes after

the collision, ten lifeboats had been lowered and ten remained aboard. At that moment Chief Officer Wilde ordered Fifth Officer Lowe to take command of boat fourteen, which had apparently filled up to capacity or as near as made no difference: the British Report places sixty-three aboard, consisting of fifty-three women, Lowe and seven crewmen. The alert reader will notice a discrepancy of two, which may have been accounted for by one stow-away and one male volunteer oarsman. On the other hand Lowe chased away two men who tried to board number fourteen when it was still level with the boat deck. As the lifeboat descended Lowe, according to his evidence on day thirteen of the inquiry in London, fired three shots from his pistol along the side of the ship to deter any further attempts to board at successive decks. The boat stalled on its falls or else its tackle jammed five feet above the water and Lowe had to free it to drop the rest of the way.

Lowe's reliability as a witness is not beyond doubt: in America he averred that he was assigned to boat number eleven but in Britain he said he had not known his boat-station, prompting a surprised interjection from the Commissioner. What is beyond dispute is the hard-nosed, wellnigh chilling resolution of the flamboyant twenty-eight-year-old (Q: Were you the Fifth Officer? A: I had that honour). He took his boat some 150 yards clear of the foundering ship to make sure it would not be caught in any suction as she went down. Then he busied himself collecting up boats four, ten, twelve and collapsible D, roping them together and interchanging passengers among his flotilla in order to empty his own boat. His intention was to go back for survivors in the water – after waiting awhile for the cries to die down and "for the people to thin out".[16] He was prepared, indeed determined, to fill up with survivors; but he was also resolved to ensure there were not enough left alive to swamp the boats. So he waited; and he certainly saved some more lives. Unfortunately his reshuffling activities followed by his additional rescue work made a major contribution to obscuring the numbers of people originally aboard each of the five boats involved.

At 1.35 a.m. the last regular lifeboats on the starboard side, numbers thirteen and fifteen, were lowered more or less simultaneously. Murdoch and Sixth Officer Moody appear to have been in charge of the loading of these boats, which were both filled to around capacity. There was a greater sense of urgency now; obviously the idea of lowering boats only partly filled and sending them to the gangways had at last been abandoned; so had the fear of boats buckling under a full load. The Captain and the Chief Officer were in all probability still on the boat deck but may well have been preventing rushes on the boats at this stage; they are referred to less and less frequently as the recorded evidence moves on from boat to boat.

Boat thirteen was placed under the command of Fred Barrett, who had safely extricated himself from the flooded forward boiler-rooms. He had four other crewmen to help him, and fifty-nine women and children, according to the British Report. But witnesses attested to the presence of four men, including the schoolmaster from second class, Lawrence Beesley, who was to write an account of the tragedy and was observing carefully. The boat was almost swamped before launch by a heavy outflow from the ship's pumps. Calls from the lifeboat halted the descent as the boat was pushed clear along the ship's side, presumably sternward, a deduction which is justified by the boat's next moment of crisis.

Despite the outflow, when the lifeboat made contact with the water below there was the previously encountered difficulty with detaching the falls and tackle because there was no swell. While thus umbilically attached to the dying mother-ship, the passengers in boat thirteen looked up and saw to their horror that number fifteen was threatening to descend on top of them. This suggests that the ship's bow-down angle had quite suddenly increased significantly, which would have had the effect of swinging the latter boat forward at the end of her seventy-five feet of falls; or else thirteen had been propelled aft (or quite possibly both). The screams and shouts from thirteen were heard on the boat deck a second time and fifteen's descent was stayed at the last moment, enabling thirteen's falls to be cut and the boat to be pulled clear.

Perhaps the most fortunate man on number thirteen was the first-class passenger Dr Washington Dodge, who had seen his wife and son Arthur safely into number seven, the first to go. Most of the rest of the boat were from third class, many of whom also saw the lights of the mystery ship pass slowly and tantalizingly out of view.

Boat fifteen was even more crowded than number eleven, with some seventy aboard, according to the British evidence, which once again is incomplete and as self-contradictory as that relating to any other boat. There were thirteen crewmen present, more than in any other lifeboat except number eight. There were ten stewards and three firemen but no seamen, whose numbers had been thinned out by distribution among earlier boats. According to George Cavell, the trimmer who had almost been overcome by coal shifted by the shock of collision, a fireman called Diamond was in charge of this boat.

His wits were possibly addled by his experience, for Bathroom Steward Samuel James Rule told the British inquiry a day later (day six) that the man in charge was Steward Jack Stewart (sic), and that most aboard were men, with only a handful of women and children among the seventy in the boat. By the time the boat was filling up, he explained, there were hardly any women to be found above-decks so Murdoch had allowed men to get in. The Commissioner and the Attorney-General expressed amazement at the paucity of women – four plus three children – out of seventy aboard, according to Rule.

The huge discrepancies between the evidence of Cavell and Rule led to the latter's recall on day nine. It turned out that Rule was the addlepate. He now recollected that nearly all the passengers in boat fifteen had been women. A lot of them were wearing odd clothes and had their backs to him, he explained feebly. Rule proved to be a positive lord of misrule when further examined by Clement Edwards, a trade-union lawyer.

Rule said passengers got in from A deck. How could that be, Edwards wanted to know, when it was an enclosed deck? After unhelpful interventions by the Commissioner, Laing for White Star, the Solicitor-General (Sir John Simon) for the Board of Trade, and Sir Robert Finlay, again for White Star, Rule said: "The windows are forward on A deck."

As if to prove that the revealed truth is inversely proportionate to the number of lawyers engaged on seeking it, Edwards now insisted that the model before the court must be of the *Olympic*. "My instructions are that on the *Titanic* the A deck is a closed deck right to the end, and is different to this model of the *Olympic*."

Finlay: "No, this model is made as it was on the *Titanic*."

Commissioner: "Then we may take this as an exact model of the *Titanic*?"

Finlay: "Yes."

Solicitor-General: "That is so" [three words being better than one when the utterer is on daily refresher fees].

Edwards: "With very great respect to Sir Robert Finlay, I trust that will be proved, because my instructions are very positive upon this point as to the character of the contents of A deck."

Commissioner: "At the proper time I suppose this model will be proved?"

Finlay: "Certainly." [If it ever was, it is not in the record.]

Edwards (to Rule): "You say A deck is an open deck?"

Rule: "Yes – aft."

Commissioner: "Did you hear his additional word,

'aft'? My recollection is that, although there are windows, they do not extend the whole length."

Just as clarity appeared to be at hand, the persistent Edwards struck again: "That is so, my Lord – on the *Olympic*."

Commissioner: "You come to a point where the windows stop, and, for all I know, this boat may have been at that point."

Edwards (doubtless doing his best to understand, to Rule): "You say that A deck is an open deck aft?"

Rule: "Yes."

Even now, Lord Mersey could not leave well alone: "Not aft – near aft," he insisted. So Edwards asked Rule to go to the model and point out where A deck was enclosed and where it was open, all in all another triumph for the Ismay screens. It was finally established (after this latest surprise intrusion of the *Olympic* in the proceedings) that A deck was open at the point where boat fifteen could be expected to pass it going down.

That the people in fifteen were the beneficiaries of at least a partial attempt to extract steerage passengers from the depths of the ship was attested by the next witness, third-class steward John Edward Hart. He said he had helped awaken women and children, rounded up twenty-five or so and led them through the labyrinthine passages up to the boat deck; he returned and performed a similar exercise, leading this party to number fifteen. Despite one or two claims to the contrary, Hart insisted there had been no physical barriers preventing third-class passengers from reaching the topmost decks (although some passengers at the American inquiry said they had to demand the removal of at least one; but the British inquiry was not interested in passengers, as we shall see).

Back on the port side, Lightoller and the obviously very active Moody, who had crossed over again, supervised the unexceptionable launching of boat sixteen, the aftermost conventional lifeboat on that side (though not the last to be launched). This boat was getting on for full, according to the British figures: fifty-six in all, counting three male crew and three stewardesses (including Violet Jessop, who was to go through all this again on the *Britannic*, by which time she was gracing a VAD nurse's uniform). Officially the only passengers were women and children, fifty in all, none first class; but a fireman was unaccountably found aboard afterwards. Mr A. Bailey, one of the ship's two masters-at-arms (responsible for discipline), was in charge, and his orders were to row towards the ship showing its lights ahead and to port of the wreck, still visible two hours after the collision. Stewardess Elizabeth Leather insisted on rowing to keep warm, one of fewer than two dozen women (stewardesses and a matron) among the crew, most of them married. The liners were one of the few contemporary workplaces where it was impossible to avoid employing women, if only because female passengers and children had to be properly looked after. How vulnerable, yet how strong-minded and self-reliant these pioneering women must have been, sur-rounded as they were by nearly 900 men and working far from home. The boat joined up with number six and they remained together until daybreak.

First Officer Murdoch was still hard at work. Having progressed forward from boat seven to five, three and one, he now had collapsible boat C attached to the davits vacated by the latter and looked round for forty-seven people to fill it. On Smith's orders, apparently, he put Quartermaster George Thomas Rowe in charge of the Engelhardt patent boat. This collapsible craft had a flat, clinker-built double bottom and low sides topped by canvas capable of being raised to a height of three feet and locked into position – an unnecessarily elaborate refinement just to reduce a lifeboat's profile by a yard. The boat was made of wood and buoyant (though not very, it seems) even without its sides raised.

The British inquiry places no fewer than seventy-one people on this boat, which would make it the most heavily laden of them all by a margin of one, even more than the larger, conventional boats eleven and fifteen, each credited with seventy. This is perhaps the most extreme illustration of the tendency among survivors to overestimate the numbers who survived with them. Those who tried to count heads in the boats in the dark, with people shivering in the bottom or else constantly moving, rowing, baling, standing up or sitting down, were bound to make mistakes; and inflationary psychological factors may also have been at work, such as guilt, wish-fulfilment and the like. Colonel Gracie's carefully researched contemporary account, which also clearly draws on the inquiry Reports, puts only thirty-nine people aboard.[17]

Rowe, a former Royal Navy man who had helped Boxhall with the distress signals and tried to contact the mystery ship by Morse lamp, told Senator Theodore E. Burton in a separate interview on day six of the American inquiry that he counted thirty-nine, including himself, a steward, a barber called Weikman, three firemen, thirty-one women and children and two male first-class passengers. He did not count, but did mention, four Chinese "stowaways", giving a total of forty-three. Murdoch was said by at least one other witness to have fired two shots to deter a crowd of men from taking over the Engelhardt.

Rowe told the British inquiry on day fifteen that Captain Smith had personally told him to take charge of collapsible C; it had been difficult to launch because there was a six-degree list to port at the time (1.40 a.m.) and the boat scraped and bumped against the ship's starboard side. The naval veteran aged thirty-two had noticed while on the bridge that the ship had put 260 miles behind her between noon and the collision, suggesting an average speed in excess of 21.75 knots (in fact over 22.25; the ship's clocks were next due to be put back again at midnight, twenty or so minutes after the collision). Rowe was sure that the ship on the port bow to which he steered was a sailing vessel.

He was less certain in London of the numbers aboard: six crew certainly, perhaps twenty-eight women and a few children, four Chinese for sure and just two gentlemen from first class: William Carter, another wealthy Philadelphian – and J. Bruce Ismay.

About Ismay there was no doubt; but considerable uncertainty remains about the circumstances under which he boarded. Ismay himself said there were no other passengers or crew about on the boat deck when the collapsible started its descent; so he stepped into it with Carter (who was not called to testify). Many years after the event the survivor John B. Thayer, seventeen at the time of the disaster, wrote in a private memoir that Ismay had pushed through a crowd of men to get on. Rather earlier than that, soon after landing in New York, Charlotte Cardeza damagingly told Associated Press that Ismay had not only got into the boat when it was virtually empty but picked her husband Thomas, a renowned amateur oarsman, to help row it (as we saw, the Cardezas, unlike Ismay, paid for their fractionally less opulent millionaire's suite, opposite his on the starboard side). Cardeza was not called either, and there appears to be no other evidence of his presence in the boat, although he and his wife undoubtedly survived. But the life which Ismay saved by stepping into collapsible C was ruined for ever by his decision. We shall return to his impossible dilemma when describing the inquiries. There may have been a rush at boat C by "foreigners" which provoked Murdoch into firing his pistol into the air to clear the lifeboat of these intruders (perhaps these were the men through whom Ismay pushed himself forward); but the women who got in instead were nearly all from the third class.[18]

Some mystery also attaches to boat two, launched under

Lightoller's tutelage at 1.45 a.m. This was the other emergency cutter, the foremost boat on the port side with a capacity of only forty, and the man given charge of it was Fourth Officer Boxhall. He was assisted by one seaman, one steward and one cook. The passengers included a single elderly man from steerage and twenty-one women from a total aboard of twenty-six. Lightoller may (or may not) have used his pistol to clear some "Mediterranean-looking" men out of the boat first (it should not be forgotten that many aboard could not speak English and were therefore precluded from acting in a "British" manner by their inability to understand such orders as "women and children only"). Whether or not such latter-day embellishments of the story are correct, it would appear from the attested loading of the boat that even at this late stage Lightoller was being strict about allowing women and children and preventing men (except the old one, who was accompanied by female relatives) from boarding. Murdoch on the other side had been much more flexible, presumably to save time. He had all but one of the starboard boats in the water by 1.40 a.m. whereas Lightoller matched that achievement on the port side only twenty-five minutes later.

Boxhall, according to his own evidence, rowed round the ship to the starboard side, which must have taken some time; perhaps he was looking for an open gangway door. After that he headed south-east, still with just twenty-six aboard. He did not see the ship go down because he was half a mile away (*sic*) at the time; from that distance, however, unless he had his back to the wreck, he would easily have been able to see the ship, even from sea-level, at least until her lights went out moments before she sank.[19] He had brought a box of green rockets aboard with him – or else he found them aboard – and fired several, which may help to explain why his was the first boat to be picked up by the *Carpathia*.

By the time number two reached the water, the sea had covered the forward well deck, presumably washing away the lumps of ice dumped there by the collision. The ship's wireless was telling the *Carpathia* that the engine-room was "full up to boilers".[20]

The last of the conventional lifeboats was launched at 1.55 a.m. – boat four, forward on the port side. Lightoller, having carried out Smith's and Wilde's orders to uncover the boats, had begun to attend to this boat seventy minutes earlier, just as Murdoch started work on the first to get away, number seven. Lightoller planned, having apparently overlooked the Ismay screen or else forgotten how it functioned, to load the boats from A deck. Number four, however, hung there empty as nobody had opened the windows in the screen;[21] number seven would thus appear to have cleared the forward end of the boat deck for the time being, at the beginning of the protracted drama of lowering the boats. Lightoller had number four hauled back up to the boat deck, thought better of it and sent it back down to A deck as he dispatched a crewman to find the special spanner-handle and open the windows. First-class women and appendages formed a decorous little queue to board number four, but the frantically busy Second Officer did not return to them for more than an hour. They included Mrs Astor, Mrs Carter, Mrs Ryerson, Mrs Thayer and Mrs Widener, with various children and maids.

When Lightoller finally came back, all the other boats and one out of four collapsibles had been sent off. The davits which had just launched number two would soon be used to lower collapsible D at the forward, port end of the boat deck. Collapsibles A and B were still lashed to the roof of the officers' house. Down came boat four to A deck, where a cable was used to pull it close enough to the listing ship's side for passengers to be able to step into it. Lightoller stood with one foot on deck and the other in the boat; Colonel John Jacob Astor helped him hand the women and children, some thirty-six of them apparently, into the boat – including the very young Madeleine Astor, expecting their child. Astor asked Lightoller if he might join her as the boat was not two-thirds full, but the officer was as firm as ever: women and children only. The multimillionaire therefore stoically bade farewell to his young bride and stepped back like a gentleman. The ship was so far gone that the boat had only to descend twenty-five feet or even less to reach the water. Astor now remembered his dog, Kitty, an Airedale, cooped up on F deck aft, and went down to set her free.[22] His widow's last view from the lifeboat of the luxurious ship on which they had planned to come home together was reportedly of their dog running about on the sloping deck. Her eyesight must have been truly remarkable.

Madeleine Astor's boat had only one crew member in it when it was at last launched. Three others, including Quartermaster W. J. Perkis, clambered hand over hand down the falls and into the boat. Once the boat was detached from the ship a male stowaway revealed himself. Perkis took command and saw to it that at least one boat remained close enough to the liner to save people in the water after she went down. Perkis and his colleagues plucked seven (possibly eight) men, all from the crew, into the boat; two of them died from exposure, leaving some forty-six in all when number four joined numbers fourteen, twelve, ten and D under Lowe, who began to rearrange the survivors as we saw above. Boat four leaked badly, making constant baling necessary; even so, some remembered sitting in water up to their shins as they rowed. Each boat had a plug in its bottom for drainage; some plugs were found with difficulty, if at all. Mrs Marian Thayer interestingly said she saw, from number four, "an overturned boat shortly after reaching the water".

The last lifeboat to be launched from the *Titanic* was collapsible boat D, forward on the port side, lowered by the davits which had handled number two twenty minutes earlier.[23] It was now 2.05 a.m. and the forecastle deck was going under; the sea was about level with B deck amidships. Chief Officer Wilde and Lightoller took charge of loading; Lightoller drew his pistol and got crewmen to link arms and form an arc round the boat to prevent a rush by the considerable numbers of men on the boat deck. They included the second-class passenger "Michel Hoffmann" who handed his two little sons, Michel and Edmond, through the human barrier. Hoffmann's real surname was Navratil, and he had boarded with the boys at Southampton in an early example of what today's tabloid newspapers would call a "tug-of-love" drama: he had snatched them from their mother. The boys survived but Navratil died in the icy Atlantic.[24] It took time to muster less than a full load of women and children now, forty in all according to the British Report, and just as the boat began to go down the deck was once more clear.

There were three crewmen, led by Quartermaster Arthur John Bright, two male passengers, a Swede and an Englishman who jumped from A deck as the boat came past, and later a male stowaway from steerage was found to be aboard. This should have given one short of a full tally for the boat (forty-seven). When D joined his *ad hoc* flotilla, Lowe removed all three crewmen and the collapsible was left without a helmsman; but Lowe's number fourteen took it in tow as the *Carpathia* hove in sight.

Before that blessed moment, Lowe and four volunteers had rowed back to where the ship had been, looking for people in the water – the only real attempt, however belated, to make up the shortfall in the lifeboats. The crew found three still alive among the corpses held up by their bulky life-jackets. One of them, William F. Hoyt, very big and very ill, died in the bottom of the boat, despite the attentions of the crew. After that, Lowe stepped the boat's mast and hoisted her sail to take advantage of the breeze which had come up.

*

Any confusion there may have been about the lifeboats actually launched is handsomely surpassed by the tangled evidence on the fate of the two collapsibles, A and B, tied to the roof of the officers' quarters above the boat deck. It is certain that there was no time to get either to a set of davits for launching and therefore that both floated off the ship as she slipped under the water. Boat B went into the water upside-down. Lightoller said he had tried to release both in turn, gave up on A (which he thought had gone down with the ship) and returned to B. Some people, all men, were on it when it floated off the dying ship and overturned. Wilde and Murdoch were last seen trying to free the boat; neither got aboard.[25]

Wireless Operator Harold Bride described how he was washed overboard and somehow ended up underneath collapsible B, trapped in an air-pocket for up to three-quarters of an hour. He swam out from under it and away and was in the water for a similar interlude (inconceivable in water at twenty-eight degrees; but time draws out enormously in such frightful conditions) before being picked up by boat number twelve. Bride's ankles were badly injured and his feet frostbitten in his struggle to survive. His superior, Phillips, made it to boat B but died of exposure in the night.

Two of the thirty or so men who managed to get onto the inverted collapsible B, both from the ship's crew, said later that they had seen Captain Smith swim across to it and actually lay a hand on it before saying, "I will follow the ship" and returning to the bridge, now about to be overwhelmed.

Lightoller was dragged under by the sinking ship but a burst of air through a grating blew him to the surface again, whereupon he scrambled aboard B. Colonel Gracie, already shocked by meeting his "tide of humanity", had a similar experience before surfacing and swimming to B. Those who joined him and Lightoller stood upright in two rows back to back in a macabre joint balancing act, with people falling overboard out of the precarious line, dying of exhaustion and exposure during the two hours they stood on their swamped support; one or two others came out of the water to replace them.[26] Joughin the Chief Baker, fortified by whisky, thought he spent an incredible two hours in the water until he reached B, whereupon he was at first pushed away before scrambling aboard. After dawn broke they were sighted by Lowe's flotilla and taken aboard lifeboat twelve, prostrate with exhaustion and in many cases suffering from frostbite.

All of which leaves us with collapsible boat A. Some crewmen were well advanced with sliding this boat down planks from the roof of the officers' house to the boat deck when the rising water relieved them of the burden. By this time Lightoller must have crossed the deck to work on B, because he saw none of this. The Engelhardt floated away with its canvas screen still down, but at least it was right side up. The British Report deduced that the last two collapsibles jointly saved some fifty lives.

Insofar as A had a commander it was first-class steward Edward Brown, who was helping to free it when he and the boat were washed overboard.[27] Brown was a witness of rare clarity at the British inquiry and what he had to say rings true. As he worked to shift the boat he looked aft and he saw the bridge begin to go under. He insisted that he heard the band playing even at this very last stage. Just before that, Captain Smith had passed on his way to the bridge, saying: "Well boys, do your best for the women and children, and look out for yourselves." He had already called at the wireless office to release Phillips and Bride from their duties; but Phillips carried on until 2.17 a.m., within minutes of the end. Bride meanwhile, according to his evidence, attacked, possibly fatally, a crewman who was trying to steal a life-jacket from the wireless room.

Although Steward Brown had earlier been on the starboard side of the boat deck helping to load lifeboats five (to which he had originally been assigned), three, one and

C, he apparently saw no ship in the vicinity (although if moving rather than stationary she might just have passed out of sight by 2 a.m. – or else the *Titanic* might have swung round so that a motionless vessel would finally have lain to port of the wreck).

But Brown did notice Ismay helping to load collapsible C and getting into it himself. The ship was still listing to port in its last throes. When Brown came back to the surface, the water round him was full of people who had been washed off the boat deck and collapsible A was low in the water with several people aboard. Its sides were never raised; the procedure must have been cumbersome, especially in the sea. Brown also said people fought each other in the water: some of his clothes were torn off him in what was presumably a scramble to get aboard the *Titanic*'s last boat. His hands swelled up in the wet and cold and his feet burst out of his boots. Nonetheless he took an oar. Those aboard came from all classes and four other crewmen may have reached it, for a possible final total of sixteen in the boat, including just one woman, Rosa Abbott from third class. Some probably died of exposure and slid or were pushed overboard. When Lowe appeared in number fourteen, there was more than a foot of water in the bottom of boat A. He took all the living still aboard off her, perhaps eleven, perhaps fourteen, and left a minimum of three dead men in the abandoned collapsible.

Having seen all the boats off the sinking *Titanic*, we should pay one more visit aboard for a few final scenes as recollected by individual survivors.

Benjamin Guggenheim and his valet, Victor Giglio, left the boats to the women and children and went below, to reappear a few minutes later in full evening dress. "We've dressed up in our best and are prepared to go down like gentlemen," said Guggenheim (quoted by survivors to *The New York Times*).

At two o'clock in the morning, Major Archie Butt and three other gentlemen – Arthur Ryerson, Francis Millet and Clarence Moore – played a last hand of cards in the first-class smoking room before going up to the boat deck.

At another table in the same room sat Thomas Andrews, managing director of Harland and Wolff. In front of him was a life-jacket. He was staring vacantly at the wall, patently exhausted or in shock, or both.

On the after end of the boat deck as the waters rose, Father Thomas Byles, a Roman Catholic, heard confessions.

The band played on to the end on the same deck, its last rendition a matter of dispute, but a hymn: "Autumn", or more likely (because more appropriate as a traditional funeral hymn), "Nearer, my God, to Thee".

The entire band of eight musicians went down with the ship. So did the entire senior engineering staff of thirty-two officers and men, who had shut down the ship and yet managed to keep the lights blazing until the very last moments. So did the entire guarantee party of Andrews and his eight helpers. So did all five postal clerks. So did the trio of senior officers from the *Olympic* who ran the ship to her doom – Smith, Wilde and Murdoch. So did whole families of many nations, and groups of crewmen from the same Southampton streets, among the one and a half thousand people whose deaths went into the fabric of the legend of the *Titanic*.

Only as she went into her final agony, with shipboard time approaching 2.20 a.m., did the lights go out. Now the only source of illumination was the exceptionally bright starlight; but the sudden extinction of the ship's own brilliant light must have made it difficult if not impossible for the survivors, who would have experienced temporary night-blindness as a result, to be absolutely sure of what they saw of this terrible maritime *Götterdämmerung*. But the stern seems to have risen almost perpendicularly into the air before it vanished; when the wreck was located in 1985, the stern section was duly found to have broken off. Many hundreds of people were clinging to the rails of the poop as it began to swing up into the air. Others were caught at the after end of the boat deck, on the lower side of the unbridgeable gulf represented by the after well deck, and were washed overboard a few moments earlier.

All witnesses agreed, even though their descriptions of it varied wildly, that the ship emitted a terrifying and protracted death-rattle. There was a series of "explosions" or loud crashes as boilers and other massive items of equipment broke loose and smashed through the buckling steel bulkheads. It is possible that the few boilers which had been kept going to power the generators exploded on contact with the cold water. Many witnesses were clearly haunted by the noise. Those who survive a shipwreck often remember the extraordinary sound of a ship's death-agony more vividly than they recollect what it looked like.

Of the 711 survivors counted by the British Report[28] 203 came from first, 118 from second and 178 from third class plus 212 from the crew. In round figures, thirty-three per cent of males and ninety-seven per cent of females in first class lived; in second class, eight and eighty-six per cent respectively; in third, sixteen and forty-six. The British Report states that all children in first and second classes survived, whereas Lorraine Allison from first was lost with her nanny, Alice Cleaver; in third, twenty-seven per cent of boys and forty-five per cent of girls were rescued. Twenty-four per cent of the crew also survived, including sixty-five per cent of the deck department, twenty-two of the engine department but only twenty per cent of the stewards. The overall survival rate was 32.30 per cent; over two-thirds of those aboard on departure from Queenstown therefore died in what was then the greatest disaster ever to have occurred in peacetime at sea and in the entire history of transport. It was not until sixty-eight years had passed that this melancholy record was surpassed, when a passenger ferry sank in the Philippines with the loss of 4,375 lives in April 1980, after colliding with a tanker.

Before turning to the rescue, we can reasonably make one observation on the basis of the foregoing boat-by-boat narrative: there was no planning involved in the evacuation. There was no advance contingency plan, at least for the eventuality which struck the ship, and neither Captain Smith nor his officers came up with an improvised strategy for evacuating the vessel. The main reason for the absence of the former was undoubtedly the general atmosphere of over-confidence engendered by buoyant technological leaps in a still innocent age. The main reason for the latter deficiency was surely the realization that, with no ship on hand to help them after all before the "unsinkable" sank, and with boats for only half those aboard, a systematic evacuation was simply unthinkable. No matter how it was organized, it would have meant condemning fifty per cent of passengers and crew to death because the total aboard could not be saved by twenty lifeboats capable of taking barely half their number. There might have been an unimaginably dreadful Darwinian struggle over the limited number of places, which no amount of officers with pistols could have controlled, especially after boats and passengers were in the water.

Clearly the senior officers tacitly decided to let the principle of women and children only (or at least first) dominate their efforts. But the principle of first come, first served, was not far behind in governing the filling of the lifeboats, if only to a limited and erratic degree. The officers were unforgivably and tragically unaware that the boats were built to be lowered fully laden. The launching of the boats was not much better than an unco-ordinated shambles, regardless of the often heroic efforts of individual officers, sailors and passengers. For this too Smith, as master, must bear the principal blame, having failed to see to it that the ship was systematically searched for enough women and children to fill the boats.

The difference between the level of inefficiency on view on the night of 14–15 April 1912 and the level of efficiency that might have been achieved had the officers been less ignorant and the crew more trained, is the difference between the one-third who were saved and the half who might have been; or indeed the 100 per cent that could have survived had the *Titanic* lived up to her unofficial specification as her own "unsinkable" lifeboat – or had the *Californian* or other ships got to her in time. We can now look at the ships which did come; and some of those which did not.

6

OF MYSTERIES AND SHIPS

Captain Arthur Henry Rostron of the *Carpathia* became the hero of the *Titanic* tragedy by default, his role contrasting so sharply with the parts played by the reckless Captain Smith and the feckless Captain Lord of the *Californian*. The United States Congress, legislature of a nation of hero-worshippers, had a special gold medal struck for Rostron, the man who brought deliverance to the survivors of the *Titanic*. The quality that earned him his accolades on both sides of the Atlantic was not so much courage as sheer, unadulterated competence: here was a true master mariner who knew exactly what to do in an emergency at sea, and who acted decisively and with awesome efficiency when called upon. One of the sadder ironies of the whole story is that Captain Stanley Lord, chief scapegoat alongside Ismay, might so easily have sailed away with Rostron's laurels at no serious risk to his ship or himself, as we shall see in this chapter.

But it was the *Carpathia* which first hove into sight at dawn on Monday 15 April 1912, bringing boundless relief and joy to the hundreds of numb and shivering survivors in the lifeboats. She was a Cunard liner of 13,600 tons, built on the Tyne in 1902–3 for the busy transatlantic emigrant traffic. She was originally designed to carry 200 second-class and 1,500 steerage passengers, mostly in dormitories. In 1905 an internal upgrading and redesign of this sound if rather basic liner meant she could now offer 100 first-class berths as well as 200 second- and 750 third-class (in a third of the net space available on the

"Olympics", which could carry up to 2,435 passengers, only 1,026 of them in steerage). The crew numbered about 325. After two years on the Anglo-American, North Atlantic route (Liverpool to Boston or New York), the *Carpathia* was diverted to the Mediterranean–New York migrant run. The *Carpathia* was no prestige ship but rather a utilitarian vessel of sturdy, not ungraceful construction with a design speed of just 14.5 knots. She was 540 feet long and sixty-five broad, with a single tall funnel painted in the Cunard colours: red, with collar and thin rings picked out in black. Her superstructure was the usual white and her hull black.

Her master was born at Bolton, Lancashire, in 1869 and learned his trade in sail before joining Cunard in 1895. He stayed with the company, apart from a brief wartime attachment to the Royal Naval Reserve, until he retired in 1931. A captain since 1907, Rostron had assumed his sixth command in five years on 18 January 1912. He had some 740 passengers aboard, 125 in first, sixty-five in second and 550 in third class, when he left Cunard's New York pier, number fifty-four on the western side of Manhattan Island, on 11 April, bound for Gibraltar and points east (luckily for the *Titanic* survivors, emigrant ships tended to be less busy eastbound than westbound).

Rostron enjoyed the services of only one Marconi operator, Harold Thomas Cottam, even younger than his *Titanic* colleagues at a mere twenty-one. He was not expected to be on duty round the clock but rather during the day; in case of real need, however, he was to be available at any time. His wireless shack, which also contained his bunk, was on top of the superstructure aft of the funnel, on the roof of the second-class smoking room. He had a busy Sunday, starting work at 7 a.m. and unable to turn in until about midnight; even then he still had his earphones in place because he had not received an acknowledgement of a message to the liner *Parisian*. Idly scanning the airwaves, he tuned in to Cape Cod, Massachusetts, and overheard transmissions to the *Titanic*.

He took it into his head to check with the ship to find out if she was receiving them. Addressing MGY, the *Titanic* call sign, he asked, in the chatty style favoured by Morse and teleprinter operators of old, "I say, OM (old man), do you know there is a batch of messages coming through for you from MCC [Cape Cod] ..."

Cottam's shocked reaction can be imagined as MGY cut across his transmission: "Come at once. We have struck an iceberg. It's CQD [emergency], OM. Position 41° 46' N, 50° 14' W." Stunned, Cottam could only ask superfluous questions: "Shall I tell my captain? Do you require assistance?" The reply to MPA (the *Carpathia*'s call sign) was immediate: "Yes. Come quick." The time was 12.25 a.m. on the *Titanic*, 12.35 on the *Carpathia*. Half-undressed, Cottam dashed forward to the bridge and alerted First Officer H. V. Dean, on watch. Together the two men clattered below to the Captain's stateroom and burst in on him without knocking. Rostron's annoyance turned into horror as he absorbed the news on the way up to the chart room. There he worked out that his ship was fifty-eight miles south-east of the reported position and began to issue a stream of incisive and systematic orders. He set a course of north 52° west or 308°.[1]

The ship's eighteen lifeboats were swung out ready for lowering. The entire crew, those off watch as well as on, were to be served with hot drinks and alerted to prepare for the reception of survivors. Chief Engineer Johnson was ordered to make steam as he had never made it before – piling on coal for maximum pressure in all boilers and shutting down as many ancillary, steam-powered facilities as possible, including radiators, so that every ounce of energy could be devoted to speed. The result was a sustained burst of 17.5 knots, an amazing three more than the ship's reciprocating engines were designed to deliver. Passengers awakened by the vibration were asked to stay out of the way in their cabins or bunks. The *Carpathia* shuddered from stem to stern as every spare corner of space was cleared for survivors, blankets were collected, hot drinks and soup prepared, the three doctors aboard put on stand-by – and extra lookouts posted. Two men took station in the "eyes" of the ship right forward at the bow in addition to the one in the crow's nest, and a volunteer extra officer stayed on the bridge with no other task but to look for ice and any sign of the wreck. Interestingly, Rostron said later that the distress message was the first indication he had received of the presence of ice on his route, which was effectively the reverse of the *Titanic*'s, except that the eastbound agreed lane or Homeward Southern Track lay to the south of the westbound or Outward. Cottam must either have missed the many warning messages or failed to ensure that his captain was informed of them.

Rostron's attention to the tiniest details as he raced to the rescue was perhaps the most impressive aspect of his intervention in the saga. He seems to have thought of absolutely everything. All potential obstructions on deck and elsewhere that might hurt people were cleared; gangway doors in the ship's sides were opened and hooked back, bosun's chairs improvised to facilitate boarding, sacks attached to ropes for hoisting children aboard, nets, ropes, ladders and lights slung . . . Even barrels of machine-oil were kept ready, to calm any rough water for the benefit of lifeboats.[2]

The last direct message from the *Titanic* to the *Carpathia* was heard by Cottam at 1.55 a.m. (*Carpathia*'s time, ten minutes ahead of the *Titanic*'s): "Engine-room full up to boilers." (On reflection, this is a curious text, since the boilers and the engines were all at the same level on the tank top, housed in huge compartments extending upwards to the underside of G deck, the engines of course being aft of the boilers; but the import was clear enough, even if Jack Phillips's idea of a steamship's propulsion system was a trifle hazy.)

SS *Carpathia* thundered on, emitting a vast plume of black smoke, skirting the ice when necessary and firing rockets over her bows as she came, to signal that rescue was at hand. Curiously, Boxhall's flares fired from boat number two were sighted aboard the *Carpathia* at 2.40 a.m. ship's time, whereas the ship's rockets (much higher in the sky, even if the lifeboats were much lower in the water) were first seen at 3.30 a.m. *Titanic* time, or one hour later. At twenty minutes before dawn, or 4 a.m. *Carpathia*'s time, not quite three and a half hours after Cottam picked up his first distress call, *Carpathia*, having navigated towards the broadcast position worked out by Boxhall, sighted the green light carried by that officer's boat. The position logged for the discovery of the lifeboats was 41° 40' north, 50° west, between seven and eight miles south-east of the Boxhall position. His boat was secured alongside ten minutes later and the survivors of the *Titanic* began to climb or be lifted aboard.

Dawn broke over an unforgettable scene. Some two dozen large icebergs (over 200 feet showing) and scores of lesser bergs were in sight, dwarfing the straggle of lifeboats scattered over a four- to five-mile area. Rostron remembered it vividly later:

> Except for the boats beside the ship and the icebergs, the sea was strangely empty. Hardly a bit of wreckage floated – just a deckchair or two, a few lifebelts, a good deal of cork; no more flotsam than one can often see on a seashore drifted in by the tide. The ship had plunged at the last, taking everything with her. I saw only one body in the water; the intense cold made it hopeless for anyone to live long in it.[3]

Between the sinking of the *Titanic* and the arrival of the *Carpathia*, collapsible boat A, which had floated off, was cleared of some thirteen survivors by boats D and fourteen and abandoned with three dead men aboard; A was not sighted by the rescuers.

Collapsible B, which went into the water upside-down, was eventually abandoned and those three dozen or so who had been standing on it transferred to boat twelve, which had been summoned by Lightoller's whistle. B was sighted, still overturned but not noticeably surrounded by wreckage, from the *Carpathia*. The Second Officer duly took command of number twelve, which had also relieved D of a few survivors, at about 6.30 a.m. and this boat was the last to transfer her now overfull load of more than seventy people to the *Carpathia*. Lightoller, the senior surviving officer, was the last to come aboard the rescue ship, at about 8.30 a.m.

Collapsible C, with Ismay aboard, had met the *Carpathia* at about 6.15 a.m., been cleared and abandoned.

Collapsible D arrived attached to Lowe's boat fourteen at about 7 a.m.; both were left in the water after their passengers were brought aboard. Boats four (still leaking badly) and fifteen were similarly abandoned.

The other thirteen boats were unloaded as they made fast to the *Carpathia*, which moved slowly and with extreme care from boat to boat, between 4.10 and 8 a.m. Boarding from the first lifeboat to be secured, number two, Boxhall went straight to the bridge to report the details of the disaster to Captain Rostron. The thirteen salvaged boats (numbers one to three, five to thirteen and number sixteen) were finally hoisted aboard the *Carpathia*; seven were placed under davits and six on chocks on the forecastle deck, for delivery to White Star in New York.

For the sake of completeness we may anticipate here that collapsible B was found, damaged on one side and surrounded by wreckage, by the recovery ship *Mackay-Bennett* on 22 April, miles away from Boxhall's position. It was not picked up. Collapsible A was sighted and picked up by the White Star liner *Oceanic* only on 13 May; the three corpses still aboard were buried at sea after a funeral service and the boat was eventually added to the thirteen already delivered to New York by Rostron.[4]

Rostron's evidence to the British inquiry about what boats he picked up is clear: he said he found thirteen lifeboats, two emergency boats and two collapsibles, as well as two (*sic*) overturned boats (a lifeboat and a collapsible). One collapsible had not got off, he said, obviously misinformed by Lightoller, who had been unaware that collapsible A had floated clear and been used for a time.

Meanwhile, aboard the *Carpathia*, the passengers had soon become aware of the tragic drama their ship was about to join. People began to come up on deck as the liner reached the boats; by the time significant numbers of survivors were coming on board, a large and silent crowd lined the rails. Soon the regular passengers were comforting the new ones, giving them spare clothes and helping the old, the young, the sick and injured, those numbed with shock and cold. J. Bruce Ismay was led to the cabin of Dr Frank McGee, the ship's surgeon, and did not emerge until the ship reached New York.

Rostron ordered a tally of the survivors and came up with a total of 705, made up of 201 first-class, 118 second- and 179 third-class passengers, and 207 crew. The British inquiry concluded that he had somehow managed to miss six from first class and made the total 711; but it seems churlish to suggest that a man of Rostron's splendid efficiency could not count. In later references to the rescue he adhered firmly and unshakably to 705, the figure now generally accepted.

As his ship passed over the putative spot where the *Titanic* went down, Father Roger Anderson, an American Episcopalian monk among the *Carpathia*'s passengers, conducted a service of commemoration for the lost and thanksgiving for the saved, in the packed first-class dining saloon. After the Cunarder had left the icefield and was on her way to New York, Anderson led a funeral service for the three *Titanic* crewmen who had died after the rescue and the one male, third-class passenger who had been brought aboard dead. The weighted bodies of the last fatalities from the *Titanic* slipped over the side.

Marconi operator Harold Cottam's exhaustion was soon verging on the terminal; his rescued colleague Harold Bride finally responded positively to Rostron's and Cottam's appeals for his help, despite his injured and frostbitten feet. He was carried up to the wireless shack and was still there when the ship reached New York. Captain Rostron however kept tight personal control of outgoing traffic, checking every message transmitted. The eastbound *Olympic*, racing to the Boxhall position from a hopeless 500 miles to the west, helped by relaying messages, including laboriously assembled lists of survivors, to New York via coastal wireless stations. USS *Chester*, a light cruiser sent to sea for the purpose by President Taft, desperate for news of his friend and aide Archie Butt, was ordered to act as a relay for *Carpathia*'s traffic. Bride complained of the slowness of the naval telegraphists.

It was Rostron too who suggested to a traumatized Ismay soon after he came aboard that he ought to notify his New York office of the disaster. Ismay wrote out a message to Philip A. S. Franklin, American vice-president of IMM: "Deeply regret advise you *Titanic* sank this morning after collision with iceberg, resulting in serious loss of life. Full particulars later." Ismay also sent a total of three messages asking that White Star's ship *Cedric*, due to leave New York on Thursday 18 April, be detained to take home the surviving crew. Their pay was unceremoniously, not to say parsimoniously, stopped under IMM/White Star conditions of service the moment the *Titanic* went under! All attempts to get information from the *Carpathia* were ignored, even when they came from the White House or were signed by Cunard's New York agent, C. P. Sumner: Rostron gave absolute priority to the survivors and their messages.

As the *Carpathia* sailed westward to New York (where we shall pick up her story again), carrying one of the two

Titanic scapegoats in a state of shock, she left the other to conduct a second careful search of the disaster area: Captain Lord of the *Californian*.

His ship hove in sight at about 8 a.m. just as the last boatloads were being taken aboard the *Carpathia*. Rostron handed over to Lord the task of checking the area one more time, on the reasonable ground that he wanted to take the survivors to New York as soon as possible. Lord's systematic search, made in increasing circles, yielded remarkably little wreckage and no bodies. On returning close to his starting point Lord counted "about" six abandoned boats in the water, of which three were regular lifeboats, two were collapsibles and one boat (not two) was upside-down. He recollected that the capsized boat he saw was a proper lifeboat, not a collapsible. Rostron, it will be remembered, saw an overturned regular lifeboat as well as a collapsible in similar condition; and Mrs Thayer also swore to having seen an overturned lifeboat shortly after her own number four finally took to the water.

Lord's tally of abandoned boats ties in numerically with the separated A and the salvaged thirteen to give a correct total of twenty; but one of the many minor mysteries of the disaster is the fact that Lord recalled seeing four regular lifeboats, three upright and one capsized. The *Titanic* carried only fourteen regular boats – of which Rostron had indisputably recovered eleven (as well as the two smaller emergency boats). The *Californian* took nothing aboard and Lord gave up looking at 11.20 a.m. To understand how different his role could have been, we have to go back once more to events preceding the rescue.

The *Californian*, a cargo vessel of 6,223 tons, was built for the Leyland Line of Liverpool (and the cotton trade) in Dundee, Scotland, in 1901–2 and measured 447 by fifty-four feet. She had a crew of about fifty-five and space for up to forty-seven passengers, with well-appointed dining and smoking saloons. There were no passengers aboard on this voyage. On a ship of this type one could cross the Atlantic at less speed, and for less money, than on a liner – but not without comforts. The ship's design speed was about 13 knots and she carried one tall funnel in Leyland's livery: pink with a black collar.

Stanley Lord, her fourth captain, was born in 1877, in Bolton like Rostron, and also learned his trade under sail, joining the West India and Pacific steamer line in 1897. The line was taken over in 1900 by Leyland, which was itself acquired by IMM shortly afterwards. Lord was given his first command, the *Antillian*, in 1906; the *Californian* was his fourth in six years. She left Liverpool carrying a mixed cargo on 5 April 1912, bound for Boston. Having received several ice alerts by the 13th, Lord was not surprised to see icebergs to the south at dusk on Sunday, 14 April. At 6.30 p.m. therefore he ordered a warning to be sent to the *Antillian*, which transmission was, as we noted, overheard aboard the *Titanic*. Lord doubled the lookout ninety minutes later (his time being twelve minutes ahead of the *Titanic*'s) and was still on the bridge when ice was sighted dead ahead.

At 10.21 p.m. Lord ordered the engines to "Full Astern" and "Stop" and had the helm swung hard a-port, bringing her round to a north-easterly heading before she stopped. In the cold, calm, clear weather he could make out no icebergs as such; but there was loose ice all around the ship and he correctly deduced he was inside the edge of a large icefield. So he decided to heave-to for the night at a position which Lord himself worked out by dead reckoning to be 42° 5' north, 50° 7' west; Lord was the only witness to his ship's stated position. Pressure was maintained in the boilers to be ready for any eventuality. If his and Boxhall's calculations were correct, his ship was nineteen to twenty miles north-north-east (by north) of the *Titanic* when she struck.

About one hour before that event, Lord saw a light approaching from the south-east, presumably of an oncoming vessel. At 11.30 p.m. *Californian* time, or at least twenty minutes before the collision occurred, Lord saw what he believed was the same ship's green or starboard navigation light (indicating a westbound ship), as well as a masthead light and some deck lighting, some five miles to the south (maximum visibility from his ship's bridge, forty-nine feet above the sea, was to a horizon eight miles away; a tall or high object would be visible at a greater distance, proportionate to its height). Third Officer Charles Groves tried to contact her by signal-lamp but got no reaction.[5]

Just after midnight Second Officer Herbert Stone saw a ship about five miles to the south and a little to the west, showing him one masthead light and her red, port-side light, which meant she was heading (either travelling or pointing) roughly east. The *Californian* meanwhile was swinging slowly clockwise from east-north-east to west-north-west, which meant her bow (and her heading) swung through an arc of at least 225 degrees. Relative to the ship as a whole, however, the points of the compass remained in the same place, although one would have to cross over to the other side of the *Californian*'s bridge after the swing to continue looking southward, the general direction from which all the allegedly observed phenomena reached the eyes of those aboard. This may seem obvious even to landlubbers, but there was a great deal of confusion at the British inquiry among such nautical terms as direction and bearing (position relative to that of the observing ship), course and heading (which way a ship is pointing, whether stationary or moving) – to say nothing of times.

There can thus be no questioning of the conclusion that it was to her south that various witnesses aboard saw either two ships, one heading west and one east, or conceivably one ship which had reversed course or heading; either way, nobody aboard could have seen the *Titanic* if both Lord's and Boxhall's reported positions were anywhere near correct. Lord, first advised of a shipwreck (but no details) at 5.15 a.m., was told its name and position within half an hour and took nearly two hours to reach the Boxhall position (which Lord found without difficulty). He had the wit to hoist his extra lookout, with binoculars, in a coal-basket all the way up the foremast, well above the crow's nest. The ship extricated herself cautiously, sailing westward to clear the ice, turning south and finally going full speed down the western flank of the field for an hour.

She found the Canadian Pacific liner *Mount Temple* with her single yellow funnel and four masts (but no sign of anything else in the water) on Boxhall's spot at about 7.30 a.m. Shortly after that the *Californian* passed another ship, with a Leyland pink funnel and two masts, sailing north: the *Almerian*, which had no wireless. Only then did Lord sight the *Carpathia*, a little to the south-east on the other side of the icefield. He made contact by wireless and sailed through the ice to meet her at 8.30 a.m., when the two captains conversed by semaphore.

But why did Captain Lord arrive so late from under twenty miles away, thus doomed to condemnation (without trial) as the other scapegoat in the *Titanic* legend? The short answer is a long chain of unfortunate events, errors, omissions, misunderstandings, distortions and perhaps outright lies. As master, Lord was ultimately responsible for everything that happened or did not happen aboard his ship. But he was ill served, as well as gratuitously traduced by the American and British authorities and media.

Under no pressure to keep to a first-class liner's tight schedule, he positively set an example to his less cautious peers by heaving-to until daylight (as the *Mount Temple* also did when she met ice on her way to the Boxhall spot) rather than ploughing on through the dark and an icefield of an extent unknown to him. Like Rostron, Lord had only one Marconi operator, a twenty-year-old by the name of Cyril Evans, who had just six months' experience. Lord mentioned the passing ship to Evans as the latter was thinking of turning in and asked him with what other ships he had been in contact. "Only the *Titanic*," said

Evans. Lord ordered him to tell her that the *Californian* was stopped and surrounded by ice; Evans started to do so but, as described earlier, was abruptly if not rudely cut off by the *Titanic*, preoccupied with sending commercial messages to Cape Race. So Evans, who had been on duty since 7 a.m., quite justifiably went to bed.[6] His ship now became electronically deaf as well as motionless, at pretty well the precise moment when the *Titanic* sideswiped her iceberg. If he had not turned in – if he had, like Cottam, had unfinished business and kept his earphones on for another forty-five minutes, if round-the-clock wireless watches had already been the rule rather than the exception, if he had remembered to leave the emergency-call alarm bell switched on ... the *Californian* could have reached the *Titanic* before she sank and saved many lives – and the reputation of Stanley Lord. As Winston Churchill was to write of another maritime fiasco in 1914, "the terrible 'Ifs' accumulate".[7]

But at the same moment as Evans pulled the plug the officer of the watch, Groves, thought he saw the deck lights of the ship in the distance go out (which might mean no more than that she had turned so as to be end-on to the *Californian*).

Fireman Ernest Gill, aged twenty-nine, who helped to look after the ship's auxiliary ("donkey") engine, came off watch and emerged on deck "at 11.56 p.m.". He purportedly saw the broadside light of a "very large steamer about ten miles away" to starboard travelling fast (although he was well below the bridge, whence surface visibility was only eight miles). He returned to the main deck about half an hour later, he said, and ten minutes after that, or about 12.40 a.m., saw what appeared to be two rockets going up seven or eight minutes apart, again ten miles to starboard. This could have coincided with Boxhall's first socket signals. In the exceptional weather conditions of that night these might just have been visible from twenty miles away, if not very far above the horizon. In such circumstances it is also possible that an extremely large ship at a greater distance might be seen as a smaller one at a lesser.

Second Officer Herbert Stone took over the watch from Third Officer Groves at midnight and Lord left the bridge to stretch out on the chart-room sofa three-quarters of an hour later, leaving the usual order that he should be called in the event of anything untoward. Half an hour after that, at 1.15 a.m. ship's time, Stone reported by voice-pipe that the ship they had both seen, apparently stationary, to their south-east, was now steaming away to the south-west; he also reported seeing some white rockets,[8] low in the sky and thus coming from a ship well beyond the one in view. Lord told him to try and raise her again and to send the apprentice, James Gibson, down to him to report any developments.

By this time the Titanic *had fifty-three minutes left to live and the* Californian *could not possibly have reached her before she sank.* The distance of nineteen and a half miles asserted by Lord (and his First Officer, George Stewart, keeper of the official log, who however was in bed at the time) now seems not to have been an over-estimate: even without the ice that would have slowed her, the *Californian* would have been just too late to save those left behind on the wreck. But she might have been in time to pluck some people from the bitterly cold water.

At five minutes past two Gibson, a cadet aged twenty, went down to the chart room to report the firing of a total of eight white rockets at intervals; meanwhile the "tramp steamer" (*sic*) that they had seen had sailed out of sight. Lord by contrast had identified this ship as one not unlike his own. Stone felt there was something odd about her because her red (port) light was higher than her green one, indicating a heel or list to starboard (the *Titanic* listed briefly to starboard after the collision, we may recall, but went over to port as she settled in the water). Lord, a strict and feared disciplinarian, recollected asking, "What is it?" when someone came into the chart room, but going back to sleep on apparently hearing no answer.

When he awoke on the sofa just after dawn at about
4.40 a.m. a steamer was visible about eight miles off, a
ship with one yellow funnel and four masts but definitely
not the one which had been on the same general bearing
as the rockets seen during the night. At about 5.15 a.m.
Stewart told Lord that the wireless had reported a ship
sunk at 41° 46' north, 50° 14' west; at 5.40 a.m. the *Mount
Temple*, source of the news, signalled again, revealing that
it was the *Titanic* that had gone down. Evans soon picked
up similar reports from the *Frankfurt* and the *Virginian*.
Lord set a course for the reported position just after 6
a.m. and, slowed by ice, was on the scene some one and
a half hours later.

What did he, as an individual, do wrong? The foregoing
summary of the role of his ship is as clear as we can make
it, given the inevitable conflicts of evidence in this as in
every other sub-plot of the legend. Yet ever since the
American and British inquiries into the disaster, both of
which condemned Lord for not going to the aid of the
stricken liner many hours sooner than he did (let us not
forget that he did act as soon as he knew), fiercely pro-
and anti-Lord factions have existed. The former proved
strong enough to bring about a reopening of the British
inquiry eighty years after the event, softening though not
quashing history's verdict. The most passionate published
"pro-Lordians" are Leslie Harrison and Peter Padfield; the
deadliest "anti-Lordian" is Leslie Reade (all three books
are listed in the bibliography). All sometimes throw logic
overboard in their keenness to win the persistent argument. We may fairly conclude that the *Californian*,
specifically Stone as officer of the watch, should have done
something about the rockets seen from her but failed to
do so. Lord was master and was therefore responsible,
not only in law but also in the light of his own faults as a
captain – arrogant, authoritarian and afraid of ice. This
assessment need not prevent us from condemning the
thankful eagerness with which both official inquiries
seized upon this dereliction of duty to make a scapegoat

of the unfortunate Lord as a diversion from other issues.

The Americans concluded that the *Californian* had been closer to the *Titanic* than nineteen miles, and that her officers had seen her distress signals and not responded, which placed "a grave responsibility" on Lord as master. The British seized on Evans's remark to Lord that he had been in touch with only one ship (the *Titanic*) and that he thought she was nearby, plus the fact that a ship (and sky signals) had undoubtedly been sighted from the *Californian*, as "proof" that the latter had sighted the *Titanic* and vice versa. The conclusion is an offence against logic, but we shall come back to how Lord Mersey and others treated Lord in our chapter on the British inquiry. Suffice it to say here that "Donkeyman Gill" allowed the *Boston American* newspaper on 25 April 1912 to run, for a consideration of $500 (equivalent to fourteen months' pay), his affidavit. It stated that he had seen a very large liner before midnight (the *Titanic* was then stopped shortly after the collision, which occurred at 11.52 p.m. *Californian* time – implying that Gill might even have been watching at the very moment of the collision). He had seen rockets being fired at about 12.40 a.m., both phenomena being "about ten miles" from the *Californian*. The affidavit was read into the American inquiry record and he stuck to its content in person at both inquiries.[9]

The American Report was published on 28 May, in the middle of a ten-day break in the British inquiry. Lord and the other witnesses from the *Californian* were examined in London on days seven and eight (14 and 15 May) but none was recalled. On day twenty-four (16 June) the Attorney-General proposed, and Lord Mersey agreed, to alter the remit of the inquiry so as to enable it to condemn Lord. Both inquiries chose to believe Gill (venal but unshakable) and Groves (inexperienced by his own admission, but patently honest, even when it seemed to be against his interests) rather than Lord (hardly objective), Stewart (asleep at the time) and Stone (like Stewart afraid of Lord). The former pair had seen a passenger ship's deck lights, which Groves had also seen go out (Lord Mersey chose to interpret this as the result of the *Titanic*'s vain turn to avoid the iceberg). But Groves never saw a green starboard light (indicating a westbound ship to the south) – only a red port one after the deck lights had gone out (since the *Titanic*'s lights stayed on to the end, he could not have seen her port-side light, meaning she would have turned round to face roughly east, without seeing her broadside lights as well – which he said had gone out!). Groves also spoke of two masthead lights. The *Titanic* had one.

Efforts were made to find the "mystery ship" during and after the British inquiry, in vain. But early in August 1912 Captain Lord received an astounding letter from a certain W. H. Baker, who served briefly as Fourth Officer on the *Mount Temple* just after the disaster but was now writing from his regular berth on another Canadian Pacific liner, *Empress of Britain*:

> I came home in the *Mount Temple* from Halifax that voyage, having been taken out of the *Empress* at ten minutes notice to fill up a vacancy ... The officers and others told me what they had seen on the eventful night when the *Titanic* went down, and from what they said, they were from ten to fourteen miles from her when they saw her signals. I gather from what was told me that the captain seemed afraid to go through the ice, although it was not so very thick. They told me that they not only saw her deck lights but several green lights between them and what they thought was the *Titanic*. There were two loud reports heard which they said must have been the "finale" of the *Titanic*; this was sometime after sighting her, I gathered. The captain said at the Washington inquiry that he was forty-nine miles away but the officers state he was not more than fourteen miles off. I must tell you these men were fearfully indignant that they were not then called upon to give evidence at the time, for they were greatly incensed at

the captain's behaviour in the matter. The doctor had made all preparations and rooms were turned into hospitals, etc., and the crew were standing by ready to help, on deck, watching her lights and what they said were the green lights burnt in the [life]boats . . . These fellows must feel sorry for you, knowing that you could not, in the face of this, have been the mystery ship.[10]

Baker's letter also indicated he was under the (mistaken) impression that he and Lord had met on a training ship; but this error hardly affects the impact of his detailed description of events on the *Mount Temple*. Either her captain (see below) or Baker was lying through his teeth. This extraordinary development was taken up with the Board of Trade by C.P. Grylls, general secretary of the Mercantile Marine Service Association (MMSA), the "officers' union", at Lord's request on 27 August 1912. This was just seventeen days after Lord himself had written, rather belatedly one may feel, to the Board (with beautiful handwriting but ugly grammar), disputing Lord Mersey's apparent misinterpretation of the inquiry evidence at considerable length. But the Board complacently refused to entertain any plea from him or on his behalf until 1992, thirty years after his death.

Lord and the MMSA would have been better advised to go public with the Baker letter and appeal for more witnesses. As it was, Lord met Baker at Wallasey on Merseyside between voyages, and was introduced by him over lunch to the man Baker had briefly replaced, A. H. Notley, the *Mount Temple*'s Fourth Officer. He *inter alia* confirmed Lord's calculation of the position of the abandoned lifeboats on the morning of 15 April as eleven miles south-east of the Boxhall position, as Lord had maintained in his evidence. But Notley, while ready to provide information, would not risk his career with Canadian Pacific by making a statement to the Board of Trade, a stance which Lord, sacked by Leyland after the two official inquiries, could surely understand. Dr Mathias Bailey of the *Mount Temple* disingenuously pleaded ignorance of navigational and nautical matters as his excuse for not helping Lord.[11]

The Baker letter, to say nothing of the corroboration it received from Notley, had it been published, would have caused a sensation, given the unsolved but highly publicized "mystery ship" aspect of the tragedy. Looking back across more than eight decades, the observer inevitably finds it astonishing that nothing more came of it, thanks to the deadening hand of the Board of Trade. But the explanation is simple: it was written after the inquiries and was never published at the time. The same cannot be said of an affidavit from a Dr F. C. Quitzrau of Toronto, Ontario, to the American inquiry. He solemnly swore:

> ... that he was a passenger, travelling second class, on steamer *Mount Temple*, which left Antwerp April 3, 1912; that about midnight, Sunday, April 14, New York time, he was awakened by the sudden stopping of the engines; that he immediately went to the cabin [*sic*], where were already gathered several of the stewards and passengers, who informed him that word had been received by wireless from the *Titanic* that the *Titanic* had struck an iceberg and was calling for help. Orders were immediately issued and the *Mount Temple* course changed, heading straight for the *Titanic*. About 3 o'clock, 2 o'clock ship time [*sic*], the *Titanic* was sighted by some of the officers and crew; that as soon as the *Titanic* was seen all lights on the *Mount Temple* were put out and the engines stopped and the boat lay dead for about two hours; that as soon as day broke the engines were started and the *Mount Temple* circled the *Titanic*'s position, the officers insisting that this be done, although the captain had given orders that the boat proceed on its journey. While encircling the *Titanic*'s position we sighted the *Frankfurt* to the north-west of us, the *Birma* to the south, speaking to both of these by wireless, the latter asking if we were in distress; that

about 6 o'clock we saw the *Carpathia*, from which we had previously received a message that the *Titanic* had gone down; that about 8.30 the *Carpathia* wirelessed that it had picked up twenty lifeboats and about 720 passengers all told, and that there was no need for the *Mount Temple* to stand by, as the remainder of those on board were drowned.[12]

This statement, sworn on 29 April 1912 before the United States vice-consul in Toronto, of which the above is the full text, is either the work of a paranoid fantasist or else an account in good faith, by a doctor, of events he felt should be drawn to the attention of the American inquiry (to which it was duly forwarded) while it was still sitting. If the doctor was looking for notoriety he was denied it because his suspicions seem to have been overlooked: they were not even put to the *Mount Temple*'s Captain at the British inquiry. But neither affidavit nor author were ever discredited either. Dr Quitzrau's sworn statement gives the impression that he was everywhere at once on the ship, whereas he clearly relied on hearsay for much of his information. But, viewed alongside the Notley/Baker evidence, this affidavit makes the *Mount Temple* a leading but not the sole candidate for identification as the "mystery ship" seen from the *Titanic*.

Captain James Henry Moore, master of the *Mount Temple*, a two-class (steerage and cabin) ship of 6,661 tons, gave evidence at both inquiries. He was not put under pressure, even though he began his testimony to the Americans by getting his position wrong for the time his ship picked up the *Titanic*'s distress call (according to Marconi operator John Durrant, at 12.11 a.m. ship's time, about four minutes behind the *Titanic*'s), giving the original, erroneous position of 41° 44' north, 50° 24' west. His latitude at the time, he said, was 41° 25' north; he first gave his longitude as 51° 15' west, but he corrected this to 51° 41', some fourteen miles further west, putting him about forty-nine miles south-west of the stricken ship.

Moore ordered a north-easterly course, which he adjusted on hearing Boxhall's amended position.

He encountered ice at 3 a.m., whereupon he doubled the lookouts, sending his Fourth Officer to the forecastle head. Shortly after that he saw a schooner showing her starboard green light across his bow a mile to a mile and a half ahead. He had the engines thrown into reverse and the helm swung hard a-starboard (i.e., he turned sharply to port, north-westward) to pass her starboard to starboard, whereupon "the light seemed suddenly to go out".

Moore had, he said, had a foreign tramp steamer of 4,000 to 5,000 tons without ensign, first seen off his port bow heading east, under continuous observation from 1 to 1.30 a.m. onwards. She gradually crossed over to starboard and in the end he saw her stern light; she had a black funnel with a white band near the top containing some kind of device (this was the ship for which a widespread search was mounted, in vain). A photograph from ahead of the Anchor-Donaldson Line's *Saturnia*, which at 1 a.m. set a course for the Boxhall position in response to the distress calls but was halted by ice only six miles from it, shows a single funnel with a horizontal white band within which three dark vertical lines can be made out.[13]

Moore said he stopped at 3.25 a.m. about fourteen miles from the *Titanic*'s reported position and let his ship drift for a while before proceeding slowly through the ice to the spot, which he reached at 4.30 a.m. The only other ship visible at that stage was the unidentified tramp, by then ahead and to the south of *Mount Temple*. Moore found no wreckage or bodies, only masses of ice in a field over twenty miles by five or six, including icebergs over 200 feet high. Moore calculated that the real last position of the *Titanic* was eight miles further east than the reported one, which would help to explain the absence of evidence at the Boxhall spot.

Clearly *Mount Temple* passengers had been talking to the press, because Moore emphatically denied that any rockets or signals had been seen from his ship around midnight on the disaster night; nothing had been sighted from the bridge and nobody had been on deck at the time, he said. On receipt of the distress messages, the lifeboats were made ready, together with gangways, ropes, ladders and lifebelts. The total capacity of the twenty lifeboats aboard was 1,000 for a ship with 2,200 berths in steerage and 166 in cabin class, plus 130 crew. For some reason never explained, the ship was carrying two extra lifeboats, Moore told the American senators; but in London he said he readied eighteen boats out of a total aboard of twenty. "I assure you that I did everything that was possible, Sir, consistent with the safety of my own ship and passengers," Captain Moore told Senator Smith.

The *Mount Temple* searched until 9 a.m. on the 15th, having sighted the *Carpathia* across six miles of ice and observing the *Californian* arriving well afterwards. The evidence clearly suggests that the Canadian ship was motionless for some three hours, from 4.30 a.m., watching the *Carpathia* doing all the work; in the light of that, Moore could surely count himself lucky not to have attracted at least some of the opprobrium so liberally attached to Lord. Moore also saw the Russian liner *Birma*, which had joined in the emergency wireless traffic during the night and come up at speed from seventy miles away.

Moore added that he had never known so much ice so far south; on receiving warnings on the 13th he had altered course to the south. He would certainly not have done what Captain E. J. Smith did, maintaining high speed after such ice-warnings as he had received (company regulations for ships on the Canadian route, where there was much more ice, were correspondingly more strict): Smith had been "most unwise", he thought. He also thought that the ice would certainly have drifted across the area of the disaster and might well have concealed bodies and wreckage. Moore gave the British inquiry a third version of his longitude on receipt of the distress call: 51° 14' west (in fairness, the "51° 41' west" of the American inquiry Report could have been no more than a misprint for

51° 14'; if it was not, the Captain was either fibbing or remarkably slapdash).

His wireless man, Durrant, said the ship had altered course a maximum of fifteen minutes after receiving the "CQD" alert. At 12.43 a.m. ship's time he heard MGY (the *Titanic*) calling MKC (the *Olympic*); at 1.06 a.m. the former signalled: "Get your boats ready, going down at the head." He heard the *Frankfurt* and the *Baltic* in touch with the doomed ship as well but neither came to the scene. He had told the *Californian* the news at 5.11 a.m., he said.[14]

In marked contrast with their treatment of Lord and the *Californian* evidence, the Commissioner and the Solicitor-General went out of their way to exonerate Moore and the *Mount Temple*. Lord Mersey remarked during Durrant's evidence: "This boat, the *Mount Temple*, was never in a position to render active assistance." Sir John Simon said: "It was forty-nine miles away [nine nearer than the *Carpathia*], and it was making for her." Mersey: "She could not possibly have reached her." Simon concurred (correctly, given the attested relative positions of the two ships): "No, not possibly. She was doing her best." Neither Dr Quitzrau nor his version of events was mentioned. It is obvious, however, that an 11.5-knot ship could not have averaged the twenty-five needed to reach the wreck before it sank from a reported forty-nine miles away in the 125 minutes between the receipt of the CQD and the sinking. Of the ships known to have been in the vicinity of the disaster, only the *Californian* could have reached the spot before the *Titanic* sank – and then only if she had kept her wireless on or reacted immediately and at top speed to the rockets.

And what of the sailing ship sighted from the *Mount Temple* and the *Titanic*? This mystery at least was apparently resolved in 1962, half a century after the disaster, by a retired Norwegian Merchant Navy officer, Captain Hendrik Naess. He made an affidavit shortly before his death, which later found its way into the Norwegian press, saying that at the material time he had been first mate on the *Samson*, a 148-foot sailing barque of 506 tons commanded by Captain C. J. Ring. A rare photograph of this ship[15] shows a wooden vessel with a long bowsprit, a tall, narrow funnel (for an auxiliary or donkey engine), two cross-rigged masts and a third rigged fore and aft. Confusingly, this ship and her skipper were officially logged in an Icelandic port on both 6 and 20 April 1912; she would have had her work cut out to cover the distance to and from the disaster in the time, donkey engine or no: the "solution" of one more mystery thus serves to open up another. Perhaps Naess belonged to that strange but well-attested minority driven to make false confessions to assuage misplaced guilt or gain attention. However, at least one fishing schooner, the *Dorothy Baird*, from Gloucester, Massachusetts, was in the general area of the disaster at the material time. Neither had wireless.

Naess "revealed" that both the *Titanic* and her rockets had been seen, though not recognized at the time, by the *Samson*. But the wooden ship was owned by a sealing company in Trondheim and had been illegally hunting seal in the waters off south-eastern Canada and the Grand Banks. The rockets might have come from a fisheries-protection or other official vessel as a signal to stop and await search. Rather than be caught red-handed, the sealer made off, presumably on its engine as conditions were so calm, and presumably with all its lights doused.[16] Such a small vessel, even with the dozen whaling boats she carried, would not have been of much use to 2,220 people on board the *Titanic*; but she would have been a great deal better than nothing at all. Such was the only "identified" vessel placed by a purported eyewitness within sight of the *Titanic* during her death-agony which could have been sighted from her (if Naess was telling the truth).

The question of who was in the neighbourhood of the *Titanic* when she hit her iceberg is in many respects the most complicated and incompletely answered one in the entire story. Some of the evidence suggests that a sailing ship and a steamer may have been seen from the *Titanic*. Two ships, a steamer and a tramp, were allegedly seen from the *Californian* between herself and the wreck. The *Mount Temple* was indisputably closer to, and earlier on, the scene than the *Carpathia*, which came later from further away but did all the rescue work; the *Mount Temple* at the very least was backward in coming forward. The *Californian* was remiss in not investigating the white sky-signals, but there was clearly a rush to judgment against Lord on both sides of the Atlantic.

That making him a scapegoat for the disaster was unfair was partly acknowledged by the British Government in 1992. The discovery of the wreck thirteen miles from the Boxhall position in 1985 and the consequent revival of the pro-Lord lobby led the Department of Transport in 1990 to order a re-examination of the *Californian*'s role. The Chief Inspector of the Marine Accident Investigation Branch, Captain P. B. Marriott, appointed an outside inspector, disagreed with his anti-Lord conclusions and had his own deputy go over the ground again before signing the Report in March 1992.[17]

It stated that the *Titanic* had been at 41° 47' north, 49° 55' west when she struck (and at 41° 43.6' north, 49° 56.9' west when she sank). The *Californian* was most likely eighteen miles away to the north. She might have seen the *Titanic* by abnormal refraction (the "mirage" effect) but probably did not; she definitely saw the distress signals and did nothing about them. Second Officer Herbert Stone was at fault for not reacting to the rockets and for not ensuring that Lord was properly awakened, informed and urged to come to the bridge to resume direct command. Lord clearly did not wake up when the apprentice, Gibson, came in, and his "What is it?" was the subconscious reaction of a sleeping man. Gibson and Stone probably did not press the matter because Lord was feared as a martinet.

The *Californian* could not have achieved more than the *Carpathia*, the Report concluded; and, unlike the *Mount Temple*, she did at least cross the ice in a bid to help the Cunarder, even if the latter by then had no need of assistance. And although Captain Lord strongly disputed the hostile findings of the two main inquiries for the rest of his long life, his ineffectual and dilatory self-defence *during and immediately after them*, when it mattered most, looks wilfully self-destructive. Leslie Reade pounces on Lord's reluctant concession to the British inquiry that the rockets seen from his bridge "might have been" distress signals as a confession; but all the answer means is that Lord recognized at that precise moment, in the witness-box, that he had been in the wrong to disregard them. It is in no sense proof that he realized this *while half asleep in the early hours of 15 April 1912 and decided to take no action*.

PART THREE

AFTER THE FACT

7

NEW YORK AND HALIFAX

Captain Rostron's wireless censorship and the sheer weight of essential transmissions from the *Carpathia*'s Marconi apparatus meant that the Cunarder kept the world waiting for the merest scrap of news about the disaster. All requests for information, and there were many, from news organizations and elsewhere, insofar as they were received at all, were not answered. As we have seen, even the President of the United States was snubbed. Only the approaching *Olympic*, as sister-ship of the casualty, was favoured with a proper summary of events (Rostron, truly the man who thought of everything, wanted Haddock to avoid upsetting survivors' sensibilities; he got Ismay to support his request to the *Olympic* to stay out of sight). Even Ismay's message to his New York office reporting the disaster was not sent until Wednesday 17 April. The results of the news famine imposed by Rostron were sometimes, if unintentionally, cruel.

That the *Titanic* was in trouble became known in New York in the very earliest hours of Monday 15 April (local time). A radio ham and news tipster, David Sarnoff, aged twenty-one, had a wireless shack on top of a downtown store's skyscraper in Manhattan from where he monitored marine wireless traffic.[1] He intercepted the news from a relay transmission and alerted his clients. Nor was he the only eavesdropper that night. The editor of *The New York Times*, Carr Van Anda, got a message from Cape Race timed at 1.20 a.m. local, under an hour after the sinking.

By that time his paper was on the streets – complete with a shipping announcement that the *Titanic* was "due 16th [i.e., Tuesday] 4 *p.m.*" and signed "White Star Line". Clearly someone expected the ship well ahead of Ismay's much cited Wednesday morning welcome, but the inquiries missed this slip.[2]

The earliest reports were based on a seriously inaccurate, multiple garble. The fact that the *Virginian* had responded to the CQD call (from 170 miles to the north) by altering course was extrapolated into a story that the passengers had been taken aboard her. Monday's evening papers were reporting that the *Carpathia* and *Parisian* had brought off a successful rescue and the wreck was being towed to Halifax, Nova Scotia. The latter fiction was probably a distortion of a message from the *Asian*, then towing the broken-down German tanker *Deutschland* to the port. For this reason the *Asian* had signalled that she could do nothing to help the *Titanic*.

Another source of confusion cited by news agency executives at the American inquiry was the term "standing by" used by several ships involved in the night's signalling; this did not mean that they were alongside the wreck but that they were doing what they could to help or were awaiting developments in case they could do anything. On the evening of Monday 15 April a telegram was sent from Manhattan to Mr J. A. Hughes of Huntington, West Virginia, a state legislator, saying: "*Titanic* proceeding to Halifax. Passengers will probably land this Wednesday; all safe", signed "White Star Line". The author of this gruesome squib was never found. In England, the father of John Phillips, the *Titanic's* senior wireless operator, got this message on the 15th: "Making slowly for Halifax. Practically unsinkable. Don't worry." This was not a hoax or a message from the lost operator, but from a well-meaning uncle, who had got wind of one of the garbles and was trying to comfort his brother.

White Star's office at number nine Broadway was first given hard information on the disaster by the *Olympic*.

Long before that, Philip Franklin, IMM's American vice-president, was telephoned at his Manhattan home at 1.58 a.m. on the 15th by a reporter looking for confirmation and reaction to the earliest intimations of catastrophe. The newspaperman said that the *Virginian* and the shore-station at Montreal (where the ship's Allan Line had an office) had reported the *Titanic* to be sinking. Confirmation from Montreal that it had *heard* the rumour that the *Virginian* had taken off the passengers was viewed by eavesdroppers as confirmation of the rumour itself. For confirmation that the *Titanic* was in trouble Franklin telephoned the Associated Press, which had heard similar, and the Allan Line at Montreal; at 3 a.m. he asked the *Olympic* to get the *Titanic*'s position.[3] But it was only at 6.16 p.m. New York time on Monday that the dread message from the *Olympic*, based on information from Rostron, got through, formally confirming the demise of her sister-ship to their owners:

> *Carpathia* reached *Titanic*'s position at daybreak. Found boats and wreckage only. *Titanic* had foundered about 2.20 a.m. in 41° 46' north, 50° 14' west. All her boats accounted for. About 675 souls saved, crew and passengers, latter nearly all women and children. Leyland Line SS *Californian* remaining and searching position of disaster. *Carpathia* returning to New York with survivors; please inform Cunard. Haddock.

Haddock told the American inquiry on its seventeenth and last day that he had ordered the dispatch of this message via Cape Race at 4.35 p.m. New York time. Franklin told the inquiry: "Immediately that telegram was received by me, it was such a terrible shock that it took us a few minutes to get ourselves together." At a press conference shortly afterwards at White Star, the room emptied thunderously when Franklin's recital of the message reached the words, "foundered about 2.20 a.m.". Here at last, some eighteen hours after the great ship had gone down in the Atlantic, was official, public confirmation by her owners of the loss. "There was not a reporter left in the room – they were so anxious to get out and telephone the news." Franklin added: "We considered the ship unsinkable, and it never entered our minds that there had been anything like a serious loss of life ... until we got this Haddock message at 6.30." Franklin ignored Ismay's pleas to detain the *Cedric* to take the surviving crew home, suggesting the *Lapland* instead.

The clatter of dispersing reporters' boots on Monday evening did not prevent a mob of journalists from returning the next morning to accuse Franklin of withholding information. It is known[4] that Captain Haddock had addressed a message to IMM, New York, at 7.45 a.m. New York time on Monday via the shore station at Sable Island, saying, "Have not communicated with *Titanic* since midnight." Franklin must have got this and could only have hoped against hope afterwards that better news might follow. But there is no evidence that he received confirmation of the actual loss of the ship before Haddock's Monday evening relay of the information from the *Carpathia*. She communicated briefly with two other would-be helpers by about 8 a.m. New York time, telling the *Baltic* and the *Virginian* that their services would not be needed as Rostron had "about 800 passengers" on board. She then sent a CQ to all ships that they need no longer stand by. The "800" figure, obviously antedating the precise head-count aboard, got into Tuesday's avid press, thanks to radio hams, professional eavesdroppers and informants at shoreside wireless stations. Only after 8 p.m. on Monday did Rostron order the curtest of messages to be dispatched to Associated Press, saying that the *Titanic* had struck an iceberg and sunk, that he had picked up "many passengers" and was heading for New York.

In London, five hours ahead of New York, the "all safe" story was broken by Tuesday's evening papers and the "800 survivors" version in Wednesday's mornings. Crowds built up outside the White Star offices in both cities, made up of the curious and those desperate for news of relatives and friends. No less anguish was on view outside the company's office in Southampton, where most of the crew lived and had been recruited. In the course of the long Monday between the "sinking" and "sunk" reports, Lloyd's was reinsuring *Titanic's* cargo at a premium of fifty per cent, according to a Dow Jones wire-service report in New York. This was strongly denied by White Star and does not appear to have been true.[5]

The real sensation, however, was going to be when the *Carpathia*, delayed by fog and then rain squalls – rather more typical spring weather in the North Atlantic – arrived in New York with the survivors on the evening of Thursday, 18 April. The story was kept going in the meantime by the trickle of facts and rumours plucked from the ether, articles on famous people known to have been aboard, descriptions of the ship and other background features, and by the lists of survivors (passengers in order of class, then crew) from the *Carpathia*, relayed via the *Olympic* and USS *Chester*.

Rostron's news restrictions were motivated by the upright and reasonable concern that survivors' names and messages should enjoy absolute priority. But the master could not control incoming traffic; and much of that was dubious. Guglielmo Marconi, the great wireless inventor himself, made several appearances before the American inquiry, which was much harder on him than the British. Having said originally that he had sent no message to the *Carpathia*, he changed his tune. Recalled on day nine, he said he had checked his records and "I found that I had sent one message" to her Marconi operator, which had been transmitted at 3.15 a.m. on the 18th and signed with his full name. The signal read: "Wire news dispatch immediately ... If this impossible ask captain give reason why no news allowed to be transmitted." He got no reply, but Harold Bride confirmed he had received it. It seems an extraordinary thing for Marconi to "forget", given the unparalleled scale of the disaster and of the public interest, to say nothing of the dramatic part wireless played in it. His explanation made his "forgetfulness" even less credible.

"I was exceedingly surprised, as everybody else was at the time," said Marconi, "that no news was coming through, and I was very much worried about it, and that day [the 18th] I did suggest that this message should be sent."[6] The great man never did get around to telling the whole truth about his company's activities after the disaster; the terrier-like Senator Smith chairing the American inquiry extracted a fuller story from several other witnesses, including Cottam and Bride (the operators on the *Carpathia*) and news executives. Several, perhaps eight, offers of money for a story were disregarded; but messages emanating from Marconi's New York office advised the two beleaguered operators to "shut up" and sell their stories in New York. Further, a Marconi representative called on the Associated Press on Thursday the 18th and offered them an exclusive story based on information requested from the *Carpathia*. The Associated Press accepted but the story never came.[7] When it became known that the two operators had indeed sold their stories, but to *The New York Times*, Marconi loftily said he had been anxious that the two young men should have the chance to earn some extra money (for all the world as if their modest salaries had nothing to do with him). The paper paid them $750 each, they said, and Bride got an extra $250 from a London newspaper which bought the British rights to his story.

Frederick M. Sammis, Marconi's Chief Engineer in the United States, accepted responsibility for the suggestion to the two operators that they should exploit their experiences by taking advantage of the unprecedented outbreak of cheque-book journalism occasioned by the unique disaster. Sammis, too, said he was glad to help a couple of modestly paid employees (£4–£4 10s. per month plus board) to make something on the side. There was no law against it in America and he got nothing out of it himself.

Sammis even told the two men to go to the Strand Hotel near the Cunard pier in Manhattan, the *New York Times* temporary headquarters for the first, and one of the greatest ever, blanket-coverage operations in modern journalism. Editor Van Anda's cultivation of contacts with Marconi paid off handsomely, as did his well-padded chequebook: the paper telephoned Sammis to ask for exclusive access to the operators and got it with Marconi's personal assistance. He smuggled a *Times* reporter aboard with him and was present when Bride was interviewed on the ship; Cottam also gave an early interview while still aboard. *The New York Times* thus left its competitors standing on this and other aspects of the *Titanic* story, especially on 17 April, the first day of full coverage of the disaster. The rivals protested very strongly and Senator Smith was no less critical; they attacked Marconi and the *Times* for suppressing news of overwhelming public interest for financial gain. The *Times* responded with attacks on Senator Smith so intemperate that they rebounded and were quietly dropped.

Scenes of pandemonium, to which the press made the principal contribution, awaited SS *Carpathia* as she entered New York's vast harbour complex. The Cunard pier was cordoned off from public and press by 200 police, including mounted officers and detectives on watch for thieves. Only a maximum of two identified close relatives of each survivor were to be allowed access to the quay. The authorities had the compassion to suspend America's traditionally tough customs and immigration formalities for the benefit of Rostron and the survivors. But for the absence of television lights and microphones, it seems to have been a remarkably modern media scene, with reporters shouting questions and cameramen jostling against barriers, police and each other, magnesium flash-guns going off and people craning and pushing for a better view of not very much at first. But it was easily the most sensational news event of its kind in history thus far. The real story was about to reach the most sophisticated and competitive news-processing centre in the world, ahead of all others in its use of telephones, ticker-tapes and newspaper production technology. Cunard said it would allow no press aboard the rescue ship.

As she emerged from the Ambrose Channel northward into Lower New York Bay, the *Carpathia* was met by a welter of official and unofficial small boats, some hired and others, even the pilot boat, infiltrated by reporters. Some of them doubtless regretted their initiative as the weather was stormy, with much wind and rain. Just one managed to get aboard, from the pilot boat. A crowd of many thousands had gathered in the rain in Battery Park at the southern tip of Manhattan to watch the ship enter the Hudson River on the western side of the island. The ship sailed slowly past pier fifty-four and stopped off White Star's number fifty-nine, where she lowered the thirteen *Titanic* lifeboats (which were looted of most removable items during the night; the ship's name was sanded off the next day). Another crowd was waiting at the Cunard pier, where the *Carpathia* was nudged into place by tugs on the north side, whence she had departed just a week and a day earlier. It was 9.30 p.m.[8]

Once the *Carpathia*'s own passengers had made their unexpected return descent upon New York, down the forward gangway and into the passenger terminal came the first-class survivors, many strangely clad in what the *Carpathia*'s passengers could spare, to be met by the vetted crowd of relatives with shouts and tears. Emerging from the landward side of the terminal they were greeted by the heaving press corps and a subdued throng of members of the public. Some passengers, including the Philadelphia railroad and business element, were taken off in limousines and taxis to private trains. Others were conveyed to their New York homes or top-class hotels. Several, including Major Arthur Peuchen, went to the Waldorf Astoria, which was convenient because it was to be the scene of the opening of the United States Senate inquiry the very next day. Senator William Alden Smith, its chairman, had arrived in New York by train too late to board the *Carpathia* from a boat and was escorted aboard when she tied up. His first action was to seek out J. Bruce Ismay for a half-hour private interview.

The second-class passengers, who disembarked next, also had the means, in most cases, to look after themselves ashore. This did not apply to many from third class, most of whom had lost everything they possessed in the wreck and had to be helped by city and charity resources. Immigration officials took more interest in these poorest survivors than the rest because most of them intended to stay in the United States. But for their convenience they were spared the customary processing through Ellis Island in New York harbour: seven inspectors went aboard to examine them on the ship. Those joining relatives were given directions and help with fares. Others were put up in hostels.

Financial aid soon became available from several sources. The Mayor of New York quickly set up a relief fund which gathered more than $161,000; the city's *New York American* newspaper and Women's Relief Committee added another $100,000 for distribution by the American Red Cross. On board the *Carpathia* first-class survivors had formed their own committee and collected a total of $4,360 for distribution among the crew (including Rostron and his officers) as gratuities in New York. This fund eventually swelled to $15,000 and was administered, piquantly one may think, by none other than J.P. Morgan.[9] The survivors also bought Rostron a silver cup and had 320 medals struck for all his crew, gold for the senior officers, silver for the juniors and bronze for the rest, presented when the ship returned to New York at the end of May. But the biggest fund of all was started by the Lord Mayor of London: the Titanic Relief Fund, which amassed £413,200 within a year and was active for more than half a century. Distribution was supervised by the Corporation of the City of London.

Southampton, the city where grief was most concentrated among the often destitute families of the lost crew members, set up its own emergency relief fund. Lists of the survivors started to go up outside White Star's office in Canute Road on 17 April: what the agonized relatives would doubtless have preferred was a list of the lost, but this could only be put together later. White Star's Liverpool office was also besieged by people seeking information as the British and American nations reacted with shock to the loss of the *Titanic*.

As King George V and President Taft sent condolences, the British press quickly picked up the themes of high speed and inadequate lifeboats, government complacency and the whole question of the hubris of contemporary technology. There was a general feeling that humanity had overreached itself and come a cropper. A national commemorative service was held at St Paul's Cathedral in London on 19 April. The London *Daily Mail* got a useful exclusive from the retired Alexander Carlisle, designer under Pirrie of the "Olympics", who collapsed in St Paul's; he revealed how his plans for far more lifeboats had been overruled.

Cottam of the *Carpathia* had gone to the Strand Hotel and *The New York Times* as soon as he could get off the ship; Bride stayed aboard the *Carpathia* to rest, before transferring to hospital as the ship resumed her interrupted voyage to the Mediterranean after two hectic days on 20 April. By that time Rostron had managed to revictual his ship, give evidence to the American inquiry and write his formal report on the rescue to Cunard (which would not accept a penny from White Star – an attitude which contrasts starkly with the latter's cheapskate and immediate termination of the shipwrecked crew's pay). Shortly before departure from New York with 743 passengers on the 20th, Captain Rostron, thoughtful to the last, had his crew assembled on the main deck to praise them for their efficient conduct of the rescue and give them their rewards from the rescued.

The sober reflection on the disaster to be found in the

majority of the British newspapers, whose coverage was massive, sometimes speculative and plain wrong in the early stages but seldom sensationalized, was markedly different from the style adopted by the American press. The country's most influential daily, *The New York Times*, as we have seen, did not shrink from using all the tricks of the trade normally associated with the "yellow press" (then a relatively new phrase). New York was the scene of a uniquely fierce circulation war that began with the general adoption of the rotary press at the end of the nineteenth century, particularly between newspapers owned by Joshua Pulitzer and William Randolph Hearst.

The latter tycoon was a pathological Anglophobe, and very early on in the post-disaster coverage his *New York American* focused its impressive supply of venom on the aristocratic-looking Englishman it chose as scapegoat. In a classic and monstrous example of "trial by newspaper", it published his photograph, ringed by pictures of *Titanic* victims' widows – all under the fat, black headline, "J. BRUTE ISMAY". It also inflated a brief conversation between its editor and Lady Duff Gordon into a "signed" first-person account by her. The intrusive antics of the British tabloids, among the worst in the civilized world by the end of the century, seem trivial when compared with this kind of treatment of a historic event, the unadulterated truth of which was more than enough to satisfy the most sensation-hungry readers.

Back in New York, the 210 survivors from the *Titanic*'s crew plus four officers had left the *Carpathia* via the aft gangway used by third class, after the passenger survivors had gone and the crowds of New Yorkers and journalists had all but dispersed. They were led to a tender which sailed north to White Star's second pier, number sixty, and were put up aboard the *Lapland*, a liner owned by IMM's Red Star line. The officers got their own cabins. Thankful though they all undoubtedly were for belonging to the surviving minority of less than a quarter of the crew, they desperately wanted to go home but still faced an enervating ordeal at the hands of authority, a secondary ordeal perhaps but much longer than what they had endured in the boats. What was worse, no sooner had authority, American style, finished with them, than an even more bureaucratic authority, British style, took over.

Senator Smith, appointed chairman of the American inquiry on 17 April, acted swiftly: subpoenas were served on the four surviving officers and twelve members of the crew that very day. Another fifteen crew were soon added to the witness list before the *Lapland* set sail on the morning of Saturday 20 April. While she was still in American waters, a tugboat with a federal marshal aboard hailed her and another five crew members were served with papers and taken off. This was quick work by the Americans, who started with little or no idea of the most useful potential witnesses to detain. When the inquiry moved from New York to Washington, the witnesses went with it.

Back in Britain, as the *Lapland* docked at Plymouth on the 29th, the 170 or so *Titanic* crew aboard found themselves still to be prisoners in all but name. A grotesque wrangle began when government and White Star officials, including Harold Sanderson, came aboard and announced that the crew would not be allowed off until every one of them had made a deposition. Representatives of the Seafarers' Union had been denied access but requisitioned a boat and a megaphone. The union's president, Thomas Lewis, urged the crew to make no statements without advice while they were boarding a tender for transfer to shore. Thus encouraged, they refused to co-operate. After a ludicrous chase round the harbour, Lewis was allowed aboard the tender to meet his members. Ashore they were confined in a third-class waiting room until the laborious process of collecting raw evidence for the British inquiry was completed; a couple of dozen were served with sub-poenas to appear before it in London. Food and bedding were delivered to the shed as an inquisitive crowd waited outside.[10] When individuals emerged from questioning, they talked and complained to the crowd and the press through the gates.

By 6 p.m. some eighty-five crew or about half present had been processed in time to board a special train for Southampton. There a huge crowd, which had attended an open-air commemoration service in the stricken city earlier in the day, swamped the train on its arrival with a great wave of emotion. Although large crowds gathered again the next evening, when the other half of the surviving crew members who had landed at Plymouth came back to Southampton, the mood was quieter and more sober.

All the British witnesses had been heard in New York or Washington by the end of April; the last was Ismay, who was recalled yet again on 30 April and then released.[11] Those held up in the United States came home in dribs and drabs on White Star ships. Ismay returned on the *Adriatic*, joined by his wife, Florence, at Queenstown on 10 May and arriving in Liverpool on the 11th. There the waiting crowd brought unexpected consolation for the rough treatment he had received in America: there were shouts of sympathy and even applause.

Asian's report that she was taking the tanker *Deutschland* to Halifax was transmogrified into the false rumour that the *Titanic* was being towed there. Preparations were made for receiving her and the survivors, and then cancelled. But the principal port of Nova Scotia and the Canadian east coast was assigned a task in the saga after all – the truly macabre one of recovering the bodies from the sea. The town is rather nearer to the scene of the disaster than New York and White Star's Halifax agent chartered a British cable-laying ship, the *Mackay-Bennett* from Plymouth (Captain F. H. Lardner) for the work. John Snow and Company Limited, the largest undertaking firm in the region, was contracted to prepare the bodies for burial and hired some forty embalmers from other firms. An Anglican canon went aboard to conduct burials at sea. The embalming work was to be started aboard ship and her cable tanks were filled with ice to bring home the bodies. The ship's crew was put on double pay and the vessel, carrying 100 coffins, cast off at lunchtime on Wednesday 17 April, two and a half days after the disaster – a very creditable piece of organization by all concerned.[12]

The Boxhall position was some 450 sea-miles east of Halifax. The cable-layer, initially slowed down by squalls and fog, typical Grand Banks weather, took about two days to cover the distance, and as she approached the general area at noon on the Friday, sent a CQ message asking all ships to report bodies or wreckage sighted. Two German liners, *Rhein* and *Bremen*, responded with sightings in latitude 42° north, a touch west of longitude 49° west, or about thirty miles east-north-east of the Boxhall position. That was good enough for Lardner, who reached the area after dark.

Soon afterwards bodies and wreckage were seen from the stopped ship, and from daybreak on Saturday fifty-one corpses were plucked from the sea, including one little blond boy aged about two, four women and forty-five men. Two dozen, unidentifiable and disfigured, were sewn into weighted sacks and buried at sea, after Canon Kenneth Hind of Halifax Cathedral led a funeral service on deck. The rest, identified if possible by their personal effects, were tagged with a number which also went on a bag containing their property. A description was entered against each number in a ledger brought for the purpose.

No work was done on Sunday, but at first light on Monday morning more wreckage and corpses in life-jackets were sighted. So was *Titanic*'s collapsible lifeboat B, which had obviously been hit by a ship as its planking was damaged; it still floated upside-down. Lardner decided to abandon it. The rest of the day yielded another twenty-seven bodies, including one identified as Colonel J. J. Astor, whose initials were on the collar of its shirt.[13]

Mysteriously, there was also a handkerchief with the initials "A.V." as well as $2,440 and £250 in notes plus several gold items (belt buckle, watch, pencil, cufflinks and diamond ring). His estate exceeded $100 million. Many of the bodies had two or more layers of clothing; Astor had a blue serge suit and brown boots with his brown flannel shirt. How strange that Astor, unquestionably on the ship after the last boat left, should turn up dead near a lifeboat. He undoubtedly died in the disaster; but was this body really his? He was not among those forced to stand on the inverted collapsible B until taken on board by boats twelve and four.

Fifteen more unidentifiable victims were buried at sea on Monday. Other ships reported more bodies, one twenty-five miles east of the Boxhall position. One ship reported sighting an empty lifeboat in good condition. Wednesday was a wasted day because of thick fog; but the *Mackay-Bennett* managed to rendezvous with the Allan liner *Sardinian* and collect more canvas and sacking. By then the cable-layer had eighty bodies in store. On Thursday eighty-seven more bodies were garnered from the sea.

Meanwhile in Halifax a second ship had been chartered to relieve the *Mackay-Bennett*: the *Minia* (Captain W. G. S. de Carteret), also a cable ship. After waiting for hurriedly carpentered extra coffins, the ship set sail just before midnight on Monday 22 April and took three days to reach the search area, where the two vessels joined forces. They parted company at noon on Friday, the *Mackay-Bennett* returning to Halifax with 190 bodies after burying 116 at sea. She docked at the Navy yard on the morning of 30 April. Church bells tolled, flags flew at half-mast while shops and offices all over the city displayed black ribbons. The bodies were taken by hearse to the Mayflower public ice-rink just over half a mile away. Among the many thoughtful preparations by the authorities, cubicles were set up for the completion of embalming work and to give the relatives who had travelled to the city a little privacy as they viewed the bodies for identification. Priority had been given to first and second class even in death in the allocation of the 100 coffins; the bodies of steerage passengers and crew were in canvas bags.

The *Minia*, frustrated by continuous bad weather, returned on 6 May with only fifteen bodies, including that of the Canadian transcontinental railroad magnate Charles M. Hays. Two unidentified crewmen had been buried at sea. On 3 May the Canadian Government sent the fishery-inspection vessel *Montmagny* to join the search; she recovered four bodies, of which one was buried at sea, and came back on the 13th. The vessel returned to the charge the next morning but found no more bodies in five days. The last sweep was made by a ship chartered by White Star from St John's, Newfoundland, the *Algerine*. She found one body, of a saloon steward, the 328th to be recovered. A total of 209 were brought back to Halifax. Curiously enough this number, added to the 705 survivors carefully counted by Captain Rostron, gives a total of 914, the sum of those counted in the lifeboats by witnesses at the British inquiry. Another coincidence, presumably – but an eerie one.

Fifty-nine of the recovered bodies were claimed and taken away. The remaining 150 were interred in Halifax, mostly at the non-denominational Fairview Cemetery, where the long lines of gravestones can be seen to this day, a specially carved one commissioned by the crew of the *Mackay-Bennett* marking the grave of the two-year-old boy. Roman Catholics were buried at Mount Olivet. Jewish victims went to the Baron de Hirsch cemetery after an unseemly tug-of-war provoked by Rabbi Jacob Walter, who went among the dead "identifying" Jews – only to be forced to accept later that several were not Jewish at all. Ten bodies were moved from pillar to post and back, with such vigour that the coffins had to be replaced. Anglicans, Catholics, Jews and Methodists all held crowded funeral services. Even the Freemasons sent a delegation, as did the Navy and the Army. The plaintive notes of "Nearer my

The men on the bridge:
Captain Edward J.
Smith and (clockwise
from top left) his watch
officers: Henry Wilde
(Chief Officer), William
Murdoch (First) and
Charles Lightoller
(Second).

Both the above quoted books were supplied to the master of the "Titanic" (together with other necessary charts and books) before that ship left Southampton.

The above extracts show that it is quite incorrect to assume that icebergs had never before been encountered or field ice observed so far south, at the particular time of year when the "Titanic" disaster occurred; but it is true to say that the field ice was certainly at that time further south than it has been seen for many years.

It may be useful here to give some definitions of the various forms of ice to be met with in these latitudes, although there is frequently some confusion in their use.

An Iceberg may be defined as a detached portion of a Polar glacier carried out to sea. The ice of an iceberg formed from a glacier is of quite fresh water, only about an eighth of its mass floats above the surface of sea water.

A "Growler" is a colloquial term applied to icebergs of small mass, which therefore only show a small portion above the surface. It is not infrequently a berg which has turned over, and is therefore showing what has been termed "black ice," or more correctly, dark blue ice.

Pack Ice is the floating ice which covers wide areas of the Polar seas, broken into large pieces, which are driven ("packed") together by wind and current, so as to form a practically continuous sheet. . Such ice is generally frozen from sea water, and not derived from glaciers.

Field Ice is a term usually applied to frozen sea water floating in much looser form than pack ice.

An Icefloe is the term generally applied to the same ice (*i.e.,* field ice) in a smaller quantity.

A Floe Berg is a stratified mass of floe ice (*i.e.,* sea-water ice).

Ice Messages Received.

The "Titanic" followed the Outward Southern Track until Sunday, the 14th April, in the usual way. At 11.40 p.m. on that day she struck an iceberg and at 2.20 a.m. on the next day she foundered.

At 9 a.m. ("Titanic" time) on that day a wireless message from the s.s. "Caronia" was received by Captain Smith. It was as follows:—

Turnbull,
16,099

> "Captain, 'Titanic.'—West-bound steamers report bergs growlers "and field ice in 42° N. from 49° to 51° W., 12th April. Compliments.—Barr."

It will be noticed that this message referred to bergs, growlers and field ice sighted on the 12th April—at least 48 hours before the time of the collision. At the time this message was received the "Titanic's" position was about lat. 43° 35' N. and long. 43° 50' W. Captain Smith acknowledged the receipt of this message.

At 1.42 p.m. a wireless message from the s.s. "Baltic" was received by Captain Smith. It was as follows:—

16,176

> "Captain Smith, 'Titanic.'—Have had moderate, variable winds and "clear, fine weather since leaving. Greek steamer 'Athenai' reports "passing icebergs and large quantities of field ice to-day in lat. 41° 51' "N., long. 49° 52' W. Last night we spoke German oiltank steamer "'Deutschland,' Stettin to Philadelphia, not under control, short of coal, "lat. 40° 42' N., long. 55° 11' W. Wishes to be reported to New York "and other steamers. Wish you and 'Titanic' all success.—Commander."

At the time this message was received the "Titanic" position was about 42° 35' N., 45° 50' W. Captain Smith acknowledged the receipt of this message also.

Mr. Ismay, the Managing Director of the White Star Line, was on board the "Titanic," and it appears that the Master handed the Baltic's message to Mr. Ismay almost immediately after it was received. This no doubt was in order that Mr. Ismay might know that ice was to be expected. Mr. Ismay states that he understood from the message that they would get up to the ice "that night." Mr. Ismay showed this message to two ladies, and it is therefore probable that many persons on board became aware of its contents. This message ought in my opinion to have been

The warnings of ice sent in vain to the *Titanic*, as recorded in the report of the British inquiry.

Life aboard the doomed ship, and how its café looked before the maiden voyage.

The key men from Marconi in the new world of wireless telegraphy: Jack Phillips (bottom), chief operator, and Harold Bride (top), his deputy, of the *Titanic*; and Harold Cottam of the *Carpathia*.

The first photographs following the sinking were taken from the *Carpathia* – here a *Titanic* lifeboat approaches.

Hero and scapegoat: *Carpathia* (above) with Captain Arthur Rostron; *Californian* and Captain Stanley Lord.

Waiting for news: (above) on Broadway outside White Star, New York; Mrs
Benjamin Guggenheim (inset) waited in vain; and at the Cunard berth in
Manhattan awaiting the *Carpathia*.

Reading the news: crew's families scan the lists of survivors at White Star, Southampton, as a newsvendor sells the story in London.

God to Thee", played by the band of the Royal Canadian Regiment, blew over Fairview.

Commemorations of the dead were also held in London's Westminster Cathedral (Roman Catholic) and churches of various denominations in Belfast, Liverpool, New York and Paris. The unique gallantry of the band, which played its collective heart out as the ship was dying and went down with her to a man, evoked a suitably special response. The body of Wallace Hartley, the band's leader, was brought from Halifax to Liverpool on 12 May by the White Star liner *Arabic*. From there he was taken by hearse to his home town of Colne for a massively attended Methodist funeral service and burial. "Nearer my God to Thee" now echoed along the Colne Valley in memory of one of the most remarkable men to go down with the *Titanic*. Nearly 500 musicians from seven orchestras, billed as "the greatest professional orchestra ever assembled", played at the *Titanic* Band Memorial Concert on 24 May 1912 in the Albert Hall in London. Secular commemorations of all the victims were staged at the Metropolitan Opera in New York, the Royal Opera House in Covent Garden, London, and at other leading theatres on both sides of the Atlantic.[14]

Less tasteful and more commercial were the appearances of several crew members at a Washington vaudeville theatre while they were detained in the city by the Senate inquiry in the latter part of April 1912. The crew, it will be recalled, were struck off the payroll by White Star with effect from 2.20 a.m., *Titanic* time, on the 15th; their allowances as Senate witnesses did not cover their living expenses at first and they were dependent on whatever handouts they could get. Elsewhere, cinematograph companies cobbled together whatever footage, including animated material, they could find for showing in picture-theatres. We have already mentioned the flood of nearly 200 postcards, mostly showing the *Olympic* (as did the films); but the name of the *Titanic* or her purported picture, or both, appeared on everything from sheet music to biscuit tins, plates and beakers. There were some 300 commemorative songs in several languages, many in execrable taste or wallowing in misplaced sentimentality. It was not only the yellow press which exploited the greatest of tragedies at sea to the limit.

One of the first visible consequences of the disaster was an immediate move by all the leading steamship companies, including White Star, to provide lifeboat space for all aboard their ships. The process began within days, nobody needing to await the findings of the governmental inquiries to see which way the wind of public opinion was blowing on this issue.

But these measures did not come soon enough to prevent a revolt on the *Olympic* on 24 April 1912.[15] Some 284 of her firemen, not hitherto renowned in White Star service for their concern about lifeboats or boat drill, refused duty and went ashore just before the ship set sail for New York. The reason for the protest was the men's misgivings about the safety standard of the forty "Berthon" col-lapsible lifeboats hurriedly added to the *Olympic*'s equip-ment because of the disaster. Captain Clarke of the Board of Trade passed them as seaworthy on the 22nd, but when sixteen were offloaded again as being superfluous to requirements (the ship was far from full) the firemen deduced that they were unsafe, vainly demanding their replacement by conventional boats.

White Star, enlightened as ever in labour matters, scoured the country for scabs, hiring 100 men in Ports-mouth and fetching 150 more from Liverpool and Shef-field by special train. The liner meanwhile, her passengers aboard, moved to a sea anchorage in the Solent to stop other crew from leaving. To reassure the remaining crew Clarke ordered another lifeboat test at breakfast-time on the 25th. It rather backfired, however, when only a few boats were launched in two hours; the fiasco was aban-doned when passengers began to take an interest in the proceedings. The substitutes were delivered to the waiting ship by tug at 10 p.m. But now another fifty-three men, mostly from the seaman branch, took advantage of the tug's presence to walk off the ship because they did not trust the scratch team of non-union, replacement firemen.

Captain Haddock formally ordered the new mutineers back to work. Efforts by Mr Lewis of the Seafarers' Union to mediate failed. When the men refused to take up their duties, Captain W. E. Goodenough of the cruiser HMS *Cochrane* was summoned in aid by a humiliated and furious Haddock. Even the might of the Royal Navy behind the threat of a formal charge of mutiny could not sway the strikers. But no force was used by either side: the crew were polite in refusing the orders of the two captains. When the tug reached Southampton, the fifty-three were charged with mutiny by the police on the 26th and brought before local justices, who remanded them until the 30th. The *Olympic*'s voyage was cancelled and the passengers compensated. On 5 May the magistrates found the mutineers guilty – but gave them an absolute discharge, in a rare display of common sense. The defence damagingly argued that installing a scab crew was tantamount to rendering the ship unseaworthy. Fear of public opinion was undoubtedly the motive behind this wise decision.[16] The *Olympic* did not sail again until ten days later, by which time she had enough proper lifeboats for all and a fully professional crew, both union-approved.

One person who understood rather better than White Star how to manipulate public opinion was Horatio Bottomley (1860–1933), journalist, financier, politician, mountebank and apotheosis of the self-made man.[17] With the gut instinct of his kind for the fears and prejudices of "the man on the Clapham omnibus", Bottomley had been making a nuisance of himself with parliamentary questions about lifeboat provision since November 1910, when he drew attention to the fact that the *Olympic* had only fourteen (plus four collapsibles and two emergency boats). Fobbed off in the traditional British ministerial manner with the irrelevant answer that the ship's lifeboats exceeded the required minimum, Bottomley expanded on his theme in *John Bull*, the popular (and populist) weekly he had founded with spectacular success in 1906. In February 1911 he was on his feet again in the House of Commons, putting a question to which he already knew the answer: When had the lifeboat regulations last been set? – 1894. But the president of the Board of Trade assured him that the issue of lifeboat provision had been referred to a committee in his department. The committee, which included as adviser and member Alexander Carlisle, retired from Harland and Wolff but still a director of the Welin davit manufacturing company, met twice and reached no conclusion.

Bottomley tabled a question as early as 16 April 1912, seeking the exact capacity of the *Titanic*'s lifeboats and what proportion of the ship's official carrying capacity it represented. His was just one of many Commons questions. To prepare answers to them, Board of Trade officials amassed piles of information from a multiplicity of sources for ministers, generating the files from which so much background information on the disaster has come.

Among this rich material is evidence of a behind-the-scenes diplomatic dispute between the London and Washington governments over the Senate inquiry which began the day after the *Carpathia* reached New York with the survivors. Here was a British-registered ship with a British captain and crew, owned by a British-registered company and lost on the high seas; where was America's jurisdiction? But the *Titanic* was really owned by an American conglomerate, the American side argued, she had been bound for New York with an American majority in first class (including some very eminent citizens) and an overwhelmingly America-bound steerage. The Senate had no trouble in coming up with legitimation in the burgeoning home-from-home of the legal profession.

The dispatches of Mr C. W. Bennett, His Majesty's Consul-General in New York City, repay close study. As early as 19 April, he wrote to Sir Edward Grey, the Foreign Secretary:

> During all this sad time, and especially during the first two days, a great deal of pain was caused to the public by the improper use of wireless by unauthorised amateurs ... [who] with imperfect instruments picked up parts of messages, and piecing them together sent messages which were very far from true. In one case, at any rate, there is hardly room to doubt that a message was forged, the one purporting to come from Mr Phillips, the wireless operator of the *Titanic*, to his mother, stating that all was well, and the vessel proceeding to Halifax. Such a message never was sent from the *Titanic*.
>
> The American press has been perfectly hysterical over the disaster, and has published the wildest and most untrue statements without taking any trouble to justify the same. The particular butt has been Mr Bruce Ismay, whose conduct has been most unjustly criticised ... one cannot help sympathising with Mr Ismay in the rough manner in which he has been handled [by the Senate as well as the press].[18]

The Consul-General made long and detailed reports on the hearings day by day, enclosing huge cuttings from the *New York Sun* which seems to have provided the lengthiest coverage. Bennett was clearly astute. Already on 16 April, amid all the contradictory rumours, he was accurately reporting the death toll at about 1,600. He suggested that the mandatory Board of Trade inquiry be held in London, "not with the idea of avoiding work" at the consulate but because it would not be possible to keep witnesses in New York for two weeks or more (little did he know of Senator Smith's subpoena plans). On 17 April Bennett was already drawing attention to the need to revise the neglected lifeboat regulations of the Board of Trade: the Consul-General had political antennae too. The Naval Attaché to the embassy in Washington, Captain C. H. Sowerby, RN, was instructed to observe the American inquiry; he soon concluded that its motive was not to prevent a recurrence of the disaster but "to incriminate someone now".

The Board of Trade meanwhile turned, via Sir Edward Grey, to the British Ambassador in Washington, the Rt. Hon. James Bryce, OM (which here means not the "old man" of the wireless operators' jargon but the Order of Merit: Bryce had been an MP and Irish Secretary):

> The Board would be glad to know particulars of the Senate inquiry into the loss of the *Titanic*, which was a British-registered vessel.
>
> Have the Senate powers to hold such an inquiry under existing law, or has a new law been passed giving them the necessary authority? Are British subjects being detained in the United States for the purposes of the inquiry?

Bryce was enough of a politician to hint that his mentors in London would be ill-advised to get on their high horses in public. "In view of public opinion here [the witnesses'] offer [*sic*] to give evidence was the best course," he advised the Foreign Office on 22 April. But in private the Ambassador joined in the general, sneering attitude of British officialdom. "Their conduct of the inquiry is so incompetent that they may before long discredit themselves and public interest may subside," he noted unrealistically on the 23rd. But the Senate had passed its resolution as early as 17 April, setting up a special sub-committee of the Committee of Commerce with full powers to investigate, determine responsibility and make recommendations for legislation to prevent a repetition of the disaster, as well as for international measures, new safety provisions, restrictions on numbers carried and inspection of ships.

In the meantime a Charles W. Jones wrote to the Foreign Secretary from Liverpool on 21 April, giving a flavour of the state of public opinion in that city:

There is a rumour in this city this evening that Mr J. Bruce Ismay has shot himself in New York ... If it is [true], there can be little doubt that his mind had become unhinged after the awful strain of the past few days ... which has been enormously increased by the very brutal examination by the United States Senate investigating committee. That a British subject and an English gentleman should be put to such indignities is causing much indignation in Liverpool, and I now most humbly beg you to make some representation to the United States government on his behalf.[19]

On 24 April Bryce reported discussing the inquiry with President Taft, bereft of Major Archie Butt, late passenger on the *Titanic*. Taft, who had sent his cruisers *Chester* and *Salem* to escort *Carpathia* into New York and excluded the press from the warships, thought Senator Smith would carry on investigating as long as there was personal publicity to be harvested. Bryce agreed with the presidential assessment of Smith as no more than a congenital publicity seeker. As we shall see, this was to underestimate the man.

Also in these contemporary Foreign Office and Board of Trade files are details of the search abroad for the notorious "mystery ship" so often seen during the fateful night. Inquiries were made for any ship sporting a black-topped funnel with a white stripe containing a strange device, in the ports of Newfoundland and the American and Canadian eastern seaboards, Scandinavia, Germany, the Netherlands, Belgium, France, Italy and Russia. The files make no mention of such a search in Britain, which was surely the most likely to yield a result. The *Saturnia*, for example, does not appear to have been investigated and nothing came of the hunt.

The same could not be said of Senator Smith's inquiry, whose potential for embarrassing the British Government had been so quickly and accurately recognized. In British terms he was a loose cannon, out of reach of the restraints on disclosure of uncomfortable facts so readily available in Whitehall and Westminster. And the country which had produced such a self-publicist as Bottomley was in no position to attack Senator Smith for his avid pursuit of the oxygen of publicity, the democratic politician's *raison d'être*. He certainly made the most of his opportunity.

8

THE SENATE HEARINGS

The American inquiry into the loss of the *Titanic* was effectively a one-man show. Senator William Alden Smith, a Republican from Michigan and a member of the upper house's Committee of Commerce, got to his feet on Wednesday 17 April 1912, and proposed the creation of a special sub-committee to investigate. By that morning the extent of the disaster had become clear, even if detail was lacking, and the resolution, number 283 of the sixty-second Congress, second session, was passed unanimously. Its proposer was then appointed chairman, with six more senators as members, three Democrats and three Republicans. Senator Francis G. Newlands of Nevada was vice-chairman. None of the legislators knew more than the average, informed lay person about marine matters, but Smith availed himself of the advice of the Supervising Inspector-General of the Steamboat Inspection Service of the Department of Commerce and Labor, George Uhler.

Determined to waste no time, Smith acted with remarkable speed. He consulted the United States Attorney-General almost immediately after the vote to assure himself that he would have powers to prevent British witnesses going home, and then called on President Taft at the White House. On the afternoon of Thursday 18 April he rushed to Union Station to catch the train to New York.

Smith's conduct of the hearings was the subject of much controversy at the time and afterwards, on both sides of the Atlantic. We have noted the fiercely partisan approach of much of the American press, most of which was hostile to the Senator. British reaction contained strong elements of pique, snobbery and xenophobia. Here was a boon-docks American politician on the make probing the loss of a British-registered ship on the high seas and holding British subjects as witnesses before Britain had a chance to mount a "proper" inquiry. We have described the patrician sneers of British officials unable to get used to American openness and keenness to tackle issues head-on. But the urgency and scope of the inquiry, however erratic its conduct, which ranged from nit-picking ignorance to relentless probing, reflected the magnitude of the catas-trophe and the urgent desire of the public to know what had gone so horrifically wrong.

It did not set the tone for the subsequent British inquiry, which could hardly have been more different in atmos-phere, but at least it ensured that some issues which might have been swept under the carpet got a full airing: the American hearings were heavily reported by the British press. And the British investigation certainly took a lead from the American on such matters as condemning Captain Lord and improving safety at sea. The funda-mental difference between the two inquiries lay in motive: the Americans were looking for someone to blame for the disaster while the main motive of the British was to establish the facts with a view to preventing it recurring. The American inquiry was conducted by politicians, the British by lawyers and technical experts (although they were dominated by the chief law officers of the Crown, whose real job as political appointees was to exonerate His Majesty's Government).

Smith had served one full, six-year term in the Senate, having entered it in 1906, after eleven years as a member of the House of Representatives for a Michigan district.[1] He was born in 1859 in Dowagiac, a small town inland of the south-eastern shore of Lake Michigan. His career was a classical American story. A bright boy from a poor background forced to contribute to family funds by working in his time out of school, he also worked his way through college and law school to become an attorney in Grand Rapids, Michigan. A populist in political style and a bit of a demagogue, he presented himself as a man of the people uncontaminated by the great centres of power, whether in big business or in Washington. He was a Republican but purported to be an independent one, refusing to take sides in the great 1912 schism between Taft and his predecessor as President, Theodore Roosevelt. But he was apparently in tune with both leaders on one great issue of the day: he was opposed to the over-mighty trusts, especially Morgan's, the most swollen of them all. There can be no doubt that Smith hoped to be able to prove negligence on the part of White Star, nominally a British company headed by the unmistakably British Ismay, so that ordinary victims of the disaster could sue for compensation in American courts. He presented himself as the tribune of the people and undoubtedly worked hard at it; but his eagerness to blame the British conveniently led him to overlook the American J. P. Morgan's role as monopolist promoter of intense and unfair competition on the North Atlantic route and financier of an unsafe ship. This may or may not have been related to the fact that Morgan helped to fund Smith, something he did for many other American politicians, including both Taft and Theodore Roosevelt. He could afford it, and such largesse doubtless led him to believe that he would always be on the winning side.

Arriving in New York as the *Carpathia* was docking at pier fifty-four on the evening of the 18th, the Senator was driven by cab straight from the station to the ship and was shown to the doctor's cabin, where an exhausted Ismay was already briefing his American vice-president, Philip A. S. Franklin, who had arrived ten minutes earlier. After barely half an hour Smith disembarked to tell reporters, pointedly perhaps, that he anticipated no obstruction of his inquiries by British or shipping-line officials. He then made his way to the Waldorf Astoria

Hotel, where he was to open the inquiry the next morning.

The great hotel's ornate East Room was jam-packed. Normally used for banquets and conferences, the room contained several long tables. The sub-committee sat down one side of the central table with Smith in the middle, and each witness sat at the narrow end to their left. To the left of the witness was a stenographer. Reporters standing round the edges of the room barely had space to apply pencil to notepad. Officials, lawyers and witnesses sat at the other tables or else in tight rows on light chairs. Photographers were allowed to take pictures showing witnesses at the main table. A diagram of the *Titanic* was on display.

According to resolution 283, the sub-committee's remit was to determine responsibility for the disaster "with a view to such legislation as may be necessary to prevent ... any repetition". Senators were to inquire in particular into "the number of lifeboats, life-rafts and life preservers, and other equipment for the protection of passengers and crew; the number of persons aboard ... and whether adequate inspections were made ... and look into the question of possibility of international agreements to protect sea traffic and to make recommendations for legislation". In other words Senator Smith had *carte blanche* to examine every aspect of the disaster, backed by the legal power to subpoena anyone within reach.[2]

Witness number one was J. Bruce Ismay, aged forty-nine, permitted to make a brief statement before submitting himself to questioning by Senator Smith. Looking pale and tired, Ismay expressed his grief over the high loss of life and welcomed the inquiry, saying he had "nothing to hide". The lost liner had been "the latest thing in shipping" with no expense spared in her construction. His first appearance at the inquiry was mercifully brief. He gave the ship's speeds in revolutions: seventy from Cherbourg to Queenstown, seventy-two on the second day, seventy-five on the third, which was never exceeded. Seventy-eight was the specified full speed of the engines but they could probably have delivered eighty. The aftermost row of five single-ended boilers had not been fired but: "It was our [sic] intention, if we had fine weather on Monday afternoon or Tuesday, to drive the ship at full speed."

Ismay said he had been the sole representative of White Star aboard. Harland and Wolff had been represented by Thomas Andrews, who had died. Ismay insisted he had "never" had occasion to consult with the Captain about the movement of the ship, or vice versa. But he had arranged before the departure from Queenstown that the ship should not arrive at the entrance to New York harbour before 5 a.m. on Wednesday 17 April. Attempting to lay to rest the charge that the ship had been trying for a transatlantic record (the Blue Riband was indeed beyond her reach), Ismay said: "The *Titanic* being a new ship, we [sic] were gradually working her up." She had been sailing on the southerly westbound route.

Questioned on the thorny issue of how he came to get away in a lifeboat when so many of his customers, including women and children, failed to do so, Ismay said that at the time he boarded his boat, no women or children were in its vicinity, so "as the boat was in the act of being lowered away, I got into it". Once in the water, "we saw a light some distance off to which we attempted to pull and which we thought was a ship". He was dressed in pyjamas, slippers, suit and overcoat.

As for the sinking superliner, Ismay said he did not see her go down because he was "pulling away" with his back to her. The land-bound committee did not find anything odd in this statement. He must have been *pushing*, not pulling, on his oar (which could have been true: lifeboat oars were commonly plied by two people, one facing ahead, the other astern). He looked back and saw her green light. "I did not wish to see her go down." He opined that "she would have been here today" had the ship struck head-on instead of a glancing blow.

Ismay's first stint as a witness was doubtless a great strain for him, but much worse was to follow. As the rambling inquiry wore on, he was to be among several witnesses to be re-examined because of evidence which cast new light, if not doubt, on their earlier testimony.

Having begun with an obvious candidate for the post of scapegoat, the sub-committee called as its second witness the man whom many already saw as the hero of the tragedy: Captain Arthur Henry Rostron, who was anxious to restart his disrupted voyage to the Mediterranean. Imposing in white-covered, gold-braided cap, frock-coat and two medals, the master of the *Carpathia* since 18 January 1912 recited from his ship's log the orders he gave on receiving the distress calls from the *Titanic* and described how the survivors were brought aboard his ship. He saw only one dead body, of a crewman, in the water, but took three more aboard from a lifeboat.

Rostron said he had known Captain Smith for fifteen years but had met him only about three times. He thought his late colleague had chosen a course both safe and wise (but made no comment on his speed). Asked about the paucity of lifeboats on liners, Rostron said: "The ships are built nowadays to be practically unsinkable, and each ship is supposed to be a lifeboat in itself. The boats are merely supposed to be put on as a stand-by." He had the *Titanic*'s lifeboats half-lowered on entering New York harbour so as to be able to offload them as quickly as possible and had asked by wireless for tugs to be on hand to take them away; he would have had difficulty in docking with the clutter of extra boats.

Otherwise he ordered no wireless message to be sent without his express authority. Priority was given to relaying the lists of passengers' names. The first- and second-class lists had been relayed via the *Olympic* and when contact with her was lost (his wireless had a range of only 150 to 200 miles), the third-class names were passed to USS *Chester*. The list of surviving crew members was sent last. Private messages from survivors were handled on a first come, first served basis and transmitted when possible. Then he allowed one signal to his own company, Cunard, one to White Star and one to Associated Press, all giving the barest facts of the disaster. Rostron added that his Marconi man would not have picked up the distress call had it come only ten minutes later because he had been on the point of going to bed. Senator Smith knew he was speaking for everybody inside and outside the hearing room when he said: "Your conduct deserves the highest praise." Captain Rostron was allowed to return to his ship, which set sail at 4 p.m., and the hearing adjourned for lunch.

In the afternoon Guglielmo Marconi (1874–1937), son of an Italian marquis and an Irish mother, made a brief initial appearance. He said he had made his first successful attempt at wireless telegraphy aboard ship in 1897. His invention had saved many lives in January 1909, when the White Star liner *Republic* had been mortally damaged on being hit by the Italian ship *Florida* in fog near the Nantucket Lightship. The rescuing *Baltic* heard the CQD and saved all but a couple of the more than 1,500 passengers and seafarers on the two ships (one of the heroes was Jack Binns, the *Republic*'s wireless operator, who sold his story and later became a journalist). Marconi remained on hand for further questioning.

His place at the end of the table was taken by Second Officer Lightoller, a Lancashire man aged thirty-eight, senior surviving member of the *Titanic*'s crew. Holder of an extra master's certificate, Lightoller was something of a swashbuckler, a seasoned seaman with an adventurous career behind (and ahead) of him. At sea since thirteen, he had sailed round the world, tried his luck in the Yukon goldfield, and survived no fewer than five shipwrecks as well as a shipboard fire. (Despite his efforts during the disaster and as an assiduous company witness at both inquiries, he was never given a merchant command, even after distinguished service in the First World War as a

Royal Naval Reserve destroyer skipper, when he sank a U-boat by ramming. His retirement before the Second World War did not prevent him from taking a motorboat to Dunkirk in June 1940, when he was sixty-seven, to help evacuate the British Army.)

The pattern of proceedings at the American inquiry was already established by the time he was sworn in. Senator Smith was asking very nearly all the questions, often going into the most minute detail and frequently rowing back over points already covered. The first subject he raised with Lightoller, who had previously served on the *Oceanic*, was the *Titanic*'s sea trials. They had lasted about seven hours in all; William Murdoch had still been Chief Officer (and Lightoller First) when the ship arrived in Southampton, even during the final inspection on behalf of the Board of Trade by Captain Clarke. Lightoller described this as a "nuisance" because it had been "so strict".

Smith's darting questions touched briefly, butterfly fashion, on one unconnected topic after another, which often made it difficult for contemporary reporters to present a coherent account of the proceedings. There had been no time to prepare a strategy, let alone tactics for handling each witness or area of evidence. The reader of the record is left with the impression of an insatiable, uncritical omnivore of information, swallowing up facts at random. Only now and again did it become clear that Smith was working to an agenda, however unfocused, and had certain themes in mind. These included the suspicion that his maritime namesake and his officers had been drinking alcohol on duty and/or been negligent in some other way and that the British authorities had been complacent about safety.

Lightoller estimated that he had, rather improbably, been in the water for between thirty and sixty minutes in his life-jacket and said that the temperature of the water had been thirty-one degrees Fahrenheit (the level at which we know that the hull was at its most brittle) as he went off watch at 10 p.m. Lightoller described how he left the sinking ship at the very last moment. Collapsible B was lifted off the roof of the officers' house and overturned by the encroaching sea. The forward funnel chose that moment to fall "about four inches" from the boat; Lightoller went under, along with Colonel Gracie, Harold Bride, Mr Thayer and others. He and Gracie had been saved by a gout of air, forced out of a "blower" (ventilator) by the water rushing into the ship's hull, and were blown to the surface. Eventually some thirty people scrambled on to the upturned boat, including Jack Phillips, Bride's superior, who subsequently died. "She was packed standing from stem to stern at daylight," he said. He saw there were people in the water after the ship went down but they were half a mile from him (which sounds like an exaggeration).

Lightoller also said he had estimated that the lifeboats could carry a maximum of only about twenty-five people while hanging from the davits. He had decided to risk exceeding this number because the boats were new (the American inquiry did not unearth the fact, by his own later account unknown to Lightoller, that the boats could be lowered full). His opening evidence took up the bulk of the afternoon. After a break the inquiry went on into the evening, hearing from Harold Thomas Cottam, aged twenty-one, the *Carpathia*'s former wireless operator (relieved by another to assist the inquiry).

Cottam said he was paid £4 10s. per month plus board, and his equipment on the Cunarder had a maximum range of 250 miles. He had been on the point of going to bed but still had the earphones on his head because he was waiting for confirmation of receipt of a message sent to the *Parisian* – only to hear the stricken liner's CQD. The last message he picked up was, "Our engine-room is filling up to the boilers." From then on he had been on duty all but continuously; on Wednesday night Bride had been brought in to help until they arrived in New York.

Still revealing no specific line of inquiry, Smith next

called Alfred Crawford, a bedroom steward on B deck (first class) aged forty-one, from Southampton, who had been in boat eight. He gave the press another pair of heroes to celebrate, the elderly Isidor and Ida Straus, who elected to die together.

Captain Smith himself had been on hand while First Officer Murdoch supervised the loading of number eight and personally ordered Crawford into it to help with the rowing: "[Smith] gave us instructions to pull to a light that he saw and then land the ladies and return, back to the ship again. It was the light of a vessel in the distance. We pulled and pulled, but we could not reach it." About thirty-five people were in the boat, which was commanded by a seaman while a woman took the tiller. There were no male passengers, said Crawford; he noticed no suction effect when the ship went under. They were still pulling for the light when they sighted the *Carpathia* and turned towards her. Crawford was the second after Ismay of the sixteen Senate witnesses to mention what became known as "the mystery ship". (Assuming that the ship seen from the *Californian* was not the *Titanic* or vice versa, there were several candidates: the *Saturnia* and the *Mount Temple* stopped in the ice near the Boxhall position; and more than one vessel may have been seen from both the *Titanic* and the *Californian*.)

The first day of the inquiry ended at last at 10.30 p.m., leaving the press with reams of sensational material for the next day's editions. Charles Burlingham, White Star's American attorney, asked that the bulk of the surviving crew should be allowed to go home but Smith was reluctant to release anyone.

Smith and Senator Newlands, his deputy, were joined by the five other members of the sub-committee only when the inquiry moved to Washington for its third day. The second day began with the recall of Cottam. Among a miscellany of points elicited by Smith, he denied sending any message that the *Titanic* was proceeding to Halifax. He estimated that he had managed a total of ten hours' sleep between the CQD and New York nearly four days later.

Next to be heard was Harold Bride, a Londoner aged twenty-two with nine months' experience with the Marconi company. His pay as second operator on the *Titanic* was £4 per month and all found; he had been expected to work six-hour watches turn and turn about with his number one, Phillips. Bride said 250 telegrams had been sent between leaving Southampton and the collision. These included a few from Ismay to his offices in Liverpool and Southampton; but Bride had had no contact with him. Asked by Senator Smith whether there had been any messages to Captain Smith from his employers concerning the movement, direction or speed of the ship, Bride said there had been none. But he had personally handed the *Californian*'s ice-warning to the Captain at about 5 p.m. on Sunday the 14th.

He had slept through the collision and awoken just before midnight, when he went to relieve Phillips. As the two operators were changing places, the Captain appeared and ordered the distress call. Phillips stayed on to send it; the *Frankfurt* was the first to respond, followed by the *Carpathia* and the distant *Olympic*. The German ship's signal was very strong, indicating that she was reasonably close (in fact nearly 200 miles away – wireless works better after dark); but Phillips grew angry with his German colleague who seemed to lack a sense of urgency, eventually calling him a "fool" and telling him to stand by and keep off the air. By then they knew *Carpathia* was nearer and on her way. Bride next explained that "CQD" was an internationally known distress call also recognized by Germany. The *Frankfurt* operator "did not know his business, that is all". The *Carpathia* had grasped the situation at once.

Bride went on to say that the *Titanic*'s wireless was still functioning ten minutes before the ship sank; five minutes before that the Captain had put his head round the door and told the two operators to look out for themselves, formally relieving them of their duties. On emerging onto the boat deck Bride said he saw a collapsible boat being pushed down from the roof of the officers' house with a view to launching. He took hold of it but went over the side when it was washed overboard, upside-down, with Bride trapped under it in an air-pocket for "thirty to forty-five minutes" (which is highly unlikely, but every minute must seem like a lifetime in such desperate straits). He managed to extricate himself and join the others standing on the boat, all of whom had been immersed first: "dozens" had struggled to get on. His colleague Phillips was there, too, but died before they were rescued: his body was left in the sea.

"The last I saw of the Captain, he went overboard from the bridge," said Bride. "He jumped overboard from the bridge when we were launching the collapsible lifeboat." Bride said he had noticed no suction although he had been swimming within 150 yards of the ship. The operator, unable to walk thanks to his injured and frostbitten feet, took up the bulk of the morning session with his often confusing evidence.

In the afternoon Herbert John Pitman, aged thirty-four, Third Officer with sixteen years at sea, briefly gave his personal details before the adjournment. By this time thirty-five subpoenas had been served on crew survivors: the four officers, Bride and Cottam and twenty-nine crewmen. The chairman closed the second day's proceedings with a statement on his stewardship of the hearing thus far.

Explaining the subpoenas, he said he had received information that certain British subjects, including the officers of the *Titanic* and Ismay, were planning to return home. Such a course would have defeated the purpose of obtaining accurate information on the disaster without delay. He had visited the *Carpathia* and seen Ismay and Franklin, who assured him they would make themselves available.

Lightoller had been called early because he had been in charge of the ship until shortly before the disaster. Bride had been heard because his injuries made it hard for him to leave New York, and Cottam because his evidence tied in with his Marconi colleague's. Ismay had been called first because of his importance to the investigation and in order to have a statement from him on the record as soon as possible. All witnesses would remain available for further questioning as necessary. Subpoenas had also been served on a number of passengers whose names were not yet available. The next session would take place in Washington on Monday 22 April, in the Capitol, said Smith.

The Senate's hearing rooms are very large; but Smith's was understandably filled to bursting on the Monday and he issued a warning against unruly conduct. Having travelled to Washington, Pitman was not yet recalled. Instead Smith summoned Philip Franklin of New York, aged forty-one, vice-president in the United States of IMM. Its capital consisted of $100 million in shares and $78 million in bonds: the combine owned the International Navigation Company of Liverpool, which owned the Oceanic Steam Navigation Company, which owned the White Star Line ... IMM had thirteen directors, including Ismay (president), Lord Pirrie, J.P. Morgan Junior and Harold Sanderson (a vice-president). Franklin was an executive but did not have a seat on the board, although he had been in charge of IMM's American operation since its inception in 1902.

After hearing these corporate details, Senator Smith plunged into a tangle of cables, signals and wireless messages. The last routine one Franklin had received from the *Titanic* on Sunday 14 April reported her to be 550 miles south-east of Cape Race, which was passed to the press as usual.

What about the cruel cable from New York to Mr

Hughes in West Virginia, the next day, reporting that the *Titanic* was on her way to Halifax, where passengers would probably land on the Wednesday: "all safe – [signed] White Star Line"? Franklin said he had ordered urgent inquiries but had failed to trace the source. There were many employees at IMM's office at number nine Broadway, and there the only concrete information about the *Titanic* had come from the *Olympic*.

Franklin himself had been alerted at 1.58 a.m. New York time, when an unidentified reporter telephoned him at home in Manhattan to say that the *Virginian* and her owners' Montreal office (the Allan Line) were reporting the *Titanic* as sinking. He telephoned Associated Press, which had heard similar, and then IMM's Montreal office, asking them to contact the Allan Line for confirmation. He also ordered a message to be sent to the *Olympic* asking Captain Haddock to establish the *Titanic*'s whereabouts: "Wire us immediately her position."

Associated Press reported accurately at 3.05 a.m. New York time that there had been a CQD at 10.25 p.m. (12.15 a.m. *Titanic* time); and half an hour later a message saying she was sinking by the head. *Virginian*, *Baltic* and *Olympic* were in touch and making for her reported position. But the *Virginian* had picked up a final plea for help which, "blurred and ending abruptly", was broken off when MGY's transmitter was forever deprived of its power. IMM's first message that night was to the *Olympic* at 3 a.m. Eastern Standard Time. She gave up trying to make contact and reported the ominous silence at 9 a.m. EST, when she was 310 miles away. Four hours later Haddock relayed a message from the *Parisian* reporting that the *Carpathia* had reached the scene and found the boats.

At 2 p.m. IMM was still hoping against hope, telling Haddock: "We have received nothing from *Titanic* but rumoured here that she proceeding slowly Halifax, but we cannot confirm this. We expect *Virginian* alongside *Titanic*; try and communicate her." The press had raised this with Franklin, who had no idea of its origin. IMM had not been in touch with Marconi, but did press the *Carpathia* for survivors' names. Finally, at 6.16 p.m. EST, came Haddock's message confirming disaster and rescue. Within a quarter of an hour IMM received a message from Ismay (to "Islefrank New York", Franklin's telegraphic address): "Inexpressible sorrow. Am proceeding straight on voyage. *Carpathia* informs me no hope in searching. Will send names survivors as obtainable. Yamsi [Ismay's obvious business code]."

As Haddock resumed his crossing to Southampton he sent a last message to Franklin at 1.45 a.m. EST on 16 April: "Please allay rumour that *Virginian* had any *Titanic*'s passengers; neither has *Tunisian*; believe only survivors on *Carpathia*; 2, 3, 4 and 5th officers and 2nd Marconi operator only officers reported saved." All attempts by IMM to extract a reply from Rostron failed.

Franklin was unable to give details of safety provisions on the lost ship as White Star was run from the United Kingdom, where the line's marine superintendents and the Board of Trade were responsible. Senator Smith then asked: "Has the company [IMM or White Star], so far as you know, or any officer or director, interest in the building company [Harland and Wolff]?"

Franklin: "I have never heard of any." The reply was a testament to the invisibility of Lord Pirrie, on the board of the former and chairman, no less, of the latter, whose name had already been mentioned as a director of IMM. There was no reason why Smith should know Pirrie's key role, but Franklin's apparent ignorance about one of his directors lacks credibility.

The definitive passenger list had gone down with the ship, Franklin went on; booking lists for each port of call could however be obtained (eventually this was done, *faute de mieux*, unsatisfactory though they proved).

Franklin claimed that the lost ship exceeded the safety standards set by Lloyd's of London. She had cost £1,500,000 and could carry even more passengers than the *Olympic*. The minimum fare in first class was $125 in a shared cabin, in second $66 and in third $40. Responding patiently to Smith's barrage of unrelated questions, Franklin said Ismay had asked him to send an officer and fourteen White Star seamen in two tugboats to take charge of the thirteen recovered *Titanic* lifeboats in New York. The IMM vice-president recollected four messages from Ismay asking that the *Cedric* be delayed to take the crew survivors home. Franklin was aware of what press and public would make of such an action amid the furore over the disaster and ignored the requests. He let the *Cedric* leave on time on 18 April and earmarked the *Lapland* for the crew instead. Ismay himself meanwhile had ordered on the Friday, the day after the *Carpathia* docked, that all IMM ships be fitted with enough lifeboats for all aboard. Nobody could have foreseen the disaster, Franklin claimed: "The ship was meant to be its own lifeboat."

She was also to an unusual degree her own insurer, being covered on the open market for only two-thirds of her cost. "She was insured for, in round numbers, £1 million, the balance being carried by the IMM Company under our own underwriting scheme," Franklin said.

Darting backwards once again, a suspicious Senator Smith wanted to know why the company had wished to rush the crew home? "Men arriving under these extraordinary circumstances, not being on articles, are very difficult at times to control because a great many people are running after them for stories, and making them presents, and taking them out in the street [*sic*]. They stray away, and they get into endless trouble; and they are not controllable as are seamen and firemen ordinarily, from a ship when it is in dock under the command of an officer," said Franklin. Since the crew were not being paid at the time this does not seem surprising.

"It is the duty of every owner ... of a steamship, under similar circumstances, to get those men out of these temptations, and to get them away to their own homes and their own people and where they can go back again and sign on another ship and go to sea." Sending shipwrecked crew home at once was accepted custom and practice, using another line's ship if one's own could not provide. "The moment a ship goes down, the men's wages cease. But we, of course, take care of them," Franklin said, a touch piously one may think. "The articles end when the ship goes down."

The questioning of Franklin continued after the lunch break. He estimated accurately that five or six compartments must have been opened to the sea in the collision and confirmed that the *Titanic* had been three or four knots slower than the fastest Cunarders. He then read out extracts from White Star's instructions to masters, including this passage:

Commanders are reminded that the steamers are to a great extent uninsured and that their only livelihood, as well as the company's, depends on immunity from accident. No precaution which insures [*sic*] safe navigation is to be considered excessive.

Franklin added: "I do not believe there is any company crossing the Atlantic that carries such a large proportion of its own insurance as the subsidiary companies of [IMM]." Unfortunately the record does not give a clue to his bearing or tone when he said this – was such high exposure a matter for pride or embarrassment? But the facts speak for themselves: any loss or damage to one of its ships hurt IMM and its subsidiaries more than its competitors because the group was uniquely exposed on the insurance front. And its main asset, White Star, had a unique tally of lost and damaged ships, thanks not least to its commodore, Captain Smith.

It is impossible to escape the conclusion that the two facts – low cover, high risk – were connected. Even the substantial bonus paid to masters and officers on ships which managed to avoid hitting anything for a year apparently had insufficient effect on the bad record. To say that a company carries "a large proportion of its own insurance" can be seen as a euphemism for its refusal – or inability – to buy comprehensive cover (for the crucial damage to the *Olympic* in the collision with HMS *Hawke*, the owners were not covered at all).

The rest of day three was taken up by the evidence of the twenty-eight-year-old Fourth Officer, Joseph Groves Boxhall, of Hull, four and a half years with White Star. He described how the lifeboats had been tested before departure from Southampton, when two boats were crewed, lowered, rowed round the dock and hoisted back aboard. Boxhall was clear in his mind that boats should not be filled before they had been swung out on the davits and lowered to the boat deck; it was a matter of opinion whether they could be fully loaded from there before launch. The boats had been fully equipped in Belfast because Boxhall had checked them himself.

The Fourth Officer assured the senators that all the officers of the *Titanic* had been good, steady and reliable. Of himself he declared: "I am of temperate habits." No, he had not sailed with Captain Smith before. Nor had anyone mentioned icebergs to him on the night of the disaster, although the Captain had mentioned the possibility a day or two before and had marked ice areas on the chart. Boxhall thought the iceberg which did for the ship was low in the water, not reaching the rail (of the well deck) which was only thirty feet above the water. He thought it was a "long-lying growler" – an iceberg deceptively low in height, but lengthy and therefore more massive than it looked. At both official inquiries one of the most consistent conflicts of evidence was the inconsistency about the instrument of the ship's fate. No two witnesses seemed able to agree on any feature – size, shape, even colour – of the iceberg. This can only mean that virtually nobody actually saw it; by the time those curious enough to emerge on deck on a cold night had investigated the impact (which was not even noticed by many), the berg would have slipped past. Professional seamen were the most likely sources of an accurate description, but even they could not agree.

When Boxhall reported that mailbags were afloat on G deck, the Captain ordered the lifeboats made ready for launching. During this period the junior officer saw the masthead and side lights of a steamer on a converging course. Instructed by the master to get into the port-side emergency boat (number two), Boxhall had it rowed to 500 yards away; later he brought it back to 100 yards off to pick up more people. Like Marconi operator Harold Bride, he noticed little suction as the ship went down, although he pulled away somewhat as a precaution. As his boat was about to be lowered away, Boxhall said, he had some green flares thrown into it (not part of the boat's official equipment). Because he had fired them the *Carpathia* steered towards him, the reason why boat two was the first to be picked up. This was the last that the Senate inquiry heard from Boxhall that day; he was excused on medical grounds.

On the fourth day Third Officer H. J. Pitman, briefly seen at the end of day two in New York, was recalled. He began with the assertion that White Star conducted no full-speed trials, which was why there had been no all-out test of the *Titanic*. Another important point in Pitman's evidence was that there had simply not been enough coal to sustain a speed of 24 knots. The crash, he went on, awoke him with a sound "like a chain running over a windlass". He was the first of many to mention the ice on the forward well deck.

As Pitman was clearing boat number five, Ismay appeared and told him, "There is no time to waste." Ismay helped some women aboard and Murdoch sent Pitman on his way. The Third Officer had the impression that as they shook hands Murdoch did not expect them to meet again, whereas Pitman took another hour to realize there was no hope for the ship. "She gradually disappeared until the forecastle head was submerged to the bridge. Then she turned right on end and went down perpendicular." He heard four reports after the ship had gone under, probably from collapsing bulkheads, but did not believe there had been boiler explosions. They would have been out for two and a half hours, he said (forgetting that a few were working until the last to feed the generators). The ship had let off steam for about forty-five minutes.

Pitman claimed he wanted to row boat number five back to the scene and the crew started to do so, but the passengers had said this would risk being swamped and was a "mad idea". So they lay on their oars. Pressed hard by a badgering Senator Smith about the cries from the water, Pitman protested three times that he would rather not be questioned about this but Smith insisted. "There was a continual moan for about an hour ... [which] died away gradually," Pitman conceded. Smith then said: "If that is all the effort you made, say so ... and I will stop that branch of my questioning." Pitman confessed: "That is all, Sir; that is all the effort I made."

The unheroic Third Officer took boat number seven, which had no officer, in tow for a while and transferred some passengers to it from his own number five before slipping its rope. He saw the lights of the *Carpathia* at about 3.30 a.m. and half an hour later, when certain she was an approaching ship, started to row towards her. Pitman too did "not think boats are ever intended to be filled from the rail" but had to be lowered into the water before being fully loaded. (The surviving officers, who had the time on the *Carpathia* to reflect on the disaster, were suspiciously unanimous on this point; the evidence shows that the lost Murdoch and Moody were less worried about overloading and let more people, including men, into the boats before lowering them.) Pitman had also seen a stationary white light some three miles off but had not identified its source and therefore had no reason to row towards it. He also told the inquiry that he had no knowledge of the bunker fire before or after the *Titanic* was at Southampton.

The next witness was of special interest to the press as well as the senators: Frederick Fleet, able seaman aged twenty-four from Southampton, a lookout with four years' experience on the *Oceanic*, whose pay was £5 per month plus five shillings per voyage lookout money. This was the man who raised the alarm, albeit too late, about the iceberg from the crow's nest to the bridge. He described seeing the iceberg as "a black mass ... a little bit higher than the forecastle head" (i.e., about sixty feet tall). Fleet then astonished his audience with the admission that "I have no idea of distances or spaces". He had not had binoculars, although they had always been available on the *Oceanic* (and on the *Titanic* from Belfast to Southampton). His colleagues Hogg and Evans had asked for their return but were told none were available. Had he had glasses, Fleet maintained, he would probably have sighted the iceberg soon enough to save the ship.

On the fourth day, Tuesday 23 April, Ismay asked Smith if he could return to England, or at least New York. He had already asked and been refused on the Saturday, and was now refused again. He therefore paid a formal call, accompanied by IMM's lawyer, Burlingham, on the Senator at his office before the inquiry resumed on Wednesday. On being turned down a third time, Ismay put his request, surely unreasonable at this suspiciously early stage, in writing, only to receive an abrasive dismissal. The row about Smith's conduct of the inquiry in both America and Britain was already raging (the Senator however was not short of sympathizers in either country, who knew a public inquiry was the best route to whatever truth was available). Ismay had to stay until the end of the month.

Next up was Major Arthur G. Peuchen, aged fifty-three, chemical manufacturer and Canadian militiaman from Toronto – the first of twenty-one passengers called by the American inquiry (the British called only two, and then only on a secondary issue). The senators rightly felt that the passengers, some of whom were voters, had to be heard from, if only because their evidence would provide a useful counterpoint to officers and crew, who were not.

Peuchen was preparing for bed in first class when "I felt as though a heavy wave had struck our ship. She quivered ... Knowing that it was a calm night and that it was an unusual thing to occur on a calm night, I put my overcoat on and went up on deck. As I started to go through the grand stairway I met a friend, who said, 'Why, we have struck an iceberg.'" (He added later that some people had said they saw the iceberg slide past their cabin portholes.) The major saw the ice on the well deck, about four feet inboard of the starboard rail. The ship was listing to port after about twenty-five minutes, so he went back to his cabin and changed out of his pyjamas into warm clothing. On re-emerging he found a number of women in tears in the hallways on C deck. He also saw how a powerfully built officer (Chief Wilde) cleared about 100 stokers off the boat deck on his own.

The sails and masts had been taken out of the lifeboats he saw being prepared on the port side. When a quartermaster called for more oarsmen, Peuchen said, he told Captain Smith that he was an amateur yachtsman and was told to get into boat six, which he did by sliding down one of the launching ropes. The quartermaster at the tiller (Hitchens) refused to row back to the ship, even when a whistle from another boat seemed to be ordering him to do so. The women in the boat had wanted to go back for more survivors. Instead they rowed towards a light sighted by the quartermaster. Peuchen watched the lights go out on the *Titanic* from about five-eighths of a mile away and heard three explosions as she went down. When the *Carpathia* arrived, there were two large "islands" of wreckage in the water, past which she steamed very slowly. Peuchen could see no bodies.

"I imagine this crew [of the *Titanic*] was what we would call in yachting terms a scratch crew, brought from different vessels. They might be the best, but they had not been accustomed to working together." This explained why there were too few crewmen on hand to load and man the boats. Peuchen's assessment applied to almost any ship; not even a prestige liner enjoyed the luxury of a permanent crew. As we have seen, even the senior officers might be moved at a moment's notice to another ship, while the bulk of the crew was recruited anew for each round trip – which did not stop men from signing onto the same ship again and again. The most unusual feature of the crew was the large number of *Olympic* veterans, which meant that the *Titanic* had a high proportion of people who knew their way about – a crew rather less "scratch" than usual. Any sloppiness with the lifeboats was due to lack of interest and attention to drill in the White Star fleet: many crewmen had no idea of the lifeboat to which they were assigned, regardless of the lists posted at the start of the voyage. Peuchen knew there should have been a boat drill on the Sunday. He had been told by Lightoller that the officers did not know the boats could be fully loaded while suspended; but he could see from the strength of the equipment that this was possible.

In another bout of delayed reaction, Senator Smith recalled Fred Fleet at the beginning of day five and questioned him about his eyes. The able seaman said that as a lookout his eyes should have been checked by the Board of Trade every year or two and he had taken a test about a year before. His eyes had been sharp enough to see, both before and after leaving the ship, a bright light to port. Lightoller had told the crew to row towards it. Confirming Major Peuchen's testimony, Fleet said the women in his boat had wanted to go back for more survivors but had been overruled by Hitchens.

After hearing Fleet for the second time, Senator Smith took time out to warn the press: "From the beginning [of the inquiry] until now there has been a voluntary, gratuitous, meddlesome attempt on the part of certain persons to influence the course of the committee and to shape its procedures. Misrepresentations have been made, I have heard. Personally, I have not seen a single newspaper since I was appointed to this committee, because I did not wish to be influenced by those papers or unduly encouraged. Neither did I wish to take on any partisan bias or prejudice whatsoever. The committee will not tolerate any further attempt on the part of anyone to shape its course. We shall proceed in our own way."

Harold Godfrey Lowe was the next witness to be heard. The Fifth Officer came from North Wales, was twenty-eight years old, had spent half his life at sea and had been with White Star for fifteen months. Both the ship and her route had been new to him; his boat station had been number eleven. Prompted by a note from someone in the hearing room claiming to have seen Lowe drinking on the night, Senator Smith confronted him and received a flat denial: he was a teetotaller. When he had understood the extent of the disaster, he went to fetch a pistol before helping to load boat five under the eyes of Murdoch. He described later how he had used his weapon to deter would-be male boarders, notably "Italians", with one sideways shot per deck as he passed A, B and C on the way down, in the boat of which he eventually took charge, number fourteen. When Ismay got in the way of the loading of number five, Lowe told him to "get the hell out of it", whereupon the hapless managing director went to boat three.

Lowe thought there were about fifty in boat five, including some ten men, when it was lowered away; he too believed it could not be filled to its capacity of sixty-five until in the water. Lowe moved on to work with number three, where Ismay was still helping to load passengers despite Lowe's rebuke. There was no rush to get into either boat before the Fifth Officer moved forward to attend to number one.

By this time Smith and Lowe were obviously rubbing each other up the wrong way; as the Senator pressed his repetitive, nagging questions, Lowe became less expansive and more irritable. This was clearly in character; but Boxhall had also been put off by the chairman's manner. Relations were not improved by the one excuse for a belly-laugh proffered at the American hearing, when Smith solemnly asked the Fifth Officer what an iceberg was made of. Lowe could not resist it: "Ice," he replied, although he must have known there was more to it than that.

Lowe said he crossed over to port to help Sixth Officer Moody with boats fourteen and sixteen. Having loaded fifty-eight people into number fourteen as it hung from the davits, he got into it and took command. He had gathered several other boats, redistributed people among them, and waited "for the people to thin out" until it was safe to head back towards the wreck in a boat empty but for a handful of volunteers at the oars. At this last moment before going back, he spotted an Italian man "dressed as a woman" (i.e., with a shawl over his head): "I caught hold of him and pitched him" into one of the other boats. He then went back to the wreckage and picked four living people out of the water. One of them died shortly afterwards. He had seen no women in the water. Alone of the lifeboats, number fourteen hoisted a sail in the breeze that had come up and was able to steer towards the *Carpathia* when she appeared. Lowe had briefly taken a collapsible, awash and inverted, in tow, transferred twenty men and a woman and abandoned it with three male bodies aboard. The survivors had been standing on it up to their ankles in water. "Another three minutes and they would have been down."

The evidence of Boxhall, Pitman and Lowe appears to have persuaded Senator Smith to recall Lightoller on the afternoon of day five. The Second Officer was questioned on a broad spread of issues, ranging from the watertight doors to the lack of women on deck when the boats were loaded. He conceded that he supported Ismay's requests to hold the *Cedric* so that the crew, who had no work, could go straight home. Had fog not delayed the *Carpathia* on the way to New York they might have made it. Lightoller said he had in mind the British inquiry, bound to be held into the loss of a British-registered ship. Had he known about the Senate inquiry he would not have suggested such messages. Lightoller did his best for Ismay himself:

> I must say that at that time [on the *Carpathia*] Mr Ismay did not seem to me to be in a mental condition to finally decide anything. I tried my utmost to rouse Mr Ismay, for he was obsessed with the idea, and kept repeating, that he ought to have gone down with the ship because he found that women had gone down ... I tried to get that idea out of his head, but he was taken with it; and I know the doctor tried too, but we had difficulty in arousing Mr Ismay, purely owing to that, wholly and solely, that women had gone down in the boat [*sic*] and he had not.

Wilde had "bundled" Ismay into the lifeboat, Lightoller said. He thought a safe load in a descending boat was twenty to twenty-five. No, he had not seen a note in the chart room warning of ice; but Captain Smith had told him that he had received one at about noon on Sunday the 14th. Lightoller expected to be in the ice zone about 11 p.m. He disclosed that if ice was known to be prevalent, the company told masters to take the extreme southern westbound track before setting sail.

It would have been the job of the two pursers and their four assistants to inform the passengers of the emergency and guide them. They were assisted by the two ship's doctors, one of whom said "Goodbye, old man" to

Lightoller in the ship's last moments: none of these people survived. While he had been helping to launch the lifeboats he saw a ship four or five miles away, two points off the *Titanic*'s port bow.

Day five was brought to a close by Robert Hitchens, the thirty-year-old helmsman from Southampton. He had been steering for one hour and forty minutes, after two hours stand-by duty on the bridge (in support of his predecessor at the wheel). The course was north 70° west. There was a list of 5° to starboard five to ten minutes after the collision. At that stage the Captain sent the ship's carpenter to sound the ship.

Hitchens, who was in charge of it, was quite definite about numbers aboard lifeboat six: thirty-eight women, one seaman (Fleet), one Italian boy stowaway, Major Peuchen and two other male passengers. He had the boat rowed away from the wreck, towards a light which he thought belonged to a "cod banker", a Grand Banks fishing schooner. They could not get nearer to it, and later he said it might have been imaginary, although he had been ordered to row towards it. He told Peuchen firmly that he was in charge and let a Mrs Mayer hold the tiller, but took it back when she allowed the boat to go athwart the choppy swell which had blown up. He "borrowed" a fireman from boat sixteen to help row when they were tied together for a while. He had heard a lot of cries in the water but denied that the women had appealed to him to go back towards the wreck. He simply stayed clear out of fear of suction. He also denied drinking excessive quantities of whisky (as Mrs Mayer had told the press): he had taken a nip from a lady's flask.

Succumbing to yet another attack of second thoughts, Senator Smith called Marconi back for further questioning on the morning of day six. He wanted to know more about how the wireless company functioned and was told that the British staff were hired, and contracts with shipowners negotiated, by the joint managing director cum general manager in London, Godfrey Isaacs, brother of the Attorney-General, Sir Rufus Isaacs (a connection which will be shown to be central to the historical repute of the British inquiry led by the latter). The company had major contracts with Britain for wireless stations there and across the Empire.

Marconi said he happened to be in New York at the time of the disaster and first heard of it on the Monday evening at about 6.45 p.m. He boarded the *Carpathia* as soon as she docked and talked with Bride in the wireless room. (Cottam had already left the ship but telephoned his chief that night seeking retrospective permission for the interviews he gave *The New York Times*. Marconi also allowed the young operator to accept money for them.) Smith was openly suspicious of the inventor, knowing that the battleship USS *Florida* had intercepted four transmissions telling the operators on *Carpathia* to keep the story to themselves. Marconi insisted there had been no such order; he did not approve of such messages. He conceded that a report of the tragedy should have been transmitted, in the public interest. As master, Rostron had the right to order such a transmission whenever he liked (as he did when he felt the time was right).

Recalled again, Cottam denied receiving any "keep quiet" message but said Bride had done so. Cottam then admitted getting a signal telling him to join Marconi at the Strand Hotel (*New York Times* headquarters for the story) and to "keep your mouth shut" meanwhile. He went to the hotel where he telephoned Marconi for permission before unburdening himself (he did not mention the reporter led to him by Marconi aboard *Carpathia*). Cottam also said that he should have overheard the *Mount Temple*'s reported answer to the CQD but did not. Senator Smith at this stage believed the ship had been "just ahead of the *Titanic* ... and in sight of its officers"; people on *Mount Temple* that night had apparently told the press they saw the lights of the *Titanic* as she went down.

(Smith may not have been reading the papers but he was obviously very well informed about what they said.)

The rest of day six was taken up with simultaneous but separate interviews with crew survivors conducted by Smith and four other senators, to speed up the proceedings. They managed to get through a total of twenty-three, all of which are in the record. Taken together they repetitively built up a kaleidoscopic picture of events aboard ship and in the lifeboats which we have already described. Among the many items elicited or repeated were: initial reluctance by passengers to board the boats; many references to the lights of another ship; the lack of binoculars after Southampton; the ice on the forward well deck; the general sobriety of officers and crew.

As these witnesses were still being put through their paces a United States marshal boarded the *Californian* at 7 p.m. just after she docked in Boston. Captain Stanley Lord and his wireless operator, Cyril Evans, were served with subpoenas to appear before the Senate in Washington the next day. The two men took the overnight train to the capital.

Franklin of IMM was briefly recalled on 26 April, day seven, by a tired and irritable Smith, to be taken over familiar ground once more: who did or did not send which messages to whom. He was followed by a witness who had already told his sensational story to the Boston press for a fat fee: Ernest Gill, the *Californian*'s second donkeyman. His published affidavit was read into the record and Gill stuck to it. He above all was the witness who led both official inquiries to believe that the *Californian* had seen the sinking *Titanic* and her distress signals and done nothing.

Next to testify was Captain Lord. He gave the position where he said he had stopped in the ice, and when, and said it had taken him two and a half hours (*sic*) to reach the *Carpathia* on the morning after the collision. He had noted a steamer with one masthead light about four miles to the south at 11.30 p.m. But his first news of the disaster had come from the *Frankfurt* at about 5 a.m., confirmed by the *Virginian* at about 6 a.m. At daylight he had seen a steamer with a yellow funnel about eight miles away (*Mount Temple* for sure). Lord's evidence comes off the page as unexceptional and uncontroversial; there is no hint in questions or answers of the tidal wave of opprobrium soon to roll over him.

He was followed by Cyril Evans, who confirmed he had picked up the awful news from the *Frankfurt*; at about the same time the Chief Officer, Stewart, had mentioned the rockets seen during the night. Evans had warned the *Titanic* of ice at about 11 p.m. on the Sunday night and been told to "shut up" for his pains; but that proved she had heard him. Evans's hearsay evidence about the apprentice, Gibson, saying he had told Lord three times about rockets being sighted was damaging for Lord. But Evans also said that Gill had told him on the evening of 24 April that he expected to sell his story for $500. Senator Smith's obvious distaste for cheque-book journalism did not lead him to treat Gill with the disdain he showed towards the Marconi men on the *Carpathia*. After their appearances, Lord and Evans went back to their ship and were not heard from until the British inquiry. By then Lord's reputation was in ruins.

No such fate awaited Captain James Henry Moore, master of the yellow-funnelled *Mount Temple*, who was called on the eighth day, Saturday the 27th. According to the printed transcript, as we have seen, he corrected his longitude from 51° 15' west to 51° 41', but this was probably an error for 51° 14'. He described hearing of the CQD, changing course, receiving the corrected (Boxhall) position while forty-nine miles away, meeting first a schooner, then ice, and stopping for the latter about fourteen miles away. He had also seen a tramp steamer of 4–5,000 tons ahead and to the south of the port bow, heading north-eastward like himself. She was a foreign ship with no ensign but a black funnel embellished by a white band containing a device of some kind, and she gradually crossed over to starboard. The same ship was the only one in sight when the *Mount Temple* reached the CQD position at 4.30 a.m. There Moore sighted a field of ice measuring more than twenty miles by five or six and including icebergs 200 feet high. He searched until about 9 a.m. on the 15th, finding nothing; but he believed the wreck had stopped eight miles further east than reported in the CQD.

Moore strenuously denied press reports, attributed to his passengers, that rockets or signal lights had been seen from his ship at midnight: nobody had been on deck at that time. When he heard of the distress signals he immediately ordered the decks cleared, ladders, ropes and lifebuoys prepared and the lifeboats made ready for immediate launching. He had sighted the *Carpathia* and saw the *Californian* arrive; he also saw his tramp steamer and the Russian liner *Birma* (yellow mast and funnel). The *Mount Temple* must have been halted from about 3 a.m. in the ice, over five miles from where the *Titanic* sank, Moore thought: if the ice had been drifting at half a mile per hour it might well have covered the spot and moved the bodies and wreckage.

At this point the chairman's butterfly mind led him to reveal that Smith (Senator W. A.) had once met Smith (Captain E. J.) and been conducted round one of his ships (by a process of elimination the *Adriatic*, but the Senator could not remember the name).

Captain Moore went on to say that he had never known ice so far south and that he would not have maintained high speed in the *Titanic* after the warnings she had received. But Moore was a veteran of Canadian waters, obviously accustomed to meeting ice on more northerly routes and no less clearly imbued with a proper respect for it. He had done all he could. Senator Smith took him at his word, passing over or failing to notice the fact that the *Mount Temple* must have been motionless in the vicinity of the catastrophe, the lifeboats and the hard-working *Carpathia* for hours. Moore went out of his way to deny press reports "inspired by a passenger from Toronto" (unnamed but probably Dr Quitzrau, whose affidavit, cited above, was appended without comment to the inquiry record).

Up to now we have reported the proceedings of the American inquiry in some detail day by day, to present a picture of how it was conducted, the atmosphere, the participants and the incomplete jigsaw they painstakingly put together. As it wore on, the Senate investigation fell victim to the law of diminishing returns, expending more and more time and energy to discover less and less; we have already passed over great swathes of repetitious material in the record, and henceforward we need mention only testimony of special significance.

Recalled on day nine, Marconi now revealed the lapse of memory which had led him to "forget" his signed demand to the *Carpathia* for urgent details of the worst disaster in the history of transport, in which his invention had played a central and positive, extremely newsworthy and commercially exploitable role. Smith piled on the questions, looking also for any message sent by Ismay and wondering aloud why no notification had been sent to White Star until the *Olympic*'s on Monday the 15th. Marconi pointed out that any message from the *Carpathia* that day would have had to be relayed, possibly via the *Olympic* and Cape Race, as the rescuing ship's wireless was too weak for anything more direct. The Senator was still worrying away at the cruel "all safe/Halifax" message signed "White Star" and sent on the Monday evening. The Marconi executives present were reluctant to disclose the content of messages but Smith insisted. Franklin offered to produce all messages to and from White Star, IMM and Ismay.

Next in the firing line was Frederick Sammis, aged thirty-five, Chief Engineer of the Marconi Company of America. He took responsibility for the messages advising the operators to keep silent and telling Cottam to go to the Strand Hotel. He was happy to help modestly paid men make extra money from the press; there was no law against it and he had received nothing himself. British Marconi operators were paid about half as much as American because of the difference between the costs of living in the two countries. The bit firmly between his teeth, Smith put the worst possible interpretation on the evidence from Sammis, who politely admitted agreeing to the request from *The New York Times* for exclusive access to the operators, with Marconi's concurrence.

No doubt thoroughly satisfied with his latest haul, Smith turned to the passengers, starting with Hugh Woolner from London, who had travelled first class. He said he told Captain Smith that the windows of the Ismay screen on A deck were closed when the lifeboats were being prepared for lowering. Until the spanner for opening them was found and applied, passengers went up to the boat deck to board. Woolner then described how First Officer Murdoch fired his pistol to drive away a large crowd of men gathering round collapsible C, the boat Ismay slipped aboard so easily soon afterwards. Smith's questioning at this point is as good an example as any of his nit-picking, half-attentive, repetitious approach:

Q: Swarming into the boat?
A: Yes.
Q: Was that into this collapsible boat?
A: It was a collapsible, yes, Sir.
Q: That was the first collapsible that was launched on the port side?
A: On the starboard side. That was the other side.
Q: You were across the ship?
A: Yes.
Q: You were then on the starboard side?
A: Yes ...

Woolner helped Murdoch clear the boat (C; Ismay's boat)

and load it with women before jumping into it himself. The collapsible was rowed to a point some 150 yards from the sinking ship, which suddenly slid under with a rumbling roar. "You could not really see a thing when the lights went out. It was all brilliantly lighted at the stern end, and suddenly the lights went out, and your eyes were so unaccustomed to the darkness, you could see nothing, and you could only hear sounds."

Harold Bride now returned to state that he had received $1,000 from *The New York Times*, including $250 from Fleet Street. He went on to repeat his second-day account of the final minutes on the *Titanic* and took the opportunity to deny that he and Cottam were listening to the baseball scores on the way to New York (an even more unlikely activity then than now for Englishmen, especially when frantically busy). Senator Smith showed his hand a little:

Q: If the operator had been on watch on the *Californian*, and the *Californian* was only fifteen miles away, and your CQD call had been received, the entire situation might have been different?
A: Yes, Sir.

Boxhall was recalled to discuss the "mystery ship", already the most vexed question thrown up by the inquiry: Boxhall's version had three or four masts (and two rather than one masthead light) and had shown him her green, starboard light from five miles away. Smith at this point asserted that the *Californian* had been no more than fourteen miles away, but Boxhall effectively said this was irrelevant, because he would not have expected to see a ship so far away, nor would he expect to be able to see rockets at such a distance.

Cottam made his fourth appearance to tell of receiving $750 from *The New York Times*. He admitted getting the Marconi request for news and ignoring it because he was too busy: he had transmitted more than 500 messages after the rescue. He had discussed the money offers with Bride; they had received two such offers as the *Carpathia* approached her New York berth.

Boxhall was called yet again, to defend his navigational calculation. He rejected Captain Moore's keen estimate that it was eight miles out. Asked again about the notorious mystery ship, he said he first saw the two masthead lights, then the sidelights; the red light (*sic*) had been visible for most of the time, all with the naked eye. The ship had approached the port side and then turned away. It was not moving quickly and might have got into the ice and swung round while drifting. Captain Smith had been with him when they concluded that she was close enough to signal by lamp – five miles. "I saw the sidelights. Whatever ship she was, she had beautiful lights. I think we could see her lights more than the regulation distance [five miles], but I do not think we could see them [for] fourteen miles."

On the tenth day, Ismay was recalled for a rather longer grilling than on the first. He described the IMM maritime empire of J. P. Morgan, which included the *Californian*'s Leyland Line and half a dozen others. There was no company or personal connection between IMM and shipbuilders Harland and Wolff. (Once again there was no mention of the latter's chairman, Lord Pirrie, also a director of IMM; Ismay, as the recipient in his own home of the Ulsterman's proposal to build the "Olympics", was surely more aware of the Pirrie connection than anyone else.) Harold Sanderson, manager of White Star and a director of IMM, had been on board for the trials but not the disastrous voyage; for Ismay it had been the other way about.

Invited to describe earlier White Star losses, Ismay recalled the *Republic* and the *Naronic* – the latter, almost new, which simply vanished at sea, had not been insured, he said (no mention here of IMM's "own underwriting scheme"). The *Titanic* had been designed to float with her two largest compartments flooded, in case she was hit exactly on a watertight bulkhead by another ship. A head-on collision could not have sunk her. Ismay then produced the texts of all the messages he had sent (eight, all to Franklin) and received (four; three from Franklin and one from his wife) while on the *Carpathia*.

The White Star chief denied trying to influence Captain Smith or the running of his ship. "I should think very few commanders crossing the Atlantic have as good a record as Captain Smith had, until he had the unfortunate collision with the *Hawke* ... I think he had an exceptionally clear record." The reader will know better.

On leaving the *Titanic* Ismay had boarded the last collapsible to be launched on the starboard side; it had by no means been full.

Q: Why did you enter it?
A: Because there was room in the boat. She was being lowered away. I felt the ship was going down and I got in the boat.

I understand that my behaviour on board the *Titanic* and subsequently on board the *Carpathia* has been very severely criticised. I want to court the fullest inquiry, and I place myself unreservedly in the hands of yourself and any of your colleagues, to ask me any questions in regard to my conduct ...

So much for the repeated requests to Smith to be allowed to go home. Ismay went on to say that Captain Smith had asked for the return of the *Baltic*'s ice-warning so that he could put it up in the officers' chart room (separate from his own). He gave it back to Smith at about 7.10 p.m. on the Sunday. Ismay's main reason for being aboard had been to look for possible improvements in passenger facilities on the "Olympics". This marked the end of Ismay's American ordeal: he was told he could go home to England and left on 30 April.

The rest of the tenth day was taken up with evidence from passengers before the hearings were adjourned for three days. The indefatigable Smith returned to the Waldorf Astoria Hotel on Friday 3 May, the eleventh day, to interview more witnesses based in New York on his own. These included Melville E. Stone, the general manager of the Associated Press, serving 800 newspapers, who provided a detailed analysis of how the story broke and was handled by the agency.

After the first tips in the early hours of the Monday from Cape Race, Newfoundland, there was a silence which drove the news agency frantic. The Dow Jones wire service put out the "all safe/heading for Halifax" rumour at 9.30 that morning; it went round the world. The story lasted through the day; it was only at about 7 p.m. on Monday the 15th that Associated Press received the report (Franklin's announcement of the *Olympic* message) that the ship had sunk with great loss of life. At that time the *Carpathia* had been out of range and all her messages had to be relayed. Associated Press strove from Tuesday to Thursday to raise her. Stone revealed the offer from Marconi's on Thursday to sell Associated Press an exclusive which never came.

On the following day Smith, still in New York, examined John R. Binns, the *Republic*'s erstwhile operator, who had made himself and his former employer, Marconi, world-famous by successfully calling for help by wireless, thus saving many hundreds of lives. He had gone on to work under Captain Smith on the *Adriatic* and *Olympic* before turning to journalism, encouraged by his freelance earnings from the *Republic* saga. His then employers had urged him to keep his story for *The New York Times* "owing to their friendly connection with the Marconi Company". Binns, now a nautical correspondent, opined that a weak point in the "Olympics" was their expansion joints, inserted to reduce vibration. He also made the astute and crucial observation that *no consideration had been given to the possibility of a collision by a glancing blow* in designing the ship. The big Cunarders had benefited from their very robust, cellular structure, a qualification for the British Government subsidy to Cunard (the Admiralty, which imposed this condition, obviously knew more about keeping damaged ships afloat than the Board of Trade).

After two more hearing days in New York, Smith was back in Washington on 9 May to chair the fourteenth day in plenary session. The managing editor of Dow Jones, Maurice L. Farrell, now gave a rundown of his service's output on the terrible story. Its source for the false "all safe" report had been the Laffan news agency of Boston (owned by the *New York Sun*), using a Montreal dateline. Another of its invented contributions to the legend was a baseless report that the lost ship was carrying $5 million in bonds and diamonds. Laffan, obviously the leading source of contemporary *Titanic* fiction, also put out the false reinsurance story. At noon on the Monday it had the *Titanic* serenely heading for New York ...

Farrell produced a Dow Jones article on IMM, based on its annual report for the calendar year 1911. It had earned $38 million and made a gross profit of $8.5 million; from the surplus of $4.5 million, $3.5 had gone on depreciation, leaving a net surplus of just $1 million (a fraction of the value of the lost ship). IMM shares had fallen fifty cents to $5.50 on Monday 15 April but recovered to $6 the same day. Preference shares were marked down to $20 but rose to more than $23, for a net loss compared with the previous business day of just seven-eighths of a cent in light trading. Even when the loss was confirmed on the Tuesday, relevant shares and bonds dropped between one and three points, and only temporarily. Since the bulk of the stock was owned by Morgan interests, this rigidity comes as no surprise.

Farrell thought a net loss in the disaster of $2–3 million would hardly break IMM. He then recited some of the Morgan conglomerate's history, from a background article by Dow Jones written in the semi-crippled, wire-service manner. Morgan had promoted IMM in October 1902; the company had "never really floated", Farrell read:

Insurance companies and other underwriters had to hold their bonds, which represented real value, and they have always sold on this side of the water for far less than replacement value of the property, to say nothing of goodwill.

On the other side of the water the capture of White Star Line by American banks aroused storm of indignation in England, and caused heavy subsidies for Cunard Steamship Company and rivalry of [*sic*] building of big ships. In a few years all steamship companies suffered an era of low rates and reduced or suspended dividends.

Recently tonnage rates over the world have been much higher, and prosperity and dividends and increased surpluses were in sight.

The record of IMM seems to be thus far the poverty of low ocean rates or, on high ocean rates, steamship disaster.

In English this seems to mean that IMM had overstated the value of its collateral, and also initiated fierce and unfair competition which decimated everybody's earnings; further, IMM was plagued either by low rates or, when rates were high, by disasters. How embarrassing and irritating this must have been for a man like Morgan, who prided himself on his Midas touch.

The last three days of the American inquiry (fifteen to seventeen) were largely taken up with reading affidavits into the record, including Dr Quitzrau's and those of Mrs M. D. Douglas and Mrs E. B. Ryerson, who swore that Ismay showed them the ice-warning message (which he had denied). Smith also examined Captain John J. Knapp, USN, Hydrographer of the Navy, about ice-warnings and charts; but he only added to the confusion about the relative positions of the *Titanic*, the *Californian* and others on day sixteen, 18 May, the last day of the Washington hearings.

The final day of the Senate inquiry came at last on 25

May, when Senator Smith was back in New York to visit the *Olympic* before she left for Southampton later that day. Captain Haddock described hearing of the disaster direct from the *Titanic* via his own wireless operator, E. J. Moore. He also received a signal from Captain Rostron during the Monday saying, "Bruce Ismay is under opiate." Marconi-man Moore gave brief evidence on the messages he had handled or overheard. The very last witness was Fred Barrett, late of the *Titanic*, who told Senator Smith of his experiences, familiar to us, both in the stokehold, when the water burst through the ship's side two feet above the floor, and then in boat thirteen.

William Alden Smith wasted no time in presenting his report to a packed Senate on Tuesday 28 May 1912. It was twenty-three pages long and was supported by an overwritten speech. It was an oration to stretch the limits even of the florid standards of old-style American political rhetoric. Here is a brief sample:

> We shall leave to the honour and judgment of England its painstaking chastisement of the British Board of Trade, to whose laxity of regulation and hasty inspection the world is largely indebted for this awful fatality ...
>
> In the face of warning signals, speed was increased and messages of danger seemed to stimulate her to action rather than to persuade her to fear.

Senator Smith was highly critical of Captain Smith, berating his "indifference to danger" and his "overconfidence and neglect to heed [*sic*] the oft-repeated warnings of his friends". Lightoller was criticized, directly over the missing binoculars and indirectly for condoning the ship's high speed and mishandling the launch of the boats.

The report itself wrongly stated that the sub-committee had heard eighty-two witnesses. We count sixty-eight plus

THE ILLUSTRATED LONDON NEWS

REGISTERED AS A NEWSPAPER FOR TRANSMISSION IN THE UNITED KINGDOM, AND TO CANADA AND NEWFOUNDLAND BY MAGAZINE POST.

No. 3811.— VOL. CXL.   SATURDAY, MAY 4. 1912.   SIXPENCE.

The Copyright of all the Editorial Matter, both Engravings and Letterpress, is Strictly Reserved in Great Britain, the Colonies, Europe, and the United States of America.

Ismay (hand to moustache) testifying at the first Senate hearing at the
Waldorf-Astoria hotel in New York. Senator William Smith, the chairman,
is reading with his right elbow on the table.

Philip A. S. Franklin, New York vice-president of International Mercantile Marine, provides cover for his chief, Ismay, on the way to the hearings.

Robert Hitchens, helmsman of the *Titanic*, spoke at both inquiries: here he makes his point in London.

Attorney-General Sir Rufus Isaacs questions Ismay at the British Inquiry, chaired by Lord Mersey.

Sir Cosmo Duff Gordon, one of his £5 cheques for a rescuer, and his wife, "Lucile".

Guglielmo Marconi (right) and the chief executive of his British company, Godfrey Isaacs, brother of the insider-dealing Attorney-General.

A view of the bow of the *Titanic* two miles beneath the Atlantic and, inset, the man who found her, Dr Robert Ballard.

Artefacts recovered from the wreck and displayed at the National Maritime Museum, Greenwich, in 1995 include a porthole - and the bell from the crow's nest which was the knell of doom for the *Titanic*.

The starboard propeller of the *Titanic* as it is today. The arrow points to the number "401".

twenty-two reappearances (some witne...
many as four times), plus three writte...
counting the affidavits on White Star'...
cancelled hire of a special train to collec...
Halifax). The salient feature which disting...
dence gathered by the pell-mell American...
that given at the ensuing, more deliberate B...
the roughly equal numbers of crew membe...
passengers and extraneous witnesses called...
short time available for organization and selec...
a remarkably balanced exercise in information...
The testimony of the passengers was a usefu...
point to some of the crew's, who might well h...
excusing themselves or going easy on their once a...
ibly future employer (had it been left to Lighto...
example, Ismay's role might well have been see...
gentler light).

The report dismissed the *Titanic*'s sea trials as...
functory and the lifeboat tests and procedures as...
more so. Here, in advance, was a necessary correctiv...
the later British findings. Captain Smith had had at le...
three ice-warnings but gave them no heed. "The spee...
was not relaxed, the lookout was not increased." But th...
Captain had asked to be wakened if anything unusual
occurred and Lightoller had warned the lookouts to keep
a special watch for ice. In the collision five compartments
had flooded almost at once. "The supposedly watertight
compartments were NOT watertight and the sinking of
the vessel followed" (Smith's emphasis). There was no
direct attack on the shipbuilders.

Ships reported in the vicinity of the wreck (in order of
nearness) had included the *Californian* at nineteen and a
half miles, the *Mount Temple* (which passed an unknown
schooner and overheard the *Titanic*'s first and last distress
messages), the *Carpathia* (fifty-eight miles), the *Birma*,
Frankfurt, *Virginian*, *Baltic* and *Olympic* at 512 miles.

Sixteen witnesses from the wreck, including officers and
experienced seamen, had seen the light of a ship, which

THE RIDDLE OF THE TITANIC

not responded to rockets or lamp signals. The US
ort went on to say:

t about the same time the officers of the *Californian*
dmit seeing rockets in the general direction of the
Titanic while several [*sic*] of the crew testify that the
sidelights of a large vessel going at full speed were
plainly visible from the lower deck at 11.30 p.m. ship's
time, just before the accident ...

The committee is forced to the inevitable conclusion
that the *Californian*, controlled by the same company,
was nearer the *Titanic* than the nineteen miles reported
by her captain, and that her officers and crew saw the
distress signals of the *Titanic* and failed to respond
to them in accordance with the dictates of humanity,
international usage and the requirements of law.

This had been "most reprehensible" and Lord had
incurred "a grave responsibility".

Had assistance been promptly proffered, or had the
wireless operator ... remained a few minutes longer at
his post on Sunday evening, [the *Californian*] might
have had the proud distinction of rescuing the lives of
the passengers and crew of the *Titanic*.

The report criticized the confusion over the loading and
manning of the lifeboats. But for that, several hundred
more could have been saved. It also noted the inaccuracy
of the witnesses who had considerably exaggerated the
numbers of survivors in each boat. Fears of suction as the
ship went down had proved exaggerated too. The senators
were inclined to accept that ice had covered and/or moved
the bodies and the wreckage with the help of currents
(preferring this theory to the idea that Boxhall's position
was wrong; the latter possibility was not mentioned). No
explanation had been found for the "most reprehensible"
hoax message about Halifax: the Western Union office

where it had been handed in was in the same building as IMM on Broadway. The committee criticized the Marconi company for helping its operators to profit from cheque-book journalism and was pleased to note that Guglielmo Marconi himself had banned any repetition.

Senator Smith and his colleagues made a series of recommendations. Calling for international action, they proposed applying stricter United States safety regulations to foreign ships calling at American ports unless owner-countries tightened up their own rules. A lifeboat place should be provided for every passenger and crew member; four crew and a specified group of passengers should be assigned to each boat; drill should be strictly and frequently enforced. Wireless should be manned round the clock, amateurs should be barred from interfering and secrecy of transmissions should be protected by law. Rockets should be fired only as distress signals. Ships should have a high double bottom or longitudinal water-tight bulkheads, giving a watertight "skin" within the hull; watertight bulkheads should extend up to a watertight main deck. These proposals were to transform safety at sea; only when the roll-on, roll-off ferry was introduced half a century later to speed up turnaround, and therefore profit, was cellular construction set aside – with tragic results for the *Herald of Free Enterprise* (1987) and the *Estonia* (1994), to name but two.

A Bill proposed later by Senator Smith tackled many of the shortcomings his sub-committee had identified and also sought to extend anti-trust law to the shipping industry, which was called upon to be more open about who owned what at sea. This was the nearest Smith came to addressing, belatedly, Morgan's covered-up role in the *Titanic* tragedy. In the end it took the Clayton Act of 1914 to plug the huge loopholes in the original anti-trust law, the Sherman Act of 1890.

Meanwhile the International Ice Patrol was set up to watch for icebergs. Run by the United States Coast Guard and funded by the North Atlantic nations, it has taken to the air but remains a most practical memorial to the *Titanic*.

Senator Smith merely deduced, albeit cogently, in his speech that the very presence aboard of Ismay from IMM/White Star and Andrews from Harland and Wolff stimulated the heedless Captain Smith to put on speed. All were British. Their government was blamed for its laxity over safety standards at sea and two British captains – one dead, the other damned without trial – were held to be negligent.

In this most important sense, given Smith's anti-trust posture and his claim to independence at the outset, his investigation was a cover-up, and the attack on the British in part a diversion. The masking of American involvement in the considerable person of J. P. Morgan and his almighty interests was a lie by omission. It was his anything-goes approach to business which, more than anything else, had latterly accentuated the traditionally competitive tendency in shipping. It was ultimately he who encouraged lines to cut more corners, save more time and not shrink from dirty tricks on the North Atlantic route, such as the cartel with the Germans aimed at destroying Cunard.

Morgan, it will be recalled, pleaded illness as his excuse for not joining the ship's first and last voyage. Two days after the *Titanic* sank, he was found by the American press at the Grand Hotel in the French spa of Aix-les-Bains, where he was taking the waters. He was in excellent health and the company of his French mistress.

Even so, the chairman's gavel was not after all transformed into a hammer of the trusts.

9

THE BRITISH COURT OF INQUIRY

The "formal investigation into the loss of the SS *Titanic*" began in London on 23 April 1912, when the Lord Chancellor appointed a Wreck Commissioner under the terms of the Merchant Shipping Acts. The Home Office on 26 April nominated a panel of five assessors, all nautical experts, to assist him. On 30 April the Commissioner was formally requested to inquire into the loss of the *Titanic* by Sydney Buxton, the President of the Board of Trade (commerce minister), whose statutory duty it was to investigate shipwrecks. It was also his department's statutory duty to regulate safety at sea, including construction standards and emergency provision, a duty in which the Board had self-evidently failed.

Ultimate responsibility for public safety lay of course with the Government as a whole which conveniently, through various departments (the more the merrier for buck-passing purposes), chose the judge, the jury (assessors), the prosecutor (the Attorney-General and learned friends) and all the official witnesses (government servants to a man) in a legal process largely concerned with its own shortcomings. Small wonder that the word "whitewash" was commonly applied to the inquiry even before it ended. The Marine Department of the Board of Trade manipulated the proceedings behind the scenes, as the files in the British Public Record Office show.

The court of inquiry convened for the first time on Thursday 2 May 1912. Its remit took the form of twenty-six questions to which it was to find answers. Neither guilt nor damages were at issue: this was neither a criminal nor a civil court but one of investigation, where the rules of procedure and evidence were rather less stringent than at a trial. The questions ranged from how many passengers and crew had been aboard the casualty to what amendments were needed to shipping law. Question twenty-four originally asked: "What was the cause of the loss of the *Titanic* and of the loss of life which thereby ensued or occurred? Was [*sic*] the construction of the vessel and its arrangements such as to make it difficult for any class of passenger or any portion of the crew to take full advantage of any of the existing provisions for safety?" This question was the only one to have its text substantially amended by an insertion very late in the investigation, as will be made clear.

What sort of a man was to preside over the British investigation, whose newsworthiness was in no sense diminished by the American inquiry that was already in full swing? On paper he was the ideal man for the job. John Charles Bigham (1840–1937), as his title, Baron Mersey of Toxteth, implies, was a Liverpool man, who worked for seven years in his father's shipping firm before reading for the Bar, qualifying in 1871. Some schooling in Germany and university in France made him trilingual. Unimposing with his reedy voice, he rose rapidly in the law thanks to sheer forensic ability, becoming a Queen's Counsel in 1883, a Liverpool MP in 1895 until made a High Court judge in 1897, and president of the Probate, Divorce and Admiralty Division in 1909. Heart trouble obliged him to give this up; he was ennobled in 1910 and became a sort of journeyman judge, serving on various commissions and the like.

His first move now was to appoint a secretary, in the dashing form of his adventurous son, the Hon. Clive Bigham (1873–1956), sometime captain in the Grenadier Guards, government courier, explorer, spy, journalist, author and polymath. Bigham swiftly and efficiently set up the necessary machinery – an administrative office; all the trappings of a court (bench, dais, witness-box and long tables); a stenographic service; arrangements for witnesses, lawyers, reporters and hundreds of spectators; a twenty-foot half-model (starboard side) of the *Titanic*, a forty-foot diagram of her layout and a vast chart of the North Atlantic. He also chose the venue, the drill hall of the London Scottish Regiment, a volunteer unit of the reserve. The building was large enough to parade troops indoors, and was typical of such Victorian premises across the country except for its smart address in Buckingham Gate, just down the street from the Palace. Bigham's best efforts in covering the brick interior walls with long burgundy drapes and hanging sounding boards from the ceiling had little effect on the appalling acoustics in the galleried hall, about which there were endless complaints.[1]

Leading counsel for the Board of Trade was the newly appointed Attorney-General himself, the Government's chief law officer, Sir Rufus Isaacs, KC, MP. He was supported by the Solicitor-General, Sir John Simon, KC, MP, Butler Aspinall, KC, Mr S. A. T. Rowlatt and Raymond Asquith, son of the Prime Minister of the day. Isaacs (1860–1935), son of a Jewish fruit merchant in the East End of London, left school at fourteen, ran away to sea at sixteen, worked as a jobber at the Stock Exchange until "hammered" (declared a defaulter on a deal) and finally settled down to read for the Bar, which he joined after studies in Brussels and Hanover. Physically and mentally gifted, he had found his *métier* as an advocate and rose swiftly in the profession, entering Parliament as the Liberal Member for Reading, Berkshire, in 1904. Six years later he was Solicitor-General; Isaacs joined the Cabinet as Attorney-General early in 1912 (he was to be Lord Chief Justice in 1913 and later served successively as Ambassador to Washington, Viceroy of India and Foreign Secretary, being made Marquess of Reading in 1926).

Isaacs and his brother Godfrey, joint managing director of Marconi's British company since 1910, developed a dubious financial relationship in the very week that the

Titanic sank, enabling the Attorney-General to make a nice profit from the disaster. In March 1912 Marconi's won its great contract to link the British Empire by wireless. Godfrey owned a large block of stock in American Marconi. On 9 April 1912 he offered to sell some of his holding to his brothers Harry and Rufus, before the London Stock Exchange was due to start trading in the shares on 19 April. Harry accepted but Sir Rufus declined. On 17 April, the day that the loss of the *Titanic* was confirmed in the British press, Sir Rufus changed his mind and bought 10,000 shares at £2 each. On the same day he assigned 1,000 shares to each of two senior colleagues, the Chief Whip of the Liberal Party and the Chancellor of the Exchequer, a certain David Lloyd George. When dealings began on the 19th the shares were quoted at £3 5s. and rising, boosted by the role of wireless in the rescue. On that same day Sir Rufus sold nearly half his holding for a splendid profit.

This and other outrageous cases of insider-dealing did not become known until the beginning of 1913, and when a House of Commons Select Committee probed the "Marconi scandal" in May that year, it did not make an issue of the significance of the date on which Sir Rufus Isaacs had bought his shares.[2] Meanwhile, whereas a suspicious Senator Smith had treated Marconi as the kind of monopolist he had dedicated himself to opposing, Attorney-General and major shareholder Isaacs was to handle him with something not unadjacent to reverence. As the British inquiry wore on, Mersey did not defer to Isaacs as such but showed willing to take his "advice" on how the hearing should proceed as well as on what and from whom it should take evidence. The Attorney-General took centre-stage at the beginning and end of the inquiry and conducted most of the examinations-in-chief.

White Star retained Sir Robert Finlay, KC, MP, Mr F. Laing, KC, Maurice Hill, KC, and Norman Raeburn. The National Sailors' and Firemen's Union, the lower deck survivors and the families of lost crew members were represented by Thomas Scanlan, MP. Clement Edwards appeared for the Dockers' Union and Mr W. D. Harbinson for the third-class passengers. Mr C. Robertson Dunlop was permitted to exercise a watching brief only, on behalf of the owners, Captain and officers of the *Californian*. These were the principal figures among a shifting population of some two and a half dozen lawyers at the front of the hall; the most significant late entrant was Henry Duke, KC, for Sir Cosmo and Lady Duff Gordon.

Several British archives hold copies of the evidence, usually in an unwieldy and sometimes crumbling, bound volume of over 900 foolscap pages. The proceedings of each of the thirty-six London hearing days were rushed out by His Majesty's Stationery Office, the government publisher and printer, as a booklet for 1s. 6d. The American evidence, also published first in sections and then in a bound version, runs to nearly 1,200 printed pages, but they are barely half the size of the British.

Lord Mersey's court was spared the over-elaborate formality of the High Court: judge and barristers were dressed in subfusc but without the wigs and gowns which remain a feature of criminal and civil proceedings in England to this day. Photographers were even allowed to take pictures inside the drill hall on the opening day, which was devoted entirely to procedural matters. Isaacs outlined the basic facts of the disaster and how the formal investigation had come into being before reading out the twenty-six questions drawn up by the Board of Trade for answering by the court. In fact most of them were multiple or subdivided; the total number of individual questions exceeded 150. Isaacs concluded:

> Those are the questions which we submit to the court at the present moment ... We are at liberty at the close of our case to supplement those questions or to modify them if we think fit.

How convenient for the Government and how brazenly manipulative. Having listened attentively but with difficulty to his learned friend, Sir Robert Finlay asked if the inquiry could be moved to a large committee room at Westminster so that everybody could hear what was going on. This proved impossible.

Isaacs was back on his feet on day two, going into the facts of the disaster in detail and starting with a description of the lost ship, her crew and passenger capacity, her lifeboats and their capacity, the numbers aboard and her watertight bulkheads. He described conditions in the Atlantic and the track followed, marked "Mail steamers outward, 15 January to 14 August" on the chart, before moving on to the ice-warnings from the *Caronia* and the *Baltic*. At this juncture Lord Mersey interposed:

> Commissioner: Mr Attorney, am I right in supposing that she ran right into the locality where the ice was after the warning that the ice was there?
> Attorney-General: Yes.

The increasing cold had been an indication of the proximity of icebergs before the collision, Isaacs said, going on to describe how the crow's nest bell tolled three times. Inadequately briefed, the Attorney-General said Captain Smith's record had been exemplary apart from the *Olympic/Hawke* collision which was still with the Court of Appeal; but Smith had not been blamed because the pilot was in charge at the time. Isaacs was not yet in full command of the facts because of the absence of so many witnesses. But he sketched the scene in the lifeboats and went on to say:

> My Lord, I think that one thing must emerge from this inquiry, and that is that if it had not been for that marvel of science, wireless telegraphy, I doubt very much if anyone would have been picked up in these boats, or

at least whether as many would have been saved as were actually saved.

Spoken like a true Marconi shareholder. One can only speculate about the reaction of Lord Mersey, who cannot be dismissed as a mere pawn of the Establishment, had he known of Isaacs's financial interest.

The Attorney-General moved on to analyse the passengers by class, gender and percentages lost and saved and added that a minimum of sixteen lifeboats was required by Board of Trade rules for a ship of more than 10,000 tons, the largest category recognized by the 1894 Merchant Shipping Act.

After the opening address by Isaacs there was enough left of the second day to examine two witnesses out of nearly 100 who would appear in the box. The first was Archie Jewell, one of the six lookouts. A coherent and self-possessed witness at eighteen, he told how the ice alert had been passed on in the crow's nest and how he had experienced the collision. He was then taken through his experiences in lifeboat number seven: "We stopped there and watched her gradually sink away. We could see the people about on the deck before the lights went out."

Thomas Scanlan, for the crew, brought out the absence of binoculars, of the Sunday boat drill and of a compass on Jewell's lifeboat. He had been to starboard of the wreck before and after leaving her but had seen no other ship until picked up by the *Carpathia*. Mersey congratulated Jewell on the quality of his evidence, a rare compliment.

The second witness, Able Seaman Joseph Scarrott, was examined by Aspinall for the Board of Trade. He told of the impact, the ice on the deck and his impression of the iceberg: like the Rock of Gibraltar as seen from Europa Point. He at least had seen people rushing about the ship: members of the crew rushed on deck, foreign men tried to rush his boat number fourteen, causing Fifth Officer Lowe to fire his pistol. When Lowe returned to the scene, Scarrott saw hundreds of corpses in life-jackets amid much wreckage. Describing how Lowe and his crew picked up four people from the water, Scarrott vividly recalled with gestures the circumstances in which they found one of them:

> He was a storekeeper; he was on top of a staircase ... he was kneeling there as if he was praying, and at the same time he was calling for help. When we saw him we were about from here to that wall away from him, and the boats, the wreckage was that thick – and I am sorry to say there were more bodies than there was wreckage – it took us a good half hour to get that distance to that man to get through the bodies. We could not row the boat; we had to push them out of the way and force our boat up to this man ... We put out an oar ... and he got hold of it, and he managed to hold on, and we got him into the boat.

One of the four they picked up died as Lowe and his men made sail and returned to the rest of the "flotilla". They saw a "raft" with up to twenty people on it and took them into the boats; they took a collapsible in tow as they made for the *Carpathia*. Answering Scanlan, Scarrott said there had been plenty of time to bring up the passengers from steerage. There was no obstruction to prevent them reaching higher decks. There was a ladder on each side of the well deck, for example, whereby they could reach the boat deck. Only four boats out of twenty were required by Board of Trade regulations to have a compass, said this veteran of eighteen years at sea; but when he looked for the lamp that should have been hanging under a thwart in his boat, it was missing.

Because the court moved to Southampton on Monday 6 May to visit the *Olympic* and gain a clearer idea of the layout and physical features of the lost ship, the third day at the drill hall was deferred to the 7th, when the first witness was Fireman George Beauchamp. He had been on duty in number ten stokehold when he heard the "roar of thunder" of the collision. "Stop" rang on the telegraph, the watertight doors closed and the order was given to draw the fires in the boilers, which took fifteen minutes. Since the water was rising in the compartment he had to escape by emergency ladder. He had no idea what boat he was assigned to so loaded number thirteen, Fred Barrett's boat, and helped to row it away from the wreck. He heard "explosions and roaring" as the ship went down, and cries in the water afterwards; but their boat was full so they did not go back. They found no light, compass, water or food in the boat.

The helmsman when she struck, Hitchens, gave evidence next. While he was on stand-by on the bridge between 8 and 10 p.m. Lightoller had ordered him, he said, to warn the ship's carpenter that the temperature was low enough to freeze the fresh water. He had relieved Quartermaster Olliver at the wheel at 10 p.m., and at 11.40 he received the order "hard a-starboard" from Murdoch. They had covered forty-five miles in the preceding two hours and were heading north 71° west. The ship had swung two points to port when she struck. One minute later the Captain appeared on the bridge.

Smith had the carpenter sent for to sound the ship; after midnight he ordered: "Get all the boats out and serve out the belts." As he took charge of boat number six, Hitchens was ordered by Lightoller "to steer for that light – there was a light about two points on the port bow, about five miles away, I judge ... We surmised it to be a steamboat ... The light was moving, gradually disappearing. We did not seem to get no nearer to it [sic]." Hitchens was not the only witness to remember multicoloured, as distinct from white, rockets going up from the *Titanic*.

William Lucas, able seaman, told the court he had joined the ship fifteen minutes before she left Southampton. After the collision he had seen a couple of tons of darkish white ice on the well deck. His allotted place had been on number one (emergency) boat, but he helped to load eight lifeboats before joining the crew of collapsible D. There had been too few women on deck to fill the boats. From his boat on the port side of the wreck he saw the faint sidelight of a moving ship, and her masthead (steaming) light, eight to nine miles away.

Leading Stoker Fred Barrett told his tale of how water burst into number six boiler-room two feet above the floor. He resumed his evidence on the morning of the fourth day, 8 May. He described how boat fifteen had been lowered thirty seconds after his own number thirteen and almost landed on top of him. "There was a bit of a current and it drifted us under number fifteen boat," he deduced as he cut his boat free of its ropes – only to face swamping from the water being discharged from the side. He concluded that the ship's forward motion as she started to go down was why boat fifteen almost pushed thirteen under. "We just got clear."

Thomas Lewis for the British Seafarers' Union took up the questioning. Barrett described how his bunker number six was empty, as the result of an order issued shortly after leaving Southampton.

Q: Was there anything wrong?
A: Yes.
Q: What was wrong?
A: The bunker was afire.
Q: Shortly after you left Southampton ...

At this point Mersey demanded to know the relevance of the fire to the inquiry and was told by the witness and lawyers that it had damaged a bulkhead.

The Attorney-General rose to his feet again to examine Reginald Robinson Lee, one of five out of six lookouts to go into the box, Fleet's companion when the iceberg was sighted. Isaacs raised the theme of the missing binoculars. Lee thought they would have seen the iceberg sooner with them. Unlike almost any other witness except Fleet, Lee said he had seen a haze ahead just before the collision. The iceberg had been higher than the forecastle (over fifty-five feet), a dark mass with a white fringe on top. As it went past its side looked black. "Going astern it seemed to be white", which could have been the result of reflected light from the ship. He stayed in the crow's nest until the end of his watch at midnight and finished up on Barrett's boat. He had seen the lights of a vessel before and after abandoning ship.

John Poingdestre, the next witness and also an able seaman, dismissed this ship as "imaginary". He had seen a light four to five miles away on the horizon from his boat number twelve which others had taken to be a ship. Despite his own scepticism, he said he had told his mainly female passengers that they would be picked up in a few minutes. He had rowed towards the sound of cries in the water but found nothing in a fifteen-minute search except hundreds of deckchairs.

The Board of Trade legal team was working to a pattern, examining crew members from every lifeboat, though in no particular order. James Johnson, a first-class saloon steward, gave evidence next on events in Boxhall's boat. He reported the wry remark he had overheard from an unidentified crewman when they felt the impact of the iceberg: "Another Belfast trip." He said that there had been a discussion in boat number two about going back; Boxhall suggested it but "the ladies said no". They had heard "shrieks" from the water but "they said they were sorry and everything".

Next, Thomas Patrick Dillon, a trimmer, described how he went down with the ship as she sank. He had been standing on the poop deck for about fifty minutes and was sucked about two fathoms under; he thought about 1,000 people had gone into the water, in which he floated for about twenty minutes before being hauled into boat four and lapsing into unconsciousness. As passengers waited for the end there had been "no disorder whatsoever". One of his rescuers was Thomas Ranger, a greaser, who remembered helping to heave seven men out of the sea. "We had to rub them to bring them round." Ranger said the emergency lighting generator had been under the aftermost or fourth funnel, and the lights had remained on almost to the end because the electric wiring was covered in rubber. Power would have failed when water reached the dynamo. "Ranger" may be a misprint: the name does not appear in the crew list.

The last witness on the fifth day was Leading Fireman Charles Hendrickson, who said he had been assigned to boat twelve but was ordered into number one, which had only twelve people in it: three male and two female passengers plus seven crewmen. The passengers, who included Sir Cosmo and Lady Duff Gordon, had objected to Hendrickson's suggestion of going back for more survivors "for fear of being swamped". Screaming and "terrible cries" could be heard from 200 yards away but "they would not hear of it". The only objectors were the Duff Gordons. The day before the *Carpathia* docked in New York each of the seven crewmen had received a £5 cheque from Sir Cosmo.

The torpor into which courts invariably sink when a hearing, no matter how dramatic its subject, has been going on for several days, was dispelled as the import of these allegations sank in. The reporters scribbled furiously. Hendrickson saw out the day in the witness-box, describing how he had brushed and rubbed black oil over the scorched and warped bulkhead in bunker six "to give it its ordinary appearance". Day six was taken up by four more seafarers describing events on various boats.

The court made a second visit to the *Olympic* on Monday 13 May, returning to the drill hall for the seventh day on Tuesday. This and most of the next day were taken up with the *Californian*, one of the key events in the inquiry, when Lord Mersey, discreetly egged on by the Attorney-General, nailed his scapegoat.

By all accounts Stanley Lord was a less than impressive witness and may have been in some respects his own worst enemy in the box, arrogant, cold and stiff.

The American Senate had yet to issue the report of its

inquiry, but the British press had been full of reports of Lord's equivocal evidence in Washington on 26 April, and had also carried Donkeyman Gill's evidence about seeing a big liner and rockets at the time of the disaster. All this was more than enough to damn the unfortunate master in Mersey's mind before he had said a word. The judge's prejudice soon showed itself, as the Attorney-General mildly cornered the dour Lancastrian, so ill equipped in such treacherous legal waters.

Lord described how he had stopped in the ice at 10.21 p.m. ship's time on Sunday 14 April. He had run his engines briefly at 5.15 a.m. before moving off at six on the 15th. He had seen a westbound steamer's white light to starboard at about 11 p.m. He then asked his Marconi man, Cyril Evans, what ships he had been in touch with and was told, "Only the *Titanic*". Of the ship then visible Lord had remarked, "That was not the *Titanic*." There was no blaze of light. Later he saw a green sidelight and a few deck lights of a ship about six to seven miles off, at about 11.30 (unfortunately for Lord, the moment the *Titanic* struck, 11.40 by its own time). He had told Evans at 11 p.m. to tell the *Titanic* that the *Californian* was halted and surrounded by ice. As he went to bed a medium-sized steamer showing a green light was clearly visible as motionless, about five miles to the south-south-east. Third Officer Groves tried to raise her by signal-lamp but there was no reaction. At 1.15 a.m. Second Officer Stone by voice-pipe reported seeing a rocket and that the ship in sight had altered its bearing towards the south-west (if Stone was correct, either the ship seen earlier had moved or else she had gone and been replaced by another; no matter which way the imperceptibly drifting and gyrating *Californian* was heading – pointing – east remained east and west, west).

At this juncture Mersey showed his colours: "What is in my brain at the present time is this, that what they saw was the *Titanic*." Isaacs disingenuously asked Lord:

Q: If he did see two lights it must have been the *Titanic*, must it not?

A: It does not follow.

It certainly did not, especially as the *Titanic* only had one such light! But the Wreck Commissioner and the Attorney-General shamelessly combined the assertions that Evans had been in touch with only one ship, the *Titanic*; that Groves had seen two masthead lights, as they wrongly said were worn by the *Titanic*; and that Lord and others had seen a ship in the general direction, relative to them, of the *Titanic*, as "proof" that Lord saw the *Titanic*. This outrage against logic would have been laughed out of court in a criminal trial. The fact that only one ship was known to be in the vicinity of the *Californian* did not exclude the presence of others with two masthead lights but without wireless or Morse lamps (we know of three dozen ships at sea on the Anglo-American route that night, and the only thing we are absolutely certain of is that our list is incomplete (see Appendix II).

Lord speculated that the rocket he knew had been seen was some kind of acknowledgement of Groves's lamp; many steamers did not use such a lamp. He had not been aware that seven or eight rockets had been sighted from his ship during the night: he had known only of one. Lord also said he had seen just one passenger steamer, the *Mount Temple*, at Boxhall's position at 7.40 a.m. on the 15th. Later he had seen wreckage at 41° 33' north, 50° 1' west, or a dozen miles to the south-south-east of that position. The interrupted voyage had been Lord's "first experience of field ice ... I was treating it with every respect."

Questioned by Robertson Dunlop for Leyland, Lord and his officers, the hapless master was able to make two points: that Donkeyman Gill had "deserted" at Boston; and that the *Californian* simply could not have reached the wreck before it sank in the time between the apprentice Gibson's visit to his cabin and the sinking. Mersey however brushed them aside with another intervention, addressed to Dunlop: "Am I to understand that this is what you mean to say: that if he had known that the vessel was the *Titanic*, he would have made no attempt to reach it?" Dunlop replied: "No, my Lord"; the captain had concluded, first, that he could not have got there in time and second, that it would have been "most dangerous" had he tried. Captain Lord would have tried, but would not have reached the scene before the *Carpathia*, even if he had known that more than one rocket had been sighted, Dunlop explained. Mersey was clearly unimpressed.

The apprentice, James Gibson, aged twenty, was next in the box, saying he had gone down to Lord's cabin at 2.05 a.m. ship's time (twenty-seven minutes before the *Titanic* sank) to report eight white rockets. He thought that the ship which sailed out of sight at that time, showing no sign of distress, was a tramp steamer; but as her red light was higher than her green, she must have had a list to starboard.

Second Officer Herbert Stone thought the rockets came from a ship beyond the one whose lights they saw. "These rockets did not appear to go very high; they were very low lying; they were only about half the height of the steamer's masthead light, and I thought rockets would go higher than that," he mused. But: "I could not understand why, if the rockets came from a steamer behind this one, when the steamer altered her bearing the rockets should also alter their bearing." One rocket of the last three he had seen had been much brighter than all the rest and must have come from the steamer seen from the *Californian*. He had seen the three at about 1.40 a.m., but the steamer under observation was moving, because her bearing (i.e., her position relative to the observer) was altering, from south-south-east through south to south-west and a half west, until she vanished after 2.40 a.m., when he reported to a somnolent Lord.

Charles Victor Groves, Third Officer, said that the ship

he had seen had extinguished her lights at 11.40 p.m., which made him think she was a passenger ship; or else she could have turned two points to port so that her lights had ceased to be visible. Mersey took this to be the moment at which the *Titanic* turned two points to port to try to evade the iceberg. After the lights disappeared, Groves said, the *port* navigation light of the ship became much more readily visible because no other lights were discernible. If this was the same ship, she must have reversed her heading, implying a turn of around 180° from west to east.

Answering the Solicitor-General, Sir John Simon, Chief Officer George Frederick Stewart said of the mystery ship: "I thought what had really happened was, she had seen a ship firing rockets to [her] southward and was replying to them." Stone had given the impression that he saw two different ships at different times – unless the original one had met ice and retraced her course. The *Californian*'s overnight position had been thirty miles north of where she sighted wreckage in the morning and between nineteen and twenty miles north of the Boxhall position. Neither the *Titanic* nor her rockets could have been seen at either distance. Mersey gratuitously interrupted here to say that in his opinion the ship seen must have been the *Titanic*. One month after the event there was still no sign of the mystery ship, he said. It was now the collective word of Lord, Stewart and Stone against Groves and Gill, plus circumstantial evidence from Gibson and wireless operator Cyril Evans, who gave evidence next. Mersey had made his choice.

Evans told his tale of going to bed exhausted at 11.30 p.m. on the Sunday evening. No, he had not been offended by the "keep out" response from the *Titanic* to his interrupted ice-warning; it was normal usage in his trade and in any case the larger, faster ship enjoyed priority over the lesser on air and was seen as senior.

The court now moved on to the *Mount Temple*. Butler Aspinall examined Captain Moore on behalf of the Board of Trade. The barrister asked no questions at all about his positions or movements at the material time. Moore said he had received ice-warnings on Saturday 13 April and altered course to the south (it had not been necessary to reduce speed; but Canadian Pacific had a standing order forbidding masters to enter field ice). On hearing of the distress call, "I immediately turned the ship round and steered east" and preparations were made for a rescue, including swinging out the boats. At 3.25 a.m. ship's time (four minutes behind the *Titanic*'s) he had been forced to stop for heavy ice. Between 1.00 and 1.30 a.m. he had seen a ship on a course parallel to his but ahead (he had seen her stern light) and to the south, a vessel with a black funnel that had a white band with a device in it. This ship had been under continuous observation until after daybreak. At about 3 a.m. the green light of a sailing vessel (but nothing else of her) had been seen when the *Mount Temple* was still some fifteen to sixteen miles from the reported position of the wreck. The *Carpathia* and *Californian* had been seen by 8 a.m.

Moore said he had been on the North Atlantic run for twenty-seven years, sailing to and from Montreal in summer and St John's (New Brunswick) in winter. Binoculars were not issued to lookouts by his line. He had never seen ice so far south, and indeed saw none until he turned north and east to go to the *Titanic*, steering north 65 east true. Invited to give his opinion about Captain Smith's speed, Moore said he thought it "most unwise" when ice was known to be ahead.

The next witness was his wireless operator, John Durrant, who testified to picking up the first distress call at 12.11 a.m. ship's time on 15 April. The ship had altered course no more than fifteen minutes later.

Lord Mersey was as certain that Captain Moore owed nobody an explanation for anything as he was that Captain Lord was guilty of dereliction of duty. The long time Moore must have kept the *Mount Temple* motionless in the ice while Rostron was straining every nerve to help the survivors apparently did not register.

Durrant confirmed that at 5.11 a.m. ship's time he had told the *Californian* the news of the disaster. He had guessed what had happened when the *Titanic* failed to reply to repeated wireless calls. The Marconi man's evidence was completed at the beginning of day nine. He was followed in the box by Bathroom Steward Samuel Rule, whose evidence generated rather more heat than light. In his original evidence on day six he had said nearly all in his boat, number fifteen, had been men but this time he said they had nearly all been women. Further, he had the lawyers floundering to work out which ship the model in court was meant to represent.

Day ten began with the recall of Charles Hendrickson, who had revealed the dubious conduct of the Duff Gordons. The character of the lay audience at the proceedings was markedly different on this day since a large proportion of fashionable London had turned up to see how the wealthy husband of the famous couturière "Lucile" would acquit himself. Hendrickson now faced cross-examination by Mr H.E. Duke, KC, on behalf of the titled couple. The leading fireman was unfazed and stuck sturdily to his story, adding a little detail about how Lady Duff Gordon had asked the crewmen of the boat to sign her lifebelt as a souvenir on the *Carpathia*, one of whose seamen had obligingly taken a photograph of the survivors from boat one. Sir Cosmo had said he was paying the crew "to make good the loss of their kit".

Next to testify was George Symons, able seaman and lookout, who had been in charge of boat number one. He recited his recollections of the disaster and surmised that the ship had broken in two as she went down to a sound like "steady thunder at a distance". Isaacs's questioning made Symons, a mere AB, appear bombastic as he emphasized how he had been "master of the situation" and had "exercised my discretion" – expressions which smack of coaching by Duff Gordon's agent. Symons said he had been surprised that nobody (*sic*) suggested going back for the people screaming in the water. They had rowed hard towards the ship's light on the lifeboat's port beam but it pulled away from them. Obviously seeking to discredit the witness, Isaacs asked: "You have realized that if you had gone back you might have saved a good many people?" Unabashed, Symons replied: "Quite so."

But Symons was not disbelieved when he described the visit he received at home in Weymouth from the man acting for the Duff Gordon family's solicitors following Hendrickson's earlier evidence. James Taylor, a fireman who had also been in boat number one and received a similar visitation, bore out Hendrickson's evidence, insisting that there had been a suggestion that they go back but a lady and two men mentioned the danger of swamping.

When Sir Cosmo Duff Gordon was examined by the Attorney-General he estimated that the boat had gone 1,000 yards from the wreck before it sank. He was clearly discomfited by questions about cries from the water and the idea of going back to save people in a boat with so few aboard. No, he had not heard anyone suggest going back, or saying they would be swamped if they did:

There was a man sitting next to me, and of course in the dark I could see nothing of him. I never did see him, and I do not know yet who he is. I suppose it would be some time when they rested on their oars, twenty minutes or half an hour after the *Titanic* had sunk, a man said to me, "I suppose you have lost everything" and I said, "Of course." He says, "But you can get some more," and I said "yes". "Well," he said, "we have lost all our kit and the company won't give us any more, and what is more our pay stops from tonight. All they will do is to send us back to London." So I said to them: "You fellows need not worry about that: I will give you a fiver each to start a new kit." That is the whole of that £5-note story.

Sir Cosmo insisted that he could not identify his inter-
locutor – one of just seven crewmen, who had all posed
for a picture with him and his wife on the *Carpathia* and
four of whom had already spoken at the inquiry. Duff
Gordon said he had told Rostron about the hand-out and
the master had said it was unnecessary.

Having spent almost the whole of day ten on this
shabby affair, Mersey said at the start of day eleven,
Monday 20 May, to Thomas Scanlan, MP, as he rose
to question Sir Cosmo: "The whole of this incident to
my mind has only a small bearing on this inquiry and
I do not want too much time spent on it." *Le tout
Londres* was back in the drill hall as the baronet
continued his evidence. He described how articles on
her *Titanic* experiences had appeared under his wife's
name in American and British publications. She had not
written a word herself; all the articles had been twisted
and based either on interviews with her or on hearsay.
One family friend told a Hearst Newspapers reporter
what he had heard at their table; the latter turned it
into a first-person account.

His offer of money had been made about twenty
minutes after the *Titanic* went down. He did not think it
would have been possible to rescue any other people.
Despite Mersey's strictures, the three remaining members
of the crew of boat one were paraded through the box.
When Fireman Robert Pusey had said Sir Cosmo had
offered the money about three-quarters of an hour after
the ship sank, the soiled saga of boat number one was
wound up after a day and a half of court time.

Four crew members, including first-class stewardesses
Elizabeth Leather and Annie Robinson, told their tales
before Lightoller was called. As senior surviving crew
member he undoubtedly influenced the findings of both
inquiries with his lengthy evidence. He told the court that
he had spent the entire century thus far with White Star,
passing his extra master's certificate in 1902. All the officers except Wilde had been at the *Titanic*'s trials, at which

she had not exceeded 18.5 knots; she had averaged 18 between Belfast and Southampton.

Captain Smith had come up to the bridge on Sunday evening at 8.55 and they discussed the flat calm (but not the ship's speed). He stayed until 9.30 p.m. and went to bed with the order to let him know if anything "doubtful" came up. Lightoller had gone to a wing of the bridge for an unobstructed view – with binoculars. He said he had never detected ice with glasses but used them to examine objects already spotted by the naked eye. At the end of his watch it was still calm and clear and the air temperature stood at freezing. "I have never known speed to be reduced in any ship I have ever been in in the North Atlantic in clear weather, not on account of ice."

When he felt "a jar and grind ... a slight bumping", he thought of ice, got out of bed, went on deck, saw nothing, realized the ship was down to about six knots but calmly went back to bed. "It was not my duty to go onto the bridge when it was not my watch." Mersey understandably intervened here to query this remarkable sangfroid: "What on earth were you doing? Were you lying down in your bunk listening to the noises outside?" Lightoller said: "There were no noises. I turned in my bunk, covered myself up and waited for somebody to come along and tell me if they wanted me." He waited for fifteen to thirty minutes. Lightoller recalled how Boxhall came into his cabin:

Boxhall: You know we have struck an iceberg.
Lightoller: I know we have struck something.
Boxhall: The water is up to F deck in the mail room.

Only then did Lightoller get dressed before going along to the bridge. By that time steam was being let off with a tremendous roar. Continuing his evidence on day twelve, the Second Officer described once again how he had helped prepare and load the boats on the port side. He remembered Chief Officer Wilde calling out at one point,

"All passengers over to the starboard side." This might have been to correct the list to port (or more likely because the starboard boats would be easier to board). The boats had not been filled before lowering away for fear that they might buckle. By the time he started on the collapsibles forward, there was only a ten-foot drop to the water. The lights of a ship were off the port bow. Just after he had crossed over to starboard, "she seemed to take a bit of a dive, and I just walked into the water". He swam towards the sinking crow's nest and then crosswise to starboard. He was pushed against a grille through which water was pouring into the ship; then he was blown free by air coming in the opposite direction.

He had repeatedly and unquestionably seen the mystery ship no more than five miles off over a period of half an hour as he worked on the lifeboats. The distress signals fired had not been rockets but like shells, which burst high in the air and scattered many white stars. The night of the disaster had been marked by "an extraordinary combination of circumstances ... which you would not meet again once in 100 years." No moon, no wind, no swell; the iceberg had probably rolled over recently and was not white but "black". With so many stars in a clear sky there should have been a little reflection from a white iceberg. Lightoller was certain there had been no haze. He said opinions differed about binoculars; they might even delay the sounding of the alarm while the lookout examined his sighting. As for warnings of ice, these were common enough; frequently no ice was seen after them.

Lightoller proved he had a cool head when he refused under pressure from Scanlan to be harried into conceding that recklessness had played a role in the catastrophe. On eye-tests, the Second Officer said White Star was unique in giving special attention to them. The Board of Trade was supposed to test the eyes of officers and quartermasters as well; the tests cost one shilling each.

Lightoller said he had heard nothing about the fire in the bunker but it would have been reported to the master.

It was the Chief Engineer's job to deal with it. The Second Officer completed his evidence, which had taken all day, by saying that it was he who had sent the boatswain to open the gangway doors in the ship's side so that passengers could board the lifeboats through them.

The inquiry worked its way down the officers in order of rank, taking Pitman, Boxhall and Lowe on day thirteen. Pitman said there was no means of giving a general alarm on the ship except to go round telling people. All the ice reports he had heard of put the danger to the north of the *Titanic*. The Captain had ordered the turn from south-west to west later than Pitman expected, which took the ship "ten miles further south" before heading for New York. Pitman had seen the stern light of a sailing ship.

Boxhall had seen a steamer, which both he and Captain Smith examined through binoculars. She had not responded to the distress signals or the Morse lamp. After he had gone down in boat two, he was called back by megaphone and told to row round the stern to the starboard side. The order was not explained (but might surely have had something to do with the abortive plan to open the gangway doors). He had noticed a suction effect at the end and the oarsmen found it hard work to keep clear; they rowed to half a mile off, in a north-easterly direction. His now famous dead-reckoning calculation of the ship's position had been based on a speed of 22 knots from a star sighting at 7.30 p.m.; he also took the ship's course into account, south 86 west from 5.50 p.m.; but the chart in court showed south $86\frac{3}{4}$ west.

"I had that honour," said Lowe when asked if he had been Fifth Officer. We have seen what he told the American inquiry; by the time of the British one he had ceased to remember to which lifeboat he had been assigned, provoking an incredulous reaction from Mersey: "Why not?" Otherwise his London evidence did not vary from his American testimony.

George Elliott Turnbull, deputy manager of the Marconi International Marine Communication Company under Godfrey Isaacs, attested that ice-warnings were logged and broadcast by the Hydrographic Office of the United States Navy. Before the disaster there had been warnings that should have been directly audible on the *Titanic* from *La Touraine*, *Caronia*, *Amerika*, *Baltic* (relaying the *Athinai* warning), *Californian* (for the *Antillian* but overheard by the *Titanic*) and *Mesaba*.

Harold Bride testified he had only heard one of the ice-warnings, from the *Californian*. Later he had told that ship to keep out because he was busy. Towards the end, his colleague Jack Phillips carried on transmitting until all power was lost. Bride added a dramatic but dubious incident to the evidence he had given in the United States: "Someone was taking the life-belt off Phillips when I left the cabin." By his appearance the man was a stoker. The two operators tackled him: "I held him and Mr Phillips hit him." It can only be assumed that the man, whoever he was, died as a result because he was presumably in no fit state to save himself; the ship had only minutes left when the two operators abandoned their post on the Captain's urging. Lightoller, Boxhall, Pitman and Lowe were all briefly recalled in turn for questioning about the ice-warnings. Lightoller said Smith had shown him the *Caronia* one at 12.45 p.m. on Sunday. Boxhall and Pitman more or less recalled seeing the same message. Lowe said he had seen a chit on the chart-room wall with "ice" and a position written on it, but nothing else at all about ice.

Harold Cottam's British evidence on day fifteen contains no surprises for those familiar with the *Carpathia* operator's American testimony. But he added that he had helped the *Titanic*'s operators with their emergency messages because they had signalled they could not hear with all the steam escaping. Furthermore, the forward expansion joint ran across the deck just outside their cabin and air was being forced up out of that as water poured into the hull below. It was he who had helped put the *Titanic* in touch with the *Olympic*.

Next in the witness-box was Lookout Frederick Fleet. He insisted that there had been a haze ahead of the ship for ten minutes before impact, even when Mersey said he thought his colleague, Lee, had invented it as an excuse for seeing the iceberg too late. Fleet said the berg had been black and a little higher than the fifty-five feet of the forecastle head. He had been seventy-five feet up in the crow's nest. Mersey repeated his suspicion that the haze was an invention. Fleet hoisted his defences and turned curmudgeonly. When Mersey put some of Lightoller's evidence to him, he assured the witness that he was not trying to "get round" him. Fleet said: "But some of them are, though." As yet another lawyer rose to his feet with questions, Fleet said truculently: "Is there any more likes [*sic*] to have a go at me?" Mersey was softer now: "Well, I rather sympathize with him. Do you want to ask him any more?" The Attorney-General protested, "Oh no." Fleet said: "A good job too." Mersey cut in again: "I am very much obliged to you. I think you have given your evidence very well, although you seem to distrust us all." Fleet's ordeal was over: any secret he was hiding remained hidden. The Attorney-General added that eye-tests were voluntary and cost each man one shilling of his own money; not surprisingly, few took them.

Seven more crew members in succession gave their evidence about the lifeboats; the fourth witness on day sixteen however was Ernest Gill, the *Californian*'s assistant donkeyman. He was smoothly introduced by Isaacs, who said: "The substance of [his Boston affidavit] is no longer in dispute, and he was fully justified in what he said in America." It had been confirmed by the evidence of officers and apprentice Gibson. There is no record of a protesting intervention by Robertson Dunlop of behalf of the absent Lord, whose interests the barrister was supposed to be watching. Gill then repeated his story about the well-lit ship up to ten miles away and the rockets he

had seen. He had been subpoenaed in America so had
been unable to rejoin the *Californian*; he had not deserted.

After Gill had stepped down, the court was hushed and
tense as Joseph Bruce Ismay went into the witness-box to
face examination by the Attorney-General. He explained
the IMM-Oceanic/White Star connection. IMM owned
seven lines, five British and two American, with a total of
nearly a million tons of shipping, of which White Star
operated almost half. Isaacs said, doubtless looking for a
useful point on behalf of the Board of Trade: "In substance
the *Titanic* was an American-owned ship?" Ismay replied:
"That is true." He had no interest in the builders, Harland
and Wolff, but told the court of Lord Pirrie's dual role.
No reaction is recorded.

Ismay gave his account of how Captain Smith had
handed him the *Baltic*'s ice-warning (which he had kept
out of sheer absent-mindedness, he insisted) and how he
(Ismay) had agreed on a full-speed run with Chief Engineer
Bell while off Queenstown (but "our intention" in America
had become "the intention" in England). He denied any
knowledge of Alexander Carlisle's original plan for many
more lifeboats; but the company's ships now had enough
for all aboard. IMM was the only major operator not
classified by Lloyd's and therefore its ships were inspected
only by the Board of Trade; IMM also paid the lowest
insurance premiums in shipping by virtue of bearing the
highest proportion of any loss itself.

We thought she was unsinkable ...
    I was standing by the boat; I helped everybody into
    the boat that was there, and, as the boat was being
    lowered away, I got in.

Ismay's insistence that he had been an ordinary passenger
was deflated by Sir Rufus Isaacs and a deceptively simple
question: had he paid his fare? Otherwise, however, the

White Star chief's experience in London did not compare with his American ordeal. He concluded his evidence on the morning of the seventeenth day, 5 June. He insisted that when he left the foundering wreck the light of another ship was to its starboard side. He did not think it could have been the *Californian*, but from the evidence he did think that ship had seen the *Titanic*'s distress signals.

His fellow IMM/Oceanic director, Harold Sanderson, was next in the box, to say that White Star ships satisfied United States as well as British regulations. Ice had reached the Outward Southern Track three times since the major shipping lines agreed on routes in 1898. Whenever ice was sighted, each line contacted the rest. But if the weather was clear, captains did not slow down on the Anglo-American route (as distinct from the Canadian, where more ice meant stricter rules). Sanderson thought that Captain Smith's decision to delay his change of course after the normal turning point, which put him some miles south of the track, was his response to the ice-warnings.

In sharp contrast with the American hearings, which passed over the issue, the British inquiry made an eight-course meal of the binoculars missing from the crow's nest. Five lookouts, Lightoller and Ismay had been asked about them, but the eighth witness, Sanderson, made a uniquely opaque contribution when examined by Sir John Simon, the Solicitor-General:

Q: We have been told by the lookout people that there were binoculars on the *Olympic*?
A: Coming from Belfast to Southampton.
Q: On the *Olympic*, I am speaking of?
A: Oh, I beg your pardon; yes.
Q: And that there were not binoculars on the *Titanic*?
A: Yes.
Q: Oh, I beg your pardon; they were [supplied] on the *Oceanic*; but on the *Titanic* they had been provided coming round from Belfast?
A: Yes.[4]

Thus, on the seventeenth day of a massively publicized inquiry into the loss of a ship called the *Titanic*, the owners' general manager still manages to confuse her with her sister. His interrogator is no less confused, like many of his learned friends at an often scatterbrained inquiry; but Sanderson's slip still seems bizarre.

He returned to the witness-box on 6 June, the eighteenth day, to state that the first he had heard of the bunker fire had come from the inquiry. He had since checked with Southampton and received confirmation that it had been burning since Belfast.

On day nineteen the court moved on to matters of construction, calling Edward Wilding, Harland and Wolff's naval architect. Questioned about the cellular structure and high double bottom of Cunard's flagship and Blue-Riband holder, the *Mauretania*, Wilding said her sides were lined with watertight coal-bunkers but added that if holed she could well develop a list that would be hard to correct because of her longitudinal bulkheads.

Wilding, whose evidence conveys a strong impression of professional competence, was "quite sure" that the *Titanic* would have survived a head-on collision, but it would have killed the firemen quartered in the forecastle. The ship would have been saved had the helm not been starboarded (i.e., without the unfortunate Murdoch's turn to port). The steamer *Arizona* had hit an iceberg head-on in 1878 and survived. Eighty to 100 feet of the *Titanic*'s bow would have been crushed, as far astern as the second watertight division (which was also the extra-strong "collision bulkhead"). Wilding's calculation was that the ice had made a hole with a total area of about twelve square feet, irregularly and uncontinuously distributed along hundreds of feet of hull but with an average width of three-quarters of an inch. There would have been 16,000 tons of sea-water aboard when the bow was forty feet down.

Wilding made the sad revelation that the *Olympic*'s lifeboats had been tested with weights in Belfast to show they could be lowered fully loaded, as Harland and Wolff had intended. Had he known the officers were unaware of this, he would have made a point of telling them.

There had been no Lloyd's inspection of the ship, but Lloyd's rules only covered ships up to 650 feet long. The Board of Trade man had inspected "two to three thousand times". The Board generally used previous practice as its yardstick. Its Bulkhead Committee had laid down the prevailing standards in 1891. He said later that White Star's *Teutonic* and *Majestic* had originally been built by Harland and Wolff with longitudinal bulkheads. These had been taken out or pierced later because of the perceived risk of an uncorrectable list.

Questioned on the lifeboat issue, the shipwright said that Axel Welin, the inventor of the patent davit, had told him each pair as fitted could handle three boats. Wilding confirmed that a bulkhead scorched by fire would be more brittle.

After Leonard Peskett, Cunard's naval architect, had briefly described the structure of the "Lusitanias" – thirteen transverse bulkheads plus longitudinal bulkheads, all extending from the keel to a watertight deck, plus a double bottom rising eight feet up each side – the Rt. Hon. Alexander Montgomery Carlisle was called.

The designer under Lord Pirrie of the "Olympics" and former general manager of Harland and Wolff said he had advised the Board of Trade on safety at sea. He had taken part in design work on the "Olympics" until he retired in June 1910. He had advised installing forty-eight boats, telling White Star that sixty-four could be placed under sixteen pairs of davits if desired. Carlisle admitted however to signing the Board of Trade committee's lifeboat recommendations, even though he did not agree with some of them.

By 11 June, the twenty-first day, there had been no evidence from passengers, apart from the Duff Gordon sideshow and Ismay's abandoned pretence to have been one. Mr W. D. Harbinson, for the third class, asked when they would be called. Mersey fell in with the Attorney-General's complacent observation that, "So far as I am aware, and from the material before us, there is no useful light which can be shed upon the facts into which we are inquiring by any passengers whose evidence is available to us." Mr Harbinson did not get his wish; instead, the first of a long series of nautical, technical and official witnesses went into the box.

Prominent among them was Sir Walter J. Howell, Assistant Secretary at the Board of Trade and head of its Marine Department, the key civil servant on matters of safety in shipbuilding and at sea. He began by taking refuge in statistics: out of three-and-a-quarter million passengers on the Anglo-American route in the decade 1892–1901, seventy-three had been lost. In the next decade, nine passengers had died out of six million, and so on. Howell remained in the box for the whole of the next day and into day twenty-three before being relieved by Sir Alfred Chalmers, master mariner, surveyor and Nautical Adviser to the Marine Department. Why, he was asked, were the 1894 rules on lifeboats still in force?

The rigidly complacent official gave seven reasons, summarized here with our comments. First, the safety record at sea had been very good (true if we exclude near misses). Ships were better and better built (false; the Cunarders were more robust than the new "Olympics"). The maximum number of lifeboats that could be launched quickly was about sixteen (false; Welin disproved this). The routes used had proved safe (true until 14 April 1912). Wireless was in general use and spreading (true). The greater the number of boats, the more otherwise "idle" men were needed to man them (false). Finally, owners usually exceeded the minimum scale set voluntarily (true but irrelevant). Were it up to him, he would not change the rules even now. When Cunard and White Star had started building their latest, huge ships he had advised referring the question to the advisory committee, but the disaster had not changed his basic view one whit.

He had been succeeded at the Board of Trade on 1 November 1911 by Alfred Young, master mariner, who agreed that the lifeboat scale should be extended to cover the much larger liners now at sea. The *Titanic* could well have carried the sixty-three boats needed to take a full load of passengers and crew. Recalled on the twenty-fourth day, Captain Young said that on taking up his post he had recommended raising the scale to 50,000 tons in 5,000-ton steps. He had sent a minute to Sir Walter Howell on 18 February 1911. This would have provided 1,907 places on the *Titanic* on the existing method of calculation (which for some reason depended not on numbers aboard but on the ship's cubic capacity).

Day twenty-four had begun with an initiative from the Attorney-General which sealed the fate of Captain Stanley Lord of the *Californian*. As he had foreshadowed in a general sense on day one, Isaacs proposed inserting some extra words in the Board of Trade's self-determined questionnaire for the inquiry. He had in mind question twenty-four, he told Mersey:

> It is important that the question should be specifically put and that Your Lordship should take it into account, and that it ought not to be passed over merely as a matter throwing some general light on the inquiry. It has been already examined into [sic], and my friend Mr Dunlop has been there representing the *Californian*, and therefore we ought to put the question and ask Your Lordship to answer it.
>
> Commissioner: Quite so. I do not suppose that I have any jurisdiction to direct that the Captain's certificate should be interfered with?
>
> Attorney-General: No, I think that only arises in a

collision between two vessels. Then there is jurisdiction.
Commissioner: Assume that I take a view adverse to
the conduct of the Captain of the *Californian*, all I can
do is to express an opinion about it?
Attorney-General: Yes. What we were going to ask Your
Lordship to do was express your view upon the evidence
which you have had, and to give us the benefit of Your
Lordship's conclusions of fact.
Commissioner: Quite.

It was as if Isaacs rather than Mersey was in real charge
of the inquiry! At any rate the Commissioner proved
resolutely compliant with the Attorney-General's wishes.
The latter was as keen to exclude criticism and comment
about the "irrelevant" conduct of the Duff Gordons and
of Ismay in leaving the ship (although his influence over
the Captain might be mentioned) as he was to include
condemnation of Lord without charge or trial. By the time
Isaacs had finished with it, question twenty-four read as
follows (the insertion is in italics):

24. (a) What was the cause of the loss of the *Titanic*,
and of the loss of life which thereby ensued or occurred?
(b) *What vessels had the opportunity of rendering assistance to the* Titanic *and, if any, how was it that assistance
did not reach the* Titanic *before the SS* Carpathia
arrived? (c) Was the construction of the vessel and its
arrangements such as to make it difficult for any class
of passenger or any portion of the crew to take full
advantage of any of the existing provisions for safety?

Nowhere in the inquiry Report, which is the most that
the vast majority of interested parties read or heard of the
investigation, is it mentioned that question twenty-four
had been altered two-thirds of the way through the
inquiry, in hindsight, in Lord's absence and in the light of
disputed evidence. Here surely was an original and devious

legal procedure: first find your answer, then dream up a question to fit it.

Interspersed with the Board of Trade witnesses as the evidential portion of the inquiry drew to a close was a series of master mariners, most of whom attested to keeping up speed regardless of ice-warnings. On day twenty-four Francis Carruthers, ship surveyor in Belfast for the Board of Trade, said that only the collision bulk-head (B) had been tested with water to the top; the rest had been checked with a "feeler" (very thin blade). The double bottom had been tested with water for leaks. He was sure the ship had been taken up to "full speed" on her trials. He could not recall her turning circle, but it had been small; people had remarked on it at the time.

William Henry Chantler, a ship surveyor at Belfast, attested to examining the lifeboats. They could be lowered with their official complement of sixty-five and could carry seventy. This information had not been marked on the boats. They were strong enough for a stress twice as great as that, he had discovered from his own calculations after the disaster.

Maurice Harvey Clarke, the Board of Trade's assistant emigration officer at Southampton, said he had checked the ship's accommodation, lifeboats and crew. They had mustered separately in their divisions of seamen, firemen, and stewards and been "reviewed" by medical officers. Two boats had been tested in the water. The last of his visitations had gone on from 8 a.m. to noon on sailing day. The bunker fire should have, but had not, been reported to him. His inspection formed part two to Car-ruthers's part one; unlike Carruthers, he was a fully quali-fied nautical surveyor (Carruthers had an engineering background). Clarke thought the Board of Trade needed twice as many inspectors as the seventeen it had. Before the disaster he had heard that only White Star firemen objected to boat drill; afterwards it had become much more popular among both firemen and stewards. Why, he was asked, did emigrant ships receive special attention?

Lord Mersey decided to answer that on behalf of the witness: "Emigrants are, very properly, treated as if they were children or sick people, and have to be looked after." In fact in the early days of mass emigration passengers were packed in insanitary conditions to maximize profits. The biggest bonanza in seaborne passenger transport since the slave trade also led to widespread insurance fraud, as we saw earlier. As Wilberforce was to slavery, so Plimsoll was to shipping in the age of steam.

William David Archer, principal ship surveyor to the Board of Trade since 1898 and a qualified shipwright, said he had supervised the hull from information sent by Carruthers. Once again the unmistakable sound of fundaments being covered with paper was heard from a civil servant: if only his minute of 28 February 1911 had been followed, the Titanic could have had forty-six boats for 3,196 people; or at least, given her watertight bulkheads, twenty-six for 1,743. He would generally recommend a lifeboat capacity of 2,500 people for a 50,000-ton ship with watertight bulkheads. This is what the Titanic would have had, because she did not have enough bulkheads to qualify for the lowest provision under his proposals. Here the Board of Trade was in effect admitting that she could well have been more robust than she was. German rules would have required places for 3,198 people on a ship that size, Archer said.

Guglielmo Marconi made his London appearance on day twenty-six, to face questions from that major private shareholder in his American company, Sir Rufus Isaacs. The issues raised were technical and non-controversial. No other lawyer incommoded Marconi, in marked contrast with the way he had been harried by Senator Smith. He said the first liner with wireless had been Kaiser Wilhelm der Große in 1900. Cunard had adopted it in 1901. Marconi's introduced the distress call CQD in 1904. Although changed to SOS by the Berlin Convention of 1908, CQD was still commonly used, which was why Titanic sent both.

The five-kilowatt set on the ship had a guaranteed range of 350 miles. The apparatus was doubled for safety, powered by a dynamo, backed by an emergency dynamo and by batteries as a last resort. His company issued a monthly diagram showing coastal stations and when and where ships on regular routes would be in range of each other, based on information from shipping companies. The established priorities for wireless messages, as laid down in the Marconi handbook for 1911–12, were: distress signals; naval and governmental traffic; information relevant to navigation; service messages; ordinary correspondence. Navigational messages were supposed to be countersigned by the master and logged. It was White Star's Sir Robert Finlay rather than the Attorney-General who oleaginously expressed the court's gratitude for "the honour of seeing Mr Marconi". Finlay did not presume to question him.

No less illustrious was Sir Ernest Shackleton, who held the contemporary Antarctic record, having reached a point less than 100 miles from the South Pole in 1909. Still only thirty-eight, the great explorer was called as an expert on ice. He said he would expect to sight an eighty-foot iceberg at five miles on a clear night and at ten to twelve by day. Some icebergs looked black because they contained earth or had become porous near the surface, and would not reflect. He had seen such phenomena in the North Atlantic, albeit only as a liner passenger. On a dead calm night one would be better off looking for bergs from as close to the water as possible. He would post a man in the stem and slow down.

"You have no right to go at that speed [the *Titanic*'s] in an ice zone ... I think the possibility of accident is greatly enhanced by the speed the ship goes." His ship, *Nimrod*, had been capable of only 6 knots, but he slowed her down to 4 in ice. He would have only one man in the crow's nest so he could concentrate better; but binoculars were unnecessary. They were for the officer to check on something reported to him. Without them you could scan the entire horizon fully in a moment; glasses localized one's view. Water temperature was no clue to the presence of ice: melted fresh water would make a film on the sea so thin that scooping a sample by bucket would not reveal it. You might be able to detect ice if the wind blew from it to the ship. If there was no wind and the air temperature fell abnormally for the time of year, ice could well be nearby. Those conditions and the flat calm which also prevailed on the night of 14 April "might never occur again". There would be no revealing splash at the foot of an iceberg. You might get a haze if there was a big difference between the temperatures of water and air (not the case in the North Atlantic at the time of the disaster). Shackleton's advice for sailing in an icefield at night was to slow down to the minimum speed still conferring full steerage way (perhaps 10 knots for the *Titanic*). He was fully aware of the pressures on masters, including competition, owners' requirements and the general taste for speed.

Day twenty-seven opened with Mersey and Isaacs enjoying another cosy public chat. The Attorney-General formally submitted a final draft of question twenty-four, saying: "The only [vessel] that gives any difficulty ... is the *Californian*. As to the *Mount Temple*, you have the evidence about that. That question will cover the *Californian*." This remark surely reveals that the *Mount Temple*'s role had been the subject of speculation if not suspicion or criticism behind the scenes, and that the authorities had decided not to pursue the matter. Isaacs was warning Mersey off.

Changing the subject, Mersey found support among many of the lawyers when he advanced the curious idea that custom precluded a finding of negligence against a dead man, namely Captain Smith. "I feel the greatest reluctance to finding [*sic*] negligence against a man who cannot be heard." Up jumped Butler Aspinall: "That is the point, my Lord. He has no opportunity of giving any explanation. He is a man with a good record [*sic*]." But exactly the same could be said of Lord who, although he outlived Smith by half a century, never got a chance to answer the allegation about to be made against him.

Another convoy of captains attested that they would not reduce speed for ice in clear weather. They were led by the retired first master of the *Mauretania*, John Pritchard, who said he had always sailed at full speed – 26 knots – in such conditions, including on the route sailed by the *Titanic*. Wilding returned to give the results of tests of the *Olympic*'s turning circle. She needed thirty-seven seconds to complete a two-point ($22\frac{1}{2}°$) turn at 21.5 knots or seventy-four revolutions; during that time she would travel 1,200 to 1,300 feet. Sailing at 18 knots and then having both main engines flung into reverse (and the auxiliary turbine stopped), she needed over 3,000 feet, and three minutes fifteen seconds, to come to a halt. He had worked out with the help of Cunard that the *Mauretania*, if damaged like the *Titanic*, would have developed a list of 15° to 20°, thanks to the longitudinal bulkheads. But calculations suggested that counter-flooding on the opposite side and aft might have corrected this.

Captain Rostron appeared on day twenty-eight. It was his first day in England since the disaster, he said, and although unprepared for questions, had no difficulty in telling the same story that he had given the Americans. He also said that, in addition to the *Californian*, he had seen three steamers on the morning of 15 April in the vicinity of the disaster: one at 3.15 a.m. two points off the starboard bow showing her port light (i.e., sailing west, ahead and to the right of him), and two more at about 5 a.m., seven or eight miles to the north of Boxhall's position – one with four masts, the other with two, both with a single funnel.

Two more old salts who never slowed down for ice brought the evidence to an end at last. The rest of the day and all of the last eight days of the inquiry were taken up with lawyers' closing addresses; Mersey did not make one as he would have done at a criminal or civil trial before a jury. Thomas Scanlan, MP, for the Sailors' and Firemen's Union, was first to the charge. He blamed Captain Smith's bad seamanship as the immediate cause of the disaster. He should have slowed down and doubled his lookouts. Too many boats had been underfilled due to lack of drill, and lack of knowledge and discipline among the officers. Crew had not been properly trained in lifeboats for want of time caused by tight schedules. The Board of Trade had been complacent and failed to keep up with shipbuilding progress.

Mr L. S. Holmes, representing the Imperial Merchant Service Guild and thus the officers (but not Smith), defended his clients' conduct as satisfactory in every respect. The juniors had been overworked in the watch-and-watch system. The inspection system was inadequate, with just one man (Carruthers), no matter how competent, responsible for just about all detailed checks on engines, hull and equipment.

Mr W. D. Harbinson, for the third class, said the disaster had been avoidable with due care. Smith had altered course by delaying his turn but he should have cut his speed after the ice-warnings. Ismay must have exerted influence on the Captain by his mere presence. He could not believe that Smith handed him the *Baltic* ice-message without comment. The officers had been slack in that one (Lightoller) had calculated they would meet ice at 9.30 p.m. while another (Sixth Officer Moody) had settled on 11 p.m. This proved negligence by the ship's navigators. Too little had been done to help the third class, a disproportionately high number of whom had died. Crews should be attached to individual ships so as to know them better and drill together.

Clement Edwards, for the Dock, Wharf, Riverside and General Workers' Union of Great Britain and Ireland, and other unions, attacked the speed of the ship. Smith's surrender of the ice-warning proved that Ismay was no mere passenger; further, when disaster struck, he went straight to the bridge. Like Harbinson, Edwards suspected that the Captain had been trying to pass responsibility for the planned high-speed run to Ismay. Had he hung on to the message in the hope that Smith would forget it and carry on with the speed-test? IMM regulations required masters to slow down in ice on the Canadian route and should have imposed the same precaution when similar conditions spread further south. The Board of Trade had been negligent in not specifying a watertight deck on top of the bulkheads.

Edwards joined Mersey and Isaacs in blaming Lord for ignoring multiple rocket signals and in believing that the *Titanic* had been seen from the *Californian*. Mersey intervened approvingly here, saying: "I think the onus of proof in this matter is upon the *Californian* ... that it will be for the *Californian* to satisfy us that those were not the signals of the *Titanic* ... "

Edwards attacked Sir Cosmo Duff Gordon for his indirect bribe, his offer of money for new kit amid the screams of the dying, by which he had sought to establish his ascendancy. As for Ismay, he had been too keen to get into a boat when he must have known full well there were more women and children aboard. It had been not his legal but his moral duty to ensure they were found.

Sir Robert Finlay spoke next, not only for White Star but also for the late Captain Edward John Smith. No blame attached to him and he thus needed no immunity from accusation. He had gone down with his ship in the finest tradition. There had been no evidence that Smith deferred to Ismay, who had not saved his own life at anyone else's expense. Was he supposed to have committed suicide? Had he done so, he would have been accused of evading blame. He had no duty to go down with the ship.

Finlay reckoned that three ice-warnings reached the officers, those from the *Caronia*, *Baltic* and *Californian*. Those from the *Mesaba* and *Amerika*, very important though they had been, did not; they might have averted the crash (he did not mention the *Rappahannock*, which had actually reported ice-damage to herself when passing the *Titanic* shortly before the collision).

What would have been said of an officer who ran his ship full-tilt at an iceberg, even though it was now known that this would have kept her afloat, if at the cost of many crew? Hindsight alone showed that starboarding the helm had been wrong; Murdoch was therefore not to blame. Full speed in ice-warning areas had been general practice for many years, and there had been no noteworthy loss as a result. Following the usual practice could never be negligence. In the past twenty years there had been 32,000 crossings involving just twenty-five accidents in which a life or a ship was lost: sixty-eight passengers and eighty sailors had lost their lives in all that time and traffic.

Still speaking at the start of day thirty-one, Sir Robert said Smith had requested special vigilance for ice and ordered that he be called in case of doubt, going only as far as his chart room to sleep. The stem of the ship had been so high that there was nothing to be gained from putting a man in the "eyes". The bridge was so far out of the water that it was not possible to see from there at night that a freakish, total flat calm, "the fatal feature", had developed. There had been only two major collisions with icebergs: the *Arizona* in 1880 and *Lake Champlain* in 1907. In both there had been damage to the bows but no loss. Finlay guessed that Smith, by sailing further south before "turning the corner", would have thought himself out of the danger indicated by the three messages he had seen. He tried hard to counter Shackleton's damaging evidence, pointing out that the explorer's experience had been in the pack-ice near the South Pole rather than the loose ice found in the North Atlantic, which he had merely sailed as a passenger.

The defence of White Star also consumed the whole of day thirty-two, 27 June, after a one-day break. Finlay began again by reiterating the extraordinary weather before the disaster and how natural, though erroneous. it had been to try to avoid the iceberg. Wilding estimated 200 deaths in a head-on collision, but 1,300 more would have been saved as the ship would not have sunk.

Finlay's point about Smith's delayed turn having been an ice-evasion measure was undermined by Mersey on the advice of his nautical assessors. They deduced that the delay took the *Titanic* only four miles further south; the ship was less than two miles south of her track and four of the indicated ice. It was even possible, the assessors thought, that Smith had not gone rather further south because he was gambling that the reported ice had drifted out of his way. Had the *Mesaba*'s warning, received at 9.40 p.m., reached the bridge, there would have been no disaster, but operator Phillips had been too busy to see its significance and pass it on. Mersey pointed out that messages affecting navigation enjoyed priority over nearly all other traffic, so negligence on the part of Phillips was arguable.

Finlay reached the end of his marathon at the beginning of the thirty-third day, Friday 28 June. He was followed by his ally, Laing, who dealt with technical issues on behalf of White Star. He asserted that the ship could have stayed afloat with three forward compartments flooded. The Board of Trade required watertight bulkheads to clear floodwater in two compartments by one and a half feet; since the bulkheads on the *Titanic* would have cleared the water in such conditions by up to three feet, she would have stayed afloat with a third compartment flooded, which showed that her construction exceeded Lloyd's requirements. Laing pointed out that only in the Navy were bulkheads subjected to pressure tests.

As Robertson Dunlop rose to speak on behalf of the Leyland Line, the master and the officers of the *Californian*, he was bluntly reminded of the forlorn hope attached to his watching brief:

Commissioner: Now, Mr Dunlop, how long do you think you will take to convince us that the *Californian* did not see the *Titanic*'s lights?

Mr Dunlop: I think, my Lord, I will take about two hours.

His opening was less than felicitous:

I am instructed by the Leyland Line, the owners of the *Californian*, to appear on their behalf and on behalf of the master, and I desire at the outset to express on their behalf their profound regret that the *Californian* was unable to, or did not, render any assistance to the *Titanic*.

Dunlop's clients might reasonably have taken the view that an argument on their behalf which began with an admission of failing to help a ship in distress was not the most robust defence.

Leyland had instructed the *Californian* to stay at the scene as long as it could help, Dunlop went on; she was, after all, also owned by IMM. Dunlop averred that the *Californian* did not see the lights or the distress signals of the *Titanic* and the *Titanic* did not see the lights of the *Californian*. Nobody had challenged Captain Lord's logged position some twenty miles north by east of the wreck. The Chief Officer, not Lord, kept the log and there was no hint "that the log has been 'cooked'", said Dunlop (thus making the very suggestion he was hoping to stifle). Once the fate of the *Titanic* was known, the *Californian* moved as quickly as possible, allowing for detours of at least ten miles round the icefield.

Lord, Stone and Gibson thought they had seen a tramp steamer. Groves and Gill thought they had seen a passenger ship, but their evidence was such that it was not possible for both of them to be right. Gill had been swayed by subsequent events in America. Meanwhile three witnesses on the *Titanic* had seen a steamer which came up and went away while eight, including Ismay, saw a fishing vessel. Yet others saw the *Carpathia* later. But while all this was going on, the *Californian* was stopped in the ice. Chief Officer Stewart at 4 a.m. saw a ship steering first south-west, then north-east; this could have been the ship seen by Boxhall. Lloyd's weekly Shipping Index had been consulted; but ships were known to be in an area only by their wireless transmissions. If they had no wireless or made no transmissions, their presence would not be recorded. It was hardly likely that anyone would come forward now to admit to having been in the area of the disaster and done nothing about it. After reciting the names and liveries of various ships known to have been in the relevant area, Dunlop pointed out that Lord could not have reached the scene, two and a half hours' sailing-time away because of the ice, before the *Titanic* went down, whether he had responded to Gibson's call at 2.05 a.m. or even to the rockets seen an hour earlier.

If the inquiry lacked the powers to take away Lord's master's ticket, it also lacked the powers to censure him. The Board of Trade had the power to proceed directly against Lord but had not done so. Lord was entitled to be charged with due notice. But there was neither a charge nor any hint of one; nor had he been made a party to the inquiry. Nor had Dunlop, who had only a watching brief:

It was not until the 14th of June, a month after Captain Lord had left the witness-box, that an intimation is given that the Board of Trade proposes to formulate a question relating to the *Californian*, which would give the court an opportunity of censuring Captain Lord ... [he] has been treated here in a way which is absolutely contrary to the principles on which justice is usually administered, or on which these inquiries are generally conducted.

Lord should have been given notice of amended question twenty-four; he should have known of the allegation against him before he gave his evidence and should have had the chance to hear the evidence of other witnesses before giving his own. If the inquiry now found against him, what chance would he stand of a fair trial? This good coda after a weak start by Dunlop fell on deaf ears.

On Saturday 29 June, the thirty-fourth day of the inquiry, the Attorney-General, Sir Rufus Isaacs, rose to his feet to open the last act in an unduly protracted drama. He began by identifying the two key issues for him: the speed of the ship and the lifeboats. Had the *Titanic* sailed more slowly, she would not have been lost, or else would have floated long enough for the *Carpathia* to arrive in time to take everyone off. Mersey interposed that while he agreed excess speed was the immediate cause of the disaster, this did not imply negligence. But why the rush, given the evidence that they were not chasing a record, his Lordship mused; they were making 22 knots but only needed to average 20 to reach New York at the predetermined time of 5 a.m. on the Wednesday.

That ice was generally expected on the bridge, Isaacs argued, was shown by Lightoller's remark about the absence of a breeze and thus also ripples that would show an iceberg's waterline; by Murdoch's order to close the hatch forward so as to conceal a light that might hamper the lookouts; and by Smith's order to be called if anything doubtful arose, which could only have referred to ice and/or haze. The accident had been foreseeable. Lightoller had said on day eleven that they had a lookout in the stem between Southampton and Cherbourg in unclear weather; in view of the ice-warnings, the *Titanic* should have cut her speed and increased her lookouts.

Because the drill hall was booked for a public examination from Monday 1 July, the inquiry moved for its last two days to a much more suitable venue – Caxton Hall in Westminster, intended for public meetings and offering better acoustics. Before Isaacs resumed his address, Mersey told Finlay that Lightoller's remark about

the effect of the absence of breeze negated Finlay's argument about the total flat calm not being visible from the
bridge, where they were clearly aware of the added danger
represented by the absence of a fringe of surf round the
iceberg's waterline. They had worked out that they would
meet ice, whether at 9.30 or 11 p.m. (the difference in
Mersey's opinion being due to Lightoller and Moody using
different warnings for their separate calculations). The
Commissioner also remarked that for more than twenty-
five years the custom had been to maintain speed in clear
weather regardless of ice-warnings, "because experience
tells them that they can always avoid it. But then there
arises the natural question: then why did you not avoid
this?"

Isaacs resumed his exposition by saying that the seriousness of the damage was known to Andrews, Smith and
Ismay by midnight, when the order to prepare boats was
given; it took another forty-five minutes to launch the
first boat (which suggests that practice was lacking). The
evidence put rather more in the boats than the 711 (*sic*)
that had been saved. The news that the *Carpathia* was on
her way led many to stay aboard. The officers had been
wrong to fear that a full boat would buckle.

The "unsinkability" of a vessel was more important
than the number of boats she carried, said the Attorney-
General; the watertight compartments (*sic*) were the key
factor. It was now clear that there should be more of
both, and committees were already looking into future
provisions of bulkheads and boats under the aegis of the
Board of Trade. Nothing had been done earlier, said Isaacs,
skating over the Board's failure to keep up with shipping
technology, because the transatlantic route had been so
utterly safe.

Resuming on the thirty-sixth and final day, Wednesday
7 July, Isaacs said that new Board of Trade rules on safety
at sea were waiting on this inquiry. Hence the fact that
nothing had yet been laid before Parliament. But all shipowners had agreed to the request of the Board to provide

100 per cent lifeboat cover on all ships over 1,500 tons. The Board was also trying to get international agreement to a conference on safety at sea, in view of the competition on the North Atlantic route. The main complaint against the Board was that it had done nothing since 1894; it had not been proved wrong until the *Titanic* disaster. Nobody had anticipated a glancing, lateral collision with ice at high speed (in sum, therefore, a calamitous demonstration of official lack of foresight, surely, if not complacency).

For the Attorney-General the final outstanding question was the *Californian*. There was simply no excuse for her failure to act on seeing distress signals. In the light of the strong criticism at the American inquiry it must have been clear to Lord he would need a lawyer. But Dunlop had merely asked for a watching brief just before relevant witnesses were to be called, and after he (Isaacs) had stated on what he would be examining them. Dunlop in his questioning had "led" Lord in such a way that it was clear he was appearing for the Captain.

Lord had admitted that rockets which might have been distress signals had been seen, that they came from the direction of the *Titanic* and that nothing was tried except a lamp-signal. The evidence was conflicting, but:

> The comment I make upon it is that for the master of a British vessel to see distress signals, whether they came from a passenger steamer or not, and whether from a passenger steamer the size of the *Titanic* or not, is a very serious matter; and because it is a serious matter we have inquired into it very carefully during the course of this investigation.

By choosing the *Californian* as his last point of substance, Isaacs was elevating its importance over less emotive but more substantial issues in a speech of some structural cunning. He could not exactly be accused of suppressing such seminal issues as safety, negligence and government inertia; but he set out to side-track Mersey and his assessors with the emotive issue of Lord's heedlessness by ensuring that this red herring, produced last, was uppermost in the court's mind as it adjourned.

The Commissioner was free to make a finding on facts, Isaacs went on; if he agreed they were correct he could mention them. "I do not ask you to do anything more." In reality Isaacs was inviting Mersey to decide that Lord was in the wrong and declare this as a fact rather than an opinion. Disingenuously at this stage, the observer might have felt, Lord Mersey conceded the point that Lord should have had the chance to avoid self-incrimination (the custom in civilized states).

Isaacs argued that the *Titanic* and the *Californian* were only seven or eight miles apart, although it was "difficult to say" and one could not be precise. He admitted reformulating question twenty-four in order to get an answer based upon the evidence heard. Lord Mersey could not have been more obliging:

> I think we are all of the opinion that the distress rockets that were seen from the *Californian* were the distress signals of the *Titanic*.

Isaacs was duly grateful to his Lordship, saying this would save him the trouble of quoting a lot of evidence. Lord had stopped in ice; he must therefore have realized that other ships could be in danger – yet he ignored possible distress signals which had then not been entered in his log. If the *Californian* saw the *Titanic*'s rockets from five to seven (*sic*) miles away (Isaacs was doing his best to close the gap), and if she could sail at 11 knots, she could have saved everybody. QED ...

Lord Mersey's Report was published quite quickly, on 30 July 1912, and consisted of the following fifty words:

The Court, having carefully enquired into the

circumstances of the above-mentioned shipping casualty, finds, for the reasons appearing in the Annex hereto, that the loss of the said ship was due to collision with an iceberg, brought about by the excessive speed at which the ship was being navigated.

So much for the best efforts of ninety-six witnesses and a phalanx of lawyers. The annex however ran to seventy-four closely printed, foolscap pages, prefaced by the twenty-six questions (as amended by Isaacs) and divided into eight sections. The first described White Star briefly and its ship in detail, ending with the passengers and crew aboard. The second section dealt with the voyage, the route, the danger of ice and the warnings received, the speed of the ship, the weather and the collision. The third described the damage, its effects and the pros and cons of watertight decks, longitudinal bulkheads and high double bottoms. Section four turned to the lifeboats and the rescue; it acquitted Duff Gordon of bribery but criticized him for not urging his crew to go back to the dying. It also forbore from criticizing Ismay for saving himself: "Had he not jumped in he would merely have added one more life, namely his own, to the number of those lost." Nor had there been any question of discrimination against third-class passengers. This emollient section ended with the rescue and numbers saved, shown by gender, class and, for crew, department.

The *Californian* got a highly critical section five all to herself; the conclusion, that she could and should have helped and might have saved "many if not all" will come as no surprise. Part six dealt with the Board of Trade, finding that its lifeboat rules were out of date and inadequate. But it included massive documentation to show that the Board had been actively considering safety rules before the disaster, even if it had done nothing since 1894 (when the largest ship in the world was the *Lucania*, already 2,952 tons over the 10,000-ton limit of the lifeboat scale). The Board was acquitted of the allegation that its inspections were inadequate. Its powers of enforcement for watertight bulkheads were, however, grossly insufficient: it could supervise this aspect of construction only by voluntary invitation from the shipowner, the Report said. This was to ignore the question why the department had not asked for more powers, an omission which was also rooted in complacency.

Section seven listed the actual findings of the court, in the form of answers to the twenty-six questions one by one. This took ten pages, five fewer than were devoted to exonerating the Board of Trade. The answers covered a range of mostly obvious issues, from numbers aboard to lifeboats, route, ice-warnings, binoculars, speed, details of the disaster, wireless traffic (at great length), survivors and the like. The insertion in question twenty-four, section (b), asking what vessels could have helped and how they did not do so, was answered as follows:

> The *Californian*. She could have reached the *Titanic* if she had made the attempt when she saw the first rocket. She made no attempt.

Question twenty-five asked whether the ship had been "properly constructed and adequately equipped as a passenger steamer and emigrant ship for the Atlantic service". Despite the mass of evidence about deficient bulkheads and lifeboats, the entire answer consisted of one word: "Yes"!

Question twenty-six invited recommendations, which were set out in the eighth and final section. The new Bulkhead Committee should investigate hull construction, Lord Mersey urged, especially watertight decks, longitudinal bulkheads and high double bottoms (a suggestion which torpedoes the "Yes" to the previous question). The Board of Trade should have increased powers to monitor construction. Lifeboat provision should depend on the numbers aboard and be for all. Boat drill should be improved and enforced. Mersey also recommended that lookouts should have regular eye-tests; that discipline for emergencies should be tightened; that wireless should be compulsory and manned round the clock; that speed should be reduced in icy areas; that masters should be reminded it was an offence not to help a ship in distress; that all foreign-going ships, not just emigrant vessels, should be subject to safety inspection; and finally that an international conference should be called on the internal subdivision of ships, life-saving apparatus, wireless provision, speed in icefields and searchlights as hazard detectors.

Was the British Report a whitewash, as has so often been claimed? It certainly was in its treatment of the Board of Trade. It was also kind to the deceased Captain Smith, finding that his acceleration into a known icefield had been "a very grievous mistake" – but not negligence, because he had been following established custom and practice by not slowing down for ice-warnings in clear weather. But such conduct would "be negligence in any similar case in the future".

That is as near as the British inquiry came to blaming any of those responsible for the regulation, construction, operation and navigation of the *Titanic*. The only person condemned, on selective evidence, was the master whose ship might have saved everybody if his wireless operator had stayed awake a little longer or her Second Officer had been competent. This was a diversion insofar as it drew attention away from the failure of Captain Smith to avoid a known danger, the failure of builders and owners to make the ship as safe as Cunard's, and the failure of government to require them to do so. To discern no negligence amid this morass of shortcomings was no mere whitewash: it was a mockery of those lost in the worst peacetime transport disaster then on record.

EPILOGUE

GRAVE DOUBTS

Among the modern world's most famous shipwrecks is the battleship USS *Arizona*, which still lies on the shallow bottom of Pearl Harbor where she was sunk by torpedo-bombers on 7 December 1941. The battleship HMS *Royal Oak* still lies on the rather deeper bottom of Scapa Flow, to which she was consigned by a U-boat on 14 October 1939. The American vessel is an official memorial for the 2,403 people killed in the treacherous Japanese attack, and can be viewed by members of the public in a special submarine. The British ship is the officially designated war-grave of 833 men, and may not be touched by the scuba-divers who visit the Flow in organized groups each summer to view the wrecks of the Kaiser's fleet, scuttled without loss of life by their own crews on 21 June 1919. Fortunately both battleship memorials lie in territorial waters and the bans on physical intrusion can be enforced. The same holds good for the *Lusitania*, sunk by a U-boat in southern Irish waters off the Old Head of Kinsale on 7 May 1915 with the loss of 1,198 lives.[1]

But her contemporary and would-be competitor, the *Titanic*, on or near which more than 1,500 people lost their lives in peacetime on 15 April 1912, lies in international waters and enjoys no such protection. The shield over her resting place provided for seventy-one and a half years by two and a half miles of Atlantic water was pierced by modern technology on 1 September 1985. Despite exhortations from Congress and other institutions in the United States and elsewhere, the site could be, and has been, not merely visited by those with the financial and technological means to do so but also plundered. Some of the results went on show in Britain for a year from October 1994 in an exhibition entitled "The Wreck of the *Titanic*" at the National Maritime Museum in Greenwich, amid controversy over whether such an institution should support what objectors saw as a stunt involving grave-robbery and pandering to voyeurism.

With commendable objectivity the museum featured in its exhibition a video-recording of the programme "Anderson on the Box" by BBC-TV Ulster in which protesters had their say. They included Miss Eva Hart, one of the dwindling handful of survivors, and Una Reilly of the Ulster Titanic Society. Ms Reilly said there was "nothing unique" on the *Titanic* to justify the wholesale removal of artefacts and accused those concerned of seeking sensation and profit. The exhibition was well presented but essentially modest, taking up a small corner of a large museum and showing just 150 of the 3,600 artefacts culled from the environs of the wreck. Another video-recording on display, taken during one of the descents on the hulk, showed that rust had unceremoniously been scraped from the bow, after Dr Robert Ballard's pioneering 1986 visit, to lay bare the ship's name. This assault on the ship is of a different order of magnitude from picking up objects in the enormous field of debris round the two sections of hull.

These controversial activities were made possible by the technological prowess of the Woods Hole Oceanographic Institute in Massachusetts (Dr Ballard) and the French IFREMER Institute (Jean-Louis Michel) who combined to locate the wreck in 1985. Pictures were obtained by remote control on that occasion, but in July and August 1986 Dr Ballard and his American colleagues took a deep-water submersible for the first visit to the wreck, bringing up stunning still and moving pictures, leaving a memorial plaque and collecting a few small souvenirs from the debris. Ballard was undoubtedly sincere when he expressed the hope that the wreck of the *Titanic* would be respected on account of her dead; but if he hoped that her precise position could be kept secret, or when revealed then left undisturbed, he was being naïve. IFREMER, with whom the Americans had fallen out, knew the location, and have shown no qualms about returning in association with RMS Titanic Inc. of New York to collect thousands of objects.

It is round some of these that the Greenwich exhibition was built. If they are the best that the *Titanic* has to offer (one assumes that the exhibitors would put the pride of their collection on display) then the result is pathetic in every sense. Degradingly, American lawyers are making money from legal actions about who has what rights to exploit the wreck. RMS Titanic Inc., which claims exclusivity, undertook not to remove objects from the hull or to sell anything it found. Nonetheless a principal purpose of the exhibition, pioneered at Greenwich and scheduled to go round the world on a purpose-built floating museum-boat, was to help raise millions of dollars. These were required to pay for the past expeditions which made the exhibition possible. The wreck of the *Titanic* has thus become an investment from which a profitable return is required, not just to meet overheads and pay employees but also to repay backers.

What is to be learned from the harvest of artefacts so far garnered? One part of the answer is the less than startling revelations that passengers on the *Titanic* carried dollar bills and pound notes in leather wallets; that some of them smoked cigarettes; that they were served from silver salvers and ate off white crockery, drank alcoholic liquors from glasses and were supplied with white chamber-pots in which to dispose of the resulting waste. They also rested on wooden deck-benches with wrought-iron supports as commonly seen in British public parks; they read newspapers, wore clothes with buttons which they packed in leather bags, wrote letters and took the occasional crafty nip of spirits from a hip-flask ...

And what of the ship herself? The *Titanic* turns out, unsurprisingly, to have been equipped with fittings remarkably similar to those of her contemporaries, whether portholes, engine-room telegraphs, the famous bell in the crow's nest (unmarked), internal telephones or fuse-boards, or even such a fascinating object as a helm indicator to tell those on the stern (docking) bridge which way the rudder was pointing. Ms Reilly is absolutely right: nothing unique there, nothing we did not already know about the Western way of life, at sea and ashore, before the First World War. The Atlantic depths give birth and a ridiculous junk-heap emerges. The objects recovered have no intrinsic uniqueness: there is only the association with the *Titanic*, which viewers must sentimentally supply for themselves.

The consortium of IFREMER and RMS Titanic Inc. made its first trawl in August 1987 at a cost of around £4 million, bringing up about 1,800 items and scraping the rust off the bow to prove they had found the *Titanic*. The first visible result was a Franco-American television "spectacular" compèred by the late Telly Savalas and broadcast to many other countries. The host's only known connection with marine archaeology was a starring role in an abysmal sequel to the successful 1972 film, *The Poseidon Adventure*. A safe raised from the ship was opened amid much spurious ceremony – and to the joy of all except those involved, proved to be empty. Some of the items on display seemed to have been detached, not to say torn, from the hull rather than picked up in its vicinity; there were vociferous protests at the time.

The next visit to the wreck was rather more respectful. A joint effort involving Americans who had been with Ballard in 1985–6, the Canadian Geological Survey and the Russian Shirshov Oceanographic Institute took two Russian submersibles down in summer 1991 to make a film shot by the Canadian IMAX process, which uses the world's largest screen. The result was *Titanica*, shown in 1992. The undersea shots, in which each submersible provided back-lighting for the camera in the other, were unquestionably breathtaking and of superb quality, all the more affecting for being displayed on a wraparound screen so huge that viewers have the visual sensation of being suspended underwater themselves. As comparisons between earlier and later films show that the wreck is visibly deteriorating, this IMAX film will stand as the best record of the *Titanic* wreck available to posterity.

IFREMER and RMS Titanic Inc. made two more visits to the site in the summers of 1993 and 1994, bringing up more than 1,000 and over 750 artefacts respectively, thus raising their total haul to some 3,600 items.[2] The declining harvest from each successive raid on the remains indicates that the exploitation of the world's most famous wreck, destroyed by collision with an iceberg, has now collided with the law of diminishing returns. A new sensation from the site is highly unlikely. Any new find will now have to be remarkable indeed to surprise sensation-seekers, ghouls and the general public so as to lure them back with their money to another expensive *Titanic* exhibition. The small army of *Titanic* enthusiasts will undoubtedly remain actively interested in anything to do with the ship; but they are not numerous enough to underpin the huge outlay that would be needed to discover or recover something really new and important – if there is anything worthwhile and accessible left to find. The films and photographs of the *Titanic* constitute a unique and justifiable historical record; the bits and bobs pilfered from her resting place do not in themselves pass the "so what?" test.

In autumn 1995 it was reported, inevitably it seems, that Hollywood had actually broken into the hull of the *Titanic*, in order to use it as a set for "an epic romance and a four-hankie, very emotional script." The London *Daily Mail* of 3 October, citing the magazine *Hollywood Reporter*, announced that James Cameron, the director of such egregious motion pictures as *Alien* and *Terminator*, was behind the intrusion, carried out with the help of Russian submersibles. He was quoted as saying: "The

Titanic is a symbol for human greed and arrogance and dependence on technology." Indeed it is – just as much at the end of the 20th century as it was at the beginning.

More significant than all the objects recovered and put on display is surely the fact that half a dozen visits to the wreck have intensified rather than clarified so many un-answered questions about the disaster. While there is now absolute confirmation of the observation by many wit-nesses that she broke in two as she sank, the straggling crack that the colliding iceberg almost certainly opened in her side is deeply buried in the ocean floor. It could not be laid bare without unprecedented expenditure of time, money and effort – an investment that is unlikely to be made for the reasons given above.

The scraping of the bow by IFREMER in 1987 to reveal the name *Titanic* may or may not be classifiable as vandalism but should have established positive identi-fication of the wreck. In fact, as we said at the end of chapter 4, there are a surprising number of reasons for wondering whether there is room for doubt on this elementary issue, even giving rise to the suspicion of a switch.

The name was embossed on a black plate on either side of the bow and embellished with gold paint. It was also picked out in black on a white plate at the rounded stern. Exchanging three name-plates amid all the other work going on aboard both ships would not have taken much time or effort. The only other obvious external features, readily changeable and actually changed more than once, by which the *Titanic* and the *Olympic* could be told apart were the sides of their A decks (originally wholly open on both, then half enclosed on the former) and their B decks (different window patterns for different internal layouts).

In Belfast the *Olympic* went into dry dock on 2 March

1912 for a routine propeller-blade replacement which would normally take a few hours – and stayed there. If we may now pursue the conspiracy theory to its conclusion, this would have given the yard's experts a chance to examine her stern and perhaps discover that there was rather more of a problem than they had suspected. The *Olympic* was not ready to leave until Thursday 7 March, which meant another cancelled return trip to New York and concomitant setback for White Star's finances. No other liner could fill the sudden gap in the schedule. If the blade-shedding episode shook up the recently repaired, brittle stern to such an extent that a major restructuring, at huge cost in time and money, was called for, this might have been the moment to send the *Titanic* to sea as the *Olympic* and patch up the real *Olympic* sufficiently for her to withstand an undemanding sea trial as the *Titanic*.

But surely there would have to be more to such a brazen substitution than three name-plates? Surprisingly enough, not much: lifebelts and lifeboats carried the ship's name but precious little else aboard did so. Each ship, as we saw, had three bells at forecastle, bridge and crow's nest; the latter, on show at Greenwich almost perfectly preserved, had nothing engraved on it at all, although one would expect the more "public" (but undiscovered) bells on bridge and forecastle to have borne the ship's name. There were forty-eight name-bearing lifebelts to throw into the sea should someone fall overboard (strangely, there is no mention of these in the evidence on the disaster, although we read of scores of deckchairs being thrown into the water for people to cling to). Lifeboats also traditionally bore the name of their ship, but switching the detachable name-boards would not have been difficult.

But what about such items as cutlery, crockery and linen? Individual ships, even White Star's, used to have their own dedicated household goods: a cup with the name *Oceanic*, obviously a souvenir of an earlier voyage, was found in one of the searches. But latterly White Star had very sensibly standardized these items, supplied at

Southampton where there was also a special laundry, so that they could be used on any liner. As for headed note-paper, menu-cards and the like, which did bear the name of the ship rather than the line, somebody would in any case have ensured that the stationery was delivered to the ship bearing the same name.

Neither Dr Ballard nor anyone else who has visited the wreck for pictorial or plundering purposes has produced a single object or photograph of anything showing the name "Titanic" – except on the bow and on one luggage-tag. The name is shown on nothing else both built into the ship and recovered or recorded so far. We found this sufficiently remarkable to invite every likely source to settle the matter once and for all by furnishing proof that the wreck was the *Titanic*. Reactions ranged from amusement via irritation to ridicule and shock that anyone would raise such a question.

Our difficulty was that a substitution, far-fetched or no, looked like a promising explanation for so many puzzles. We know, for example, that White Star insisted on adding to the *Olympic*'s already alarming damage deficit by fight-ing the Admiralty all the way to the House of Lords. Since IMM managed to make a small profit in 1911, thanks mainly to White Star which more than made up for losses elsewhere, Morgan and Ismay had no *need* of the Navy's money. Nor was there any legal or commercial principle at stake as the collision was an isolated occurrence with no outside implications. Only a change in the law could have opened the way to compensation for pilot error which, as things stood then, meant that the ship was held responsible in law even though her owners and master were blameless. The bitter battle for damages can only have been an attempt to recover the losses run up by the *Olympic* in, after and because of her imbroglio with the cruiser (although it may also have been a reflection of the wounded *amour propre* of IMM/White Star in general and Captain E.J. Smith, who urged them on, in particular). We know that an undamaged *Olympic* would have had to work hard for six years to pay for herself; one badly damaged at the start of her career and thus absent from the battle against Cunard at a crucial time would have needed rather longer. She would surely have been seen as an irritating liability by Morgan. The case dragged on for three and a half years, long after the *Titanic* (and the *Hawke*) had sunk and the *Olympic* had gone to war. Morgan was proud of his Midas touch and was a bad loser. IMM must have *wanted* the money desperately, need or no need.

In chapters 8 and 9 we recorded the interest, greater in America than Britain, of the official inquiries in personal financial links between the builders and the owners of the *Titanic*. On day three of the American hearings Philip Franklin of IMM did mention that Lord Pirrie was a director of his company. But the invisible man in the *Titanic* legend clearly did not register with Senator Smith as also being the chairman of Harland and Wolff; the British merely noted but took no notice of the close connection. White Star was the yard's principal and most precious customer, its every order bound by contract to yield a cost-plus profit of five per cent. Interdependence does not come much closer than that, regardless of who might or might not hold directorships or shares in what. Struggling to keep his yard going in the new century, Lord Pirrie gained access to J.P. Morgan's capital by encouraging the American monopolist to absorb White Star into his IMM combine; Pirrie then persuaded Morgan and his surrogate in shipping matters, Ismay Junior, to invest in gigantic new Harland and Wolff ships for a no-holds-barred assault on Cunard's position as market leader in transatlantic shipping. But White Star suffered one setback after another, including the extra bills run up by the *Olympic* at the worst possible time. Meanwhile

Cunard called on the British Government for aid and went from strength to strength with its Blue-Riband winners. The victory of speed over splendour proved permanent, the Morgan bid for Atlantic supremacy failed and White Star was eventually sold to a triumphant Cunard at a loss. The only other winner was Pirrie's beloved yard.

The perfunctory trials of the *Titanic*, a pale imitation of the *Olympic*'s, were followed by an outbreak of fire in bunker number ten. It could have been dealt with at Southampton, with all a great port's fire-fighting facilities and without affecting sailing time; instead, an extra twelve firemen were specially signed on to deal with it at sea.[3] The blaze, as we saw in chapter 9, was concealed from Clarke, the Board of Trade inspector. Why did Smith not have the fire put out as soon as possible? Why did he hide it? Come to that, why did his ship consistently show a slight list to port in a calm sea before the collision, as noted by several aboard?[4] Was there some undeclared damage to account for this – a leak in the weakened stern, for example? Why after the collision did Smith run the engines slow ahead for some minutes, as attested by witnesses, a move which would have exacerbated the flooding of the forward compartments? Why was counter-flooding not attempted as a means of keeping the ship on an even keel for longer? Why did Dr Ballard find a bulkhead not on his plan of the *Titanic* when exploring the wreck?[5]

Nor should we forget Chief Officer Henry Wilde, hauled against his will out of his berth under Captain Haddock (who surely needed him more) to serve again under Captain Smith. We related in chapter 3 how Wilde was very unhappy about the transfer. He wrote to his sister (in time to catch the post offloaded at Queenstown) to say, "I still don't like this ship ... I have a queer feeling about it." How could he *still* not like a ship on which he had never sailed and which he first boarded at Southampton on departure day? We can only speculate as to the origin of his "queer feeling"; from what little is known of the man, he does not seem to have been the nervous or superstitious type. Nor was his sister the only recipient of his anxiety: he told friends who advised him to accept the transfer that he was only doing so with "much misgivings".[6] What had he heard or seen?

Wilde's arrival of course meant that Murdoch was demoted to First Officer while Lightoller, the only one of the three seniors with an extra master's certificate, was moved down to Second. This voluntary adjunct to a master's ticket was effectively essential for command of a large steamer, especially a liner, which may explain why Wilde and Murdoch never became captains. But then neither did Lightoller, lucky to survive the disaster but unlucky to be forever associated with it (which did not deter the Royal Navy from entrusting him with command of a man-of-war in battle). The blighting of his career seems scant reward for his steadfast loyalty to his employers as displayed at the inquiries; but then loyalty to a company is commonly unrequited. Lightoller's demotion for the maiden voyage forced erstwhile Second Officer Blair off the ship altogether, for which he was doubtless truly thankful; but his disappearance coincided with that of the lookouts' binoculars, locked away on Smith's order in what now became Lightoller's cabin. There is one other point to be made about Lightoller: as a survivor of several earlier shipwrecks and holder of an extra master's ticket, he must have known more about the latest lifeboats and launching equipment than he ever admitted.

It was not only Wilde who was patently reluctant to go on the "maiden voyage". We drew attention to the high number of *Olympic* veterans below deck as well as on the bridge (to the manifest inconvenience of Captain Haddock). But of the firemen serving the great boilers on the preliminary run from Belfast to Southampton, who were most likely to have known of the bunker fire, only *one* signed on again at Southampton.[7] The rest, even though they must have been short of money as a result of the long coal strike just ended, forwent the chance of continued employment and preferred to seek out other ships. Fireman John Coffey, who did sign on at Southampton, took extraordinary pains to desert at Queenstown, burrowing under the mailbags containing the last, unhappy letters from Wilde and Beedem.

But in terms of interest and importance, J. P. Morgan, the real owner of the ill-fated ship, is the outstanding absentee, topping the unusually lengthy list of fifty-five passengers known to have cancelled their bookings at the eleventh hour. He was too ill to sail on the world's most lavish liner, but well enough to reunite with his mistress at Aix-les-Bains, where he was found "in excellent health" by a reporter "just after the ship went down".[8] Asked about the disaster, he "indicated extreme distress". He had arrived at the French resort after a Nile cruise and visits to Rome and Florence; the news confirming the disaster broke on his seventy-fifth birthday, 17 April. Fortunately a large part of his art collection, kept in Europe to avoid American import duty (happily eased just as Britain introduced death duties), happened to miss the ship "because of last-minute hold-ups in crating".[9] The ultimate owner of the lost ship was thus twice blessed: to him that hath shall be given.

Also missing, if in a different way altogether, was Fireman Thomas Hart of 51 College Street, Southampton, whose enlistment on 6 April was mentioned in chapter 2. His name failed to appear on the list of survivors and was therefore posted on the bulletin board outside White Star's Southampton office a dozen days later. But on 8 May 1912 there was a knock at the door of his house. When the missing man's mother opened it, there stood Thomas

Hart himself, safe and well if somewhat dishevelled. The story he told his astounded family and the police was that his discharge certificate must have been stolen while he was drunk and used by someone else to get a berth on the *Titanic*. Hart recalled nothing else, but he claimed to have been living rough ever since, afraid to reveal himself amid all the furore about the disaster.[10] The name of the man who took over his identity and died in his stead was never discovered. One oddity about Hart's story is that half a dozen other men from College Street were on the lost ship; the impostor thus ran a high risk of exposure. Hart belonged to the notoriously reluctant tribe of firemen. He might have ducked the voyage on hearing something disturbing from the all but 100 per cent of his colleagues who decided not to re-enlist at Southampton, selling his book for the money he must have needed to live on for four weeks.

Smith took his ship on the "Outward Southern Track" in use from 15 January to 14 August. Yet when ice was present on the route from about April to June or July for three years running in 1903–5 (but not in such great amounts or so far south as in 1912), the turning point was shifted from 42° to 41° north, still on longitude 47° west – sixty miles due south. As a veteran master Smith must have known this, as well as the even more unusual ice threat reported even before he set sail on the 10th. "The field ice was certainly at that time further south than it had been seen for many years," the British Report said. Smith's delayed turn cannot be regarded as an evasive measure; on the contrary, given currents and the size of the field, it made sure he would meet the ice.

Even if Captain Smith believed his ship "practically unsinkable", the flooding of no fewer than five compartments simultaneously (to say nothing of a sixth when a fire-weakened bulkhead burst) and the gloomy prognosis of Thomas Andrews would have disabused him. He had this information within twenty-five minutes of the collision, but waited another twenty minutes before starting the pumps. In fact the ship's efforts to save herself look remarkably feeble. It is possible that concentrated pumping forward and judicious counter-flooding aft might have kept the ship closer to an even keel and afloat for longer: Lord Mersey and his expert assessors thought so.[11] Work was done on bringing forward the movable suction pump through the reopened watertight doors, presumably with a view to using the aft pumps to help the forward ones; but this plan seems to have fizzled out in the same ineffectual way as the idea of opening the gangway doors and filling up the lifeboats through them.

The whole process of preparing and lowering the boats was a bodge. Had the collision happened in rough weather rather than a flat calm, one is left with the impression that hardly anyone would have survived. No systematic search of the ship was made to ensure that as many women and children got off as possible.

Temperatures of twenty-eight degrees Fahrenheit in the water and thirty-one in the air meant that people, even well wrapped up and clinging to each other or rowing, would survive for no more than minutes in the sea and not very much longer if immersed before getting into a boat. The idea that Bride could have spent up to three-quarters of an hour with his head in an air pocket under a capsized boat is simply ludicrous. His foot injuries (as distinct from frostbite) were never explained; nor was his disappearance from all known records in 1922. Bride also saw things that nobody else saw. Lightoller and Colonel Gracie, who were pulled under and then blown back to the surface by the sinking ship, since they manifestly lived to tell the tale in the witness-box and in books, can only have spent a very few minutes in the water, even if they seemed like years at the time. It is irritating that neither public inquiry sought clarity on such points.

The United States Senate found Smith negligent and a series of court hearings ensued. The United States District Court for New York by January 1913 logged claims totalling $16,804,112; against this could be set $97,772 and two cents, the net salvage value of the *Titanic*'s legacy (lifeboats, prepaid eastbound freight charges, fares and the like) as computed by White Star. It was to this pitiful amount that the line petitioned to have its liability limited. This would fail if negligence were proved. The court set a higher limit of $663,000. But in the end, which came only in 1916, all American claims were settled out of court when White Star admitted liability and agreed to pay a total of $2,500,000, to be divided pro rata among the claimants: the maximum for a death was fixed at $50,000 in first class and $1,000 for a migrant. White Star suffered no such delay in recovering £1 million from the insurers as their share of the cost of the lost hull.

Ironically it was in Britain, whose inquiry had studiously avoided a finding of negligence, that the High Court decided otherwise. Under the Merchant Shipping Acts, White Star were liable for lost cargo and baggage worth £123,711. But Thomas Ryan sued the line for compensation for his lost son Patrick, a third-class passenger. In June 1913 the jury found Captain Smith negligent as to the speed of his ship, though not as to lookouts, and awarded Ryan a modest £100, a revealing assessment of the value of a third-class life. Other bereaved relatives won similar amounts in actions consolidated into the Ryan case. White Star appealed, as was their wont, and lost, as was their wont, in February 1914.[12] These judgments doubtless influenced their decision to settle American claims out of court there, rather than in court in England. But the finding of negligence against their commodore stood; Lord Mersey's cover-up fell away. But some people were never compensated: the *Independent* newspaper of London reported in January 1995 that relatives of Lebanese migrants on the *Titanic*, for example, have never seen a penny. The disappearance of the line's archive after Cunard took over did not help.

Among many lesser mysteries still unsolved is that of the capsized lifeboat (as distinct from collapsible) seen by Marian Thayer, Captain Rostron and Captain Lord but otherwise unaccounted for. The discovery, by the *Mackay-Bennett* on Monday 22 April in the vicinity of the damaged collapsible B, of twenty-seven corpses, including J. J. Astor's, is another conundrum. Astor – if it was he and not a thief who ransacked his stateroom – was seen (by his own wife, no less) to be aboard the *Titanic* after the last boat had left. But his body turned up among a group of passengers and crew who in all probability had been in a lifeboat: they were found together near one, most had had the forethought to dress warmly, several had food and/or tobacco and matches in their pockets.

The lifeboat muddle even extends to the *Mount Temple*, which normally carried twenty. These were swung out for a possible rescue as she headed for the Boxhall position; but for some unexplained reason, on the night of the disaster the ship was carrying two extra boats, which were not swung out (presumably because there were no spare davits). So said Captain Moore at the American inquiry on its eighth day. By day eight of the British inquiry, eighteen days later, Moore was saying that he had a total of twenty lifeboats aboard, of which eighteen had been swung out.

The Captain seems also to have been unusually vulnerable to being misheard, misreported or misprinted. The American record has him amending his longitude from 51° 15' west to 51° 41', an error of fourteen miles (but an easy misprint for 51° 14', a difference of only 1,100 yards); in Britain he was reported as saying that, when he got the distress signal, "we were then about fifteen miles from where the *Titanic* foundered." If we now give him the benefit of the doubt a second time and read fifty for fifteen, about correct for the distance between his and

Boxhall's references, we are still left with the fact that Moore said he stopped for ice at about 3 a.m. at what must have been a rather shorter distance from the wreck – and stayed put while the *Carpathia* did all the work on the Monday morning. Several witnesses on the Canadian Pacific vessel that night swore that the *Titanic* and her lights had actually been sighted from her.

Moore himself was one of many witnesses who saw a "mystery ship". There must have been several unidentified vessels in the vicinity of the wreck, given the number of sightings irreconcilable as to position, time, type of ship, course and/or heading; Moore's had the single dark funnel with the strange device in the white band. This description snugly fits the Anchor-Donaldson Line's *Saturnia*, westbound from Glasgow to St John's, New Brunswick; she turned back to assist but reportedly *stopped in the ice six miles away from the wreck site*.[13] The Board of Trade scoured the world for Moore's and Lord's and Rostron's mystery ship(s), seen by so many witnesses; why did it not look in its own backyard?

The mystery only becomes more mysterious with the passage of time. Out of the blue in *National Geographic* magazine in 1986 there appeared a letter from one Geraldine Hamilton of Calgary, Alberta:

> My father, now almost 89 years of age, left England in early April 1912 to come to Canada (aboard the liner *Victorian*). He claims, and has claimed for years, to have witnessed the flares from the *Titanic*. This ship may well have been the mystery ship and closest witness to this tragedy.[14]

Sideswiping an iceberg or other object was the one foreseeable contingency the *Titanic* was not built to withstand; she was meant to survive head-on collisions, either involving her bow running into something, or the bow of another ship running into her. A head-on crash would undoubtedly have cost many lives. Her double bottom should have kept her dry had she run aground. But a lateral collision might conveniently dispose of a damaged hull with negligible risk to the human life aboard, as a shipwright such as Lord Pirrie or Thomas Andrews must have known (the *ex post facto* proof being that nobody on the wreck was killed or even injured by the impact itself). They could be confident that the ship would float long enough in the busy North Atlantic for another ship or ships to come up and take everybody off – something which indeed could easily be organized in advance for safety's sake. There is no need to postulate a mass-murder plot for the conspiracy theory: only an insurance fraud which went horribly wrong.

Captain Smith did not sidestep the icefield but certainly cut things too fine, as was his wont. His ship met a barely perceptible iceberg in freak conditions earlier than he envisaged, or else even he with his record would surely have taken evasive action. He must have expected to sight ice because he had been told it lay ahead and close to, if not across, his track. Had there been a plot to write off the ship and lift off the passengers onto other IMM ships (for example, the *Californian*), they would have been caught unawares by a premature crash brought on by Smith's recklessness. One might also wonder whether Wilde was trying to prepare his sister for a shock announcement about the ship he disliked so much ...

As Chief Officer, Wilde was responsible for the ship's log. He of course was lost; but four officers survived, and Captain Smith was on deck to the last, encouraging here, ordering there, freeing the Marconi men of their duties and telling every man to look out for himself at the very end. Why was the log allowed to go down with the ship, a document of unique value to the inquiry bound to be held into the disaster? It could so easily have been placed in a boat with one of the officers.

The log would almost certainly have proved Ismay a liar about the doomed ship's speed and his role in increasing it. We noted that someone rather let the cat out of the bag by inserting a notice in the shipping columns of *The New York Times* that the *Titanic* was expected on Tuesday afternoon rather than Wednesday morning. The source of this can only have been a wireless message from the ship herself. Ismay's denial that she was going for a record and his assertion that she never exceeded seventy-five revolutions have been accepted because she was incapable of wresting the Blue Riband from the *Mauretania*. But boasting after her maiden voyage that the *Titanic* was not only even bigger and more luxurious but also faster than the *Olympic* would have been good advertising copy; and it was open to the *Titanic* to bid for a record on the Outward Southern Track. The British Titanic Society obtained evidence from two seafarers, Fireman John Thompson and Trimmer William McIntyre (not called to give evidence at either inquiry), that on the Sunday, 14 April, revolutions reached seventy-seven.[15]

The difficulties thrown up by a conspiratorial theory of the loss of the *Titanic*, no matter how many mysteries it may seem to explain, are obvious. Who did it, who needed to know, was the recovery of £1 million by writing off the *Olympic* on the *Titanic*'s insurance worth the huge risks? – to name but three. In the end it was Harland and Wolff who provided an acid test. The *Titanic* had the hull-number 401 which, they said, would have been stamped on major parts built into the ship. The IMAX film shows a 401 on the port propeller. Yes; but the *Titanic* was cannibalized for parts when the *Olympic* was damaged: could this not have been one of them? However that may be, one of the more arcane exhibits at Greenwich – the helm indicator from the stern bridge mentioned above – clearly showed the number 401 stamped deeply into its bronze stand ...

A conspiracy theory arises after a disaster because many people find it impossible to believe such a tragedy could just *happen*. Indeed for some a conspiracy theory is a psychological necessity, to help them come to terms with a shocking event. There is a manifest need for formal recognition of a widespread phenomenon which we could call "specific post-traumatic paranoia", whereby people of sound mind, whether victims, their relatives or merely concerned observers, exhibit temporary and/or par-ticularized paranoid symptoms as their way of coping with a disaster. It is undeniable that catastrophes almost never merely "happen" but are *caused*, whether by metal fatigue, other technical failure or human error. Such "acts of God" as floods, landslides, famines, epidemics and even climatic changes are now also increasingly blamed on human error.

One does not have to believe that organized crime, the right wing, the left wing, the CIA and the KGB combined to murder President John F. Kennedy in order to suspect there must have been more to it than one assassin with an old rifle. The fact that some disasters, such as the explosion of Pan Am flight 103 over Lockerbie in Scotland at Christ-mas 1988, are the result of criminal or terrorist plots only encourages the conspiracy theorists. So does the fact that it is commonly impossible to draw a line between degrees of human error ("error" in the broadest sense, including sins and crimes) on what is undoubtedly a sliding scale encompassing forgetfulness, carelessness, recklessness, wilful negligence, malevolence, sabotage and all the way to mass murder. The loss of the *Titanic* falls squarely in the middle of this scale: she died of wilful negligence.

The present authors do not accept that the hole in her bow discovered by IFREMER in 1987 was caused by her burning bunker exploding, for two reasons. The first is that the seat of the fire was at least 150 feet astern of the hole; the second is that there is no need to. There being no massive object from inside the ship in the vicinity to account for the hole, it must have been caused by the hull buckling on hitting the bottom at an angle.

And even if the explosion theory, advanced by George Tulloch of RMS Titanic Inc. during a British television documentary shown in March 1995,[16] were correct it is still a diversion from the central fact. SS *Titanic* hit an iceberg and sank because her master, urged on by her absent owner's agent, sent her careering blindly into a known icefield. There was no reason for him to do this.

When all the contradictions and complications, the mixed motives and the theories are stripped away, and as the eerie, ravished hulk slowly and silently crumbles two and a half miles under the Atlantic, that is what we are left with: the eternal riddle of the *Titanic*.

APPENDICES

APPENDIX I

Passenger List
(amended and consolidated)

These lists are known to contain many errors; it has not been possible to correct them all.
Those saved are shown in bold.
Names in brackets are variants shown on list of survivors.
Names in square brackets are servants.

First Class

Adams, Miss E.
Allen, Miss E. W.
Allison, H. J., Wife, Daughter, Son, Maid and **Nurse**
Anderson, Harry
Andrews, Miss C. I.
Andrews, Thomas
Appleton, Mrs E. D.
Artaga-Veytia, R.
Astor, Col. J. J., **Wife**, Man and **Maid** [Bidois, Miss]
  Aubert, Mrs N. and **Maid** [Segisser, Miss Emma]
Barkworth, O. H.
  (Barkworth, A. H.)
Bauman, J.
Baxter, Mrs J.
Beattie, T.

Beckwith, R. T. and **Wife**
  (Beckwith, R. L.)
Behr, K. H.
Birnbaum, Jakob
Bishop, D. H. and **Wife**
Bjornstrom, H.
Blackwell, S. W.
Blank, Henry
Bonnell, Miss C.
Bonnell, Lily (Bonnell, Miss Elizabeth)
Borebank, J. J.
Bowen, Miss
Bowerman, Elsie
Brady, John B.
Brandies, E.
Brayton, George
Brew, Dr A. J.
Brown, Mrs J. J.
Brown, Mrs J. M.

335

Bucknell, Mrs S. W. and Maid
(Bucknell, Mrs W.)
Butt, Major A.
Calderhead E. P.
Cardell, Mrs C. (Candee)
Cardeza, Mrs J. W. M. and
Maid [Hard, Anna]
Cardeza, T. D. M. and Man
[Lesneur ?]
Carlson, Frank
Carran, F. M.
Carter, Lucille
Carter, Master
Carter, W. E., Wife and Maid
[Serepeca, Miss]
Case, Howard B.
Cassebeer, Mrs H. A.
Cavendish, T. W., Wife and
Maid [Barber, Miss]
Chaffee, H. F. and Wife
Chambers, N. C. and Wife
Cherry, Miss G.
Chevro, Paul (Chevré)
Chibnall, Mrs E. M.
Chisholm, Robert
Clark, W. M. and Wife
Clifford, G. Q.
Colley, E. P.
Compton, Mrs A. T.
Compton, A. T. Jr.
Compton, Miss S. W.
(Compton, Miss S. R.)
Cornell, Mrs B. C. (Cornell,
Mrs R. C.)
Crafton, John B.
Crosby, E. G., Wife and
Daughter
Cummings, J. B. and Wife
Daly, P. D. (Daly, P. B.)
Daniel, R. W.
Davidson, T. and Wife
Devilliers, Mrs B.

Dick, A. A. and Wife
Dodge, W., Wife and Son
Douglas, Mrs F. C.
Douglas, W., Wife and Maid
(LeRoy, Miss)
Dulles, William O.
Earnshew, Mrs B.
Eganhiem, Mrs A. F. L.
(Fleganhiem)
Endres, Miss C.
Eustis, Miss E. M.
Flynn, J. I.
Foreman, B. L.
Fortune, M., Wife, three
Daughters and Son
Franklin, T. P.
Frauenthal, Dr H. and Wife
Frauenthal, T. G.
Frolicher, Miss M.
Futrelle, J. and Wife
Gee, Arthur
Gibson, Miss D.
Gibson, Mrs L.
Giglio, Victor
Goldenberg, S. L.
Goldenberg, Mrs S. L.
Goldshmidt, G. B.
Gracie, Col. A.
Graham, Mr
Graham, Miss M. E.
Graham, Mrs W.
Greenfield, Mrs L. D.
Greenfield, W. B.
Guggenheim, B.
Harder, G. A. and Wife
Harper, H. S., Wife and
Servant [Hammond ?]
Harris, H. B. and Wife
Harrison, W. H.
Haven, H.
Hawksford, W. J.
Hays, C. M., Wife, Daughter

and **Maid** [Pericault, Miss]
Head, Christopher
Hilliard, H. H.
Hippach, Mrs I. S.
Hippach, Miss J.
Hogeboom, Mrs J. C.
Holversoh, A. O. and **Wife**
  (Holverson, Mrs A. O.)
Hopkins, W. E.
Host, W. F.
Hoyt, F. M. and **Wife**
Icham, Miss A. E.
Ismay, J. Bruce and Man
Jones, C. C.
Julian, H. F.
Kent, Edward A.
Kenyon, F. R. and **Wife**
Kimball, E. N. and **Wife**
Klaber, Herman
Lambert, W. S.
Leader, Mrs A. (Leader, Mrs
  F. A.)
Levy, E. G.
Lines, Mrs E. H.
Lines, Miss M. C.
Lindstrom, Mrs J.
Long, Milton C.
Longley, Miss G. F.
Loring, J. H.
Madill, Miss G. A. (Mrs
  Madill)
Maguire, J. E.
Marechal, Pierre
McCaffry, T.
McCarthy, T. J.
McGough, J. R.
Melody, A.
Melsom, H. M.
Mervin, D. W. and **Wife**
  (Marvin)
Meyer, Edward J. and **Wife**
  (Meyer, Edward G.)

Millet, Frank D.
Minnehan, Dr W. E., **Wife** and
  Daughter
Moore, C. and Man
Morgan, Mr, Wife and **Maid**
  (Duff Gordon)
Natsch, Charles
Newell, A. W.
Newell, Miss Alice
Newell, Miss M.
Newsom, Miss Helen
Nicholson, A. S.
Ostby, E. C.
Ostby, Miss H. R.
Ovies, S.
Parr, M. H. W.
Partner, Austin
Payne, V.
Pears, T. and **Wife**
Penasco, V., **Wife** and **Maid**
  [Olivia, Miss]
Peuchen, Major A.
Porter, W. C.
Potter, Mrs T. Jr.
Reuchling, J. G.
Rhiems, George
Robert, Mrs E. S. and **Maid**
  [Kenchen, Amelia]
Roebling, W. A. 2nd
Rolmans, C. (Rolmane, C.)
Rood, Hugh
Rosenbaum, Miss
Ross, J. Huge
Rothes, Countess and **Maid**
  [Maloney, Mrs]
Rothschild, M. and **Wife**
Rowe, Alfred
Ryerson, A., **Wife, two**
  Daughters, Son and **Maid**
  [Chandanson]
Saalfeld, Adolph (Saalfield)
Saloman, A. L. (Saleman)

Schabert, Mr (Schabert, Mrs)
Schutes, Miss E. W
Seward, Frederick
Silver, W. B. and Wife (Silvey, Mrs W.)
Silverthorne, Mr
Simonious, Col. A.
Sloper, William T.
Smart, John M.
Smith, J. Clinch
Smith, Mrs L. P.
Smith, R. W.
Snyder, J. and Wife
Speddon, F. O, Wife, Son and Maid [Wilson, Helen]
Spenser, W. A., Wife and Maid
Stalelin, Dr Max
Stead, W. T.
Steffanson, Mr H. B.
Stehli, M. F. and Wife
Stengel, C. E. H. E. and Wife
Stephenson, Mrs W. B.
Stewart, A. A.
Stone, Mrs G. M. and Maid [Picard, Miss Benoit]
Straus, I., Wife, Maid and Man
Sutton, Frederick
Swift, Mrs F. J.
Taussig, E. and Wife
Taussig, Ruth
Taylor, E. S. and Wife (Taylor, E. Z.)
Thayer, J. B, Wife and Maid
Thayer, J. B. Jr.
Thorne, G. and Wife
Tucker, G. M. Jr.
Uruchurtu, Mr
Vanderhoef, W.
Walker, W. A.
Warren, F. M. and Wife
Weir, J.

White, M. J.
White, P. W.
White, R. F., Wife, Maid and Man (White, J. Stuart)
Wick, Mr George and Wife
Wick, Miss Mary
Widener, G. D., Wife, Maid and Man
Widener, Harry
Willard, Miss C.
Williams, Duane
Williams, N. M. Jr. (Williams, R. M.)
Woolner, Hugh
Wright, George
Young, Miss M.

Total: 317
Total Saved: 198

Second Class

Abelson, Hannah
Abelson, Samson
Andrew, Edgar
Angle, W. and Wife (Mrs Florence)
Ashby, John
Baily, Percy
Balls, Ada R.
Bambridge, Mr (Baimbridge)
Banfield, F. J.
Bateman, R. J.
Beane, Edward
Beane, Ethel
Beauchamp, H. J.
Beesley, L.
Belker, Mrs A. O., and three Children (Becker)
Bentham, Lillian
Berreman, W.
Bliss, Kate (Buss, Kate)

Botsford, W. H.
Bowenur, S.
Brito, Jose de
Brown, Mildred
Bryl, Carl
Bryl, Dagmar
Butler, Reginald
Byles, Rev. T. R. D.
Bystrom, K.
Caldwell, A. F.
Caldwell, A. G.
Caldwell, Sylvia
Cameron, Clear
Carbines, W.
Carter, Rev. E. C.
Carter, Lillian
Chapman, Charles
Chapman, Miss E.
Chapman, J. H.
Christy, Alice
Christy, Julia
Clarke, C. V.
Clarke, Ada M.
Coleridge, R. C.
Collender, Erik
Collett, Stuart (Collett, Mrs)
Collyer, Miss C. (Collyer, Mrs)
Collyer, Harvey
Collyer, Miss M.
Corbett, Irene
Corey, Mrs C. P.
Cotterill, Harry
Danbury, H.
Donton, W. J.
Davies, Charles
Davis, Agnes
Davis, J. M.
Davis, Mary
Deacon, Percy
De Carlo, S.
Def, Lena N.

Dibden, W.
Doling, Ada
Doling, Elsie
Drachstedt, Baron von
Drew, J. V.
Drew, Lulu
Drew, M.
Duran, A. (Duran, Miss)
Duran, F. (Duran, Miss)
Fahlstrom, A.
Faunthrope, H.
Faunthrope. L. (Faunthorpe, Mrs Lizzie)
Fillbrook, C.
Fjunk, Annie (Funk)
Foxe, Stanley
Fynney, Joseph
Gale, Henry
Garsido, Ethel (Garside)
Gaskoll, Alfred (Gaskell)
Gavey, Lawrence
Gilbert, W.
Giles, Edgar
Giles, Fred
Giles, Ralph
Gill, John
Gillespie, W.
Givard, H. K.
Greenberg, B. (Greenberg, F.)
Hamaliner, Anna and **Child** (Hamalainer)
Harper, John
Harper, Nina
Harris, George
Harris, Walter
Hart, Benjamin
Hart, Esther
Hart, Eva
Herman, Alice
Herman, Jane
Herman, Kate
Herman, Samuel

Hewlett, Mary D.
Hickman, L.
Hickman, S.
Hiltuner, Martha
Hocking, Eliza
Hocking, George
Hocking, Nellie
Hodges, Henry P.
Hoffman, Mr and **two Children**
Hold, Annie
Hold, Stephen
Hood, Ambrose
Howard, B.
Howard, Ellen T.
Hunt, George
Ilett, Bertha
Jacobsohn, Amy F. (Jacobson)
Jacobsohn, S. S.
Jarvis, John D.
Jeffert, Clifford (Jefferys)
Jeffery, Ernest
Jenkins, Dr J. C.
Jenkins, Stephen
Kano, Nora A. (Keane, Nora A.)
Kantor, S. and **Wife** (Kenton, Mrs Miriam)
Karnes, F.
Keane, Daniel
Kelly, F. (Kelly, Mrs)
Kirkland, Rev. Charles
Kvilner, J. H.
Lahtigen, W. and Wife
Lamb, J. J.
Lamore, Amelia
Laroche, J. and **Wife**
Laroche, Louise
Laroche, S.
Learnot, Rene
Lehman, Bertha
Leitch, Jessie (Leach)

Levy, R. F.
Leyson, R. W. N.
Linjan, John (Lingan)
Louch, Alice
Louch, Charles
Mack, Mary
Malachard, Noël
Mallet, A. and **Wife**
Mallet, Master A.
Mantvila, Joseph
Marshall, Mr
Marshall, Mrs
Masgiavacci, E.
Mathews, W. J.
Maybery, F. H.
McCrie, James
McKane, Peter
Mellers, William
Mellinger, E. and **Child**
Meyer, August
Milling, Jacob
Mitchell, Henry
Moraweck, E.
Moudd, Thomas (Mudd)
Myles, T. F.
Nasser, N. and Wife
Nesson, L.
Nicholls, J.
Norman, Robert D.
Nye, Elizabeth
Otter, Richard
Oxenham, T.
Padro, Julian
Paine, Dr Alfred
Pallas, Emilio
Paris, Mrs L.
Parker, Clifford
Pengelly, F.
Phillips, Alice
Phillips, Robert
Ponzell, Martin (Ponesell)
Portaluppi, E.

Pulsaum, Frank (Pulbaum)
Quick, Jane
Quick, Phyllis
Quick, Vera W.
Reeves, David
Renouf, Lillie
Renouf, Peter H.
Reynolds, Miss E.
Ribsdale, Lucy (Ridsdale)
Richard, Emilie (Emile)
Richards, Emily
Richards, G.
Richards, W.
Rogers, Harry
Rogers, Selina
Rugg, Emily
Sedgwick, F. W.
Sharp, P.
Shelley, L. M. (Shelley, Miss Imanita)
Silven, Lillie (Miss Lyyli)
Sincock, Maud
Sinkkonen, Anna
Sjostedt, E. A.
Slayter, H. M.
Slemer, R. J. (Slemen)
Smith, A.
Smith, Marion
Sobey, Hayden
Stanton, S. Ward
Stokes, Phillip J.
Swane, George
Sweet, George
Tervan, Mrs A. T.
Tooney, Ellen (Toomey)
Trant, M. E. L. (Trant, Mrs Jessie)
Tronplansky, M. A.
Trout, Miss E.
Turpin, Dorothy
Turpin, W. J.
Veale, James

Walcroft, Nellie
Ware, Florence L.
Ware, J. J.
Ware, W. J.
Watt, Bertha
Watt, Bessie
Webber, Susie
Weisz, Leopold
Weisz, Matilda
Wells, Mrs A. (Wells, Miss Addie)
Wells, Miss J.
Wells, Ralph
West, Ada
West, Arthur E.
West, Barbara
West, Constance
Wheadon, E.
Wheeler, Edwin
Wilhelm, C.
Wilkinson, A. C.
Wilkinson, Mrs G.
Williams, C.
Wright, Marion
Yodis, Miss H.

Total: 258
Total Saved: 112

Third Class

Abbott, Eugene
Abbott, Rosa (Abbott, Mrs Rose)
Abbott, Rossmore
Abbing, Anthony
Abelseth, Karen (Abelseth, Koran)
Abelseth, Olaus (Abelseth, Olans)
Abrahamson, August
Adahl, Mauritz

Adams, J.
Ahlin, Johanna
Ahmed, Ali
Aks, Filly
Aks, Leah
Alexander, William
Alhomaki, Ilmari
Ali, William
Allen, William
Allum, Owen G.
Anderson, Albert
Anderson, Alfreda
Anderson, Anders
Anderson, Carla (Corla)
Anderson, Ebba (Child)
Anderson, Ellis
Anderson, Erna
Anderson, Ingeborg (Child)
Anderson, Samuel
Anderson, Sigrid (Child)
Anderson, Sigvard (Child)
Anderson, Thor
Andersson, Ida Augusta
Andersson, Paul Edvin
Angheloff, Minko
Arnold, Joseph
Arnold, Josephine
Aronsson, Ernest Axel A.
Asim, Adola
Asplund, Carl (Child)
Asplund, Charles (Osplund,
   C. Anderson)
Asplund, Felix (Child)
   (Astlund, Felix)
Asplund, Gustaf (Child)
Asplund, Johan (Asplund,
   William)
Asplund, Lillian (Child)
   (Asplund, William)
Asplund, Oscar (Child)
Asplund, Selma (Astlund,
   Selma)

Assaf, Marian (Assim,
   Marriam)
Assam, Ali
Attala, Malake
Augustsan, Albert
Backstrom, Karl
Backstrom, Marie
Baclini, Eugene (Boklin,
   Eugene)
Baclini, Helene (Boklin,
   Helena)
Baclini, Latifa (Boklin, Latifa)
Baclini, Maria (Boklin, Marie)
Badman, Emily (Batman,
   Emily)
Badt, Mohamed
Balkic, Cerin
Banoura, Ayout
Barbara, Catherine
Barbara, Saude
Barry, Julia
Barton, David
Beavan, W. T.
Benson, John Viktor
Berglund, Ivar
Berkeland, Hans
Betros, Tannous
Billiard, A. van and two
   Children
Bing, Lee
Bjorklund, Ernst
Bostandyeff, Guentcho
Boulos, Akar (Child)
Boulos, Hanna
Boulos, Nourelain (Bolos,
   Monthora)
Boulos, Sultani
Bourke, Catherine
Bourke, John
Bowen, David
Bradley, Bridget
Braf, Elin Ester

Braund, Lewis
Brobek, Carl R.
Brocklebank, Owen
Buckley, Daniel
Buckley, Katherine
Burke, Jeremiah
Burke, Mary
Burns, Mary (Burns, Miss
O. M.)
Cacic, Grego
Cacic, Luka
Cacic, Manda
Cacic, Maria
Calie, Peter
Canavan, Mary
Canavan, Pat
Cann, Ernest
Car, Jeannie
Caram, Joseph
Caram, Maria
Carlson, Carol R.
Carlson, Julius
Carlsson, August Sigfrid
Carr, Ellen
Carver, A.
Celotti, Francesco
Chartens, David
Chehab, Emir Farres
Chip, Chang
Christman, Emil
Chronopoulos, Apostolos
Chronopoulos, Demetrios
Coelho, Domingos Fernardeo
Cohen, Gurchon (Cohen,
Gust)
Colbert, Patrick
Coleff, Fotio
Coleff, Peyo
Conlin, Thomas H.
Connaghton, Michel
Connors, Pat
Conolly, Kate

Conolly, Kate
Cook, Jacob
Cor, Bartol
Cor, Ivan
Cor, Ludovik
Corn, Harry
Coutts, Winnie and **two
Children**
Coxon, Daniel
Crease, Ernest James
Cribb, Alice (Cribb, L. M.)
Cribb, John Hatfield
Dahl, Charles
Dahl, Mauritz
Dahlberg, Gerda
Dakic, Branko
Daly, Eugene
Daly, Marcella (Daly,
Marsella)
Danbom, Ernest
Danbom, Sigrid and Son
Danoff, Yoto
Dantchoff, Khristo
Davies, Alfred
Davies, Evan
Davies, John
Davies, Joseph
Davison, Mary (Davidson,
Mary)
Davison, Thomas H.
Dean, Bertram F.
Dean, Hetty, Daughter and
Son (Dean, Ettie)
Delalic, Regyo
Denkoff, Mito
Dennis, Samuel
Dennis, William
Derkings, Edward (Dorking,
Edward)
Devaney, Margaret (Devany,
Margaret)
Dewan, Frank

Dibo, Elias
Dimic, Jovan
Dintcheff, Valtcho
Dooley, Patrick
Dowdell, Elizabeth (Darnell, Elizabeth)
Doyle, Elin
Drapkin, Jenie (Draplin, Jennie)
Drazenovie, Josip
Driscoll, Bridget
Dugemin, Joseph (Dugenon, Joseph)
Dyker, Adolf
Dyker, Elizabeth
Ecimovic, Joso
Edwardsson, Gustaf
Eklunz, Hans
Ekstrom, Johan
Elias, Joseph
Elias, Joseph (Elias, Nicola)
Elsbury, James
Emanuel, Ethel
Emmeth, Thomas
Everett, Thomas J.
Fabini, Leeni (Falnai, Ermaulman)
Farrell, James
Fat-ma, Mustmani
Finote, Luigi (Ferole, Luigi)
Fischer, Ebehard
Flynn, James
Flynn, John
Foley, Joseph
Foley, William
Foo, Choong
Ford, Arthur
Ford, Miss D. M.
Ford, E. W.
Ford, Maggie
Ford, Margaret
Ford, M. W. T. N.

Fox, Patrick
Franklin, Charles
Gallagher, Martin
Garfirth, John
Gerios, Assaf
Gerios, Youssef
Gerios, Youssef
Gheorgheff, Stanio
Gilinski, Leslie
Gilnagh, Katie (Gallenagh, Kate)
Glynn, Mary
Godwin, Frederick
Goldsmith, Emily A.
Goldsmith, Frank J.
Goldsmith, Frank J. Jnr.
Goldsmith, Nathan
Goncalves, Manoel E.
Goodwin, Augusta
Goodwin, Charles E.
Goodwin, Lillian A. and four Children
Green, George
Gronnestad, Daniel D.
Guest, Robert
Gustafson, Alfred
Gustafson, Anders
Gustafson, Johan
Gustafsson, Gideon
Haas, Aloisia
Hadman, Oscar (Hedman)
Hagardon, Kate
Hagarty, Nora
Hagland, Angvald O.
Hagland, Konrad R.
Hakkurainen, Elin (Hokkronen, Ellen)
Hakkurainen, Pekko
Hampe, Leon
Hankonen, Eluna (Hankonen, Elin)
Hanna, Mansour

Hansen, Claus
Hansen, Henry Damgavd
Hansen, Janny (Hanson,
Jenny)
Harknett, Alice
Harmer, Abraham
Hart, Henry
Healy, Nora
Hee, Ling (Hip, Ching)
Heininen, Wendla
Hemming, Nora
Hendekovic, Ignaz
Henery, Delia
Henriksson, Jenny
Hervonen, Helga and
Daughter (Herronen,
Hilda)
Hickkinen, Laina (Hakaonen,
Line)
Hillstrom, Hilda (Hillsfrom,
Hilda)
Holm, John F. A.
Holton, Johan
Horgan, John
Howard, May (Mary)
Humblin, Adolf
Hyman, Abraham
Ilieff, Ylio
Ilmakangas, Ida
Ilmakangas, Pista
Ivanoff, Konio
Jansen, Carl
Jardin, Jose Netto
Jensen, Carl (Jenson, Carl)
Jenson, Hans Peter
Jensen, Nilho R.
Jensen, Svenst L.
Jenymin, Annie (Jermyn,
Annie)
Johannessen, Bernt
(Johanson, Verent)
Johannessen, Elias

Johansen, Nils
Johanson, Oscar (Johannson,
Oscar)
Johanson, Oscar L.
(Johnnanson, Oscar L.)
Johansson, Erik
Johansson, Gustaf
Johnson, A.
Johnson, Alice and **Daughter**
(Johnnanson, Alice)
Johnson, Harold (Johnsen,
Harold)
Johnson, W.
Johnsson, Carl
Johnsson, Malkolm
Johnston, A. G.
Johnston, Mrs, Daughter and
Son
Jonkoff, Lazor
Jonsson, Nielo H.
Joseph, Mary
Jusila, Erik (Johnsila, Eric)
Jusila, Katrina
Jutel, Henrik Hansen
Kallio, Nikolai
Kalvig, Johannes H.
Karajic, Milan
Karlson, Einar
Karlson, Nils August
Karun, Anna (Child) (Kuram,
Anna)
Karun, Franz (Kuram, Frans)
Kassan, Housseing (Casem,
Boyen)
Kassein, Hassef (Cassen,
Masef)
Kassem, Fared
Keefe, Arthur
Kekic, Tido
Kelly, Annie C.
Kelly, James (Southampton)
Kelly, James (Queenstown)

Kelly, Mary
Kennedy, John
Kerane, Andy
Khalil, Betros
Khalil, Zahie
Kiernam, John
Kiernam, Phillip
Kilgannon, Thomas
Kink, Anton
Kink, Louise and Daughter
   (Kink, Louisa)
Kink, Maria
Kink, Vincenz
Klasen, Hilda and Daughter
Klasen, Klas A.
Kraeff, Thodor
Laitinen, Sofia
Laleff, Kristo
Lam, Ali (Lam, Hah)
Lam, Len
Landegren, Aurora
   (Lundgreen, Aurora)
Lane, Patrick
Lang, Fang
Lang, Hee
Larson, Viktor
Larsson, Bengt Edvin
Larsson, Edvard
Lefebre, Frances, three
   Daughters and one Son
Leinonen, Antti
Lemberopoulos, Peter
Lemon, Denis
Lemon, Mary
Leonard, L.
Lester, James
Lindablom, August
Lindahl, Agda
Lindell, Edvard B.
Lindell, Elin
Lindqvist, Einar
Linehan, Michel

Ling, Lee
Lithman, Simon
Lobb, Cordelia
Lobb, William A.
Lockyer, Edward
Lovell, John
Lulic, Nicola (Lulu, Nella)
Lundahl, John
Lundin, Olga (Lunden, Olga)
Lundstrom, Jan (Lundstrom,
   Imrie)
MacKay, George W.
Madigan, Maggie
Madsen, Fridjof (Mathesen,
   Frithiof)
Maenpaa, Matti
Mahon, Delia
Maisner, Simon
Makinen, Kalle
Malinoff, Nicola
Mampe, Leon
Mangan, Mary
Mannion, Margaret
   (Marrion, Margaret)
Marinko, Dmitri
Markim, Johann
Markoff, Marin
McCarthy, Katie
McCoy, Agnes
McCoy, Alice
McCoy, Bernard
McCormack, Thomas
McDermot, Delia
McElroy, Michel
McGovern, Mary (McGovan,
   Mary)
McGowan, Annie
   (McGowan, Miss A.)
McGowan, Katherine
McMahon, Martin
McNamee, Eileen
McNamee, Neal

Meanwell, Marion O.
Mechan, John
Meek, Annie L.
Meeklave, Ellie (Mocklaire, Ellen)
Melkebuk, Philemon
Meme, Hanna (Mauman, Hanne)
Meo, Alfonso
Messemacker, Emma (Messewacker, Arcina)
Messemacker, Guillaume (Messewacker, Guilliam)
Midtsjo, Carl (Midtago, Carl)
Mikanen, John (McKaren, John)
Miles, Frank
Mineff, Ivan
Minkoff, Lazar
Mirko, Dika
Mitkoff, Mito
Moen, Sigurd H.
Monbarek, Hanna
Moncarek, Omine and two Children (Montharck)
Moor, Beile (Moore, Belle)
Moor, Meier (Moore, Neciman)
Moore, Leonard C.
Moran, Bertha
Moran, James
Morgan, Daniel J.
Morley, William
Morrow, Thomas
Moss, Albert
Moussa, Mantoura
Moutal, Rahamin
Mulder, Theo
Mullens, Katie (Mullen, Kate)
Mulvihill, Bertha
Murdlin, Joseph
Murphy, Kate

Murphy, Mary (Murphy, Maggie J.)
Murphy, Nora
Myhrman, Oliver
Naidenoff, Penko
Naked, Maria (Neket, Mariu)
Naked, Said (Neckard, Said)
Naked, Waika (Naseraill, Adelia)
Nancarrow, W. H.
Nankoff, Minko
Nasr, Mustafa
Naughton, Hannah (Nyhan, Anna)
Nedeco, Petroff
Nemagh, Robert
Nenkoff, Christo
Nichan, Krikorian (Muhun, Erikorian)
Nicola, Jamila and Son (Nicola, Jancoli)
Nieminen, Manta
Niklasen, Sander
Nilson, Berta (Nelson, Bertha)
Nilson, Helmina (Nelso, Helmina J.)
Nilsson, August F. (Nelson, Carlo)
Nirva, Isak
Nosworthy, Richard C.
Novel, Mansouer
Nyoven, Johan (Niskenen, John)
Nyston, Anna (Nysten, Anna)
O'Brien, Denis
O'Brien, Hannah
O'Brien, Thomas
O'Connell, Pat D.
O'Connor, Maurice
O'Connor, Pat
Odahl, Martin
O'Donaghue, Bert

Sadowitz, Harry
Sage, Ada (Child)
Sage, Annie
Sage, Constance
  (Child)
Sage, Dorothy
Sage, Douglas
Sage, Frederick
Sage, George
Sage, John
Sage, Stella
Sage, Thomas (Child)
Sage, William (Child)
Salander, Carl
Saljilsvik, Anna (Salkjelsock,
  Anna)
Salonen, Werner
Samaan, Elias
Samaan, Hanna
Samaan, Youssef
Sandman, Johan (Sundman,
  Julian)
Sandstrom, Agnes and **two
  Daughters**
Sarkis, Lahowd
Sarkis, Mardirosian
Sather, Simon
Saundercock, W. H.
Sawyer, Frederick
Scanlan, James
Scrota, Maurice
Sdycoff, Todor
Seman, Betros (Child)
Shabini, Georges (Georges,
  Shabini)
Shaughnessy, Pat
Shedid, Daher
Sheerlinck, Jean (Schurlinch,
  Jane)
Shellard, Frederick
Shine, Ellen
Shorney, Charles

Sihvola, Antti
Simmons, John
Sivic, Husen
Sjoboom, Anna (Sjablom,
  Annie)
Skoog, Anna, two Daughters
  and two Sons
Skoog, William
Slabenoff, Petco
Sleiman, Attalla
Slovovski, Selman
Smiljanic, Mile
Smyth, Julian (Smyth, Salia)
Sohole, Peter
Solvang, Lena
  Jacobsen
Somerton, Francis W.
Sop, Jules (Sap, Jules)
Spector, Woolf
Spinner, Henry
Staneff, Ivan
Stankovic, Jovan
Stanley, Amy
Stanley, E. R.
Storey, T.
Stoyehoff, Ilia
Stoytcho, Mihoff
Strandberg, Ida
Stranden, Jules (Strinder, Julo)
Strilic, Ivan
Strom, Selma (Child)
Sunderland, Victor
Sutehall, Henry
Svensen, Olaf
Svensson, Coverin (Svenson,
  Severin)
Svensson, Johan
Syntakoff, Stanko
Tannous, Daler
Tannous, Elias
Tannous, Thomas
Theobald, Thomas

Thomas, Charles
Thomas, John
Thomas, Tamin and Child
Thomson, Alex
Thorneycroft, Florence
Thorneycroft, Percival
Tikkanen, Juho
Tobin, Roger
Todoroff, Lalio
Tomlin, Ernest P.
Tonfik, Nahli
Tonglin, Gunner
Torber, Ernest
Torfa, Assad
Trembisky, Berk (Trenobisky, Berk)
Tunquist, W. (Turnquist, H.)
Turcin, Stefan
Turgo, Anna (Turgen, Anna)
Twekula, Hedwig (Tukula, Hedvig)
Useher, Baulner
Uzelas, Jovo
Vagil, Adele Jane
Van de Velde, Joseph
Van de Walle, Nestor
Van der Planke, Augusta
Van der Planke, Emilie
Van der Planke, Jules
Van der Planke, Leon
Van der Steen, Leo
Van Impe, Jacob
Van Impe, Rosalie and Daughter
Vartunian, David
Vassilios, Catavelas
Vereruysse, Victor
Vestrom, Huld A. A.
Vook, Janko
Waelens, Achille
Ware, Frederick
Warren, Charles W.

Wazli, Yousif
Webber, James
Weller, Abi
Wende, Olof Edvin
Wennerstrom, August (Wimhormstrom, Amy E.)
Wenzel, Zinhart
Widegrin, Charles
Wiklund, Jacob A.
Wiklund, Karl F.
Wilkes, Ellen
Willey, Edward
Williams, Harry
Williams, Leslie
Windelov, Einar
Wirz, Albert
Wiseman, Philip
Wittenrongel, Camille
Yalsevae, Ivan
Yasbeck, Antoni
Yasbeck, Celiney (Yaslick, Salamy)
Youssef, Brahim (Jousef)
Youssef, Hanne, one Daughter and one Son (Jousef)
Zabour, Hileni
Zabour, Tamini
Zarkarian, Maprieder
Zievens, Rene
Zimmermann, Leo

Total: 709
Total Saved: 175

Officers and Crew of the Titanic

The following is the White Star list of the officers and crew of the *Titanic*. Unless otherwise stated they lived at Southampton.

Names in brackets (on right) are as amended on the lists of survivors or witnesses. Even so, both lists contain many errors.

Crew saved are printed in bold.

E. J. Smith, Captain
H. T. Wilde, Liverpool, Chief Mate
W. M. Murdoch, First Mate
C. H. Lightoller, Second Mate
H. J. Pitman, Somerset, Third Mate
J. G. Boxhall, Hull, Fourth Mate
H. G. Lowe, Fifth Mate
J. P. Moody, Grimsby, Sixth Mate
W. F. N. O'Loughlin, Surgeon
J. E. Simpson, Belfast, Surgeon
J. Bell, Chief Engineer
W. Farquharson, Senior Second Engineer
J. H. Hesketh, Liverpool, Junior Second Engineer
N. Harrison, Junior Second Engineer
G. F. Hosking, Itchen, Senior Third Engineer
E. C. Dodd, Junior Third Engineer
L. Hodgkinson, Senior Fourth Engineer
J. M. Smith, Itchen, Junior Fourth Engineer

B. Wilson, Senior Assistant Engineer
H. G. Harvey, Junior Assistant Second Engineer
J. Shepherd, Junior Assistant Second Engineer
C. Hodge, Senior Assistant Third Engineer
F. E. G. Coy
J. Fraser, Junior Assistant Third Officer
H. R. Dyer, Senior Assistant Fourth Engineer
A. Ward, Romsey, Junior Assistant Fourth Engineer
Thomas Kemp, Assistant Fourth Engineer
F. A. Parsons, Senior Fifth Engineer
W. D. Mackie, Forest Gate, Junior Fifth Engineer
R. Millar, Alloa, Fifth Engineer
W. Moyes, Stirling, Senior Sixth Engineer
W. M. E. Reynolds, Belfast, Junior Sixth Engineer
H. Creese, Deck Engineer

T. Millar, Belfast, Assistant
Deck Engineer

G. Chiswall, Itchen,
Boilermaker

H. Fitzpatrick, Belfast, Junior
Boilermaker

Peter Sloan, Chief Electrician

A. S. Alsopp, Second
Electrician

H. Jupe, Assistant Electrician

Alfred Middleton, Sligo,
Assistant Electrician

A. J. May, Northampton

J. Hutchinson, Joiner and
Carpenter

A. Nicholls, Bosun

J. Maxwell, Carpenter

A. Haines, Boatswain's Mate
(J. Haines)

T. King, Master-at-Arms

H. Bailey, Master-at-Arms

J. Foley, Storekeeper

S. Hemmings, Lamp Trimmer
(S. Hennings)

C. Procter, Chef

A. Bocketay, Assistant Chef

H. Stubbings, Cook

H. Maynard, Cook

H. W. McElroy, Purser

R. L. Barker, Purser

C. Holcroft, Clerk

E. W. King, Clones, Clerk

F. R. Rice, Crosby, Clerk

G. F. Turner, Chiswick,
Stenographer

F. G. Phillips, Godalming,
Telegraphist

H. S. Bride, Telegraphist (not
on survivor list)

L. Gatti, Manager of
Restaurant

Francisco Nanni, Finsbury

Park N., Head Waiter

Giuseppi Bochet, London,
Second Head Waiter

R. Boroker, Cheshire, First
Cashier (Miss R. Bowker)

M. E. Martin, Acton, Second
Cashier (Miss M. Martin)

W. A. Jeffrey, Acton,
Controller

H. Vine, Acton, Assistant
Controller

Albert Irvine, Belfast,
Assistant Electrician

William Kelly, Dublin, Writer

William Duffy, Itchen, Writer

A. Rous, Writer

R. J. Sawyer, Window Cleaner

W. Hardie, Window Cleaner
(W. Horder)

Total: 74
Total Saved: 13

Mess Stewards

W. A. Makeson

John Coleman, Itchen

S. Blake (? Blake)

George Gumery

C. W. N. Fitzpatrick (W.
Fitzpatrick)

Total: 5
Total Saved: 2

Quartermasters

S. Humphreys

W. Wynn (not on survivor list)

A. Oliver (F. Oliver)
R. Hitchens, Dongola
G. Rowe
A. Bright (R. Bright)
W. Perkis (J. Perks)

Total: 7
Total Saved: 6

Lookout Men

S. Symons (G. Symons)
F. Fleet (F. Flett)
J. A. Hogg (P. Hogg)
F. Evans (S. Evans)
A. Jewell
R. R. Lee (J. Lee)

Total: 6
Total Saved: 6

Able Seamen

W. Weller (W. Wimie)
W. Lucas
F. Bradley
G. Moore (L. Moore)
W. H. Lyons
J. Forward
A. Horswick (J. Horsewell)
E. Archer
F. Osman
Stephen J. Davis
C. Taylor
F. Crouch, Cornwall
B. Terrell
W. McCarthy, Cork
T. Jones, Liverpool
E. Buley (J. Bewly)
C. H. Pascoe (C. Hascoe)

H. Holman
D. Matheson
F. Clench (not on survivor list)
G. Church (F. Church)
F. Tamlin
Robert Hopkins (V. Hopkins)
W. C. Peters
J. Anderson
W. Smith
F. O. Evans
J. McGough (G. McGough)
J. Scarrott
P. Vigett
W. Brice
J. Poingdestre (J. Poing
   Derstoc)

Total: 32
Total Saved: 20

Storekeepers

A. Kenzler
A. Foster
H. Rudd
C. Newman
Edward Parsons
H. H. Thompson
J. W. Keran
F. W Prentice
G. Ricks
Arthur J. Williams, Walton
C. F. Morgan, Birkenhead
E. J. W. Rogers
S. A. Stap (Miss S. Strap)

Total: 13
Total Saved: 1

Firemen

W. Small, Liverpool

353

James Keegan, Liverpool
T. Threlfall, Liverpool
F. Walker
Thomas Ford, Liverpool
C. Hendrickson
   (? Hendricksen)
W. Mayo
T. Davies
J. Norris
T. Graham
E. Watetridge
J. Wyett
J. Thomas
C. Otken
John Jactopin
C. Altrams
C. Painter
H. Sparkman
   (? Sparkman)
F. Reeves
W. Lindsay
W. Jarvis
R. Price
W. Brugge
T. Knowles, Lymington
W. Butt
G. Rickman
H. Smither
E. McGaw
J. Haggan
G. Combes (? Combes)
W. Light
A. Mayzes
R. Pusey (? Puen)
R. Triggs (? Triggs)
R. Cooper (? Cooper)
F. Young
J. Dilley (? Dilley)
E. Gradidge
A. Blatherstone
A. Tizard
A. Shiers

E. Hannan
E. Harris
George Nettleton
F. Mardle
H. Siniar, Clapham
W. Watson
F. M. McAndrews
S. Graves
R. Hopgood
D. Hanbrook
J. Podesta
W. Neithear
N. Toas
Thomas James
J. Blaney
J. Taylor
A. Head
J. J. Moore (? Moore)
J. Barnes
J. Diaper (? Draper)
T. Bradley
E. Tegs
J. Ward
F. Barrett (? Barrett)
J. Mason
P. Pugh
T. Blake
W. Ferris
H. Cooper
W. Cherrett
E. Williams
J. McGregor
G. W. Bailey
J. Fraser
J. Chorley
T. Hart
T. Hunt
F. W. Barrett (not on survivor
   list)
W. Ball
T. Laley, East Dulwich
G. Kemish (? Kerrish)

A. Streets (? Striet)

G. Roberts

B. Moss

George Milford

E. Blien

T. Instance

W. Saunders

C. Rice

R. Turley

W. McCaslan

A. Black

C. Biddlescomb

B Hands

M. Golder

William McQuillan, Belfast

John Noon

B. Cunningham

C. Hewert

Thomas Shea

J. Hall

C. Barlow

G. Beauchamp (? Beacha)

F. Saunders

Thomas McAndrill

J. Cummins (? Crummins)

G. Marget

S. Sullivan

C. Biggs

Archibald Scott

W. McRae

R. Adans

D. Cacceran

F. Harris, Gosport

A. May

F. Shafper

W. Mintram

G. Hallett

H. Olliver (? Oliver)

G. Snelgrove

Charles Barnes

Frank Painter

C. Judd (? Judd)

J. Brown

E. Flarty

F. Rendell

G. Thresher (? Thresher)

J. Taylor

W. Bessant

W. Major

G. Burnett

E. McGurney

F. Wardner

W. Hurst

Thomas Kerr

F. Mason

A. Burroughs (A. Burrage)

A. Witcher

G. Godley

T. Morgan

W. Vear

H. Vear

H. Allen

W. Cross

F. Drel

J. Pearse (? Pearce)

E. Burton

W. H. Taylor

W. H. Noss

S. Doyle (? Doel)

E. Denville

W. Clet

W. Hodges

J. Priest

H. Blackman

L. Dymond (? Dymond)

G. Pond

C. Light

William Murdock

J. Thompson, Liverpool (? Thompson)

J. Canner

A. Curtis

S. Collins

F. Taylor

H. Stubbs
J. Richards

Total: 167
Total Saved: 35

Trimmers

J. Dawson
W. McIntyre
W. Hinton
James McCann
T. Casey
W. Evans
J. Haslin
F. Carter
W. Saunders
A. Foyle
F. White (? White)
R. Proudfoot
S. Maskell
B. Gosling
J. Read
J. Brooks
William Wilson
H. Lee
A. Farrang
G. Cavell
R. Morrell
J. Bevis
A. Morgan
H. Brewer
R. Reid
H. Coe
H. Perry
Thomas P. Dillon (not on
  survivor list)
A. Dore (? Dore)
E. Smith
E. Tegs
A. Hunt (? Hunt)
F. Harris

J. Bellows
W. Morris
S. Webb
W. Snooks
A. Hebb
R. Moore
B. Mitchell
C. Shillaher
H. Stocker
A. J. Fagle
F. Watts
H. Ford
W. Skeater
F. Sheath (? Sheath)
A. Penney
H. Calderwood
W. Binstead (? Pinstead)
G. Kearl
H. Wood
J. Hill
F. Long
E. Perry (? Perry)
P. Blake
T. White
H. Crabb
W. Long
S. Gosling
E. Snow
T. Preston
G. Pelham
G. Green
E. Ingram
J. Avery
J. Cooper
G. Allen
W. Fredericks
  (? Fredericks)
R. Carr
E. Elliott

Total: 71
Total Saved: 10

Greasers

A. White
J. Jukes
Fred Kanchensen
C. Keare
G. Phillips
F. Beattie
A. Self (? Self)
T. Palles
O. Eastman
A. Veal
G. Prangnell
T. Rungem
W. Pitfield
C. Olive
F. Godwin
F. Woodford
M. Stafford
A. Morris
W. Bott
J. Couch
T. McInerney
J. Kirkham
T. Fay
J. Jago
J. Tozer
R. Baines
R. Moores
D. Gregory
E. Castleman
F. Scott (? Scott)
F. Goree
J. Kelly
J. Dannon

Total: 33
Total Saved: 2

Stewards

A. Latimer, Chief

George Dodd, Second
J. S. Wheat, Assistant Second
 (not on survivor list)
W. T. Hughes, Assistant
 Second
William Moss, Saloon
W. Burke, Second Saloon
A. J. Goshawk, Third Saloon
W. Osborne
John Strugness
A. Dubb
W. Rovell, Liverpool
J. Smillin, Glasgow
James Johnson (J. Johnston)
A. A. Howe
C. D. MacKay (not on
 survivor list)
Henry Ketchley
W. Dyer
W. Brown
C. Whalton, Liverpool
 (? E. Wheelton) (not on
 survivor list)
E. Brown, Holyhead
A. Kutchling
B. Oaket
A. Best
W. House
H. Cove, London
W. Lucas, London
Tom Weatherstone
E. Spinner
A. W. Barringer
A. McMickea
 (A. McMichen)
F. D Ray
H. I. Lloyd
J. Shea
F. Allsop
J. H Boyes
G. Knight
A. J. Littlejohn

Ernest T. Barker, Harringay
R. Jones
H. Bristow, Kent
B. Boughton
P. Keen
F. Crafter
J. McMullin
H. Fairall, Ryde
William Lake
S. Nicholls
F. Toms
B. Thomas
J. E. Cartwright
R. G. Smith
M. Rowe (? Rue)
George Evans
T. Turner
G. Cook
A. Coleman
J. Symons
J. Ranson
W. Cherubin, Isle of Wight
H. Crisp
William Burrows, London
J. H. Stagg
J. L. Pury
L. White
S. Rummer
A. Stroud
L. Hoare
A. Lawrence
E. Hendy
A. Derrett
A. M. Bagot
C. Casswill
W. Pryce
W. Ward
L. Whiteley, Highgate
E. Burr
T. Veal
F. Wormald
P. Dewlands

James Toshuch
W. Taylor
W. F. Kingscote
T. Warwick
A. E. Lane
A. C. Thomas
R. Butt
J. McGrady
P. Ahler
H. Bruton
F. Hartnell
C. Lydiatt
A. Mellor
E. Bagley
George Lefevre
D. E. Saunders
A. D. Harrison
H. Yearsley
G. F. Crowe (not on survivor list)
J. Boyd
J. Butterworth
J. W. Robinson
J. R. Diveridge
F. C. Simmons
Joseph Dolley
Thomas Holland (L. Hyland)
T. W. H. Cowles
Ernest E. T. Freeman
W. Boston
W. Hawksworth
P. W. Fletcher
E. Abbott
R. E. Burke, Chandlerford
C. Back
Brooke Webb
E. Hamilton
J. Stewart (W. Seward)
A. T. Broome
T. Wright, Shepherd's Bush
E. Bessant

J. Painton
Ernest R. Olive
S. Holloway
W. Carney, Liverpool
Alfred King
T. Allen
L. Perkins
W. A. Watson
C. H. Harries
A. Barrett
A. Mishelany
E. T. Corben
Samuel Ryler
F. Morris (not on survivor list)
H. Broome
E. Major
F. Pennol
Thomas Baxter
John P. Penrose
W. Gwann
A. Hayter
T. Clark (? Clark)
R. Wareham
R. Allen
F. McCarthy (P. McCarthy)
W. Anderson
G. R. Davis
R. Ide
R. C. Geare
H. Wittman
S. Gill
J. Hill
E. Harris, Winchester
C. Edwards
J. W. Marriott
J. Akerman
S. Stebbings
H. Fellows
C. Jackson
W. Henry
E. J. Guy (E. J. Gay)
J. Scott

S. Hiscock
F. Hopkins
W. Bunnell
E. Hogue, Dulwich Common
(? Hogan)
C. Light, Christchurch
J. A. Bradshaw
P. Ball
Donald Campbell, Clerk
W. F. Janaway
A. Cunningham
T. Hewitt, Aintree
A. Crawford (H. Crawford)
P. P. Ward
W. Bishop
E. Ward
T. Donoghue
Charles Culling (C. Cullen)
William Faulkener
Thomas O'Connor
W. McMurray
C. Stagg, Liverpool
H. Roberts, Bootle
Charles Crumplin
S. C. Siebert
A. Thussinger (A. Tessinger)
W. Bond
E. Stone
H. Etches
G. Brewster
J. Walpole
B. Tucker
G. Levett
F. Smith
F. B. Wrayson
J. Monks
John Hardy, Highfield, Chief
Second-Class
(? Harty)
H. Jenner
R. Sconnell
P. W. Conway, South Hackney

M. Rogers, Winchester
R. J. Davies
H. Philliene (H. Phillamore)
G. Bailey, Shepperton
Alan Franklin
R. Parsons
R. Russell, Redbridge
G. E. Moore
W. Ridout
F. H. Randall
A. Whitford
A. Jones
W. G. Dashwood
M. V. Meddleton, Putney
T. Seaton
N. Daughty
C. Harris (? Harris)
F. Benham
E. Stroud
C. Jensem
W. E. Ryerson, Walthamstow
(W. E. Eyerson)
R. Pirrafen
John Charman
Joseph Heinen, Lewisham
C. W. Samuel
Peter Alinger
J. Hawksworth
Jacob V. Gibbons, Studland
Bay
F. Terrell (F. Tirrel)
W. Williams
H. Christmas
B. Lacey, Salisbury
J. T. Wood, Upper Clapton
C. Andrews
G. Robertson
H. Humphreys
G. H. Dean
R. Owen
H. Gunn
W. T. Kerley, Salisbury

W. H. Nichols (S. H. Nichols)
R. J. Pacey
F. Kelland, Bitterne, Library
Steward
F. W. Edge
J. Witter (J. Whitter)
H. Bulley
J. Chapman
W. Perren
G. Hinckley
J. G. Widgery (J. G. Willgery)
G. Barrow
F. Ford
C. Smith
W. Boothby
? Mackie
J. Byrne, Ilford
C. Reed
G. Beeden, Harlesden
E. W. Hamblyn
H. Bogi, Eastleigh
E. H. Petty
E. F. Stone
W. Suvary
C. Cook
A. Harding
J. Longmuir, Eastleigh
Arthur E. Jones
F. Hambley
A. Burray
Mrs Snape, Sandown
Mrs Wallis
James Kiernan
S. F. Geddunary
L. Mullar, Inspector and
Steward
A. Pearcey
W. Dunford
J. Brookman
H. P. Hill
F. Ford
C. Taylor

R. Bristow
F. Edbroke, Portsmouth
J. Mabey
A. D. Nichols
G. Chitty
V. Rice
S. G. Barton
W. D Cox
A. Ackerman
J. A. Prideaux
H. J. Flight
S. Daniels
R. Mankle
E. B. Ede
W. Sivier, Paddington
L. Knight, Bishopsgate
A. Mantz (Mansea)
H. Ingrouville
J. Hart
G. Talbot
W. E. Foley (C. Foley)
F. Port
H. Finch
M. Thaler, Croydon
W. H. Egg
E. Hilemot
M. Leonard, Belfast
Richard Halford (W. S.
  Halford)
H. R. Baxter
A. E. Peasel
T. Mullin
C. J. Savage (P. J. Savage)
G. Evans
H. Prior
A. Pugh
C. Cecil
H. Ashe
C. Crispin, Eastleigh
J. White (J. Whitter)
W. Wright
W. Willis

A. Lewis (A. E. R. Lewis)
T. Ryard
W. T. Fox

Total: 324
Total Saved: 46

Stewardesses

M. Slocombe, London
A. Caton, London
K. Gold
Annie Martin, Portsmouth
E. L. Leather, Port Sunlight
M. Bennett (K. Bennett)
M. Gregson
V. C. Jessop
M. Sloan, Belfast
E. Marsden
T. E. Smith
M. K. Roberts, Nottingham
H. McLaren
A. Pritchard, London
A. Robinson
B. Lavington, Winchester
E. Bliss
K. Walsh

Total: 18
Total Saved: 17

Cooks

W. Sammons
F. Gallop
C. Ruskimmel
W. Slight
J. Lovell
W. Caunt
J. Hutchinson
J. R. Ellis
G. Ayling

J. Orr
H. E. Beverly
H. Welch
C. Coombs
William Thorley
H. Jones
W. Bedford

Total: 16
Total Saved: 1

Scullions

F. A. J. Hall
W. Bull (P. Bull)
J. Collins, Belfast
H. Ross, London
F. Martin, Fareham (F.
   Marten)
Joseph Colgan
W. Platt
G. Allen
G. King
W. Inge
Reginald Hardwicke
   (R. Hardrick)
William Beere
C. Smith
Harry Shaw, Liverpool
A. Simmons

Total: 15
Total Saved: 6

Bakers

C. Joujhi, Chief (J. Joughin)
J. Giles
J. J. Davies
W. Hine, Lyndhurst
C. Burgess

H. Neal
J. Smith
L. Wake
G. Ching
F. Barnes
A. Barker, Winchester
E. Farenden, Emsworth
A. Lauder
G. Feltham

Total: 14
Total Saved: 3

Butchers

A. Mayhew
T. Topp, Farnborough
F. Roberts
C. Mills
T. Parker
W. Wilsher
H. G. Hensford

Total: 7
Total Saved: 1

*Attendants, Barbers,
Waiters, Ship's Cooks,
etc.*

J. B. Crosbie
W. Ennis, Southport
Leonard Taylor,
   Blackpool
A. H. Whiteman
   (G. Whiteman)
A. White, Portsmouth
H. Keene
P. Gill
H. Johnston
H. Hatch
Ernest Brice, Acton

Charles Furvey, Acton
J. Phillips, Southampton
E. Yorrish, Gatti
C. Scavino, Gatti
Angelo Knotto, Gatti
P. Pourpe, Gatti
R. Urbini, Gatti
Ertera Vahassori, Gatti
Narsisso Bazzi, Gatti
Enrics Ratti, Gatti
Guito Casali, Gatti
Geno Jesia, Gatti
Giovani Batihoe, Gatti
Robert Nieni, Gatti
V. Gilandino, Gatti
Benjamin Theyn, London
E. Poggi
Orovello Louis, Gatti
Alonzo B. Aptix Di Antonio,
  Gatti
David Beux, Gatti
B. Bernardo, Gatti
Louis Biatti, Gatti
J. Monros, Gatti
Alfonso Meratti, Gatti
G. Lavaggi, Gatti
Lornetti Mario, Gatti
Rinaldo Ricadone, Gatti
Abele Rigozzia, Gatti
Giovanni de Martiro, Gatti
Maurice de Treacq, Gatti
Albert Provatin, Gatti
Sebastino Serantino, Gatti
Itile Donnati, London
Aber Pedrini, Southampton
P. Rousseau, Gatti
G. Biatrix, Gatti
Henri Bollin, Gatti
Auguste Contin, Gatti
Claude Janin, Gatti
Adrian Charboisson, Gatti
Jean Vicat, Gatti

Total: 51
Total Saved: 2

*Other men engaged by
  Messrs. Gatti were:*

Henry Jaillet
Georges Jouanwault
Pierre Vilvarlarge
Morel Conraire
Louis Dornier
Jean Pachera
Giovanni Monteverdi
Louis Desornini
Adolf Maltman
H. Voegelin
Gerald Groxlaude
Jean Blumet
George Aspilagt
C. Teitz
Carlo Leiz
F. Bertoldo
Paul Mange, Secretary (Paul
  Mauge)
G. Salussolia
E. Testoni
Tazez Sartori

Total: 20
Total Saved: 1

*Survivors who do not appear
  on the crew list*

S. J. Rule (not on survivor or
  crew list)
W. Mells
? Pelboun
? Casper
? Nutlearn

? Fryer
S. Humphreys
J. Piggott
F. Louis
R. P. Fropper

T. **Ranger** (T. Granger)
Total: 11
Total Crew Aboard: 884
Total Crew Saved: 183

The following, who had "signed on", did not sail with the *Titanic*:

A. Haveling
W. Sims
V. Penny (W. Penny)
C. Blake
A. Slade
Thomas Slade
D. Slade
W. Burrows
J. Shaw
F. Holden
B. Brewer

E. di Napoli
B. Fish
P. Kilford
W. W. Dawes
P. Ettlinger (not on crew list)
R. Fisher
A. Manley (not on crew list)
W. J. Mewe
P. Dawkins
F. T. Bowman
J. Coffy

The following were taken on as substitutes:

Renny Dodds
L. Kinsella
E. Hosgood, London
W. Lloyd
H. Witt
D. Black

A. **Windebank**
A. Locke
J. Brown, Eastleigh
F. O'Connor
W. Dickson
T. Gordon

The following names are on the list of survivors picked up by the *Carpathia* and taken to New York, but do not appear on the passenger list. Taking this list with that of surviving crew, we are left with ninety-eight survivors too many as compared with the official findings.

Ajal, Bemora
Akelseph, Alous
Aloum, Badmoura
Anton, Louisa

Argenia, Mrs Genova and two
  Children
Artonon, V.
Asplund, William

Barawich, George
Barawich, Harren
Barawich, Marian
Barlson, Rinat
Bassette, Miss
Behr, Mr K. H.
Billa, Maggie
Bockstrom, Masy
Bonas, John
Bridgett, Ros
Brown, Miss E.
Burns, Miss O. M.
Bury, Richard
Casem, Boyen
Cassebeer, Mrs H. A.
Chandanson, Miss Victorine
Charles, William E.
Charters, John
Cheang, Foo
Choonson, John
Collett, Mr D.
Collier, Gosham
Crosby, Miss Harriet
Daly, Charles
Daniel, Sarah
Deanodelman, Delia
Domunder, Theodore
Doyt, Agnes (or Mrs A. A. Dick)
Eldegrek, Leonek
Emearmaslon, Mr Renardo
Fastman, Daniel
Frolicher, Max
Frolicher, Mrs
Fulwell, Mrs J.
Hamann, Maria
Hanson, Miss Jeannie
Hemvig, Croft
Holverson, Mrs A. O.
Hosono, Mr Masabumi
Jacques, Mrs
Jap, Jules

Jermyn, Miss Mary
Jerserac, Inay
Joblom, S.
Josburg, Siline
Joseph, Katherine
Joseph, Nigel
Jusefa, Carl
Jusefa, Manera
Kenton, Miriam
Kesorny, Florence
Kinorn, Krikoraen
Kockovaen, Erickau
Kolsbottel, Anna
Koucher, Miss Emile
Krigesne, Jos
Lang, Hee
Lare, Eleoneh
Lesneur, Mrs Gustav
Ludgais, Amo
Maioni, Miss Ruberta
Malle, Bertha
Maloney, Mrs R.
Manga, Margaret
Manga, Mr Paula
Manv, Julio
Maran, Bertha
Marlkarl, Hauwakan
Marrigan, Margaret
Marshall, Miss Katey
Marson, Adele
Massey, Marion
Mathgo, Karl
McCoy, Ernest
McDearmont, Miss Leila
McGovan, Anna
Merrigan (Harrigan)
Messelmolk, G. D.
Messelmolk, Anna
Missulmona, Amina
Mock, Mrs Phillippe
Modelmot, Celia
Moubark, Burns

Muhun, Erikorian
Nern, Hannah
Nevatey, Margaret
Nouberek, Halin
Noubarek, Jiron
Nubulaket, Samula
Nyhan, Anna
Oamb, Nicola
Olivia, Miss
Ollmson, Sourly
Olman, Virma
Ongalen, Helena
Ornout, Alfred F.
Osplund, C. Anderson
Oumsun ?
Patro, Hobesa
Pericault, Miss A.
Person, Eames
Picard, Benoit
Pinsky, Miss Rose
Ranelt, Miss Appic
Reibon, Anna
Renago, Mrs Naman J.
Schurbint, John

Scunda, Assed
Scunda, Famine
Segisser, Miss Emma
Serepeca, Miss Augusta
Seward, Frederick K.
Shine, Axel
Sibelrome, Agnes
Sibelrome, Rose
Simpson, Miss Anna
Sindo, Beatrice
Smith, Mrs L. P.
Sofia, Anna
Steffanson, H. B.
Strinder, Julo
Submaket, Fituasa
Sulici, Nicola
Waters, Miss Nellie
Wilson, Miss Helen
Wimhormstrom, Amy E.
Zenn, Phillip
Zuni, Fabin

*Total not included in
passenger list*: 135

The Various Totals Reported Saved

1   Minimum number saved according to Board of Trade before inquiry: 703
2   Number saved according to Captain Rostron: 705
3   Official number saved according to British Inquiry Report: 711
4   Number saved and named on official White Star list published 20 April 1912: 757
5   Total number saved according to official White Star list, inquiry witnesses, newspaper statements and lists transmitted by *Carpathia*: 803

APPENDIX II

Ships at Sea on the North Atlantic on the Night of the Disaster

GRT = Gross Register Tons.
* = owned by IMM.

Almerian: 2,948 GRT, 351.5 feet long, Leyland Line, Great Britain*

Amerika: 22,622 GRT, 669 feet long, Hamburg-Amerika Line, Germany

Antillian: 5,608 GRT, 421 feet long, Leyland Line, Great Britain*

Asian: 5,614 GRT, 421 feet long, Leyland Line, Great Britain*

Athinia: 6,742 GRT, 420 feet long, Hellenic Trans-Atlantic Steam Navigation, Greece

Baltic: 23,876 GRT, 709 feet long, White Star, Great Britain*

Birma: 4,859 GRT, 390 feet long, Rotterdamsche Lloyd, Holland

Bruce: 1,553 GRT, 250.5 feet long, Reid Newfoundland Company, Great Britain

Californian: 6,223 GRT, 447.5 feet long, Leyland Line, Great Britain*

Campanello: 9,291 GRT, 470 feet long, H. W. Harding, Great Britain

Caronia: 19,687 GRT, 650 feet long, Cunard, Great Britain

Carpathia: 13,603 GRT, 540 feet long, Cunard, Great Britain

Celtic: 20,904 GRT, 681 feet long, White Star, Great Britain*

Deutschland: 3,710 GRT, 339 feet long, Deutsch-Amerika Petroleum, Germany

Dora: Could be any one of twelve small vessels with the same name. Most likely, 2,662 GRT, 291 feet long, H. Schuld, Germany

Dorothy Baird: (3-masted sailing ship), 241 GRT, 118.5 feet long, James Baird, Great Britain

Etonian: 6,438 GRT, 475.5 feet long, Wilson & Furness – Leyland, Great Britain

Frankfurt: 7,431 GRT, length ?, Norddeutscher Lloyd, Germany

La Provence: 13,753 GRT, 602 feet long, Compagnie General Transatlantique, France

Memphian: 6,305 GRT, 400 feet long, Leyland Line, Great Britain*

Mesaba: 6,833 GRT, 482 feet long, Atlantic Transport, Great Britain

Mount Temple: 8,790 GRT, 485 feet long, Canadian Pacific Railway, Great Britain

Olympic: 46,359 GRT (altered in register from 45,324 GRT), 882.5 feet long, White Star, Great Britain*

Parisian: 5,395 GRT, 441 feet long, Allan Line, Great Britain

Paula: 2,748 GRT, 283 feet long, Deutsch-Amerika Petroleum, Germany

Pisa: 4,959 GRT, 390 feet long, Hamburg-Amerika, Germany

Premier: 374 GRT, 155 feet long, Merritt & Chapman, Great Britain

President Lincoln: 18,168 GRT, 599 feet long, Hamburg-Amerika, Germany

Prinz Friedrich Wilhelm: 17,082 GRT, 455 feet long, Norddeutscher Lloyd, Germany

Rappahannock: 3,884 GRT, 370 feet long, Furness Withy, Great Britain

Samson: 506 GRT, 148 feet long, Saefaenger Co., Norway

Saturnia: 8,611 GRT, 456 feet long, Saturnia Steam Ship Co. (Donaldson Brothers), Great Britain

Trautenfels: 4,699 GRT, 390 feet long, Deutsche Dampfschiffahrt, Germany

Victorian: 10,635 GRT, 520 feet long, Allan Line, Great Britain

Virginian: 10,757 GRT, 520 feet long, Allan Line, Great Britain

Ypiranga: 8,103 GRT, 448 feet long, Hamburg-Amerika, Germany

NOTES

Chapter 1: The "Olympic" Class

1 *The Shipbuilder*, vol. VI, Midsummer 1911, special number, ed. A. G. Hood, p. 19 onward; reproduced in *Ocean Liners of the Past: Olympic and Titanic* (see bibliography for full references to books etc.). Henceforward referred to as *Shipbuilder*.

2 Ibid., p. 26, col. 1.

3 "Proceedings on a Formal Investigation into the Loss of the SS *Titanic*", HMSO 1912 (record of the British inquiry, henceforward BI), Day 16, evidence of Ismay.

4 Van der Vat, *The Atlantic Campaign*, pp. 19–22.

5 "Report on the Loss of the SS *Titanic*", HMSO 1912 (report of the British inquiry or British Report, henceforward BR), pp. 16–17; see also BI, Day 20, evidence of L. Peskett, Cunard's naval architect.

6 *Shipbuilder*, figs. 34 and 35.

7 *Oxford Classical Dictionary*, ed. M. Cary et al., Oxford 1949.

8 John P. Eaton and Charles A. Haas, *Titanic – Triumph and Tragedy* (a "bible", henceforward referred to as Eaton & Haas), p. 57, footnote.

9 Ibid., p. 31; *Shipbuilder*, Epilogue by John Maxtone-Graham, *passim*.

10 BR, p. 22.

11 *Shipbuilder*, pp. 123–7.

12 BR, p. 18.

13 Eaton & Haas, p. 32; BI, Day 20, evidence of A. Carlisle.

14 *Shipbuilder*, p. 129.

15 Eaton & Haas, p. 38.

16 Public Record Office, Kew (PRO), Admiralty file ADM 116/1163C.

17 Jane's *Fighting Ships*, 1914, under "Old British Cruisers".
18 PRO, op. cit.
19 PRO, ADM 116/1163A.
20 Ibid.
21 Ibid.
22 Merchant Shipping Act, 1894, section 633; reference kindly supplied by Trinity House. Pilot immunity was repealed in 1918.
23 ADM 116/1163 C and D.
24 See e.g., Eaton & Haas, p. 32.
25 Eaton & Haas, *Falling Star* (henceforward referred to by title), p. 132.
26 *Falling Star*, p. 134.
27 Simon Mills, *RMS Olympic*, p. 23.
28 Paper no. 15, Centennial Meeting of the Society of Naval Architects and Marine Engineers, New York, 14–19 September 1993: "Deep Underwater Exploration Vehicles – Past, Present and Future", by William H. Garzke, Dana R. Yoerger, Stewart Harris, Robert O. Dulin, David K. Brown. Quoted by kind permission of Mr Garzke.
29 *Falling Star*, p. 134.
30 *Shipbuilder*, p. 131.
31 Eaton & Haas, p. 33.
32 Ibid., p. 42.
33 *Falling Star*, p. 136.
34 George M. Behe, *Titanic Tidbits* (no. 2), pp. 19–20.

Chapter 2: Roots of Disaster

1 Described in e.g., Barbara Tuchman, *The Proud Tower*, *passim*.
2 Van der Vat, *The Grand Scuttle*, Part I, refers.
3 Tuchman, Chapter 7, *passim*.
4 Van der Vat, op. cit., Chapter 2.
5 Eaton & Haas; Michael Davie, *The Titanic*, both *passim*.
6 BI, Day 23, evidence of Sir Alfred Chalmers, Board of Trade.
7 *Shipbuilder*, Introduction, *passim*.
8 See countless reports in e.g., *The Times*, *Daily Mail* etc. at British Newspaper Library, Colindale. *The New York Times* etc. also refer.

9 *Falling Star*, Chapter 1, pp. 9–13.
10 *Shipping and Mercantile Gazette*, Liverpool, 1864 (quoted in *Falling Star*).
11 *Falling Star*, Chapter 2, pp. 14–31.
12 *Shipbuilder*, p. 5.
13 *Falling Star*, p. 31.
14 Op. cit., p. 5.
15 *Falling Star*, *passim*.
16 *Dictionary of National Biography*, 1931–40 supplement.
17 Stanley Jackson, *J. P. Morgan*, pp. 11–12.
18 Ibid., Preface.
19 Davie, pp. 24–5.
20 BR, p. 7.
21 Eaton & Haas, p. 13; Davie, Chapter 1, *passim*.
22 Jackson, Chapter 2.
23 Ibid., Chapter 16.
24 Ibid.
25 Davie, Chapter 1; *The Ismay Line* by Wilton J. Oldham, pp. 160–1.
26 See especially BI, Day 16, evidence of J. Bruce Ismay.
27 Davie, Chapter 1; Jackson, Chapter 16.
28 *Dictionary of National Biography* supplement for 1922–30; article by Alfred Cochrane.
29 *Journal of Commerce*, Liverpool, 15 April 1994. *The New York Times* was among many other papers to report this.
30 *Falling Star*, Chapter 11.
31 *Oxford Classical Dictionary*.
32 Letter to Gardiner, 18 March 1994.
33 See *Who Was Who*, A & C Black Ltd, London, 1929–40 volume.
34 Eaton & Haas, *Destination Disaster*, p. 56.
35 Davie, Chapter 1.
36 *Shipbuilder*, *passim*.
37 Eaton & Haas, Chapter 3.
38 Charles Herbert Lightoller, *Titanic and Other Ships*, p. 124.
39 *The New York Times*, 16 April 1912, p. 7.
40 Material on Smith in Eaton & Haas; *Falling Star*; Davie: all *passim*; Richard A. Cahill, *Disasters at Sea*, Chapter 1.
41 Lightoller, op. cit.
42 Eaton & Haas, Chapters 3 and 4; *Shipbuilder*, *passim*.

43 Wyn Craig Wade, *The Titanic – End of a Dream*, p. 22.
44 Cahill, p. 13; Eaton & Haas, pp. 71–2; Davie, Chapter 3.

Chapter 3: All Aboard

1 BR, p. 64; American inquiry (AI), Part 4, evidence of lookout Frederick Fleet, AB.
2 BI, Day 4, evidence of Leading Stoker Frederick Barrett.
3 BI, Day 17 (Appendix); AI, part 1, testimony of C. H. Lightoller.
4 BI, Day 15, evidence of George Alfred Hogg, AB.
5 Conversation with van der Vat.
6 BI, Day 25, evidence of Sir Walter Howell and Sir Alfred Chalmers, Board of Trade.
7 PRO, Kew, file BT100/259.
8 Behe, p. 20.
9 Quoted by Cahill, op. cit., p. 14; Geoffrey Marcus, *The Maiden Voyage*, p. 58.
10 Our special thanks to Steve Rigby and Geoff Whitfield of the British Titanic Society for providing copies of this and other material.
11 *Shipbuilder*, Epilogue; Eaton & Haas, Chapters 5 and 6, both *passim*.
12 Davie, Chapter 3.
13 Quoted in Eaton & Haas, p. 72.
14 Ibid., p. 100.
15 Davie, Chapter 2.
16 PRO, Kew, BT100/259.
17 BR, p. 62.
18 AI, Part I, Day 1, Ismay's testimony.
19 AI, Part II, Day 10.
20 BI, Day 16, Ismay's evidence.
21 BI, Day 17, Ismay's evidence (continued).
22 Behe, p. 4.
23 BR, pp. 26–9.
24 BI, Day 17, p. 465.

Chapter 4: Nemesis on Ice

1 Eaton & Haas, p. 101.
2 "Report of the Hearings before a sub-committee of the

Committee on Commerce", United States Senate, 62nd
Congress, report no. 806: *Titanic* Disaster (American
Report, henceforward AR), p. 7.

3 AI, Part I, Day 1, Ismay's testimony; BR, p. 29.
4 Eaton & Haas, Chapter 10.
5 Davie, p. 85.
6 BI, Day 13, evidence of Third, Fourth and Fifth Officers
(Pitman, Boxhall, Lowe).
7 BI, Day 10, evidence of Symons.
8 Behe, pp. 7–17.
9 BR, pp. 26–8.
10 Ibid., pp. 28–9.
11 BI, Day 4, Barrett's evidence (continued).
12 Ibid., Day 5.
13 BI, Day 2, evidence of A. Jewell.
14 BR, p. 37.
15 BR, p. 27.
16 *The Discovery of the Titanic* by Dr Robert D. Ballard,
p. 221.
17 BR, pp. 28–9.
18 Ibid., p. 30.
19 Ibid., pp. 30–1.
20 AI, *passim.*
21 BI, *passim.*
22 Both cited in Davie, pp. 94–8.
23 BI, evidence of e.g., Quartermaster Hitchens (Day 3),
Fourth Officer Boxhall (Day 13).
24 BR, p. 66.
25 See "Plimsoll" in *Oxford Companion to Ships and the
Sea*.
26 Public Record Office, Belfast, Harland and Wolff papers,
D2805/MIN/A/1.

Chapter 5: The Quick and the Dead

1 BR, p. 38.
2 *Oxford Companion to Ships and the Sea*, p. 413.
3 Michael Davie unearthed Marian Thayer's fascinating
affidavit on the shipwreck and quotes it in extenso in
Chapter 3. We refer to it again below.
4 BI, Day 2, evidence of Jewell.

5 Quoted by Eaton & Haas, p. 150.

6 BI, Day 19, Wilding's evidence.

7 AI, Part 4, Day 4, Pitman (recalled).

8 Walter Lord, *A Night to Remember*, pp. 56, 97, 100, 102–3; Davie, Chapter 6; BI, Day 3 (Hitchens), Day 12 (Lightoller).

9 BR, p. 38; Lord, p. 100; BI, Day 6, evidence of Steward S. J. Rule.

10 BI, Day 5, Hendrickson; and (especially) Day 10, Symons, Taylor and Sir C. Duff Gordon; Day 11, Duff Gordon (continued). See also Davie, Chapter 3; Eaton & Haas, p. 151.

11 See Archibald Gracie's *The Truth about the Titanic*, p. 141 and *passim*. Gracie says number eight preceded number six into the water.

12 Lord, p. 99.

13 BI, Day 11, Wynn's evidence. See also Gracie, pp. 279–87; Eaton & Haas, p. 152.

14 BI, Day 11, Mrs Robinson; AI, Day 6, Steward Edward Wheelton; Eaton & Haas, p. 153; Gracie, pp. 283–7.

15 Quoted in Eaton & Haas, p. 147.

16 AI, Day 5, Lowe's own testimony.

17 Gracie, op. cit., p. 300.

18 See Davie, Chapter 6, *passim*; Gracie, pp. 301–4; AI, Days 1 and 10; BI, Days 16 and 17 (all Ismay).

19 BI, Day 13; AI, Day 3.

20 BR, p. 67.

21 Eaton & Haas, pp. 149 and 156.

22 Eaton & Haas, pp. 23–4.

23 BI, Day 3, evidence of William Lucas, AB; AI, Day 6, testimony of Chief Second-Class Steward John Hardy.

24 Eaton & Haas, pp. 156–7.

25 BI, Day 12, Lightoller (continued).

26 Ibid.; Gracie, pp. 64–5, 78–81, 207–27, *passim*.

27 BI, Day 9, E. Brown.

28 BR, pp. 42 and 70.

Chapter 6: Of Mysteries and Ships

1 Rostron's evidence to AI, Part I, Day 1; and BI, Day 28.

2 See Eaton & Haas, Chapter 13, for detailed reconstruction.

3 Rostron, *The Loss of the Titanic*, in Titanic Signals Archive, 1991, pp. 20–1.
4 This analysis is compiled from British inquiry evidence and many references in Davie, Eaton & Haas, Gracie, Lord and Wade.
5 Eaton & Haas, Chapter 12.
6 BI, Day 8, C. F. Evans.
7 See van der Vat's *The Ship that Changed the World*, p. 177. The Royal Navy's inexcusable failure to stop two German warships reaching the Black Sea and shelling the Russian coast under the Turkish flag led to the Gallipoli disaster and the economic strangulation of Russia.
8 Leslie Harrison, *A Titanic Myth – the Californian Incident*, Chapter 1, *passim*; BI, Day 7, Stanley Lord, Herbert Stone, James Gibson; Day 8, Charles Groves, G. F. Stewart.
9 AI, Day 7, BI, Day 16 (Gill).
10 PRO, Kew, file MT9/920F, Board of Trade, Titanic inquiry correspondence.
11 Harrison, pp. 131–3. This author took up Lord's case most effectively on his retirement as general secretary of the MMSA.
12 AI, appended to Day 14 evidence.
13 AI, Day 8; BI, Day 8: evidence of J. H. Moore.
14 BI, Days 8 and 9; Durrant.
15 Eaton & Haas, pp. 174–5.
16 Ibid., p. 167; Harrison, pp. 195–7. See also Leslie Reade, *The Ship that Stood Still*, Chapter 18.
17 "*Titanic* – Reappraisal of Evidence ...": see Bibliography.

Chapter 7: New York and Halifax

1 Eaton & Haas, p. 181.
2 British Titanic Society, "Atlantic Daily Bulletin", no. 1, 1994, p. 10.
3 AI, Day 3, Franklin.
4 BR, p. 68.
5 AI, Day 14, evidence of Maurice Farrell of Dow Jones.
6 AI, Days 1, 6 and 9 (evidence of Guglielmo Marconi).
7 Ibid., Day 11, testimony of Melville Stone (AP).
8 Eaton & Haas, p. 182.
9 Ibid., pp. 184 and 205 (footnote).

10 Ibid., Chapter 17.
11 AI, Day 10.
12 Eaton & Haas, Chapter 16, *passim*.
13 Davie, Chapter 11, *passim*.
14 Eaton & Haas, Chapters 17 and 20, *passim*.
15 *Daily Mail*, 27 April 1912.
16 PRO, Kew, file M9/920 A; Mills, RMS Olympic, pp. 27–8.
17 See, e.g., Chambers *Biographical Dictionary*, 5th edition, 1990.
18 PRO, M9/920 B.
19 PRO, FO 369/522.

Chapter 8: The Senate Hearings

1 Davie, Chapter 8; Eaton & Haas, Chapter 15, both *passim*.
2 The factual material for the rest of this chapter is derived from "*Titanic* Disaster: Hearing before a sub-committee of the Committee on Commerce, US Senate, 62nd Congress, 2nd Session", S. Doc. 933 (62–2), serial no. 6179; and "Report of Hearings before a sub-committee of the Committee on Commerce, US Senate, 62nd Congress, 2nd session, report no. 806: *Titanic* Disaster", serial no. 6127.

Chapter 9: The British Court of Inquiry

1 Davie, Chapter 9; Eaton & Haas, Chapter 18, both *passim*.
2 Davie, ibid.: excellent material on Isaacs.
3 The factual material for the rest of this chapter is derived from "Proceedings on a Formal Investigation into the Loss of the SS *Titanic*" and "Report on the Loss of the SS *Titanic*", Cmnd. no. 6352, both HMSO, 1912.
4 BI, p. 478, questions numbered 19, 342–5.

Epilogue: Grave Doubts

1 See van der Vat's *Pacific Campaign*, pp. 20–1 (Arizona); and his *Stealth at Sea: the History of the Submarine*, pp. 170–2 (*Royal Oak*) and pp. 70–3 (*Lusitania*).

2 Many articles in British press, 1994. See in particular *Financial Times*, 26 November; *Independent on Sunday*, 25 September; *Guardian*, 10 June.

3 Richard O'Connor, *Down to Eternity*, pp. 59–60.

4 Lawrence Beesley, *The Loss of the SS Titanic*, p. 34; Terry Coleman, *The Liners*, p. 71.

5 Private conversation with van der Vat, 7 October 1993.

6 Marcus, p. 81.

7 Eaton & Haas, p. 56.

8 Davie, Chapter 3.

9 Jackson, pp. 296–301.

10 Eaton & Haas, *Destination Disaster*, pp. 72–3.

11 BR, p. 35.

12 Eaton & Haas, Chapter 19; Davie, Chapter 6, *passim*.

13 See photograph and text in Eaton & Haas, pp. 174 and 265.

14 *National Geographic*, April 1986.

15 British Titanic Society, "Atlantic Daily Bulletin", no. 1 of 1994, pp. 9–10.

16 *Encounters: Explorers of the Titanic*, a John Gau production for Channel 4 TV, directed by Alexander Lindsay and Simon Normanton, first shown on Channel 4 (UK) on 5 March 1995.

ACKNOWLEDGEMENTS

The authors accept full responsibility for any error, but would like to express many thanks to the following for advice and assistance, encouragement and information.

Dr Robert D. Ballard of the Woods Hole Oceanographic Institute, Massachusetts; Frederick Banfield; British Titanic Society (Steve Rigby of Golborne, Lancs., and Geoff Whitfield of Liverpool); Annette Boon; John Clifford of the *Cork Examiner*; John P. Eaton of New York City; Geological Survey of Canada, Ottawa; Lynn Gardiner; Don Lynch of the Titanic Historical Society, Redondo Beach, California; Tommy McCluskie of Harland and Wolff, Belfast; Ken Marschall, Redondo Beach; John Miller; Michael Shaw of Curtis Brown; Ion Trewin, colleagues and staff of Weidenfeld & Nicolson and the Orion Publishing Group; George Tulloch of RMS Titanic Inc., New York City; Ralph White of Los Angeles; Dinah Wiener of Dinah Wiener Ltd.

We should also like to thank the staffs of the Bodleian Library, Oxford; Guildhall Library, City of London; Lloyd's Register Library, London; the London Library; National Archive, Washington, DC; National Maritime Museum, Greenwich; Public Record Offices, Belfast and Kew, Surrey; Oxford and Richmond (Surrey) public libraries; Trinity House, London; the Witt Library at the Courtauld Institute, London.

Grateful acknowledgement is due to the following for quotations from copyright works (see also bibliography).

Robert D. Ballard for *The Discovery of the Titanic*; George M. Behe for *Titanic Tidbits* (no. 2) – "The Bridge paid No Attention to my Signals"; A & C Black Ltd for *Who's Who* and *Who was Who*; Michael Davie for *The Titanic – the Full Story of a Tragedy*; John P. Eaton and Charles A. Haas for *Titanic – Triumph and Tragedy*, and for *Falling Star*; Stanley Jackson for *J. P. Morgan – the Rise and Fall of a Banker*; *National Geographic* for its April 1986 issue; Oxford University Press for *Dictionary of National Biography*; Patrick Stephens Ltd and *Shipping World and Shipbuilder* for *Ocean Liners of the Past – Olympic and Titanic*; Studio Editions Ltd for Jane's *Fighting Ships of World War I* (1990 reproduction); Titanic Signals Archive for *The Loss of the Titanic*.

In the event of any omission from the above lists, we apologize and ask for notification, whereupon we shall make every effort to correct matters in future editions.

BIBLIOGRAPHY

ANDERSON, Roy, *White Star* (Stephenson, Prescot, Lancs., 1964)

ANGELUCCI, Enzo and CUCARI, Attilio, *Ships* (Macdonald & Jane's, London, 1975)

BALLARD, Dr Robert D., *The Discovery of the Titanic* (Hodder & Stoughton, London, 1987)

BEESLEY, Lawrence, *The Loss of the S.S. Titanic – Its Story and its Lessons* (William Heinemann, London, 1912)

BEHE, George M., *Titanic Tidbits* (no. 2) (Titanic Historical Society, Redondo Beach, California, 1993)

BOYD-SMITH, Peter, *Titanic – From Rare Historical Reports* (Brooks Books, Southampton, 1992)

BRISTOW, Diana, *Titanic RIP – Do Dead Men Tell Tales?* (Harlo Press, USA, 1989)

BULLOCK, Shan, *A Titanic Hero – Thomas Andrews, Shipbuilder* (Maunsel, Dublin and London, 1912, and reprinted 7C's Press, Riverside, Connecticut, 1973)

CAHILL, R. A., *Disasters At Sea – Titanic To Exxon Valdez* (Century, London, 1990)

CARY, M. et al. (ed.), *Oxford Classical Dictionary* (Oxford University Press, 1949)

COLEMAN, Terry, *The Liners* (Allen Lane, Penguin Books, London, 1976)

DAVIE, Michael, *The Titanic – the Full Story of a Tragedy* (The Bodley Head, London, 1986)

Dictionary of National Biography (Oxford University Press, various dates)

DODGE, Washington, *The Loss of the Titanic* (7C's Press, Riverside, Connecticut, 1912)

EATON, John P. and HAAS, Charles A., *Titanic – Triumph*

and Tragedy (Patrick Stephens/Haynes Publishing, Sparkford, 1986)

EATON, John P. and HAAS, Charles A., *Titanic – Destination Disaster* (Patrick Stephens/Haynes Publishing, Sparkford, 1987)

EATON, John P. and HAAS, Charles A., *Falling Star – Misadventures of White Star Ships* (Patrick Stephens/Haynes Publishing, Sparkford, 1989)

GARDNER, Joseph L. (ed.), *Great Mysteries of the Past* (Reader's Digest, New York, 1992)

GARRETT, Richard, *Atlantic Disaster – The Titanic and Other Victims of the North Atlantic* (Buchan & Enright, London, 1986)

GIBBS, Philip, *The Deathless Story of the Titanic* (Lloyd's Weekly News, London, 1912)

GRACIE, Archibald, *The Truth about the Titanic* (Mitchell Kennerley, New York, 1913, reprinted 1985)

HARRISON, Leslie, *A Titanic Myth – The* Californian *Incident* (William Kimber, London, 1986)

HOBSON, Dominic, *The Pride of Lucifer: Unauthorized Biography of a Merchant Bank* (Hamish Hamilton, 1990)

HOOD, A. G. (ed.), *The Shipbuilder – the White Star Liners* Olympic *and* Titanic (special issue, London, 1911, reproduced by Patrick Stephens/Haynes Publishing, Sparkford, 1988)

HUTCHINGS, David F., *RMS Titanic – A Modern Legend* (Waterfront Publications, Blandford Forum, 1993)

HYSLOP, Donald, FORSYTH, Alastair and JEMIMA, Sheila, *Titanic Voices: the Story of the White Star Line, Titanic and Southampton* (Southampton City Council, 1994)

JACKSON, Stanley, *J. P. Morgan – The Rise and Fall of a Banker* (William Heinemann, London, 1984)

JANE'S *Fighting Ships of World War 1* (reproduced by Studio Editions, London, 1990)

KEMP, Peter (ed.), *The Oxford Companion to Ships and the Sea* (Oxford University Press, Oxford, 1976)

LIGHTOLLER, C. H., *Titanic and Other Ships* (Nicholson & Watson, London, 1935)

LORD, Walter, *A Night to Remember* (Longmans, Green, London, 1956)

LORD, Walter, *The Night Lives On – New Thoughts and Revelations about the Titanic* (Allen Lane, Penguin Books, London, 1987)

LYNCH, Don, *Titanic: An Illustrated History*, Paintings by Ken Marschall (Hodder & Stoughton, London, 1992)

MAGNUSSON, Magnus (ed.), Chambers *Biographical Dictionary* (Chambers, Edinburgh, 1990)

MARCUS, Geoffrey, *The Maiden Voyage* (Allen & Unwin, London, 1969)

MERSEY, Viscount, *A Picture of Life 1872–1940* (John Murray, London, 1941)

MILLS, Simon, *RMS Olympic – the Old Reliable* (Waterfront Publications, Blandford Forum, Dorset, 1993)

MOSS, Michael, *Shipbuilders to the World – 125 years of Harland & Wolff, Belfast, 1861–1986* (Blackstaff Press, Belfast, 1987)

O'CONNOR, Richard, *Down to Eternity* (Fawcett Publications, New York, n.d.)

OLDHAM, Wilton J., *The Ismay Line* (Journal of Commerce, Liverpool, 1961)

PADFIELD, Peter, *The Titanic and the Californian* (Hodder & Stoughton, London, 1965)

PELLEGRINO, Charles, *Her Name Titanic – the Untold Story of the Sinking and Finding of the Unsinkable Ship* (Robert Hale, London, 1990)

PRESTON, Antony, *History of the Royal Navy* (Hamlyn Bison, London, 1983)

READE, Leslie, *The Ship that Stood Still* ((Patrick Stephens/Haynes Publishing, Sparkford, 1993)

ROSTRON, Sir Arthur, *The Loss of the Titanic* (Titanic Signals Archive, Westbury, Wiltshire, 1991)

STENSON, Patrick, *'Lights' – The Odyssey of C. H. Lightoller* (The Bodley Head, London, 1984)

THAYER, John B., *The Sinking of the S.S. Titanic* (7C's Press, Riverside, Connecticut, 1974)

TUCHMAN, Barbara, *The Proud Tower* (Hamish Hamilton, London, 1966)

VAN DER VAT, Dan, *The Grand Scuttle – the Sinking of the German Fleet at Scapa Flow 1919* (Hodder & Stoughton, London, 1982)

VAN DER VAT, Dan, *The Ship that Changed the World* (Hodder & Stoughton, London, 1985)

VAN DER VAT, Dan, *The Atlantic Campaign* (Hodder & Stoughton, London, 1988)

WADE, Wyn Craig, *The Titanic – End of a Dream* (Weidenfeld & Nicolson, London, 1979)

WATSON, Arnold and Betty, *Roster of Valor – the Titanic–Halifax Legacy* (7C's Press, Riverside, Connecticut, 1984)

WOODROFFE, David and MACDONALD, Fiona, *Titanic* (Macdonald & Co., London, 1989)

YOUNG, Filson, *Titanic* (Grant Richards, London, 1912)

Reports

JOURNAL OF COMMERCE: "Report of British Official Inquiry into the Circumstances Attending the Loss of the RMS *Titanic*" (Liverpool and London, 1912)

UNITED STATES SENATE: "Report of Hearings before a sub-committee of the Committee on Commerce" (Report no. 806: *Titanic* Disaster, Government Printing Office, Washington, DC, 1912)

UNITED STATES SENATE: "*Titanic* Disaster: Hearings before a sub-committee of the Committee on Commerce" (Document no. 726, Government Printing Office, Washington, DC, 1912)

MERSEY, Lord: "Report on the Loss of the SS *Titanic*" (Cmnd. no. 6352 HMSO, London, 1912)

MERSEY, Lord: "Proceedings on a Formal Investigation into the Loss of the SS *Titanic*" (HMSO, London, 1912)

"TITANIC – Reappraisal of Evidence Relating to SS *Californian*" (Marine Accidents Investigation Board (HMSO, 1992)

Periodicals

National Geographic: April 1986, December 1986 and October 1987

Proceedings of the Institute of Mechanical Engineers (July 1985), *Titanic Signals News* (White Star Publications, Winter/Spring, 1994, Patrick Stenson)

INDEX